*Studies in Economic Transition*

*General Editors*: **Jens Hölscher**, Reader in Economics, University of Brighton; and **Horst Tomann**, Professor of Economics, Free University Berlin

This series has been established in response to a growing demand for a greater understanding of the transformation of economic systems. It brings together theoretical and empirical studies on economic transition and economic development. The post-communist transition from planned to market economies is one of the main areas of applied theory because in this field the most dramatic examples of change and economic dynamics can be found. The series aims to contribute to the understanding of specific major economic changes as well as to advance the theory of economic development. The implications of economic policy will be a major point of focus.

*Titles include:*

Lucian Cernat
EUROPEANIZATION, VARIETIES OF CAPITALISM AND ECONOMIC PERFORMANCE IN CENTRAL AND EASTERN EUROPE

Irwin Collier, Herwig Roggemann, Oliver Scholz and Horst Tomann (*editors*)
WELFARE STATES IN TRANSITION
East and West

Bruno Dallago and Ichiro Iwasaki (*editors*)
CORPORATE RESTRUCTURING AND GOVERNANCE IN TRANSITION ECONOMIES

Bruno Dallago (*editor*)
TRANSFORMATION AND EUROPEAN INTEGRATION
The Local Dimension

Hella Engerer
PRIVATIZATION AND ITS LIMITS IN CENTRAL AND EASTERN EUROPE
Property Rights in Transition

Saul Estrin, Grzegorz W. Kolodko and Milica Uvalic (*editors*)
TRANSITION AND BEYOND

Hubert Gabrisch and Rüdiger Pohl (*editors*)
EU ENLARGEMENT AND ITS MACROECONOMIC EFFECTS
IN EASTERN EUROPE
Currencies, Prices, Investment and Competitiveness

Oleh Havrylyshyn
DIVERGENT PATHS IN POST-COMMUNIST TRANSFORMATION
Capitalism for All or Capitalism for the Few?

Jens Hölscher (*editor*)
FINANCIAL TURBULENCE AND CAPITAL MARKETS IN TRANSITION COUNTRIES

Jens Hölscher and Anja Hochberg (*editors*)
EAST GERMANY'S ECONOMIC DEVELOPMENT SINCE UNIFICATION
Domestic and Global Aspects

Iraj Hoshi, Paul J.J. Welfens and Anna Wziatek-Kubiak (*editors*)
INDUSTRIAL COMPETITIVENESS AND RESTRUCTURING IN ENLARGED EUROPE
How Accession Countries Catch Up and Integrate in the European Union

Mihaela Keleman and Monika Kostera (*editors*)
CRITICAL MANAGEMENT RESEARCH IN EASTERN EUROPE
Managing the Transition

Emil J. Kirchner (*editor*)
DECENTRALIZATION AND TRANSITION IN THE VISEGRAD
Poland, Hungary, the Czech Republic and Slovakia

David Lane (editor)
THE TRANSFORMATION OF STATE SOCIALISM
System Change, Capitalism, or Something Else?

David Lane and Martin Myant (*editors*)
VARIETIES OF CAPITALISM IN POST-COMMUNIST COUNTRIES

Jens Lowitzsch
FINANCIAL PARTICIPATION OF EMPLOYEES IN THE EU-27

Tomasz Mickiewicz
ECONOMIC TRANSITION IN CENTRAL EUROPE AND THE COMMONWEALTH OF INDEPENDENT STATES

Milan Nikolić
MONETARY POLICY IN TRANSITION
Inflation Nexus Money Supply in Postcommunist Russia

Julie Pellegrin
THE POLITICAL ECONOMY OF COMPETITIVENESS IN AN ENLARGED EUROPE

Stanislav Poloucek (*editor*)
REFORMING THE FINANCIAL SECTOR IN CENTRAL EUROPEAN COUNTRIES

Gregg S. Robins
BANKING IN TRANSITION
East Germany after Unification

Johannes Stephan
ECONOMIC TRANSITION IN HUNGARY AND EAST GERMANY
Gradualism and Shock Therapy in Catch-up Development

Johannes Stephan (*editor*)
TECHNOLOGY TRANSFER VIA FOREIGN DIRECT INVESTMENT IN CENTRAL AND EASTERN EUROPE

Horst Tomann
MONETARY INTEGRATION IN EUROPE

Hans van Zon
THE POLITICAL ECONOMY OF INDEPENDENT UKRAINE

Hans van Zon
RUSSIA'S DEVELOPMENT PROBLEM
The Cult of Power

Adalbert Winkler (*editor*)
BANKING AND MONETARY POLICY IN EASTERN EUROPE
The First Ten Years

---

**Studies in Economic Transition**
**Series Standing Order ISBN 978 0–333–73353–0**
(*outside North America only*)

You can receive future titles in this series as they are published by placing a standing order. Please contact your bookseller or, in case of difficulty, write to us at the address below with your name and address, the title of the series and the ISBN quoted above.

Customer Services Department, Macmillan Distribution Ltd, Houndmills, Basingstoke, Hampshire RG21 6XS, England

---

# Financial Participation of Employees in the EU-27

Jens Lowitzsch

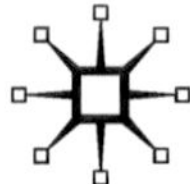



First published 2009 by
PALGRAVE MACMILLAN

Palgrave Macmillan in the UK is an imprint of Macmillan Publishers Limited,
registered in England, company number 785998, of Houndmills, Basingstoke,
Hampshire RG21 6XS.

Palgrave Macmillan in the US is a division of St Martin's Press LLC,
175 Fifth Avenue, New York, NY 10010.

Palgrave Macmillan is the global academic imprint of the above companies
and has companies and representatives throughout the world.

Palgrave® and Macmillan® are registered trademarks in the United States,
the United Kingdom, Europe and other countries

ISBN: 978-0-230-22412-4      hardback

This book is printed on paper suitable for recycling and made from fully
managed and sustained forest sources. Logging, pulping and manufacturing
processes are expected to conform to the environmental regulations of the
country of origin.

A catalogue record for this book is available from the British Library.

A catalog record for this book is available from the Library of Congress.

10   9   8   7   6   5   4   3   2   1
18  17  16  15  14  13  12  11  10  09

Printed and bound in Great Britain by
CPI Antony Rowe, Chippenham and Eastbourne

# Contents

# Figures

# Tables

# Foreword

Working people have long dreamed of owning the companies that employ them. In 1885, John Bates Clark, founder of the American Economic Association, wrote: 'Productive property owned in undivided shares by labouring men [...] is the ideal which humanity has approached, abandoned and approached again.' This ideal inspired the worldwide Cooperative Movement, exemplified by Mondragon in Spain, as well as France's national program of financial participation – *la participation* – which General de Gaulle instituted in 1959. Now, as the world contends with the effects of a deepening financial crisis that could turn into another Great Depression, the long-deferred ideal of broadened ownership assumes new relevance as a practical means of preserving the European economy.

Consider this: in 2006 the European Commission predicted that within the next ten years one-third of the EU's ageing entrepreneurs, mainly heads of family businesses, would withdraw. This means that up to 690,000 enterprises, affecting 2.8 million workers, will be sold or transferred to new owners every year. Who will these new owners be? Leveraged buyout firms? Sovereign wealth funds? Hedge funds? Oligarchs? European conglomerates eager to expand their manufacturing capacities and market reach? Or the companies' own employees?

Does it matter to Europe who the buyers of its old-line firms are? Does it matter who gains and exercises the rights of property – the right to control, the right to receive the earnings of the thing owned, the right to sell, remove, abandon or even destroy? The sum of these rights is economic power. Those who have it command; those who do not, serve.

Small and medium-sized businesses are the economic backbone of the Member States; they are vital to a united Europe's prosperity and economic power. Thus the identity of the new owners is already a serious policy question. Might Europe be better served by initiatives that enable present and future employees to buy, when feasible, the small and medium-sized enterprises coming up for sale?

In a globalised, competitive environment, employee-owned companies have an intrinsic advantage. They anchor both production and distribution in local communities. They generally do not move their headquarters or manufacturing operations to countries with the lowest costs. Thus the income arising from production – paid to workers as wages, to suppliers as payments for goods and services and to shareholders as dividends – ends up in the pockets of those more likely to spend their income in the places where they live and work. Profits distributed to employee shareholders generally do not end up in off-shore accounts.

Europe's small and medium-sized businesses – the *Mittelstand* – are mostly family firms, deeply rooted in the small cities and towns where they were founded, often several generations ago; they may well be the area's largest employer. Their employees are highly skilled; often the products they make are prized for their quality all over the world. These employees are the natural stewards of the company's reputation, standards and traditions. They are the company's natural shareholders.

The empirical findings presented in this book, stemming from the PEPPER IV Report, present conclusive evidence, regardless of data source, that the past decade has seen a significant expansion of employee financial participation in Europe. This is true of both profit sharing and employee share ownership, although profit sharing is more widespread. Despite the fact, however, that employee share ownership is the apex of employee financial participation, working people can rarely reach it through wages alone, even when augmented by profit sharing. To buy a going concern requires capital credit; capital credit requires savings large enough to ensure repayment of the acquisition loan and interest. People rich enough to guarantee this risk have always been few. We need look no further to identify the institutional cause of capital concentration, and its social consequences. As Professor Herwig Roggemann points out, 'The ownership society is at the same time the non-ownership society.'

In 1956, however, the American lawyer Louis Kelso invented the Employee Stock Ownership plan (ESOP). Through the ESOP, employees of a profitable company could buy and pay for shares in their employer company without wage deductions or recourse to rainy-day savings. Future earnings of the shares acquired repaid the acquisition costs. Over a working lifetime, employees could accumulate enough shares to retire in comfort. At the same time, the ESOP offered retiring owners a new way to 'cash out' at market price – at once or in stages for those wishing to exit gradually. This double-edged transaction equally benefited employees and employer, unifying interests once considered irreconcilable. Media reports on this wondrous new financial innovation regularly began with the assurance: 'ESOP is no fable'.

The ESOP model could counter or ameliorate some of the negative domestic effects of Globalisation. Although promoted as a new concept, Globalisation has certain features in common with the old Mercantile system which Adam Smith wrote *The Wealth of Nations* to repudiate. That system enabled powerful nations, through forced colonisation if necessary, to control the industry, resources and trade of weaker nations. Globalisation seeks the same ends through modern means. Advanced electronic and financial technologies have made standing armies, pro-consuls, tax collectors, resident administrators and other encumbrances of empire obsolete. Now the 'Send' key of a computer or fax machine can instantly transfer any amount of money to any account anywhere in the world. Earnings of profitable companies are the prize sought today.

A European ESOP could play the role of Europe's White Knight, as the US ESOP did during the merger and take-over frenzy of the 1970s. Warding off hostile takeovers by financing share ownership for employees, who would have been 'sold' along with the company, the US ESOP rescued both workers and companies alike from Wall Street predators – the 'players' whose financial gamesmanship, it turns out, helped bring on the present world economic crisis.

When I teamed up with Louis Kelso in 1963, there were only three ESOPs in existence; by the end of the 1970s, there were hundreds, and by the end of the 1980s, tens of thousands. No one knows how many millions of dollars American employees have earned from their ESOP holdings over 50-plus years. Currently, however, some 11 million US employees are ESOP participants, whereas ESOP assets are valued at between 60 billion and 80 billion US dollars. ESOP companies hire more people and pay more taxes than their non-ESOP counterparts. Not least, they regularly appear on best-places-to-work lists.

Now Dr. Jens Lowitzsch has designed a modular approach to financial participation at the European level, including a version of the US ESOP which EU Member States can adapt to their own specific needs and circumstances, and which transnational firms can also use to extend financial participation to workers in other States. In making working families better consumers, both employee shareholding and profit sharing address the Achilles' heel of the free market, known variously as the production–consumption gap, under-consumption, purchasing power insufficiency, etc., but essentially the same old problem that was obvious to Chief Sitting Bull 125 years ago. As he explained to sharpshooter Annie Oakley, 'The White man knows how to make everything but he does not know how to distribute it.'

Neo-mercantilists will complain that an EU-policy intended to enlarge the consumer power of working families in its own Member States is 'protectionism.' However, they should re-read their professed mentor Adam Smith. He believed, 'Consumption is the sole end and purpose of all production; and the interest of the producer ought to be attended to only so far as it may be necessary for promoting that of the consumer. The maxim is so perfectly self-evident that it would be absurd to attempt to prove it. But in the mercantile system the interest of the consumer is almost constantly sacrificed to that of the producer; and it seems to consider production, and not consumption, as the ultimate end and object of all industry and commerce.'

Building ownership of productive assets into a nation's own working families makes good free-market sense. We think the Sage of Glasgow would approve. The financial crisis engulfing our world is, at bottom, a consumption crisis. It is brought on by too little money in the pockets of those who are eager to buy the goods and services merchants are eager to sell and producers to supply. Once investment capital had to be painfully hoarded from savings squeezed from current consumption. Today there is more capital in the world than opportunities to invest it. Meanwhile, the economies of the world contract and decline from lack of consumer demand.

In enlarging economic opportunity for the many through share ownership, ESOPs, together with profit sharing and other forms of employee financial participation, work to create a more just society. General de Gaulle said, 'To stick to wages alone is to maintain a permanent class struggle.'

Patricia Hetter Kelso

# Preface

Twenty years have passed since the Commission of the European Communities expressed an interest in promoting an EU instrument to facilitate financial participation of employees.[1] Over this period a series of PEPPER Reports have documented the diverse experience of the growing number of EU countries.[2] Consequently, in its Resolution of 5 June 2003, the European Parliament called on the European Commission to investigate further the issue of a European framework for the promotion of employee financial participation.[3] Today, the topic and especially its European dimension has gained importance across the European Union, as the President of the European Parliament, Hans-Gert Pöttering, in his foreword to a study published in 2008,[4] points out:

> The radical reforms of the legal and economic order in Europe that have occurred in the process of the EU's eastward enlargement, together with privatisation and globalisation, have led not only to economic progress but also to widening social fissures. To counter the growing discrepancy in some member states between the few who are rich and the many others whose economic existence is being rendered insecure, the concept of financial participation of employees in Europe is becoming increasingly significant. [...]

This book is a response to the above cited report of the European Parliament, which called on the Commission to undertake studies focusing on specific questions, for example, the feasibility of financial participation in small and medium-sized enterprises, or the possibility of implementing share ownership schemes based on the British and Irish ESOP model (Employee Stock Ownership Plans) in other EU member states.

Preliminary results of the current PEPPER IV project, which is benchmarking financial participation of employees in all 27 EU member states, reveal a positive trend over the past 10 years. Against this background, by providing ample information and recommendations on how to implement and extend financial participation of employees, and thus on 'asset formation' at a European level, this book makes an important contribution to the debate.

Of particular value is the flexible concept of a building block approach to promoting a European platform for financial participation, based on the principle of voluntariness. I hope that the discussion of the advantages and disadvantages of the different national financial participation schemes will invigorate the search for feasible models at the European level.

Furthermore, employee financial participation is seen more and more as an economic instrument to enhance productivity and competitiveness of the European economies. As the Vice-President of the European Commission, Günther Verheugen, in his foreword to the 2006 PEPPER III Report puts it:

Two years after the 10 new Member States joined the European Union, it is clear that the enlargement has acted as a catalyst of economic dynamism and modernisation for the EU, helping the economies of old and new Member States to face better the challenges of globalisation, while the predicted major shocks or disruptive impacts have not taken place. However, important challenges remain for both old and new Member States, namely the ageing population and the strain it puts on public finances and the further increasing global competition. [...]

To address both challenges, we need to enhance the productivity and competitiveness of our economies, making the EU a more attractive place to invest and work in. The framework conditions set by legislators are an important factor enhancing innovation and entrepreneurial activity, productivity, and finally growth and jobs. The EU strategy for growth and jobs, which is also known as the 'Lisbon strategy', lays out an integrated framework to bring this about. [...]

[...] A stronger link between pay and performance can be one of the possible ways to reform the labour markets. Such performance pay schemes can come in many forms. Employee participation in profits and enterprise results (PEPPER) is one possibility to entice workers to be productive and adaptive to change.

[...] I hope that the experiences with financial participation schemes in the new Member States and the candidate countries as presented in this PEPPER III Report will serve as a catalyst for new developments and dynamism in other EU countries and thus deliver a contribution to the success of the reviewed strategy for growth and jobs in the EU.

Finally, Jean Claude Juncker, President of the "Euro Group" of the ministers of finances and economy of the euro area, in his foreword to the PEPPER IV Report, stresses the importance of employee financial participation in the context of the financial crises: '[...] As we have been witnessing since late 2008, employees often bear much more than just a fair share of the pain in an economic downturn. Tools allowing them to share the gain when the financial results of their employer are growing are, apart from all other aspects, part of a basic fairness in the relationship between employer and employee. The development of such mechanisms therefore needs to continue. [...]'

Thus all three, Jean Claude Juncker, Hans-Gert Pöttering and Günther Verheugen expressly endorse the idea of employee financial participation, especially in the context of the Lisbon Strategy. Because of the significant political initiatives currently under way at both European and national level, we believe that the conditions for further developing the financial participation of employees are now especially favourable.

Jens Lowitzsch

## Notes

1. See 'Communication from the Commission concerning its Action Programme relating to the implementation of the Community Charter of Basic Social Rights for Workers', COM (89) 569 final, Brussels, 29 November 1989.
2. Named after the resulting acronym of the title 'Promotion of Employee Participation in Profits and Enterprise Results' of the first Report by M. Uvalić (1991, EU-12) and subsequently covering more member countries (PEPPER II, 1997: EU-15 and PEPPER III, 2006: 10 New Member States/4 Candidate Countries) the reports were summarised in the PEPPER IV Report covering all EU-27 (J. Lowitzsch, I. Hashi and R. Woodward (eds), *The PEPPER IV Report – Assessing and Benchmarking Financial Participation of Employees in the EU-27*, Berlin Inter-University Centre, 2008).
3. European Parliament resolution on the Commission communication to the Council, the European Parliament, the Economic and Social Committee and the Committee of the Regions on a framework for the promotion of employee financial participation, P5-TA (2003) 0253.
4. J. Lowitzsch et al. (2008) *Financial Participation for a New Social Europe*, Rom/ Berlin: International Association for Financial Participation (IAFP)/European Federation of Employee Share Ownership (EFES). The book was distributed in the European Parliament in French, German and English.

# Acknowledgements

This book has been written by Jens Lowitzsch in co-operation with a core team of experts in the field of Financial Participation. Patricia Hetter Kelso, who, together with her husband, Louis O. Kelso, invented the ESOP more than 50 years ago, oversaw content and editing. The 'Building Block Approach' to a European model of Financial Participation is based on initial research (Lowitzsch, 2004) supported by the Kelso Institute, which was extended in the PEPPER III Report (Lowitzsch, 2006), a survey of Financial Participation in the New Member States and Candidate Countries of the EU and then finalised in the project 'A European Platform for Financial Participation of Employees' (Lowitzsch, 2008). The empirical findings presented in this book stem from the PEPPER IV Report 'Assessing and Benchmarking Financial Participation in the EU-27' (Lowitzsch, Hashi and Woodward (eds) 2009). The individual contributors of this book were involved in these research projects which were all supported by the European Commission's Directorate General Employment, Social Affairs and Equal Opportunities and the Kelso Institute for the Study of Economic Systems.

# Contributors

**Axel Bormann** is a lawyer, researcher and regional country manager for Romania with the Institute for East European Law, Munich. He specialises in labour law, commercial and privatisation law as well as insolvency law. Axel Bormann has participated in legal reform projects of the World Bank as well as the EU.

**Stefan Hanisch** is a lawyer and research associate with the Inter-University Centre at the Institute for Eastern European Studies of the Free University of Berlin specialising in East European and Central Asian law. Furthermore, he has participated as an international legal expert and consultant in various development co-operation projects with the Post-Soviet countries.

**Dr Iraj Hashi** is Professor of Economics at Staffordshire University Business School, UK. He obtained his Ph.D. in Economics from the University of Keele in 1980. His chief research interests include the restructuring of East European economies (especially Albania, Poland, the Czech Republic and the former Yugoslav Republics), enterprise behaviour during the transition period, the privatisation of state-owned enterprises, the theory of labour-managed firms and employee-owned enterprises and the economics of bankruptcy.

**Dr Jens Lowitzsch** is a lawyer and assistant director of the Inter-University Centre at the Institute for Eastern European Studies, Free University of Berlin, where he obtained his doctoral degree in law in 2002. As a specialist in civil law, insolvency law, European law and employees ownership he acquired an economic background in various research and consultancy projects. As project director and supervisor he led the above-mentioned EU-projects concerning Financial Participation of Employees.

**John D. Menke** is founder and president of Menke & Associates, Inc., one of the oldest and most prominent firms specialising in Employee Stock Ownership Plan (ESOP) buyouts. He has over 30 years of broad experience in investment banking, mergers and acquisitions and private equity transactions. He has supervised or participated in more than

1,500 ESOP transactions, representing more than 10 per cent of the ESOPs in existence in the United States today.

**Dr Herwig Roggemann** is Professor emeritus of law at the faculty of law and the Institute for Eastern European Studies, Free University of Berlin, and the director of its Inter-University Centre. He was the director of the Institute for Eastern European Studies during 1993–7. He is a specialist in civil and business law, comparative and East European law and International Criminal Law. He has an ample experience of supervising research projects, especially in Eastern European countries.

**Natalia Spitsa** is a lawyer specialising in civil and business law of Central and Eastern European countries and Germany, comparative law and EU Law. She has gained extensive experience in managing international legal projects at the German Foundation for International Legal Co-operation. Furthermore, she has worked as legal researcher within projects at the Institute for Eastern European Studies.

**Dr Richard Woodward** is an economist, specialising in transition economies, capital market development, privatisation, restructuring and development of the banking sector. He has more than nine years of research experience with CASE foundation in Warsaw. His consulting and research work in the area of municipal government development included municipal budgeting, municipal finance and municipal bond markets. He is currently lecturer in international business at the University of Edinburgh Management School and Economics.

# Network of Affiliated Country Experts

For individual countries' chapters, an extensive use was made of the country chapters of the previous PEPPER I–IV Reports and the contributions from our network of affiliated country experts which have co-operated in past projects:

| | |
|---|---|
| **Belgium** | Tom Vandenbrande HIVA / Marc Mathieu, EFES |
| **Bulgaria** | Spartak Keremidchiev, Bulgarian Academy of Science, Sofia / Stela Ivanova, Institute for East European Law, Munich |
| **Croatia** | Srečko Goić, University of Split / Darko Završak & Ratko Brnabić, University of Split |
| **Cyprus** | Loizos Papacharalambous, Papacharalambous & Angelides, Nicosia / Haris Kountouros, Brussels |
| **Czech Republic** | Lubomír Lízal & Ondřej Vychodil, Charles University, Prague / Stephan Heidenhain, bnt – Pravda, Noack & Partner, Prague |
| **Denmark** | Niels Mygind, Copenhagen Business School |
| **Germany** | Natalia Spitsa, Inter-University Centre, Free University of Berlin / Bernd Waas, Goethe University Frankfurt / Heinrich Beyer, AGP, Kassel |
| **Estonia** | Raul Eamets, University of Tartu |
| **Greece** | Christos Ioannou, OMED Athens |
| **Spain** | Izaskun Alzola & Fred Freundlich, Mondragon University |
| **France** | Paul Maillard, FONDACT, Paris / Marco Caramelli, INSEEC, Paris / Francis Kessler, University Paris 1 |
| **Hungary** | László Neumann & Dorottya Boda, National Employment Office, Budapest / Zoltan Vig, Central European University, Budapest / Erika Kovac & Zoltán Bankó, PTE, Pécs |
| **Ireland** | George Tutthill, ProShare / Anthony Kerr, University College, Dublin / Seamus Milne, Department of Finance, Dublin |
| **Italy** | Andrea Borroni, Somaglia / Emanuela Di Filippo CISL, Rome / Domenico Paparella, CESOS, Rome |

| | |
|---|---|
| **Latvia** | Tatyana Muravska, Centre for European & Transition Studies, Riga / Theis Klauberg, bnt Legal and Tax Consultants, Riga |
| **Lithuania** | Valdonė Darškuvienė & Tomas Davulis, Vytautas Magnus University, Vilnius |
| **Luxembourg** | Gary Tunsch, Departement Travail et Relations Professionnelles |
| **Malta** | Saviour Rizzo, University of Malta, Valletta / David Borg Carbott, Ganado & Associates – Advocates, Valletta |
| **Netherlands** | Pascale Nieuwland-Jansen, Nederlands Participatie Institut |
| **Austria** | Max Stelzer, Voestalpine, Linz |
| **Poland** | Richard Woodward, CASE Foundation, Warsaw / Leszek Mitrus, Jagiellonian University, Kraków |
| **Portugal** | Ana Filipe, SIMA, Lisbon |
| **Romania** | Lucian Albu, Romanian Academy of Sciences, Bucharest / Raluca Dimitriu, Academy of Economic Studies, Bucharest |
| **Slovakia** | Lubomír Lízal & Alexander Klein, Charles University, Prague |
| **Slovenia** | Aleksandra Gregoric, University of Ljubljana / Šime Ivanjko, University of Ljubljana / Grit Ackermann ZDS, Ljubljana |
| **Finland** | Tina Sweins, Helsinki University / Anders von Koskull, Hanken School of Economics, Helsinki |
| **Sweden** | Tina Sweins, Helsinki University / Mia Ronnmar, University of Lund |
| **Turkey** | Elif Tunalı & Yasemin Atasoy, Capital Markets Board of Turkey, Antalya |
| **United Kingdom** | Andrew Pendleton, Essex University |

# Part I  A European Platform for Financial Participation

# 1
# The Building Block Approach to a Common European Model

*Jens Lowitzsch*

> *If then, we regard economic freedom as a good, our objective must be thus to restore property. We must seek political and economic reforms which shall tend to distribute property more widely until the owners of sufficient means of production ... are numerous enough to determine the character of society.*
>
> Hilaire Belloc, *The Servile State*, 1913

## 1.1   Introduction

In every political system based on a market economy, the concept of property, and especially the legal institution of private property, plays a determining role. However, privatisation, increasing concentration, unequal distribution and internationalisation of property have created economic, political and social problems, which so far have defied solution. The creation of a 'New Social Europe' and the recent inclusion of no less than ten Eastern European states make the property question even more urgent. Financial participation (in the form of employee ownership as well as profit-sharing) based on an appropriate legal framework addresses these problems at their source. Instead of eliminating private property and thereby destroying the market economy, wage-dependent employees can be enabled to acquire productive property as shareholders in successful business corporations.

In the EU-15, more than 19 per cent of employees in the private sector currently participate financially in the enterprise for which they work. These existing schemes constitute a pillar of the European Social Model. A generally favourable attitude within a given country has usually led

3

to some supportive legislation for PEPPER schemes, which in turn has spread their practice. This suggests a clear link between national attitudes, legislation and diffusion. However, the European Union (EU) still lacks a unified legal foundation on which to build a European system of financial participation.

A quite different situation obtains in the new EU member and candidate countries (see the PEPPER III Report). Very few laws specifically address employee financial participation, and these refer almost exclusively to employee share ownership; legislation on profit-sharing is rare. Although employees were frequently offered privileged conditions for buying shares of their employer companies, the purpose was not to motivate employees to become more efficient and productive. Nor was there more than mild concern for social justice. Rather, this method was simply an expedient for privatising state-owned enterprises for which at the time there were no buyers. Essentially it was a decision made by default.

In the European Reform Treaty signed on 13 December 2007 in Lisbon, the EU for the first time expressly commits itself to the European Social Model as one of the pillars of its policy. Thus, Article 3 III states that the Union 'shall work for the sustainable development of Europe based on [...] a highly competitive social market economy, aiming at full employment and social progress' and that 'It shall combat social exclusion and discrimination, and shall promote social justice and protection'.

In 2006, in his foreword to the PEPPER III Report, the Commission's Vice-President, Günther Verheugen, postulated a stronger link between pay and performance as one of the possible ways to reform the labour markets. Further, in September 2007, Mrs Christine Lagarde, the French Minister for Economy, Finances and Labour, announced that on assuming the Presidency of the EU in July 2008, France wished to launch a European Model of financial participation supported by the member countries.

This book sets forth both a policy and a detailed proposal for a European concept of employee ownership and profit-sharing, one that provides a broad incentive system made up of diverse and flexible alternatives, which correspond to existing national systems. Our goal is a general scheme suitable for use throughout the EU, derived from the best practices of national legislation and customs.

We would like to stress that we are particularly emphasising the development of Employee Stock Ownership Plans (ESOPs) and related schemes. Originating in the United States, ESOPs are – with the exception of Ireland, the United Kingdom and Hungary – still little known in Europe. ESOPs are financial tools that, among other advantages, provide access to capital credit; they also tend to enhance the entrepreneurial commitment of both employers and employees.

## 1.2 Objective and context

### 1.2.1 Socio-economic background

Both the European Commission and the European Parliament recently launched a new initiative, manifested in the opinion of the Economic and Social Committee of 26 February 2003,[1] on the Commission communication 'on a framework for the promotion of employee financial participation'.[2] Given this remarkable political initiative by the European policymakers, we surmise that the conditions for improving the legal framework for financial participation of employees (and therefore for the transformation of non-owners into shareholders) are now especially favourable.

The European Parliament called on the Commission to submit studies on the issues raised in its Resolution of 5 June 2003,[3] including a study on setting up a European monitoring body. Our proposed European Concept ideally complies with the request for analysing and describing the overall framework of employee participation in general, and already existing financial participation schemes in particular. As an alternative to the creation of a European Recommendation or Directive on financial participation, we suggest the application of existing national company law rooted in the second Council Directive on Company Law.[4] Further, the amendment[5] of existing European company law, that is, the European Company Statute,[6] is considered. Advantages and disadvantages of financial participation schemes at the national level are discussed in support of the promotion of such schemes on a European level.

#### 1.2.1.1 The function of ownership[7]

Ownership of capital property is the material foundation of individual political and economic freedom. As the German Federal Constitutional Court has ruled: 'The guarantee of ownership shall preserve – in the field of property rights – a free sphere for the bearer of fundamental rights, and thus it shall enable the individual to develop and self responsibly conduct his life'.[8] This reaffirms ownership as a fundamental constitutional right indispensable to individual freedom and economic opportunity.

Most citizens in industrial societies do not own any kind of productive property. Thus they are impeded from wider participation in civil society and from access to economic opportunity, as well as from the attainment of economic security and leisure. The challenge of the 'New Social Europe' is to create a new proprietary society of functional owners, incorporating those who have so far been excluded by a closed system of ownership.

The Economic and Social Committee and the Commission both emphasised that broad forms of financial participation can greatly benefit the European business system by reducing conflict in industrial relations.[9] Both bodies believe that financial participation can help achieve the objective, laid down by the March 2000 Lisbon summit, of making the European economy 'the most competitive and dynamic knowledge-based economy in the world, capable of sustainable economic growth with more and better jobs and greater social cohesion'.[10]

### 1.2.1.2   *Capital concentration is dysfunctional*

The question of how much economic concentration and inequality of property distribution a democratic society can or even should tolerate remains to be answered. On the other hand, the thesis that democracy requires a wide distribution of wealth is widely accepted. Both social justice and free market distribution require a minimum standard of democratic equality to achieve social stability and maintain the market system. Present social policy has not yet responded to the growing concentration of wealth[11] and the resulting dramatic increase in 'non-owners'; no regulations have come into force either on a national or a European level. Social attention so far has been focused on the growing wealth of the few (for example, anti-monopoly legislation) without acknowledging the corresponding increase in the number of those who do not own. It needs to be recognised that the 'society of owners' is simultaneously a 'society of non-owners'.[12]

What gives legitimacy to the current discussion of new forms of financial participation is the incontrovertible failure of the Marxist solution to the property problem. The problem of concentrated ownership cannot be solved by eliminating private property. The result is a dysfunctional economic system that, in abandoning a market economy, finds itself unable to satisfy either the basic human and consumer needs of its people or the basic requirements of democracy. Similar structural problems in Western Europe (for example, Germany) have led to the legal and political conclusion that 'the prevention of a dysfunctional concentration of private property possibly not only requires legislation against concentration of economic property, but also an active public promotion of asset formation'.[13]

The counter-model representing the solution to this problem of property distribution was proposed as early as 1958 by the American lawyer and investment banker Louis Kelso.[14] It uses the existing financial infrastructure of a free market democracy. Kelso's alternative goes to the root of the problem: instead of depriving owners of their private property, non-owners should be enabled to become owners through an effective opportunity to participate in the success of their firm not only as wage-earners but also as shareholders.

### 1.2.1.3   Insufficient legal foundations

The basic concept of civil society as a society of private property owners has not (yet) been sufficiently recognised in European law.[15] Since the adoption of the European Charter of Fundamental Rights (as part of the Treaty of Nice in 2001), ownership has been more precisely defined in Article 17 of the Charter.[16] However, not until the ratification of the European Reform Treaty and the inclusion of the European Charter of Fundamental Rights as part of it will the Charter become binding European law.

So far, the only explicit support for a framework for financial participation is to be found in the Council Recommendation of 27 July 1992[17] and in Part 7-II of the Action Programme for Implementing the Community Charter of the Fundamental Social Rights of Workers.[18] Title XI (Social Politics) of the additional protocol of the European Human Rights Convention of 1952, however, contains no recognition of the financial participation of employees. It merely states principles of protection of labour, equal opportunities and co-determination, although Article 139 (former 118b) ECT permits agreements between social partners on a community level. A rare exception to the general silence is the second Council Directive on Company Law.[19] In summary, the community law appears deficient concerning employee participation in general and financial participation in particular.

### 1.2.2   European initiatives

### 1.2.2.1   The PEPPER Reports

The foregoing problems were previously discussed at the European level and addressed by several measures in the early 1990s, including the following:

- the European Commission PEPPER I Report (Promotion of Employee Participation in Profits and Enterprise Results) in 1991;[20]
- the Recommendation of the Council of the Union of 27 July 1992,[21] concerning the promotion of employee participation in profits and enterprise results; and

- the Resolution of the European Parliament of 9 April 1992, concerning the proposition of the European Commission for the aforementioned recommendation of the Council of the Union.[22]

Despite these initiatives, however, the PEPPER II Report of 1997[23] found no major changes in national policies for the promotion of employee financial participation schemes. Large differences between the countries – especially in the role of the state in the development of PEPPER systems – still exist. A systematic information exchange on a larger scale has generally not succeeded beyond perhaps a few narrow studies. With the exception of Great Britain and France, the variety of incentive systems offered was rather small.[24]

This assessment was extended to the new Member States and candidate countries in 2006 with the PEPPER III Report.[25] In both the non-transition countries and the former socialist states, the few laws enabling forms of employee financial participation refer almost exclusively to employee share ownership, whereas in the latter they are mainly linked to privatisation. There have been only a few cases of legislation on profit-sharing. The general attitude of governments and social partners shows the lack of concrete policy measures supporting PEPPER schemes by policymakers, and limited interest both by trade unions and employers organisations.

In 2008 the PEPPER IV Report[26] for the first time provides an overview on employee participation in its entirety in all member and candidate countries of the EU. Furthermore, it offers comprehensive empirical data on employee participation in the 27 EU Member States and two candidate countries, its significance in economic practice; legal obstacles, and future possibilities. The Report consists of three complementary basic components that build on each other:

- Description of the legal environment, fiscal or other incentives and social partners attitudes in country profiles.
- Benchmarking financial participation, that is, the scope and nature of financial participation schemes against the background of the country profiles.
- Comparative analysis of the national policies and characteristics that affect the environment for financial participation, providing a contextual frame of reference for each single profile.

The PEPPER Reports analysed schemes promoted by the EU. These were all company level, broad-based plans dependent on company performance (at the same time not excluding participation in company assets). Thus gain-sharing, irregular cash-based profit-sharing, share option schemes not broadly based and executive stock option schemes were excluded.

### 1.2.2.2 Finding solutions for a 'New Social Europe'

A variety of concepts have been established in the Member States, where the executive and legislative branches and the social partners (as well as particular companies) have made great efforts to advance 'employee participation in productive property'.[27] This is not only true of countries led by social-democratic governments. In Germany the conservative government, before being voted out of office on 27 September 1998, had accepted a draft for a Third Law on Property Participation[28] and the current 'Große Koalition' under Chancellor Merkel has just passed a new law on financial participation.[29] This suggests that the debate has transcended the classical political battlefields of left and right. Furthermore, it seems that the dogmatic frontiers between employers and employees – at least in the area of financial participation – are starting to erode.

Within the EU as a whole, reinforcing the integrational function of ownership by making ownership more broadly accessible requires a legal foundation for the implementation and support of financial participation schemes. This involves two main goals:

- firstly, to develop regulations concerning financial participation at the Directive level, providing for a broader incentive system to support financial participation more actively and to overcome national differences in taxation policy; and
- secondly, to attain a general inclusion of the principle of financial participation of employees in the legal framework of the European Social Constitution.[30]

### 1.2.2.3 Summary of the postulate of the European policymakers

The Commission communication seeking a 'framework for the promotion of employee financial participation'[31] sets forth the following essential principles for financial participation schemes:

- Participation must be voluntary for both enterprises and employees.
- Access to financial participation schemes should in principle be open to all employees (no discrimination against part-time workers or women).
- They should be set up and managed in a clear and comprehensible manner with emphasis on transparency for employees.

- Share ownership schemes especially will almost inevitably involve a certain complexity, and in this case it is important to provide adequate training for employees to enable them to assess the nature and particulars of the scheme in question.
- Rules on financial participation in companies should be based on a pre-defined formula clearly linked to enterprise results.
- Unreasonable risks for employees must be avoided or, at the very least, employees must be warned of the risks of financial participation arising from fluctuations in income or from limited diversification of investments.
- The scheme must be a complement to, not a substitute for, existing pay systems.
- Financial participation schemes should be developed in a way that is compatible with worker mobility both internationally and between enterprises.

Financial participation involves not only opportunities but also risks and difficulties, in particular the following:

- The dual risk that employee shareholders might lose both their jobs and the value of their shares in the event of the company's bankruptcy.
- Organisational and other obstacles, for example, in the areas of taxation law, social security law and labour law in transnational enterprises.
- In small and medium-sized enterprises (SMEs), both the cost and the administrative problems may be considered prohibitive.

The Commission and Parliament further identified the following transnational obstacles to both the development of a European model and to cross-border plans for financial participation:[32]

- Differences in taxation systems can give rise to double taxation issues. This is primarily a problem of determining the optimal time to tax share options depending on when they are exercised.
- Differences in fiscal systems can also entail substantial administrative costs for enterprises wishing to introduce multi-national financial participation schemes.
- Social security contributions on income from financial participation and investment holdings are assessed in various ways.

- Legal questions arise from differences in the laws on securities and prospectuses and in labour as well as social security laws.
- In an international context, the general lack of mutual recognition usually impedes offering these schemes to employees in other countries.
- Blocking periods restrict the time when employees may dispose of their shares.
- Cultural presumptions regarding the social partnership vary widely.

Except for shareholding schemes in the context of the ongoing privatisation processes, almost none of the new member countries provide either a legal or fiscal framework for employee participation.[33] According to the Commission communication, several specific obstacles exist in Central and Eastern Europe:

- Employee-owned enterprises often face severe financial difficulties, especially in cases where employee ownership emerged by default rather than by design.
- Interest in employee share ownership on the part of employees tends to be limited, as evidenced by employees very often preferring to sell their shares almost immediately.
- With the completion of privatisation, favourable tax arrangements offered by some countries for the purposes of employee buyouts are expiring.
- Techniques for increasing the awareness of employee participation need development in countries where private ownership is a relatively new concept.

### 1.2.3   The current reform process

*1.2.3.1   Actual tendencies of property development – A challenge
          for social policy*

The current development of the legal system of ownership in Europe can be described as bearing the following tendencies:

- Concentration of ownership, which reached new extremes in the 1990s, is continuing in several European countries.[34]
- In some Western European countries (for example, Germany, France, Italy, Austria) the privatisation of big companies (especially in the infrastructure, energy and telecommunication sectors), although leading to

a diversification of ownership to some extent, only slowed down, but did not reverse, the process of concentration of ownership.[35]
- In the course of the post-socialist (re-)privatisation in Eastern and Central Europe, unusual forms of financial participation have been developed as a result of social privatisation methods.[36] They have, however, been carried out with only varying success. In Eastern Germany, forms of participation have been limited to the management buyout.[37]
- In Central and Eastern Europe, as well as in Eastern Germany, the (re-)privatisation of economic assets previously held by the state, by society or by co-operatives at first appeared to broaden ownership. However, this process did not, despite legislative intentions, lead to progressively more equality in ownership distribution, but promoted new ownership concentration.

### 1.2.3.2   *Status quo*

In the EU-15, more than 19 per cent of employees in the private sector currently participate financially in their employer firms through profit-sharing or share ownership.[38] These existing schemes constitute a pillar of the European social model based on partnership and seeking to overcome the rivalry between capital and labour. So far, only participation in decision making has been incorporated in the legal framework of the EU treaties.[39] The Commission's PEPPER II Report (1997) concluded that there is more diversity than uniformity in models of financial participation. The analysis of the legislative framework in the ten new EU members and the four candidate countries[40] (PEPPER III, 2006) has shown that there are practically very few laws specifically dedicated to employee financial participation. Because no specific legal foundation yet exists, there is no European framework for financial participation until now.

There is a need, however, for co-ordination of current practices through the development of guidelines and agreements on general principles. These should maintain the flexibility of individual countries' policies to ensure compatibility so as not to impede workers' mobility, particularly across national borders. Solutions must be found on a community-wide basis to the issues of taxation of share ownership and to the valuation of shares for social security purposes. Management may be induced to introduce share ownership or profit-sharing for several reasons[41]:

- to make employees more motivated and productive;
- to make enterprises more competitive through improved capital structure, better liquidity for the company (that is, to enhance working capital), and easier access to external capital.

Yet a significant breakthrough can probably be achieved only with the help of government incentives, such as tax concessions. All these considerations must be incorporated into the development of a specific legal framework for the financial participation of European employees in the enterprises for which they work.

### 1.2.3.3  *Recent studies*

To formulate a more focused strategy, several studies have recently been undertaken, including:

- the working document of the European Parliament Secretariat, 'Employee Participation in Profits and Ownership: A Review of the Issues and Evidence';[42]
- studies by the European Foundation for the Improvement of Living and Working Conditions on the subject of employee financial participation;[43] and
- the report of the Committee on Employment and Social Affairs and the opinions respectively of the Committee on Economic and Monetary Affairs, the Committee on Industry, External Trade, Research and Energy, and the Committee on Women's Rights and Equal Opportunities.[44]

Based on these studies, the European Parliament reiterated its proposal that 'employee share ownership, which creates jobs, is more deserving of state support than profit-sharing handed out in cash to employees'. Triggered by a motion of the Committee on Employment and Social Affairs in its Resolution of 5 June 2003,[45] the European Parliament advocates, in addition to fiscal solutions, savings bonuses to encourage personal asset formation on the grounds that savings bonuses benefit workers who pay little or no tax while bonus systems are easier to reconcile in transnational participation models. The Resolution's proposal for increasing employee ownership starts from the premise that the value added by an enterprise is created by all the factors of production working together. Therefore the European Parliament proposes that stock options should not be restricted to management and calls for studies on the feasibility of making share options available to all employees and, if this is practicable, what forms of options would allow employees to share in the growing value of the companies for which they work.

   The European Parliament would also welcome studies on the forms of financial participation that now exist or would be appropriate for

SMEs.[46] It further recommends that studies be conducted on the suitability of trusteed programmes such as ESOPs and Employee Stock Ownership Trusts (ESOTs) (which operate in Ireland and Great Britain), on funds that combine several SMEs, as well as on existing workers' co-operative models.[47]

### 1.2.4   The path to a European regulation

The American experience in institutionalising techniques for broadening the ownership of capital, valid in all of the 50 American states, provides a model for such a trans-jurisdictional framework. In its communication the Commission refers to this experience by stressing the 'important impact financial participation can have in terms of economic growth, fostering industrial change and making sure that all workers participate in this growing prosperity'. Furthermore, the Commission states that 'especially when compared to the experiences in the USA, there exists still a huge, largely unused potential for the further development of financial participation as part of an overall strategy aimed towards stimulating the growth of new, dynamic companies'.[48] Two relevant issues are currently under consideration in the EU:

- Can broadened ownership of capital through ESOPs or similar vehicles help EU companies become more competitive in the world market? One field of action already identified in this context, in the Council Recommendation of 7 December 1994,[49] are transfers of businesses to employees as a way to facilitate business succession in SMEs.[50]
- Assuming that broadened ownership of capital is desirable from a social and economic standpoint, what is the best way to amend legal structures in the EU so as to create a legal foundation for employee share ownership as part of property rights legislation, and thus the *acquis communautaire* itself?

#### 1.2.4.1   *Focus: Legislating financial participation schemes*

Although tax incentives are the most common way of encouraging financial participation schemes, a common European legal framework imposing such tax incentives would collide with the national legislative sovereignty over taxation. Under the EU each Member State retains exclusive power over all matters involving taxation; any Directive involving taxation requires the unanimous consent of the Member States. Therefore a European approach to the problem must provide a broad incentive system going beyond the classical instruments of tax legislation. Establishing such schemes through legislation is of primary importance, as it gives companies a distinct legal entity and provides them with a clear framework for company decisions and actions. At the same time, establishing a legal framework delineates what is possible for companies without inviting sanctions from regulatory, legal or taxation authorities.[51]

### 1.2.4.2 *Unanimous decision versus majority vote*

Diverse national approaches to both financial participation and participation in decision making constitute further impediments to change. For obvious reasons, it is very difficult to reach a unanimous supranational compromise either in the Commission or in the Council. The law of European Treaties in general permits majority vote decisions in a few cases, recently extended by the Treaty of Nice.[52] No less than 27 provisions have been changed completely or partly from unanimity to qualified majority voting, among them measures to facilitate freedom of movement for the citizens of the Union (Article 18 ECT) and industrial policy (Article 157 ECT). As for taxation (Articles 93, 94 and 175 ECT), however, the requirement of unanimity for all measures is maintained across the board. In the field of social policy (Articles 42 and 137 ECT), despite maintenance of the status quo, the Council, acting in unanimity, can make the co-decision procedure[53] applicable to those areas of social policy which are currently still subject to the rule of unanimity.[54] Therefore the search for a legal foundation at the Directive level has to focus on those 'majority vote' regulations if it is to be successful. This is further true because the position of the governments in relation to the social partners, their role in society and their relation to each other varies significantly in the different member countries.[55]

### 1.2.4.3 *Different contexts, different approaches: The building block approach*

A strict distinction about suitable options and legal procedure to create solutions at the European level has to be made between participation in decision making and financial participation of employees. Participation in decision making, whatever its form at the national level, is as a rule obligatory for enterprises in the given country.[56] Because community law would be equally binding, a supranational compromise can encompass only the smallest common features of the diverse national regulations.[57] Financial participation on the other hand is traditionally an optional instrument for improving company performance and corporate governance; enterprises are therefore free to introduce financial participation schemes.[58] Thus, provided they are granted voluntarily at the national level, a supranational concept can offer a variety of incentives from which to choose.

A European regulation should thus encompass a broad incentive system that provides different and flexible solutions, compatible with those already established in the Member States. An adaptable scheme can provide for a solution suitable for use throughout the EU, comprising best practices of national legislation and customs.[59] Combining them in a single programme with alternative options leads to a 'Building Block Approach', with the different elements being mutually complementary.

These building blocks consist of the following three basic elements:

- profit-sharing (cash-based, deferred and share-based);
- individual employee shareholding (stock options and employee shares);
- ESOPs as collective schemes.

Although profit-sharing schemes, stock options and employee shares are relatively widespread in the EU, ESOPs are predominantly to be found in countries with an Anglo-American tradition, for example, the United Kingdom and Ireland.[60] Originated in the United States as a technique of corporate finance, the ESOP, using borrowed funds on a leveraged basis, has the capacity to create substantial employee ownership and can be used to finance ownership succession plans, an important feature, especially for European SMEs.[61] Furthermore, it can be used to refinance outstanding debt, to repurchase shares from departing plan participants, or to finance the acquisition of productive assets.[62] The last two functions are also both possible on an unleveraged basis. In the unleveraged case, of course, less stock can be acquired in any given transaction.

## 1.3   The current situation in Europe

### 1.3.1   Policy issues

With the advent of a new European Constitution, the structural problems described above have led to the postulate that, in addition to legislation discouraging concentration of economic property, an active public promotion of asset formation[63] is required on a European scale. Nevertheless, up to now no appropriate conclusions have been drawn from the fact that the social groups of owners and non-owners are drifting apart dramatically. No regulations actively supporting the implementation of a European concept for employee financial participation have been enacted at the national level of the Member States or at the supranational European level. At the end of the 1990s, in the countries of the EU-15, no major changes in the national policies were to be observed, and up to now large differences between the countries exist. In the new Member States of Central and Eastern Europe, local approaches embracing different forms of mass privatisation and employee shareholding (not contemplated in (Eastern) Germany[64] or in other Western European states) were undertaken with varying degrees of success.[65]

The influence of private property on the political system,[66] especially the observation that widely diffused private property may have a decentralising, power-sharing and power-limiting effect, leads to the conclusion that 'ownership, being by nature autocratic, becomes republican when it is implanted into a political society'.[67] The arbitrary intrusion on private ownership reduces the confidence of the citizen in the state. Thus a reasonably stable but also fair system of property plays an important part in political peace. This link between the political system and the property system makes the current but not always successful privatisation process in the post-socialist transformation states a touchstone for real (as opposed to only formal) system transformation.

The concentration of the most important property assets in the hands of only a few individuals or in the hands of the state is a threat to any democratic pluralistic society, especially to the emerging social system and civil society in Central and Eastern Europe. Nevertheless, legal and political priorities differ considerably between East and West, because changing the socialist economic system through privatisation and re-privatisation is the first priority of post-socialist legislators.[68]

### 1.3.2   Problems related to the legal framework and transnational obstacles

As previously mentioned, as of now the only explicit support of financial participation is to be found in the Council Recommendation of 27 July 1992[69] and in Part 7-II of the Action Programme for implementing the Community Charter of the Fundamental Social Rights of Workers. The Charter of 9 December 1989, also signed by the United Kingdom in 1998, is neither a binding legal act nor a treaty among the signatory states.[70] Together with the action programme, which has also been approved by the heads of state or government, it is used by the Commission as a basis for justifying many of the Directives it proposes. Overall, the community law seems to be deficient in respect to employee participation in general and financial participation in particular.

A second deficiency is that the development of financial participation schemes across the EU is strongly influenced by national policies, in particular by the availability of an appropriate legal framework, tax incentives and other financial advantages.[71] As a result, different laws, and sometimes mandatory rules, in the different countries often require specific forms of financial participation, forcing companies to tailor the design of an international plan accordingly.[72] At the end of 2003, a High Level Group of Independent Experts[73] classified the barriers to cross-border plans for financial participation into seven broad categories.

- Existing legal framework:
  Legal obstacles embrace such different issues, such as the following examples: employee involvement in the introduction of plans; legal statute of companies or groups; plan coverage; limits, thresholds and criteria for calculation; eligibility criteria; fixing of withholding or retention periods as well as rules and vehicles for investment and administration of funds.
- Taxation and social security issues:
  Diverse tax treatment of the various types of financial participation plans across the EU, linked to general differences in taxation systems, represent another very important barrier to the implementation and spread of plans. Combined with the existence or absence of tax-favoured plans, the differences most importantly concern incidence and timing of taxation, uncertainty and/or complexity of fiscal treatment, and differences in tax treatment and social security contributions for employers and/or employees as well as double taxation or double exemption.
- Securities laws:
  Different securities laws can impose substantially different obligations on enterprises to provide information to employees when offering shares in different Member States.
- Labour or employment laws:
  In some countries, labour or employment laws foresee the necessity of consulting with employee representatives, trade unions or works councils and negotiating plans with them at the company level as well as of providing information to employees. Likewise, the definition of pay, the impact of plans on pension rights, the existence of 'acquired rights' and employee data protection are often regulated differently at the national level.
- Financial market regulations:
  Member countries have different requirements for stock exchange disclosure rules, levels of compliance and shareholder and regulatory approval, as well as the entitlement of the employees' legal representatives to information.

- Social and cultural traditions:
  Differences in industrial relations practice as well as cultural differences relating to savings patterns and risk aversion, which affect the willingness of employees to invest in their employer firm.
- Introduction and operating costs:
  Installation and maintenance costs may be high when financial design and company appraisal, employee communications, legal and tax advice, compliance obligations and annual administration must comply with different national requirements under one plan.

### 1.3.3   The national level

*1.3.3.1   The situation in the old Member States of the EU – Table 1.1*

*1.3.3.2   The situation in the new Member States and candidate countries – Table 1.2*

## 1.4   Towards a European concept of financial participation

### 1.4.1   Choosing a building block approach

Regardless of the form profit-sharing takes, the resulting funds may be used to create employee share ownership, as in the case of share-based deferred profit-sharing practised in various other combinations in France, the United Kingdom and Ireland. The existing variety of national profit-sharing schemes (often involving an institutional infrastructure) would be compatible with a supranational concept resting basically on the two forms of employee share ownership: individually held or held through a trust.

Therefore the building blocks should consist of the three basic PEPPER elements:[74]

- profit-sharing (cash-based, deferred and share-based);
- employee shareholding (stock options and employee shares);
- ESOPs as collective schemes.

Referring to the catalogue of minimum requirements (for example, being transparent, broad-based, and so on) the basic scheme reflects the existing postulates of the European policymakers (see 1.2.2.3) and neither relies on nor excludes tax incentives. All of the different elements are voluntary for both enterprises and employees. They can be put together in any combination with the different building-blocks tailored to the specific needs of the given enterprise (see Figure 1.1).

*Table 1.1*   The old Member States of the EU

| Country | General attitude<br>[A] Social Partners<br>[B] Government | Legislation and Fiscal or other Incentives | Schemes and their Incidence<br>CRANET: Offered in Firms with more than 200 employees<br>EWCS: Take-up Rate of Employees |
|---|---|---|---|
| Belgium | [A] TU opposed, but relatively more support for profit-sharing; EA in favour<br>[B] Since 1982, legislation for ESO; amendment 1991; since 1999 legislation for stock options; since 2001 new law on ESO and PS | All plans: EmpC maximum 20% of after – tax profit per year; maximum 10% of total gross salary<br>ESO: NCL – discounted ES in JSC, financing by firm possible; in capital increases: maximum 20% of equity capital, ES discount limit 20%; NTL – (restricted stock grant) value reduced by 16.7%, taxation deferred if two years not transferable, 15% tax on benefit, no SSC; (stock purchase plan) benefit tax base 83.33% of fair market value<br>SO: NTL – since 1999 taxed at grant on a lump sum basis, no SSC<br>PS: NTL – tax 15% for PS in an investment savings plan, 25% for other plans | 2005 CRANET: ESO 21%, PS 3.7%<br>2005 EWCS: ESO 4.3%, PS 5.9% firms involved mainly from financial sector, large firms and multinationals<br>SO 2005 CRANET: 2%; EU Report 2003: 75,000 employees benefit; most of 20 largest Belgian firms operate plans; 40% of firms with more than 50 employees |
| Denmark | [A] TU indifferent to FP; EA opposed to any extension of employee participation | ESO: NCL – ES in JSC: discounted, maximum 10% of salary per year, seven-year holding period, free | 2005 CRANET: ESO 36%, PS 7.3%<br>2005 EWCS: ESO 2.4%, PS 6.4%<br>SO 2005 CRANET: 2%; EU Report |

| | | | |
|---|---|---|---|
| | [B] Employee Funds discussed in 1970–80s, PS popular; later support for ESO and SO; in 2000s government support for share-based schemes | maximum DKK 8,000 per year; financing by firm possible if qualified plan; in capital increases deviation from subscription or pre-emption rights possible; NTL – deferred taxation of benefit; EmplC: discount tax deductible<br>PS: NCL – SPS; NTL – maximum 10% of annual salary<br>SO: NTL – broad-based maximum DKK 8,000, five-year holding period; individual maximum 10% of annual salary or maximum 15% difference between exercise price and market price | 2003: 20% of 500 largest firms by 1999, one-third of quoted firms 2000 |
| Germany | [A] TU sceptical or partly hostile because of 'double risk'; EA support individual firms<br>[B] Traditional focus on savings plans (total capital higher than that of ES firm plans); FP since 2006 on political agenda of all parties | ESO: NCL – discounted ES in JSC, financing by firm possible; state savings bonus of 18% of maximum EUR 400 (EUR 72 per year) invested in employer stock; no tax and SSC on maximum EUR 135 per year employer matching contribution<br>PS: None<br>SO: NCL – in capital increase, nominal amount restricted to 10%, that of increase to 50% of equity capital | 2005 CRANET: ESO 11%; PS 45%<br>2005 EWCS: ESO 0.8%, PS 5.3%<br>2005 IAB: ESO 3%, PS 12%<br>2003 WSI: PS in one-third of firms<br>ESO: 2006 AGP, 3,000 firms, 2.3 million Empl., EUR 19 billion<br>SO: EU Report 2003, in over two-thirds of DAX-listed firms |

(*Continued*)

*Table 1.1*    (Continued)

| Country | General attitude<br>[A] Social Partners<br>[B] Government | Legislation and Fiscal or other Incentives | Schemes and their Incidence<br>CRANET: Offered in Firms with more than 200 employees<br>EWCS: Take-up Rate of Employees |
|---|---|---|---|
| Greece | [A] TU moved from scepticism to support in 1980s; EA indifferent, low priority not a current topic<br>[B] Some regulations on CPS (1984) and ESO (1987); since 1999 more attention on SO; not a current issue | ESO: NCL – ES in JSC discounted or free; within capital increase for three years not transferable, up to 20% of annual profit; NTL – no PIT/SSC on benefit<br>SO: NCL – free or discounted; NTL – taxable at exercise; tax exempt if qualified plan<br>PS: NTL – maximum 15% of company profits, 25% of employees' gross salary; no PIT, but SSC | 2005 CRANET: ESO 23.6%; PS 9.4%<br>2005 EWCS: ESO 1%, PS 2.8%<br>SO: 2005 CRANET 2%; SO EU Report 2003: only a limited number of firms |
| Spain | [A] Low priority: TU oppose income flexibility; EA ambivalent, fear information disclosure requirements<br>[B] Long tradition of social economy: COOPs (new law 1997) and EBO; PS supported in 1994 then shift to ESO/SO; active support | ESO: NCL – ES/SO in JSC, financing by firm possible; NTL – tax benefits on PIT after three-year holding period<br>PS: NLL<br>SO: NTL – after two-year holding period 40% reduction of taxed plan benefit<br>EBO: 'Workers Companies' with | 2005 CRANET: ESO 5.7%, PS 17%<br>2005 EWCS: ESO 0.5%, PS 6.4%<br>ESO: 2003 CNMV 20% of large firms with share purchase plans<br>SO: 2005 CRANET: 19%; EU Report 2003: plans in 40 firms of which 50% in IBEX 35<br>EBO: 2003 Heissmann, circa 15,000 'Workers Companies' |

| France | [A] TU show mixed attitudes: sceptical but actively involved, favour if not substitute to pay; EA generally in favour, especially if voluntary [B] PS/ESC strong continuous support since 1959; also in privatisations; climate FP friendly, focused policy | more than 51% ESO, 10–25% of profits in Reserve Fund; NTL – if 25% reserve, tax exempt from capital transfer tax, tax on formation and capital increase, notary fees ESO: PrivL – 5% ES-reserve, maximum 20% discount; NCL – discounted ES in JSC, financing by firm possible, also capital increase; Save-as-you-earn schemes; NTL – flat rate tax of 7.6% and 10% on returns, no SSC; SO: NCL – capital increase; NTL – tax on exercise gain 26–30% after four-year holding period ESOP/EBO: Law on Trusteeship 2007; NCL – special reserve for EBO possible PS: DPS compulsory, CPS voluntary; NTL – flat rate tax 7.6–10% if paid to firm savings-scheme or fund after five-year holding period | 2005 CRANET: ESO 34%, PS 92%; 2005 EWCS: ESO 5.3%, PS 12% 2004 FONDACT: DPS covered 53% of non-agriculture private sector firms employees (that is 6.3 million) SO: 2005 CRANET 3%; SO EU Report 2003: circa 50% of quoted firms and 28% of limited companies, total circa 30,000 employees |



(*Continued*)

*Table 1.1*   (Continued)

| Country | General attitude<br>[A] Social Partners<br>[B] Government | Legislation and Fiscal or other Incentives | Schemes and their Incidence<br>CRANET: Offered in Firms with more than 200 employees<br>EWCS: Take-up Rate of Employees |
|---|---|---|---|
| Ireland | [A] EA strong support; TU support if financial and intrinsic reward to employees; managers and employees pragmatically motivated; Lobby groups and institutions, for example banks, for ESO<br>[B] Support in privatisation; improvements in 1995 and 1997; promoting voluntary adoption of SPS, for example Approved Profit-Sharing Scheme (APSS) | ESO: PrivL – 14.9% ESOT stock paid for by loan or by state; NCL – ES/SPS in JSC, financing by firm possible; NTL – New Shares: limited PIT tax base deduction for Empl., no SSC<br>SO: Savings Plan: bonus/interest on savings tax-free, no PIT on grant/exercise, no SSC; Approved Plan: no PIT at exercise, no SSC<br>ESOP: Trust Act – taxed 15% interest, 10% investment; NTL – ESOT: tax incentives as for APSS if ESOT part of APSS<br>PS: NTL – APSS: at transfer no PIT, no SSC up to limit, salary foregone – up to 7.5% of gross salary deductible | 1999 CRANET: ESO 14%, PS 15%<br>2005 EWCS: ESO 5.3%, PS, 9.2%<br>SO: 2002 IBEC: 90 firms with SAYE schemes, 15 firms with Approved Share Option Schemes<br>PS: 2002 IBEC: 400 firms with APPS<br>ESOP: Not specified |
| Italy | [A] TU mixed attitudes, recently interested in topic, EA mostly supportive | ESO: CivC – discounted ES in JSC, financing by firm possible; in capital increases deviation from | 2005 CRANET: ESO 13.7%, PS 6.2%<br>2005 EWCS: ESO 1.4%, PS 3.1%<br>SO: 2005 CRANET 1%; EU Report |

|  |  |  |  |
| --- | --- | --- | --- |
|  | [B] Trilateral agreement 1993 supported PS; then shift to support ESO/SO; recently discussed on political agenda | pre-emption rights and preferential 'ES' possible; NTL – PIT & SSC exemption up to max EUR 2,065 after three-year holding period; in limited liability companies free share up to EUR 7,500 tax exempt<br>PS: NCL – no SSC on maximum 5% of total pay<br>SO: NTL – SSC exemption after five-year holding period | 2003, circa 6% of employees involved |
| Luxemburg | [A] TU/EA growing interest in 1990s, not supportive of share schemes; EA support profit-sharing<br>[B] FP not a current issue | ESO: NCL – ES in JSC, financing by firm possible<br>SO: NTL – 'Tradable Option Plans' reduced tax burden<br>PS: None | 2005 EWCS: ESO 3.7%, PS 13.5%<br>PS: PEPPER II, 1995 CPS in 25% of firms, mainly banks<br>SO: EU Report 2003, estimates 25% of firms – mainly financial sector<br>ESO: n. a. |
| Netherlands | [A] TU/EA generally in favour; TU support if supplement to pay, prefer PS to ESO<br>[B] Traditional focus on savings plans; support for SO in 2003 | ESO: NCL – ES in JSC, financing by firm possible; NTL – up to EUR 1,226 from pre-tax salary after four years in a savings plan 15% flat tax, no SSC<br>PS: NTL – up to EUR 613 from pre-tax salary after four years in a savings plan 15% flat tax, no SSC<br>SO: NTL – specific tax incentives abolished<br>IEnt: Qualified Savings Funds | 2005 CRANET: ESO 20%, PS 44.8%<br>2005 EWCS: ESO 1.5%, PS 13.8%<br>PS: 3 million participants in 2000<br>SO: 2005 CRANET 4%; EU Report 2003, more than 80% of all listed firms |

(Continued)

*Table 1.1*   (Continued)

| Country | General attitude<br>[A] Social Partners<br>[B] Government | Legislation and Fiscal or other Incentives | Schemes and their Incidence<br>CRANET: Offered in Firms with more than 200 employees<br>EWCS: Take-up Rate of Employees |
|---|---|---|---|
| Austria | [A] TU/EA currently support FP and co-operate; different views about participation in decision making<br>[B] Legislation since 1974; first tax incentives since 1993; more active support since 2001 | ESO: NCL – discounted ES in JSC; financing by firm possible; NTL – PIT/SSC allowance for benefit; CGT or 50% PIT for dividends; tax exemption for share sale gain<br>IEnt: NCL – Empl. Foundation: EmpC buys own stock, sheltered in IEnt, dividends paid out; NTL – EmpC: contribution to IEnt, setting-up and operation cost deductible; IEnt: tax allowance on contributions; Empl.: CGT on dividends<br>SO: NCL – capital increase: nominal amount maximum 10%, increase maximum 50% of equity capital; maximum 20% of equity capital for total amount of shares receivable; NTL – 10% of benefit per year, but maximum 50% of total benefit tax-free and carry forward of taxation for the remaining amount<br>PS: None | 2005 CRANET: ESO 12%, PS 32.8%<br>2005 EWCS: ESO 1.2%, PS 5.4%<br>2005 WKÖ/BAK: ESO 8%, PS 25%<br>SO: 2005 CRANET: 2%; 2005 WKÖ/BAK: 1% |

| Portugal | [A] TU/EA Indifferent, low priority: TU prefer PS to SO<br>[B] ESO mainly supported in privatisation, especially around 1997; not on the Agenda; FP is generally ignored | ESO: PrivL – discounted ES; NCL – ES in JSC, financing by firm possible; in capital increase: suspension of pre-emptive right of shareholders for 'social reasons' possible<br>PS: NLL – not remuneration, no SSC<br>SO: NTL – 50% of share sale gain liable to PIT | 2008 PEPPER IV: ESO 5.3%, PS 28%<br>2005 EWCS: ESO 0.9%, PS 1.9%<br>SO: EU Report 2003, from 60 firms listed at Euronext Lisbon Stock Exchange, about 22% have implemented SO |
| Finland | [A] TU/EA generally support FP, especially desire to improve the environment for Personnel Funds; other forms not discussed<br>[B] Discussions on FP since the 1970s; 1989 law on Personnel Funds (the major form until now) | ESO: NTL – discount tax-free, no SSC; tax relief for dividends<br>SO: None<br>PS: Cash-based none; NCL – share-based Personnel Funds: in firms with more than 30 employees, if all participate, registration with Ministry of Labour, after five-year blocking period up to 15% per year can be withdrawn; NTL – 20% of payments to employee tax-free; earnings of fund tax-free | 2005 CRANET: ESO 14%, PS 66%<br>2005 EWCS: ESO 0.7%, PS 11%<br>PS: 2007 54 Personnel Funds with 126,000 members<br>SO: 2005 CRANET 5%; 2003 EU Report: 84% of companies listed at Helsinki Stock Exchange |

(Continued)

*Table 1.1*   (Continued)

| Country | General attitude<br>[A] Social Partners<br>[B] Government | Legislation and Fiscal or other Incentives | Schemes and their Incidence<br>CRANET: Offered in Firms with more than 200 employees<br>EWCS: Take-up Rate of Employees |
| --- | --- | --- | --- |
| Sweden | [A] TU neutral or opposed, advocated Wage-Earner Funds; EA favour PS for wage flexibility, but no active support<br>[B] 1992–7 tax incentives for PS in firms; since then no support | ESO: NCL – ES in JSC, financing by firm possible; in capital increase suspension of pre-emptive right of shareholders possible<br>PS: Cash-based none; NCL – share-based Profit-Sharing Foundations: one-third of employees on similar terms, after dissolution assets to be distributed; NTL – for the employer 24.26% payroll tax instead of 32.28% SSC<br>SO: None | 2005 CRANET: ESO 16%, PS 26%<br>2005 EWCS: ESO 1.6%, PS 15%<br>PS: 2003 Heissmann: 15%<br>Wage-Earner Funds created in 1983 were abolished in 1991 |
| United Kingdom | [A] Climate FP friendly and supportive; TU involved, but reservations: prefer SO to PS; EA positive, favour flexibility with regard to form of schemes; employees interested | ESO: NTL – Share Incentive Plan (SIP) discounted: no PIT/SSC; no dividend tax if dividends reinvested in shares, generally no SSC; no CGT if sale immediately after taking shares out of the plan | 2005 CRANET: ESO 19%, PS 13%<br>2005 EWCS: ESO 1.9%, PS 6.4%<br>2006 ifsProShare: ESO/SO approved plans in 5,000 firms, some with ESOPs; SIP in 830 firms; SPS: 2002 1 million Empl. under approved schemes, average per capita less than GBP 700 |

| | | |
|---|---|---|
| [B] Long tradition of FP, especially ESO and ESOP; now more active support for SO, that is SAYE and Sharesave; 2000 new of Enterprise Management Incentives EMI; very little participation in decision making | SO: NTL – Savings-Related SO Plan, Firm SO Plan: generally no PIT at grant or exercise, no SSC; SAYE: tax bonus on savings; EMI: no PIT, no SSC at grant or exercise (NCL – Empl. Benefit Trust used)<br>ESOP: NCL – maximum GBP 125 per month shares for pre-tax salary in Trust, EmpC maximum two matching shares and share worth maximum GBP 3,000 per year; NTL – shares exempt from income tax and SSC after five years; EmpC contribution to trust tax deductible<br>PS: NTL – approved PS; tax benefits abolished in 2002 | SO: 2005 CRANET 2%; 2006 ifsProShare: Savings-Related Plans in 1,300 firms, 2.6 million Empl.; Company Plans in 3,000 firms; EMI in 3,000 firms |

*Sources* PEPPER I–IV and CNMV 2003; CRANET 2005/1999 (firms with more than 200 Empl.); EU Stock Options Report 2003; EWCS 2005 (take-up rate); FONDACT 2004 Heissmann 2003; IAB 2005; IBEC 2002; ifsProShare 2006; WKÖ/BAK 2005; WSI 2003; please note that the country data of the different surveys is incoherent due to inconsistencies in methodology and definitions. Excluded from studies: management buyout, general savings plans, consumer and housing co-operatives.

*Abbreviations* AI = anecdotal information only; CGT = capital gains tax; CivC = Civil Code; CPS = cash-based profit-sharing; CS = case studies; DPS = deferred profit-sharing; EA = employer associations; EBO = employee buyout; EmpC = employer company; Empl. = employee; ES = employee shares; ESO = employee share ownership; ESOP = Employee Stock Ownership Plan; FP = financial participation; IEnt = intermediary entities; JSC = joint-stock companies; MEBO = management-employee buyout; NCL = national company law; NLL = national labour legislation; NTL = national tax legislation; PIT = personal income tax; PrivL = privatisation legislation; PS = profit-sharing; SO = stock options; SPS = share-based profit-sharing; SSC = social security contributions TU = trade unions.

*Table 1.2*   The new Member States and candidate countries

| Country | General attitude<br>[A] Social Partners<br>[B] Government | Legislation and Fiscal or other Incentives | Schemes and their Incidence<br>CRANET: Offered in Firms with >200 Empl.<br>EWCS: Take-up Rate of Empl. |
|---|---|---|---|
| Bulgaria | [A] TU open to FP, EA indifferent; not a current topic on either of their agendas<br>[B] ESO strong support 1997–2000 since then ignored; in 2002 PrivL incentives abolished; FP generally ignored | ESO: None; NTL – Uniform 7% dividend tax<br>PS: None; NTL – SPS personal income tax exempt | 2005 CRANET: ESO 38%, PS 5%<br>2005 EWCS: ESO 1.8%, PS 6.3%<br>ESO: 10% Mass Privatisation, 4–5% Cash Privatisation; low, decreasing<br>MEBO: 1,436, 28% privatisations; managers took over most<br>PS: AI, few cases survey evidence;<br>SO: 2005 CRANET 14% |
| Cyprus | [A] FP not an issue on TU/EA agendas<br>[B] FP so far ignored | ESO: NCL – discounted ES in JSC; financing ES by firm possible; NTL – dividends and gains from share sale tax-free<br>PS: None | 2005 CRANET: ESO 10%, PS 7.7%<br>2005 EWCS: ESO 1.2%, PS 2.7%<br>SO: 2005 CRANET: 4%<br>ESO/PS: AI, insignificant |
| Czech Republic | [A] TU/EA indifferent to FP, not a current topic on their agendas<br>[B] ESOP discussed in 1990; FP ignored after introduction of voucher concept | ESO: NCL – discounted ES/SPS in JSC; not considered public offering; ES discount limit: 5% of equity capital, financing by firm possible; NTL – uniform 15% dividend tax<br>PS: NCL – CPS/SPS in JSC; NLL: negotiable in collective bargaining agreements | 2005 CRANET: ESO 14%, PS 27%<br>2005 EWCS: ESO 1.6%, PS 11%<br>SO: 2005 CRANET: 3%<br>ESO: Insignificant; 0.31% of the privatised assets<br>PS: AI, insignificant |
| Estonia | [A] TU indifferent to FP, EA opposed to any extension of employee participation | ESO: NCL rights attached to shares issued before 1 September 1995 remain valid; no public prospectus | 2005 CRANET: ESO 9.6%, PS 11%<br>2005 EWCS: ESO 2%, PS 11%<br>ESO: 2005 2% (1995 after |

| | | | |
|---|---|---|---|
| | [B] PrivL supported ESO until 1992 after 1993 FP ignored | for ES needed; NTL Empl.: no income tax on dividends from resident firms; EmpC 22% on distributed profit, only 'bonus issue' in capital increase exempt PS: None | privatisation 20%) of firms majority employee-owned, 20% minority PS: AI, survey evidence, very few cases |
| Hungary | [A] FP for managers means to avoid external control, for employees to preserve workplace; TU lobbied ES/ESO in privatisation, recently passive; EA indifferent [B] ESOP/ES strong support in PrivL until 1996; climate FP friendly but lack of concrete economic policy decisions | ESO: PrivL – preferential sale; discount maximum 10% firms assets and 150% of annual min. pay, instalments; Decree Egzisztencia Credit; NCL – specific ES in JSC, discounted or free, maximum 15% of equity capital, financing by firm possible; since 2003 tax-qualified stock plans, first HUF 0.5 million free, then 20% tax, three-year holding period SO: NTL – PIT base is value at exercise ESOP: ESOP Law 1992 preferential credit; corporate tax exempt until end 1996; contribution to plan maximum 20% tax deductible; tax base lowered PS: None | 2005 CRANET: ESO 15%, PS 15% 2005 EWCS: ESO 1%, PS 3% ESO: 1998 1% of assets privatised; preferential privatisation in 540 firms; CS strong decline; now AI, 30% of firms (70% SO, 30% ES), mostly foreign ESOP: initially 287 employing 80,000, in 2005 151 left; 1.2% of employment by private firms PS: AI, 20% of firms, mostly foreign, only 10% of entitled receive profit SO: 2005 CRANET 27% |

(Continued)

*Table 1.2*   (Continued)

| Country | General attitude<br>[A] Social Partners<br>[B] Government | Legislation and Fiscal or other Incentives | Schemes and their Incidence<br>CRANET: Offered in Firms with >200 Empl.<br>EWCS: Take-up Rate of Empl. |
|---|---|---|---|
| Latvia | [A] TU/EA indifferent to FP, not a current topic on their agendas;<br>[B] Little support for ESO in PrivL; FP so far ignored | ESO: PrivL – maximum 20% ES; specific ES in state and public firms; NCL – preferential ES in JSC free and discounted, in capital increases maximum 10% of equity capital non-voting stock<br>PS: None | 2005 EWCS: ESO 0.6%, PS 8.5%<br>ESO: PrivL 110.6 million vouchers to 2.5 million people; AI, 1999 16% of 915 firms dominant ESO but falling over time<br>PS: AI, 7% of firms; mostly IT, consulting, real estate |
| Lithuania | [A] Climate FP friendly; TU interested, lack of actions; EA support individual firms<br>[B] ESOP/ES strong support in PrivL until 1996; now FP not on political agenda of parliament and government | ESO: PrivL – 5% ES deferred payment maximum five years; NCL – in corporations ES for three years non-transferable and non-voting, financing by firm possible; NTL – uniform 15% dividend tax; after holding period profits from sale of shares not taxed<br>PS: None | 2008 PEPPER IV: ESO 4%, PS 36%<br>2005 EWCS: ESO 0.9%, PS 4%;<br>ESO: low and decreasing; AI, 2000 36% (1995 92%) privatised firms dominant ESO, falling over time;<br>PS: AI; CPS mostly foreign (IT, consulting, advertising, and so on); DPS few cases 2005 linked to employee savings plan |
| Malta | [A] TU support schemes in practice; FP not a current topic in national tripartite dialogue<br>[B] FP collateral effect of nationalisation (1980s) and privatisation (1990s) not a current issue | ESO: NCL – ES in corporations, exempt from prospectus and investment rules; maximum 10% discount, financing by firm possible; NTL – SO only taxable at exercise<br>ESOP: Trust Act refers to FP; taxed 15% interest, 10% investment<br>PS: mentioned in NLL | 2005 EWCS: ESO 0.7%, PS 3.9%<br>ESO: AI; banking sector: ES, SAYE scheme, SO,<br>ESOP: AI, Trust Funds in Bank of Valetta and Malta Telecom<br>PS: AI; 2004 public sector (shipyard 1,761 employees); private (foreign) firms, mostly reserved for management |

| | | | |
|---|---|---|---|
| Romania | [A] TU support individual cases; EA avoid topic; tripartite council tackled FP sporadically<br>[B] ESO supported until 1997 especially MEBO; then support declined; current government gives little support and has other priorities | ESO: PrivL – aim 30% of privatised assets vouchers and ES; vouchers free; 10% discount ES; NCL – ES in JSC, financing by firm possible; NTL – 10% dividend tax<br>ESOP: PrivL on Empl. Associations; leveraged transaction, preferential credit, maximum interest rate 10%<br>PS: Ordinance – CPS compulsory in state and municipal firms | 2008 PEPPER IV: ESO 6%, PS 42%<br>2005 EWCS: ESO 1.6%, PS 5%;<br>ESO: ES 10% of shares issued at privatisation, decreasing<br>ESOP: 1998 one-third of privatisations, most frequently used single method 2000: 2,632 firms, average 65% ESO, 1,652 majority ESO<br>PS: estimated 1.2 million Empl. in public sector covered |
| Poland | [A] TU/EA indifferent to FP; managers and employees pragmatically motivated; Lobby groups and institutions, for example banks, for ESO<br>[B] FP Supported in early privatisation period; ESO in most privatisations, since mid-1990s decreasing support; PS increased emphasis in the context of collective bargaining agreements | ESO: PrivL – 15% ES for free, two years non-transferable, maximum value 18-month minimum pay National Investment Funds 1995 (NIF), shares for symbolic fee; NCL – ES/SPS in JSC, financing by firm possible; NTL – uniform 15% dividend tax<br>EBO: PrivL – Leveraged lease buyout (LLBO), anticipated ownership transfer possible; interest 50% of refinance rate; interest part of lease payments are costs; Insolvency law – buyout right<br>PS: NCL – CPS/SPS in JSC | 2008 PEPPER IV: ESO 40%, PS 26%<br>2005 EWCS: ESO 0.7%, PS 5%<br>ESO: low and declining; AI in privatised firms, 2000 circa 11.4% (1998 12.7%); NIF adult citizens one share in 15 funds<br>EBO: LLBO 2002 one-third of privatisations, most frequently used single method, 1,335 firms employing 162,000, 14% over 250 Empl.<br>PS: AI, limited to management |

(Continued)

*Table 1.2* (Continued)

| Country | General attitude<br>[A] Social Partners<br>[B] Government | Legislation and Fiscal or other Incentives | Schemes and their Incidence<br>CRANET: Offered in Firms with >200 Empl.<br>EWCS: Take-up Rate of Empl. |
|---|---|---|---|
| Slovakia | [A] TU/EA indifferent to FP, not a current topic on their agendas<br>[B] ESOP discussed in 1990; EBO concept failed 1995; FP now generally ignored | ESO: NCL – discounted ES and SPS in JSC; maximum 70% discount or financing by firm possible<br>PS: NCL – CPS/SPS in JSC | 2005 CRANET: ESO 12.7%, PS 17%<br>2005 EWCS: ESO 2.3%, PS 28%<br>SO: 2005 CRANET 10%<br>ESO: Insignificant; AI, banking sector and new privatisations<br>EBO: AI, in privatisation, usually management-led |
| Slovenia | [A] TU/EA very supportive to FP; Employee Ownership Association lobbies legislation; active support by works councils and the Association of Managers<br>[B] Strong political support to FP; draft laws 1997/2005 in parliament rejected; new law on FP in 2008 | All schemes: since 2008 70% tax relief for PS and ESO with one-year holding period (100% relief with > three-year); maximum 20% profits or 10% total salaries per year and maximum 5,000 EUR per employee<br>ESO: PrivL – maximum 20% ES for vouchers; vouchers free, shares for overdue claims; NCL – ES/SPS in corporations; discount and financing by firm possible<br>EBO: maximum 40%, shares four years non-transferable; worker association proxy organisation under Takeover law<br>PS: PrivL – SPS in internal buyout | 2005 CRANET: ESO 14%, PS 20%;<br>2005 EWCS: ESO 2.6%, PS 18%<br>ESO/EBO: 90% of privatised firms; CS 1998 60% majority ESO while only 23% of capital (2004 18% strong decline)<br>PS: CS, in statutes of 32% of firms, but unexploited in 22%; for board members 20% of listed firms<br>SO: 2005 CRANET 4% |

| Croatia | [A] TU recently promote ESO in revision of privatisation; EA indifferent to FP; long tradition of self-management<br>[B] ESO supported until 1995, since then FP ignored; ESOPs planned in new PrivL | ESO: NCL – ES in JSC financing by firm possible; NTL – dividends tax exempt; profits from sale of shares not taxed<br>ESOP: general rules of NCL apply<br>PS: None | 2008 PEPPERIV: ESO 34%, PS 29%<br>ESO: 2005 more than 10% of value of privatised firms (1996 20%); 2004 12% firms with majority ESO<br>ESOP: Survey evidence, ESOP elements in 9,4% of firms (52 out of 552), completed ESOP circa in one-fourth of them<br>PS: AI |
| Turkey | [A] Climate FP friendly; TU supportive, EA undecided, split; employees interested<br>[B] FP issue 1968 in Tax Reform Commission; some attention to individual privatisations; 2002 programme, lack of concrete measures | ESO: PrivL decrees for individual firms; discount and instalments; NTL – after one year share-sale profits not taxed; for SO limited tax on dividends and profits from sale<br>IntE: NCL/CivC 'welfare/mutual assistance funds' of firms; financing by firm profits and contributions<br>PS: NCL/CivC both CFS and SPS; maximum 10% prior reserve | 2005 EWCS: ESO 1.3%, PS 2.4%<br>2005 CRANET: ESO 4.4%, PS 8.9%, SO, 1%<br>ESO: AI, PrivL 12 cases 9–37% ESO, one case majority, up to 15% discount; SO/ESO private firms mostly foreign (26 registered, 35 applications) 2007 survey evidence: 3–4% of publicly traded companies<br>IntE: Not specified<br>PS: AI, retained profits as dividends widespread; CS 38 out of 50 listed firms; 2007 survey evidence: 20% of publicly traded companies |

*Sources*: PEPPER I–IV and: CNMV 2003; CRANET 2005/1999 (firms with more than 200 Empl.); EU Stock Options Report 2003; EWCS 2005 (take-up rate); FONDACT 2004 Heissmann 2003; IAB 2005; IBEC 2002; ifsProShare 2006; WKÖ/BAK 2005; WSI 2003; please note that the country data of the different surveys is incoherent due to inconsistencies in methodology and definitions. Excluded from studies: management buyout, general savings plans, consumer and housing co-operatives.

*Abbreviations*: AI = anecdotal information only; CGT = capital gains tax; CivC = Civil Code; CPS = cash-based profit-sharing; CS = case studies; DPS = deferred profit-sharing; EA = employer associations; EBO = employee buyout; EmpC = employer company; Empl. = employee; ES = employee shares; ESO = employee share ownership; ESOP = Employee Stock Ownership Plan; FP = financial participation; IEnt = intermediary entities; JSC = joint-stock companies; MEBO = management-employee buyout; NCL = national company law; NLL = national labour legislation; NTL = national tax legislation; PIT = personal income tax; PrivL = privatisation legislation; PS = profit-sharing; SO = stock options; SPS = share-based profit-sharing; SSC = social security contributions; TU = trade unions.

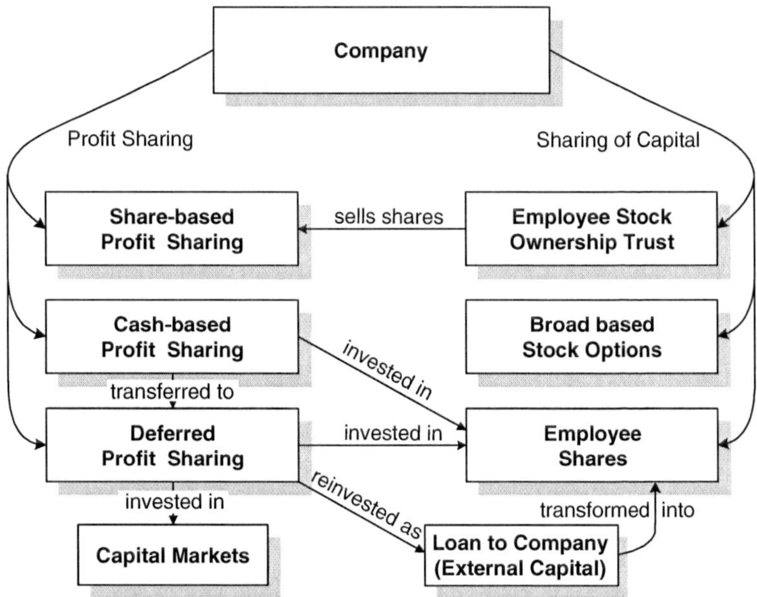


*Figure 1.1*   The building block approach.

### 1.4.1.1   *Module One: Profit-sharing (cash-based and deferred)*

In cash-based profit-sharing (CPS) and deferred profit-sharing schemes (DPS), part of an employee's remuneration is directly linked to the profits of the enterprise. In contrast to individual incentives, this concept involves a collective scheme that generally applies to all employees. The formula may include profits, productivity and return on investment. Bonuses are normally paid in addition to a basic fixed wage and provide a variable source of income. They may be paid out in cash or on a deferred basis into a company saving scheme, and can be invested in the capital markets or the company's shares (see Figure 1.2).

A considerable body of evidence suggests that the introduction of profit-sharing correlates with a rise in the level of productivity in a company.[75] The consistency of the findings on the incentive effect on profitability is remarkable. Profit-sharing is associated with higher productivity levels in every case regardless of the methods, model specification or data used.[76] Although profit-sharing schemes operate successfully, even without tax or social security exemptions (for example, in Germany), a disadvantage of these schemes in the context of a European Concept is their dependency on the necessary administrative

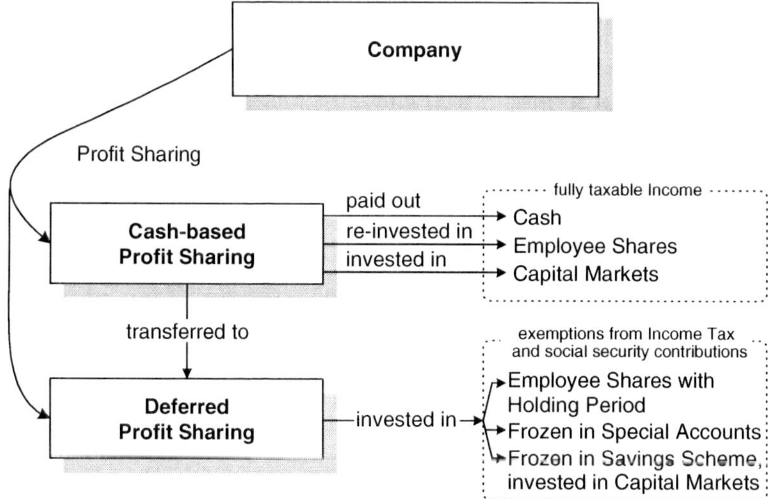

*Figure 1.2*  Profit-sharing.

infrastructure. A further downside in cross-border plans is the fact that they are typically based on individual firms rather than on controlled group profits.[77]

Financial participation schemes, and in particular profit-sharing bonuses that are paid in cash, should also have the effect of making total remuneration more flexible and therefore more responsive to macroeconomic shocks. This wage flexibility is seen as a means of reducing the risk of unemployment in periods of recession and therefore promoting greater employment stability.[78] In some Western countries, recent findings have confirmed this effect while, in contrast, other studies suggest no relationship, or question the methods and outcome because of the periods of investigation.[79]

### 1.4.1.2   Module Two: Employee shareholding (employee shares and broad-based stock options)

In share ownership plans, shares may be distributed for free or may be sold at the market price or under preferential conditions. The latter may include sale at a discount rate (discounted stock purchase plan), sale at a lower price through forms of delayed payment (usually within a capital increase), or by giving priority in public offerings to all or a group of employees. To defer the valuation problem in unlisted SMEs,[80] capital participation may initially take the form of an employee loan

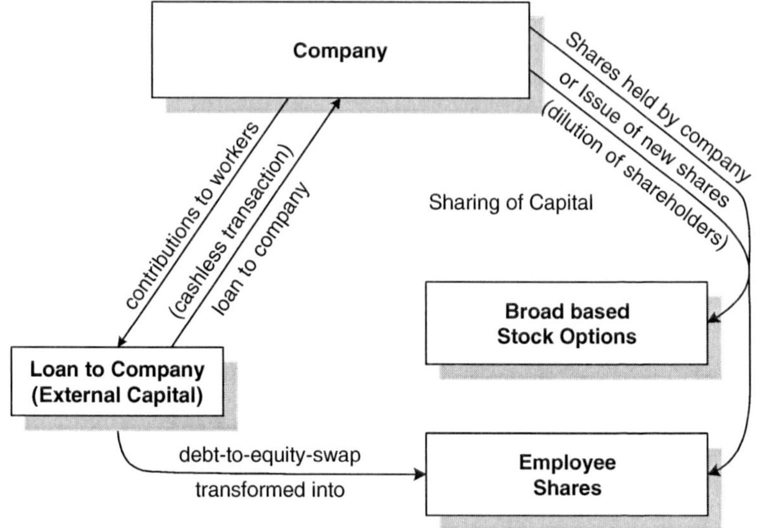



*Figure 1.3*   Employee shareholding.

to the company, creating corporate debt (external capital) subsequently converted into company shares.[81] Valuation of the shares designated for acquisition through the loan can be postponed until the moment of the actual conversion into shares (debt-to-equity) without impeding the implementation of the scheme (see Figure 1.3).

Employee stock options,[82] unlike executive stock options granted to reward individual performance, are broad-based. The company grants employees options that entitle them to acquire shares in the company at a later date, but at a per share price fixed at the time the option is granted. Potential gain from rising stock values is the primary reward conferred by options. Unlike conventional options, employee stock options as a rule cannot be traded, and the holder cannot usually hedge against the risk of a decline in value. Furthermore, employee stock options are normally subject to forfeiture before vesting should the employee voluntarily leave the firm.

When a company contributes newly issued stock to its employees, the current stockholders suffer a dilution in equity per share. Theoretically, this dilution can be compensated for by increased productivity and profitability as a result of higher employee motivation and increased working capital, which increases the value of all company shares. Although some studies[83] confirm this result, the issue remains widely disputed (except in 100 per cent ESOPs or in buyouts where no newly issued shares are involved).

Sceptics voice concern that share ownership subjects employees to an additional risk. Because they are encouraged to put a part of their wealth into the shares of their own companies, rather than other companies, risk is concentrated rather than diversified.[84] The advocates of share ownership maintain that reasonable investment in shares of their own companies represents a good portfolio allocation, because these shares are positively correlated with a return on their most valuable asset, their own work. On the whole, this theoretical debate has not yet produced decisive results. It seems that collective investment funds operating on a branch level,[85] or investment and credit insurance backed by the government,[86] could spread the risk and thus compensate for the 'double-risk'. However, the risks are very limited if the scheme only involves a benefit in addition to the basic wages.

### 1.4.1.3  *Module Three: ESOPs and share-based profit-sharing*

Share-based profit-sharing (SPS) is a form of deferred profit-sharing with the profit share being paid in shares of the company, which are usually frozen in a fund for a certain period of time, after which workers are allowed to dispose of them. Similarly, ESOPs are funded by the company either contributing shares to the plan, contributing cash that the plan uses to buy shares, or by having the plan borrow money to buy new or existing shares. The schemes may be combined (see Figure 1.4), resulting in the following essential structure:[87]

- The company establishes an ESOT in favour of its employees.
- The trust is usually financed by a combination of company contributions and borrowings. Company contributions often are part of a profit-sharing agreement with the employees. The trust may borrow money directly from a bank or from the company, which in turn may take a loan from a bank or other lender. Shares are either acquired directly from the existing shareholders or by a new share issue. The trust loan is usually guaranteed by the company, but in some cases it is without recourse to the company.
- The shares are held collectively in the trust, and are only allocated to individual employees accounts, or distributed, after a particular holding period. This holding period may be either a matter for the trustees to determine, or it may be driven by the need to repay borrowings before distributing shares, or it may be driven by tax holding periods before the shares can be distributed free of income tax. Most commonly, it is a combination of all three.

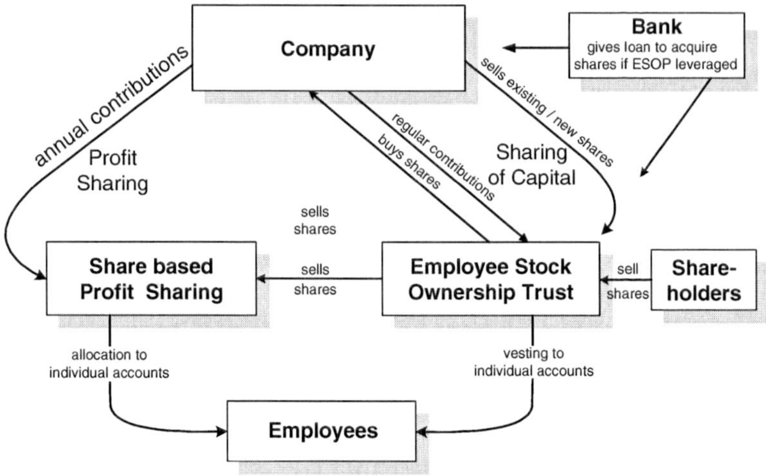


*Figure 1.4*   Employee Stock Ownership Plans and share-based profit-sharing.

- When a share-based profit-sharing scheme is used to distribute the shares, the shares are usually transferred by the ESOT to the profit-sharing scheme without the profit-sharing scheme being required to pay for them. Alternatively the company can make a payment to the profit-sharing scheme to allow the scheme to acquire the shares from the trust. In either case, the shares will be vested in individual employees once they are transferred to the profit-sharing scheme.
- The loan may be repaid by direct cash contributions from the company to the trust, monies received from sale of shares to the share-based profit-sharing scheme, or dividends on the shares held in the trust.

### 1.4.1.4   *Specific features of ESOPs*

Unlike a pension plan, which as a rule requires diversification, an ESOP is specifically designed to hold employer securities. An ESOP can be used by a company that does not have a listing for its shares to create an internal market for the employees to buy and sell the company's shares. This can be done if the ESOP both distributes shares to the employees and operates a market whereby employees can sell their shares and acquire further ones. Usually, a process such as a bi-annual share auction is used. The ESOP can provide liquidity to this internal market if it is also a buyer of shares in this internal market. The shares that the ESOP buys will then be distributed to employees in subsequent distributions. The creation of a market for the shares of an otherwise illiquid company makes the ESOP a financial tool that benefits both employees and the employer company.

In this context, an important feature of an ESOP is that it can be leveraged by taking out an external loan to buy shares in the employer company. This leverage potential is most important because it can accommodate large transactions for the company and its shareholders while creating particularly sizeable capital ownership in employee accounts. The ESOP debt is funded by appropriately timed contributions from the company to the ESOT. Of course, any dividends earned by the stock may also help to pay off the loan, but this is more of a complementary element.[88] As with any other bank loan, ESOP loans must be repaid, regardless of whether the dividends on the stock are sufficient to pay off the loan. By making the loan payments tax deductible to the corporation, as, for example, in the USA, the loan is repaid with tax-free income, in contrast to a conventional re-capitalisation loan that must be paid back with after-tax income.[89]

Utilising corporate credit to guarantee the loan which funds the acquisition of employee shares by the ESOT and writing off loan repayments as expenses deductible from taxable corporate income substantially reduces the financing costs.[90] Given the additional advantage that the shares are not sold to outsiders, thus eliminating the risk of loss of control, the ESOP solution in most cases will be preferable to a conventional bank loan. Of course, any of the objectives of an ESOP, resulting in any percentage of shareholding from 1 per cent to 100 per cent, can be achieved on an unleveraged basis over time.

An ESOP, considered only as an umbrella term to cover a trust set up by a company to put shares in the hand of its employees, is similar in many ways to a share-based profit-sharing scheme but most importantly is not as limited. Whereas the latter has only one source of funds (that is, direct contributions from the employer company), the ESOP can be financed from such different sources as:

- a loan from the employer company, from a selling shareholder or from a financial institution such as a bank;
- dividend earnings;
- sale of shares to its related share-based profit-sharing scheme;
- contributions from the employer company.

Share-based profit-sharing schemes, while providing the company with a vehicle to deliver shares to the employees, offer a very limited market for those shares. The ESOP not only provides a new source of shares that can be sold to a profit-sharing scheme, but it also has the advantage of providing workers with an internal market to which they can sell their shares, which at the same time recycles shares for the accounts of future employees. This internal market is of major importance in unlisted SMEs for which no other ready source of liquidity exists.

Leveraged employee share ownership, on the other hand, as in the case of ESOPs, involves an additional element of risk. Whereas profit-sharing plans represent a variable financial burden, leveraged schemes require fixed loan amortisation payments regardless of the company's financial performance – a condition similar to taking on debt. In fact, such loans are treated as a liability if the company guarantees the loan or commits to future contributions to service it. Thus, if a company is not growing or becomes unprofitable, the repayment obligation can threaten its ability to survive. Furthermore, closely held companies may be obliged to purchase the shares of departing plan participants because of the absence of a public market for their stock.[91] In such a case, the repurchase liability in a successful company generally increases over time as the appraised value of the company's stock rises, although it does not usually increase as a percentage of the company's free cash flow.[92] If a company does not plan adequately to meet this liability, it may be forced to make a public offering of its stock to eliminate the repurchase obligation, an expedient that is not only very expensive but also involves a loss of control and independence and the loss of opportunity to future employees.[93] A better alternative is the creation of a 'sinking fund', although in small companies it may be difficult to develop accurate actuarial assumptions.[94] Where a relatively large portion of the repurchase liability is attributed to a few plan participants, the use of life insurance may be appropriate.[95]

Finally, the costs of designing and implementing a financial participation scheme can be considerable. To these must be added the ongoing costs for administration, legal services and employee communication. An additional expense for closely held companies arises from the need for an annual appraisal of the company's value by an outside expert. For a medium-sized US ESOP company, the installation costs are approximately USD 40,000 with the annual administration costs, including appraisal, ranging to about USD 15,000.[96] Generally speaking, unless a company is medium-sized, these costs may outweigh possible tax advantages.[97]

### 1.4.2   Options for creating the legal foundations of a European concept

*1.4.2.1   Recommendation according to Article 249 Paragraph 1 (1) ECT*

The European Concept could be framed as a Recommendation according to Article 249 paragraph 1 (1) ECT. The downside of such a solution, however, is that Recommendations according to Article 249 paragraph 5 ECT are not legally binding and thus implementation in the Member States would be far from certain. On the other hand, legislation of such schemes in any form whatsoever is a major step forward, as it sets up a distinct legal entity for companies to refer to and provides a framework for company decisions and actions in those countries that approve the European Concept.

One possible solution to the problem of national implementation would be a recognition procedure by Member States for financial participation similar to that proposed by the High Level Group of Independent Experts.[98] As a result of this procedure, single Member States would recognise single elements from the European Concept drawn up in the Recommendation as equivalent to a plan drawn up under its own laws and provide equivalent benefits. In this way, they would provide companies operating under their legislation with a legal framework that delineates what is possible without invoking sanctions from regulatory, legal and taxation authorities. Recognition is nonetheless a major step and would require considerable co-operation between the Member States and the Commission.

*1.4.2.2   Directive level: Amending existing European company law*

Considering the difficulties in passing and implementing European Directives, especially in sensitive areas where unanimous decisions may be required, it seems preferable to amend existing European legislation. Because employee share ownership fits into the framework of company law, rules to implement it could be proposed as an amendment of the European Company legislation. Like the European Company Statute[99] (ECS), which provides an option for forming a supranational company, there could be an amendment to the ECS permitting such companies to create 'European Employee Shareholding' as an option.[100] This option could be easily extended to other companies that do not fall under the ECS, provided that national legislation would then be adapted to the requirements of the supranational statute.

The EU Member States would have an incentive to implement legal rules pertaining to the 'European Employee Shareholding Statute' as an amendment to the ECS, choosing from a variety of incentives, possibly including tax breaks as well as other preferential treatment:

- Unlike the supplementary rules to the ECS concerning participation in decision making, those on 'European Employee Shareholding' would be totally voluntary; they would apply only if the company decides to adopt one of the existing models of financial participation.
- As in the case of the supplementary rules to the ECS on participation in decision making,[101] the scheme would be, at first hand, proposed by the employers to their employees; in other words, a negotiated proposition. If the proposed scheme does not correspond to a catalogue of minimum requirements, or the parties so decide, a statutory set of standard rules would apply as a 'safe harbour'.

The mechanism of the 'default standard rules' concerning participation in decision making, foreseen in the ECS for resolving potential conflict while not imposing a solution, would even be suitable in the field of financial participation:

- As for the 'standard rules' for private and/or unlisted SMEs, an ESOP trust would be feasible because it may provide a relatively non-controversial solution to the question of employee voting rights and may buffer potential risk more easily, while solving the problem of business succession.
- As for the 'standard rules' for quoted medium-sized and large enterprises, a restricted broad-based employee stock option or stock purchase scheme (as practised in the United Kingdom) seems to be feasible since there has already been substantial development in European harmonisation on the one hand (see below), and a remarkable initiative put forward by the Directorate-General for Enterprise and Industry on the other.[102]

### 1.4.2.3   *National level: Building on existing national company law*

Given the difficulties in arriving at a supranational compromise either in the Commission or in the Council that have been described above, in order to reach a regulation at the supranational level, the simplest solution is to build on existing national legislation originating in the *acquis communautaire*. A rare example of such legal 'common ground' is some of the national rules on listed and unlisted joint-stock companies originating in the implementation of European law that is the second Council

Directive on Company Law 77/91/EEC, dating back to 13 December 1976. Article 19 paragraph 3, Article 23 paragraph 2 and Article 41 paragraphs 1 and 2 of the Directive allow Member States to deviate from the European legal framework of joint-stock companies in order to encourage employee financial participation. Although primarily referring to share ownership schemes these – optional – regulations also leave room for combination with profit-sharing schemes.

Article 19 paragraph 3 allows Member States to deviate from the restrictive rules governing exemptions from the general prohibition against a company acquiring its own stock. When the shares acquired by the company are earmarked for distribution to that company's employees or to the employees of an associate company, a general shareholders assembly decision is not obligatory although such shares must be distributed within 12 months of acquisition.[103]

Member States may lift the limit of the nominal value of the acquired shares of 10 per cent of the subscribed capital (including shares previously acquired by the company and held by it, and shares acquired by a person acting in his own name but on the company's behalf) though, according to Article 41 paragraph 1.

As an exception to the general prohibition against a company leveraging the acquisition of its own shares, Article 23 paragraph 2 allows Member States to permit companies to advance funds, make loans and provide security (financial assistance), with the intention of selling these shares to company employees. Article 41 paragraph 1 further allows for deviations from general rules and restrictions to encourage employee financial participation during the process of raising additional capital. An example is the financing of the share issue from the companies' own funds or through a profit-sharing scheme. Finally, the opening clause of Article 41 paragraph 2 of the Directive providing for the possibility of suspension of Articles 30, 31, 36, 37, 38 and 39 for companies under a special law issuing collectively held workers' shares, has not been used except in the case of France[104].

As Table 1.3 illustrates, a surprisingly large majority of Member States have adopted national legislation permitting a company to acquire its own shares in order to transfer them to its employees (implemented in 17, possible in 25), and to facilitate this acquisition by financial assistance (implemented in 23). Despite the fact that this legislation has rarely been used in some countries, the existence of corresponding regulations across the EU may serve as a foundation for a European Concept.

*Table 1.3*   Implementation of the Second Council Directive on Company Law 77/91/EEC

| Country | Article 19 paragraph 3 permission to acquire companies own shares for its employees | Article 23 permission to advance funds, make loans, provide security (financial assistance), with a view to acquisition | Article 41 paragraph 1 derogation to encourage financial participation in case of capital increases | Other general provisions in company law to promote financial participation |
|---|---|---|---|---|
| **EU-15** | | | | |
| Belgium | Without decision of general assembly | Value of financial assistance within distributable reserves; net assets must not become less than subscribed capital; also firms founded by employees who hold more than 50% of voting rights | Five years not transferable, limit: 20% of equity capital; maximum 20% discount | No |
| Denmark | Limit: equity capital exceeds distributional dividend; share capital less own shares held must amount to not less than DKK 500,000 | If qualified stock purchase plan; also acquisition from employees; to extent that shareholders' equity in firm exceeds amount of not distributable dividends | According to articles of association issue of new and bonus shares; also subsidiary employees; authorisation up to five years each; also other than by cash payment | Deviation from subscription and pre-emption rights by decision of general assembly (two-thirds of votes and equity capital) for benefit of employees |
| Germany | Without decision of general assembly; also (former) employees or of affiliated firms; reserve | Yes | Stock options for firms' and affiliated firms' employees; general assembly decision; | In firms with individual share certificates number of shares to be increased to the same extent as |

| | | | | |
|---|---|---|---|---|
| | fund necessary without reducing equity capital or reserve funds | | nominal amount of options restricted to 10%, that of increase to 50% of equity capital | equity capital is increased |
| Greece | Also personnel of ancillary firms | No | Shares and stock options, free and discounted; three years not transferable without general assembly approval | No |
| Spain | Also for stock options | Yes | No | No |
| France | In context of share-based profit-sharing scheme, share savings plan or stock option scheme | Also in subsidiaries or companies included in a group savings scheme | For all schemes; general assembly decision required; no public offering | Employee stock options; share-based deferred profit-sharing; save-as-you-earn schemes |
| Ireland | Not specific for employees, generally possible | Firm and group firm; provision of money and loans under share scheme; present and former employees and members of families | No | Finance Acts: share-based profit-sharing; save-as-you-earn and share purchase schemes |
| Italy | No | Value of financial assistance within distributable reserves | Pre-emptive right of shareholders can be suspended for up to 25% of new shares with majority general assembly vote; more than 25% require majority of capital held | Special 'Employees Shares' can be issued in capital increase with specific rules for form, tradability and rights |

(Conitnued)

*Table 1.3*   (Continued)

| Country | Article 19 paragraph 3 permission to acquire companies own shares for its employees | Article 23 permission to advance funds, make loans, provide security (financial assistance), with a view to acquisition | Article 41 paragraph 1 derogation to encourage financial participation in case of capital increases | Other general provisions in company law to promote financial participation |
|---|---|---|---|---|
| Luxembourg | As minimum requirements of Directive | Limit: net assets of firm not lower than amount of subscribed capital plus reserves | No | No |
| Netherlands | Also employees of group firm; without decision of general assembly, if articles of association provide; equity capital reduced by acquisition price not less than amount paid for shares plus reserve funds | Yes (but restrictions for closed JSC) | No | No |
| Austria | Also employees of affiliated firms; reserve fund for own shares to be established without reducing of equity capital or other reserve funds; stock options without decision of general assembly, but consent of Supervisory board | No | Stock options for firms and affiliated firms employees; general assembly decision; nominal amount of options restricted to 10%, that of increase to 50% of equity capital; limit of 20% of equity capital for total amount of shares receivable | In firms with individual share certificates the number of shares has to be increased to the same extent as equity capital is increased |

| Portugal | Not specific for employees, generally possible, if partnership contract does not provide for anything else | Also to employees of affiliated firms; liquid assets must not become less than subscribed capital plus not distributable reserves | General assembly may limit and abolish pre-emptive right of shareholders for 'social reasons' | No |
| --- | --- | --- | --- | --- |
| Finland | Not specific for employees, generally possible | Yes, if interest rate is less than the reference interest rate, difference is taxable benefit and subject to social tax | No special regulation with a view to employees | Act on Personnel Funds |
| Sweden | Not specific for employees, generally possible | Employees of firm and group firm; total value limited; min. 50% of firms' employees covered; advance and loan to be repaid within five years | General assembly can suspend shareholders pre-emptive right of; also group firm; also wife, husband and children | No |
| United Kingdom | Not specific for employees, generally possible | Firm and group firm; provision of money and loans under share scheme; present and former employees, also family members; net assets must not become less than subscribed capital; value of financial assistance within distributable reserves | No | Finance Acts: share-based profit-sharing; save-as-you-earn and share purchase schemes |



(Conitnued)

*Table 1.3*   (Continued)

| Country | Article 19 paragraph 3 permission to acquire companies own shares for its employees | Article 23 permission to advance funds, make loans, provide security (financial assistance), with a view to acquisition | Article 41 paragraph 1 derogation to encourage financial participation in case of capital increases | Other general provisions in company law to promote financial participation |
|---|---|---|---|---|
| **New Members** | | | | |
| Bulgaria | Not specific for employees, generally possible | No | No | No |
| Cyprus | Without decision of general assembly | Advance funds and make loans to employees | No | No |
| Czech Republic | Without general assembly decision provided for reserve | In accordance with articles of association | Financing from company profits or profit-sharing; not considered public offering | Discount limit: 5% of equity capital, covered by firms own resources |
| Estonia | Not spec. for employees, generally possible | No | No | No |
| Hungary | Not specific for employees, generally possible | Also employees of controlled firms or organisations founded by employees | Both, free and discounted special employee shares, not considered public offering | Free and discounted employee shares; limit: 15% equity capital; not transferable; obligation to sell back |
| Latvia | Firm may fully pay up stock, not transferable; for maximum six months | No | Non-voting shares, maximum 10% of equity capital, covered by firms profit; no public offering | Employee shares in municipal and state firms; not transferable; obligation to sell back |

| | | | | |
|---|---|---|---|---|
| Lithuania | Not specific for employees, generally possible | Advance funds or loan paid back by deductions from employees' salary | Non-voting shares for maximum three-year period in which share sale only to other employees | No |
| Malta | Without decision of general assembly | For employees of firm and group firm; provided it does not endanger firms own funds | No | Free and discounted shares of parent firm for employees; no prospectus needed |
| Poland | Also retired employees and affiliated firms; reserve needed | Reserve needed, also employees of affiliated companies | Financing from firms' profits and profit-sharing; not considered public offering | No |
| Romania | Financed by profits and/or distributable reserves | Yes | No | No |
| Slovakia | In accordance with articles of association | Provided it does not endanger company's own funds | By decision of the general assembly | Discounted share offers, discount maximum 70% covered by firms' own resources |
| Slovenia | Also retired employees and of associate firms | Also employees of associate companies | Financing from profit-sharing possible | No |
| **Candidate countries** | | | | |
| Croatia | Also employees of associated firms; reserve from profits needed | Reserve needed; must not endanger equity capital | Among others to fulfil employees' claims to acquire shares | No |
| Turkey | Not specific for employees, generally possible | No | No | No |

## 1.5   Conclusions and summary

### 1.5.1   Compliance with the postulates of the European policymakers

*1.5.1.1   Achieving competitiveness while maintaining diversity*

Financial participation of employees is closely linked to the objectives of the Lisbon summit for making the European economy 'the most competitive and dynamic knowledge-based economy in the world, capable of sustainable economic growth with more and better jobs and greater social cohesion'.[105] Our proposed European Concept refers – as does the Commission – particularly to the experience in the USA that demonstrates the impact such a model can have 'in terms of economic growth, fostering industrial change and making sure that all workers participate in this growing prosperity'.[106] Therefore, in order to harness the potential – still largely unexploited in Europe – of the further development of financial participation as part of an overall strategy for stimulating the growth of new, dynamic companies as the Commission requires, we advocate the development of ESOPs.

Although the thesis that democracy requires a broad distribution of wealth is widely accepted, present social policy has not yet responded to the growing concentration of wealth; no regulations have come into force either at a national or a European level. Social attention so far has been focused on the growing wealth of the few (for example, anti-monopoly legislation). Given this context, an open, modular concept ideally responds to the need for developing regulations at the supranational level in order to support financial participation more actively and to overcome national differences in taxation policy. At the same time, such a legal framework, while providing a broader incentive system, delineates what companies may do without inviting sanctions from regulatory, legal and taxation authorities.

A legal foundation at the European level has to focus on 'majority vote' regulations if it is to be successful. Thus it should encompass a broad incentive system that provides different and flexible solutions compatible with those already established in the Member States:

- Relatively widespread in the EU are profit-sharing schemes, stock options and employee shares.
- In countries with an Anglo-American tradition, for example, the United Kingdom and Ireland, ESOPs are also to be found.
- Central and Eastern European countries have developed share ownership systems (rather than profit-sharing schemes) with shares being

distributed for free or sold at the market price or under preferential conditions.

The apparent difference in legal and political priorities between East and West is because the first priority of post-socialist legislators is to change the socialist economic system through privatisation and re-privatisation. Therefore the development of these schemes does not necessarily constitute a progressive evolution of their pay system or their work organisation process.

The Building Block Approach reflects this diversity, while opening national practice to new forms of financial participation.

### 1.5.1.2   *The building block approach: Meeting essential principles ...*

The proposed Building Block Approach fully complies with the essential principles of financial participation schemes that the Commission sets forth in the cited communication:

- All elements of the building blocks are voluntary for both enterprises and employees (this does not, however, conflict with the French compulsory regulations at the national level).
- The building blocks can be put together in any combination depending on the specific needs of the given enterprise so as to produce individually tailored, clear and comprehensible plans.
- Discrimination, for example, against part-time workers or women, would exclude any national company scheme from being integrated into the supranational European Concept.
- The proposed share ownership schemes that have been established in the United States and the United Kingdom for decades include adequate training programmes and educational materials, which allow employees to assess the nature and details of the schemes.
- Unreasonable risks for employees are buffered by the diversity of the concept. The dissemination practices for employee information aim at, among other objectives, raising the awareness of the risks of financial participation resulting from fluctuations in income or from limited diversification of investments.
- By collecting the best practice of national legislation and customs, the rules on financial participation at the company level are based on a pre-defined formula clearly linked to enterprise results.
- Each building block is a complement to, not a substitute for, existing pay systems.

- It is the explicit aim of the Building Block Approach to be used throughout the EU and as such to be compatible with worker mobility both internationally and between enterprises.

### *1.5.1.3   ... and overcoming transnational obstacles*

At the same time, the Building Block Approach seeks to address transnational obstacles identified by the Commission and Parliament[107] as imposing barriers to the development of a European model and to cross-border plans for financial participation:

- By providing a broad incentive system going beyond the classical instruments of tax legislation, the modular approach neither relies on nor excludes tax incentives.
- Despite the difficulty of implementing tax incentives, these still remain a powerful tool for enhancing and broadening financial participation. They could be voluntarily granted by countries singly or in groups, creating in the process an increasingly favourable environment. The pro-activism of countries with an advanced tradition like France or the United Kingdom would at the same time encourage others to emulate them.
- The benchmarking project we undertook[108] across the EU provides the first ever complete overview of employee participation in all member and candidate countries of the EU and thus facilitates the avoidance of transnational obstacles, for example, blocking periods when employees may not dispose of their shares.
- Our project, by providing information in a systematic way with reference to the experience of the EU-15, is also helping to overcome the cultural differences in the social partnership as well as raising the new member countries' awareness of employees.

### 1.5.2   ESOPs: A thrust for innovation

In addition to well-known forms of financial participation (for example, employee shares and profit-sharing), the Building Block Approach introduces a lesser-known but flexible form of collective share ownership: the ESOP. Whereas, for example, share-based profit-sharing schemes have only one source of funds (that is, direct contributions from the employer company), the ESOP can obtain financing from such different sources as:

- a loan from the employer company, a selling shareholder or from a financial institution such as a bank;

- dividend earnings;
- sale of shares to its related share-based profit-sharing scheme;
- contributions from the employer company.

A full or partial ESOP buyout provides an ideal vehicle to facilitate transitions in ownership and management of closely held companies. This field of action has been highlighted as one of the main objectives of the Council Recommendation of 7 December 1994[109] and recently by the European Commission, explicitly stressing the importance of ownership transfers to employees as a specific measure for facilitating business succession in SMEs.[110] The ESOP creates a market for retiring shareholders' shares, which is of major importance to unlisted SMEs having no other ready source of liquidity.

Whereas share ownership generally involves additional risk for employees, the ESOP avoids this consequence. Although employees, as in other share ownership schemes, are encouraged to allot part of their wealth into the shares of their own companies rather than those of other companies, resulting in concentrated rather than diversified risk, there is this fundamental difference: ESOP debt is funded by appropriately timed contributions from the company to the ESOT. Thus the scheme provides an additional benefit to basic wages. The employee's salary remains unaffected. There is an additional advantage to the company: shares are not sold to outsiders; thus there is no risk of loss of control and the company remains local.

Finally, ESOPs make employees more motivated and productive while making enterprises more competitive.[111]

### 1.5.2.1   ESOP as a vehicle for business succession

ESOPs may easily buyout one or more shareholders while permitting other shareholders to retain their equity position. This is one of its major advantages from the shareholders' perspective. At the same time, ESOPs give business owners the opportunity to diversify their investment portfolios without the costly process of going public.[112] Furthermore, there is no dilution in equity per share of current stockholders because no new shares are issued and all shares are bought at fair market value.[113]

As stated above, if the ESOT borrows money to buy shares, the company repays the loan by combining any dividend income of the trust with its own tax-deductible contributions to the plan. As the loan is repaid, several shares equal to the percentage of the loan repaid that year are allocated to employee accounts, usually on the basis of relative compensation (see Figure 1.5). In this way the ESOP creates a market for

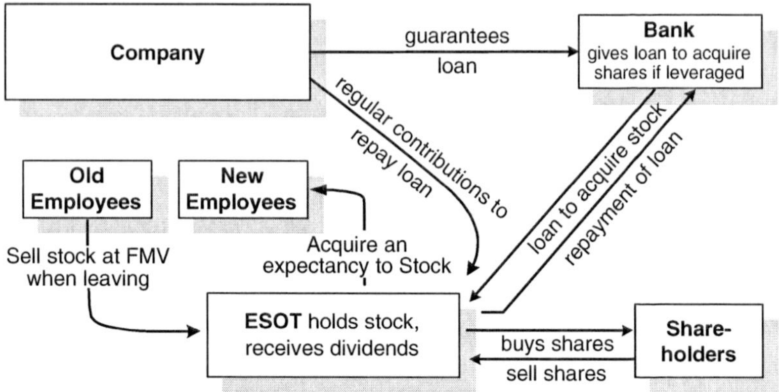



*Figure 1.5*   ESOP as a vehicle for business succession.

retiring shareholders' shares at a price acceptable to the owner – a market that otherwise might not exist. At the same time, when a change of control is appropriate, ownership is transferred to motivated employees who have a vital interest in the company's long-term success.

Thus the ESOP may be an attractive alternative to selling the business to outsiders, especially when there is a desire to keep control of the business within a family or a key-employee group.[114] As a trusted plan, the ESOP is designed to separate control over the shares in the trust from the 'beneficial owners'. The trustee exercises the voting rights while the employees are the financial beneficiaries of the trust. The trustee may, in fact, be the very person who has just sold some or all of his shares to the trust. For smaller firms especially, it is much easier to contemplate a gradual transfer of ownership by creating a market for the shares of those who wish to sell at the present moment, while enabling those who wish to hold their shares to retain their equity interest permanently or at least until some later date. The result is the opportunity of gradually cashing out without giving up immediate control.[115]

The virtue of an ESOP is that it can easily accomplish a 100 per cent buyout over time without subjecting the company at any given moment to 100 per cent leverage.[116]

### 1.5.2.2   *ESOP enhancing cash flow*

The ESOP may also be used to enhance working capital for any legitimate corporate purpose. This involves the issuance of new shares or the sale of existing stock held in the company treasury. Besides creating employee shareholding, the employer company, under certain circumstances, by

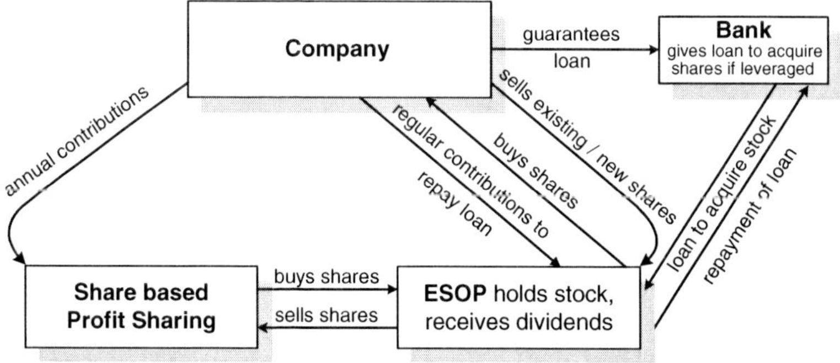



*Figure 1.6*   ESOP enhancing cash flow.

selling shares at full market value to the trust, receives an equity injection. This is the case when tax advantages are available for paying off leveraged principal with tax-deductible plan contributions. It also occurs when the company acquires cash from the employees directly. However, even without these conditions, the company, through its contributions, fully funds the 'equity' (see Figure 1.6).

Usually the dilution of the current stockholders is partly offset by any available tax advantages. It can further be compensated for by increased productivity and profitability of the company as a result of higher employee motivation, which in the process raises the value of its stock. An increase in working capital can occur if the ESOP is replacing some other programme which would have diverted cash out of the company (for example, a pension or profit-sharing plan invested in non-employer securities). The same is true if, in the absence of an ESOP, the company has to purchase shares from a departing founding shareholder with after-tax income rather than pre-tax income.

### 1.5.2.3   *The private equity buyout versus the ESOP*

A recent Commission Communication from 2006[117] stated that with the aging of Europe's population, 'one third of EU entrepreneurs, mainly those running family enterprises, will withdraw within the next ten years.' This portends an enormous increase in business transfer activity which could affect up to 690,000 SMEs and 2.8 million jobs every year.[118] It is anticipated that as a consequence of the new forms of business finance now coming into use, transfers within the family will decrease, while sales to outside buyers will rise. The entrance of international investors into what used to be primarily domestic markets will broaden the range of potential buyers for European SMEs. However, these enterprises are the backbone of Europe's national economies, cultures and traditions. Their sale to impersonal private equity funds[119] and strategic investors will affect not only the working lives of Europeans, but also their material well-being and the quality of their communities. This process is likely to threaten the successful regional structure of European (family-owned) businesses[120] and will profoundly affect the European Community itself – its values, its vision and its effectiveness.

The growing number of private equity firms targeting Europe's SMEs[121] makes a comparison of an alternate leveraged buyout tool of immediate strategic importance. This alternate vehicle is the ESOP. Although the ESOP and the private equity fund have some features in common[122], the two markedly differ in one crucial respect: they benefit different constituencies and have different economic and social effects. The private equity buyout concentrates ownership of productive enterprises and the income they produce, while the ESOP broadens both the economy's ownership base and the distribution of income. The private equity buyout increases the wealth of its own narrow constituency, whereas the ESOP improves the material well-being and economic security of working people and their families. The private equity buyout is a short-term transaction aiming at restructuring and selling the target company to a third party – that, in turn, may be just another private equity fund. The ESOP is a long-term commitment that ensures the continuity of the enterprise.

Quick profits for a few investment consortiums, whose participants are already well-capitalised, or incomes rising over time for employees motivated by the ESOP to make their enterprises more profitable and competitive? This is the choice confronting the EU as it prepares for a massive transformation of ownership of the business enterprises that generate its economic prosperity.

The leveraged buyout (LBO) exploits the fact that productive capital repays its formation or acquisition costs out of its own future earnings; that is, it is self-financing. However, this vehicle has two forms, either of which may be used to transfer SMEs to new owners. In both cases the owner sells at fair market value with the control premium.[123] As has already been noted, however, the two forms serve different purposes with radically different economic and social effects (see Figure 1.7).

Although both kinds of LBOs use debt-financing up to 80 per cent[124] of the purchase price to acquire partial or total ownership of the target company, the time horizon is entirely different. The goal of the private equity firm is generally short-term profit gained from restructuring or

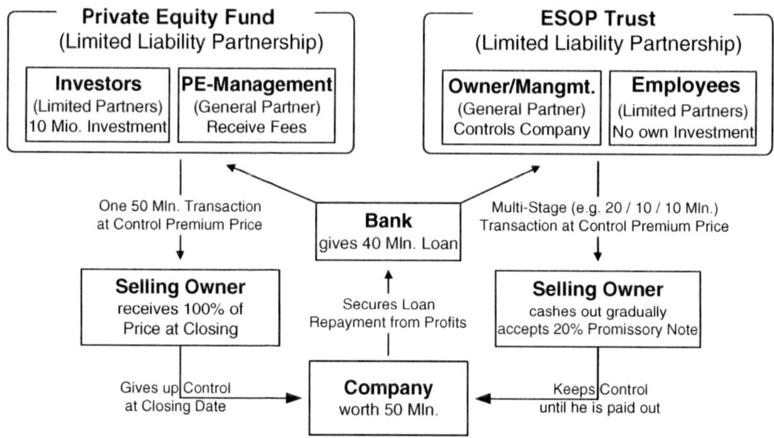



*Figure 1.7* Leveraged buyout – comparison of an ESOP to a private equity transaction

'down-sizing' the company for resale; therefore retaining control of the company at closing is a prerequisite. The ESOP by comparison is a multi-stage, long-term transaction extending over a period of five to seven years during which the buyout loan enables the selling owner to cash out gradually without giving up control immediately.

The flexibility of the ESOP can greatly benefit owners of SMEs who do not want totally to sever their connection with an enterprise which perhaps has been family-owned for generations and to which they may be bound by sentimental as well as economic ties. Selling their company to the ESOP in instalments, they may delegate some management functions while retaining a vital role in the control of the company until they wish completely to retire. This option involves sharing the risks involved with the bank that financed the acquisition loan; employees themselves incur no additional risk.

The exit strategy of private equity funds of restructuring and then selling the enterprise may lead to management buyouts, initial public offering, secondary sale, buy back, trade sale or even a write-off. Ideally the whole cycle is no longer than five years.[125] The ESOP trust by contrast 'warehouses' shares, thus creating an in-house market in non-listed companies which can be used to buy shares from retiring employees while offering shares to new employees.

Private equity transactions may increase liquidity in capital markets; they also create wealth for the limited partners, investment bankers, outside investors and senior managers who structure and participate in this type of buyout.[126] However, middle managers and lower-echelon employees may lose their jobs during the restructuring process; the home community may lose consumers and taxpayers. Production, under globalisation, may be relocated elsewhere or even 'off-shored' to another country.

The ESOP-leveraged buyout offers continuity and stability. If 'modernisation' or restructuring is necessary, as is usually the case with an old established business in need of new technology and methods, the enterprise will still remain in the community. It will be owned by local residents, consumers and taxpayers. More of the income it produces will remain in the community as well.

Studies over the years have found that firms in which employees have an ownership stake are more profitable, create more jobs and are better taxpayers than their counterparts with no employee ownership. These findings suggest that the ESOP-leveraged buyout could be an important tool for implementing the goal of the Lisbon Agenda, namely making European SMEs more competitive.

## Notes

1. SOCI 115, Employee Financial Participation, CESE 284/2003.
2. COM (2002) 364 Final.
3. P5-TA (2003) 0253.
4. The Directive of 13 December 1976, 77/91/EEC allows various derogations designed to encourage the financial participation of employees in joint-stock companies.
5. As proposed in the European Parliament Resolution of 5 June 2003 (P5-TA (2003) 0253), 31. IV; similar to the Council Directive 2001/86/EC of 8 October 2001, 'supplementing the Statute for a European Company with regard to the involvement of employees', Official Journal, L 294/22, but with regard to financial participation.
6. Council Regulation (EC) No. 2157/2001 of 8 October 2001 on the Statute for a European company (SE); Official Journal, L 294/1.
7. See H. Roggemann (1999a) 'Functional Change in Property Rights in the Welfare State: Lessons from the Federal Republic of Germany', in I. Collier, H. Roggemann, O. Scholz and H. Toman (eds) *Welfare States in Transition – East and West* (New York: St. Martin's Press), pp. 25–40.
8. See the Federal Constitutional Court in the case concerning the possession of rented apartments of 26 May 1993, BVerfGE, Vol. 89, p. 1, especially p. 6; compare also BVerfGE, Vol. 24, p. 267, especially 389; Vol. 50, pp. 290, especially 339; Vol. 53, pp. 257, especially 289.
9. See Opinion of the *Economic and Social Committee* of 26 February 2003, on the Commission communication 'on a framework for the promotion of employee financial participation', European Parliament, Social Affairs Series, SOCI 115, Employee Financial Participation, CESE 284/2003, p. 4.

10. See point 1.5 of the Presidency Conclusions of the Lisbon European Council (23–24 March 2000).
11. For Germany see *Die Zeit*, No. 40, 23 September 2004, Economy 'Where do the rich stand?' and No. 34, August 2004, Economy 'Only the rich get richer'; for emerging countries see *Le Monde*, Dossier and Documents No. 334, September 2004, 'Les riches des pays émergents'.
12. See H. Roggemann (1999a), pp. 25–40.
13. See H. J. Papier (2008) in Th. Maunz, G. Dürig and R. Herzog (eds) *Commentary on the Basic (Constitutional) Law of Germany* (Bonn: Beck), Article 14, No. 17; compare also the Resolution of the *European Parliament* (P5-TA (2003) 0253) on the Commission communication to the Council, the European Parliament, the Economic and Social Committee and the Committee of the Regions 'on a framework for the promotion of employee financial participation', COM (2002) 364, 2002/2243 (INI).
14. See L. Kelso and P. H. Kelso (1991) *Democracy and Economic Power: Extending the ESOP Revolution through Binary Economics* (Lanham, MD: University Press of America).
15. One reason is that Article 295 (former 222) of the Treaty of Amsterdam excludes private property as a legal institution from the law of European contracts. However, de facto the treaties do deal with the subject of private property, especially by regulating derived rights and related areas.
16. Nevertheless the Charter as a mere list of policies is not genuine *jus cogens* and thus has no *res judicata* effect.
17. Concerning the promotion of participation by employed persons in profits and enterprise results (including equity participation), 92/443/EEC, Official Journal L 245, 26 August 1992, pp. 53–5.
18. The Charter of 9 December 1989, which was also signed by the United Kingdom in 1998, is neither a binding legal act nor is it a treaty among the signatory states. It is merely a solemn declaration which should nonetheless serve as an aid to the interpretation of the provisions of the EC Treaty, because it reflects views and traditions common to the Member States and represents a declaration of basic principles which the EU and its Member States intend to respect. Together with the Action Programme, which has also been approved by the Heads of State or Government, it is therefore used by the Commission as a basis for justifying many of the Directives it proposes.
19. See Articles 19 paragraph 3, 23 paragraph 2, 41 paragraphs 1 and 2 of the Directive 77/91/EEC, dating back to 13 December 1976 which allow derogations from the European legal framework for joint-stock Companies designed to encourage the financial participation of employees (see below Part 1, IV. B.3.).
20. By M. Uvalić (1991) *The PEPPER Report: Promotion of Employee Participation in Profits and Enterprise Results in the Member States of the European Union* (in English, French and German), Supplement 3/91 to the brochure 'Social Europe' (Luxembourg: Office for Official Publications of the European Communities).
21. 92/443/EEC, Official Journal, L 254 of 26 August 1992, p. 53.
22. Official Journal, C 245 of 20 September 1992.
23. The report was designed to give a review of the effects of the previously mentioned recommendation of the Council of the European Union 92/443/EEC in the Member States; see PEPPER II Report (1997), COM (96) 0697 C4-0019/97.

24. With preference generally given to profit-sharing models in France and share ownership models in Great Britain.
25. J. Lowitzsch (2006) *The PEPPER III Report – Promotion of Employee Participation in Profits and Enterprise Results in the New Member and Candidate Countries of the European Union* (Rome and Berlin: Inter-University Centre Split/Berlin), distributed by the European Foundation for the Improvement of Living and Working Conditions.
26. The Commission funded project, led by the author of this book, closes the gap between PEPPER I/II (1991 EU-12/1997, EU-15) and PEPPER III (2006 ten new Member States and four candidate countries) that currently prevent a full profiling of financial participation policy and practice and rolls out the benchmarking indicators developed by the European Foundation for the Improvement of Living and Working Conditions.
27. For details see PEPPER II Report (1997), COM (96) 0697 C4-0019/97.
28. BGBl. I/1998, No. 61, p. 2647, on which the Committee for Labour and Social Policy of the German Bundestag had conducted a hearing of experts.
29. Nevertheless resulting from the substantial differences that divide the two member parties of the Grand Coalition the new 'Law on Capital Participation of Employees' which came into force in April 2009 merely increased existing insignificant fiscal incentives.
30. EU Treaties in the actual form of the Nice Treaty. See Title XI, Article 136 et seq.; Title XVII, Article 158 et seq.
31. COM (2002) 364 Final, 5 July 2002.
32. See European Commission (2003a) Report of the High Level Group of independent experts on cross-border obstacles to financial participation of employees for companies having a transnational dimension, December (Brussels: European Commission), p. 17.
33. See J. Lowitzsch (2006).
34. For example, for Germany see *Die Zeit*, No. 40, 23 September 2004, Economy 'Where do the rich stand?'.
35. See J. Winiecki in *Rzeczpospolita*, 16 August 2004, Economy 'Kapitalistyczna karawana idzie dalej' [The capitalist caravan is moving on], comparing the share of public property and privatisation in OECD countries.
36. See J. Lowitzsch (2002) *Privatisierung und Beteiligung in Mittelosteuropa – Am Beispiel des polnischen, slowakischen und tschechischen Modells* [Privatisation and Capital Participation in Central Eastern Europe – The Example of the Polish, the Czech and the Slovak Model] (Berlin: Berlin Verlag Arno Spitz GmbH).
37. See F. Barjak, G. Heimpold et al. (1996) *Management-Buyout in Ostdeutschland*, (Halle: Institut für Wirtschaftsforschung).
38. A5-0150/2003, Report of the *Committee on Employment and Social Affairs of the European Parliament* on the Commission communication 'on a framework for the promotion of employee financial participation', COM (2002) 364, 2002/2243 (INI), p. 12.
39. For example, in the context of the European Company Statute in the Council Directive 2001/86/EC of 8 October 2001, 'supplementing the Statute for a European company with respect to the involvement of employees', Official Journal, L 294/22.
40. Cyprus, Czech Republic, Estonia, Hungary, Lithuania, Latvia, Malta, Poland, Slovakia and Slovenia as countries that joined the EU on 1 May 2004 and Croatia, Bulgaria, Romania and Turkey as candidate countries.

41. For a recent, comprehensive overview of the positive economic evidence (especially for ESOPs) see J. R. Blasi, D. Kruse and A. Bernstein (2003) *In the Company of Owners* (New York: Basic Books); they find an average increase of productivity level by about 4 per cent, of total shareholder returns by about 2 per cent and of profit levels by about 14 per cent compared with firms without PEPPER schemes.
42. SOCI 109, European Parliament, Directorate-General for Research, Luxembourg, 2002.
43. *Employee Share Ownership and Profit-Sharing in the European Union*, 2001; *Recent Trends in Financial Participation in the European Union*, 2001; *Financial Participation in the EU: Indicators for Benchmarking*, 2004; *Financial Participation for Small and Medium-Sized Enterprises: Barriers and Potential Solutions*, 2004; *Financial Participation: The Role of Governments and Social Partners*, 2004.
44. Of 5 May 2003 (FINAL A5-0150/2003), Rapporteur: Winfried Menrad.
45. P5-TA (2003) 0253.
46. For France see P. Maillard (2007) *Rapport sur la Participation dans les Èntreprise de moins de 50 Salariés*, Report to Prime Minister Dominique de Villepin, April; compare also European Commission (2003b) *Transfer of Businesses – Continuity Through a New Beginning*, Final Report of the MAP 2002 Project (Brussels: European Commission, Directorate-General Enterprise and Industry).
47. In this context the question of employee involvement is mentioned. As the study E. Poutsma (2001) *Recent Trends in Financial Participation in the European Union* (Dublin: European Foundation for the Improvement of Living and Working Conditions) showed, there is a clear connection between successful employee financial participation and participative structures in the enterprise; see pp. 42–5.
48. COM (2002) 364 Final, 5 July 2002, pp. 3, 10.
49. On the transfer of small and medium-sized enterprises, 94/1069/EEC, with explanatory note, Official Journal No C 400, 31 December 1994, p. 1.
50. One of the key areas defined in European Commission (2003b).
51. See A. Pendleton et al. (2001) *Employee Share Ownership and Profit-Sharing in the European Union* (Dublin: European Foundation for the Improvement of Living and Working Conditions), p. 9.
52. The Treaty of Nice has extended the scope of co-decision. This procedure will be applicable to seven provisions which change over from unanimity to qualified majority voting (Articles 13, 62, 63, 65, 157, 159 and 191; for Article 161, the Treaty stipulates assent). Accordingly, most of the legislative measures which, after the Treaty of Nice, require a decision from the Council acting by qualified majority will be decided by the co-decision procedure.
53. See Chapter 3 of this volume.
54. This 'bridge' cannot, however, be used for social security.
55. For example, the consensual continental contrasts with the Anglo-American confrontational model; likewise the strong position of the state in France contrasts with the powerful role of the German 'Tarifpartner' (collective bargaining parties, such as trade unions and employer associations). See A. Pendleton and E. Poutsma (2004) *Financial Participation: The Role of Governments and Social Partners* (Dublin: European Foundation for the Improvement of Living and Working Conditions).

56. As, for example, the German 'Mitbestimmung' and the Works Councils in France and the Netherlands.
57. This problem is well illustrated by the prolonged controversy over the so-called European Workers Council, and as a consequence the rather minimal compromise of the regulation in the European Company Statute.
58. A rare exception exists in France where enterprises with more than 50 employees are required to establish a participation fund. See PEPPER II Report (1997), COM (96) 0697, C4-0019/97, pp. 19–20.
59. Compare White and Case (2001) *The European Company Statute*, p. 4.
60. For Ireland, see J. Shanahan and L. Hennessy (1998) *Underpinning Partnership at the Workplace – An MSF Guide to Profit-Sharing, ESOPs and Equity Participation* (Dublin: Amicus-MSF), p. 9.
61. One of the key areas defined in European Commission (2003b).
62. From an entrepreneurial point of view, see D. Ackermann (2002) *How to Cash Out Tax-Free, Yet Keep Your Business … ESOPs – A Practical Guide for Business Owners and Their Advisors*, Conference Paper for the National Center for Employee Ownership, San Francisco, California.
63. See H. J. Papier (2008) in Th. Maunz, H. Dürig and R. Herzog (eds) *Commentary on the Basic Law of Germany* (Bonn: Beck), Article 14, No. 17.
64. East Germany has confined itself almost solely to forms of management buyout. See F. Barjak, G. Heimpold et al. (1996).
65. In some cases it has become obvious that these local approaches to greater equality in the distribution of property may lead to a renewal of socialistic structures of ownership and bureaucratic hindrance of market economy structures (for example, Czech Republic, Slovakia, Russia, Croatia and Bulgaria). With regard to the voucher privatisation in the Czech Republic, see J. Lowitzsch (2001) *Restructuring Strategy and Insider Ownership as Determinants of Privatisation Models in Poland and the Czech Republic*, Conference Paper, Enterprise in Transition, Split, Croatia. As to problems of privatisation in Slovakia, see I. Mikloš (former Minister of Privatisation) (1995) *Corruption Risks in the Privatisation Process*, Klub Windsor Paper, Bratislava.
66. 'Speaking one's mind declines when property holding declines, and with it those who are free of necessity disappear from sight', S. de Grazia (1962) *Of Time, Work and Leisure* (New York: The Twentieth Century Fund).
67. For the power-limiting and 'peace-making' function of private property see also H. J. Papier (2008), Nos 4 and 5.
68. See H. Roggemann (1997a) *Functional Changes of Property Rights in East and West – Comparative Remarks to Post-Socialist Transformation in Eastern and Western Europe*, CERGE EI Working Paper (Prague: Charles University); H. Roggemann (1997b) 'On the Relation between Ownership and Privatisation in the Post-Socialist Countries' in University of Split, Faculty of Economics (ed.) *Enterprise in Transition II* (Split: Faculty of Economics, University of Split), p. 193; H. Roggemann and J. Lowitzsch (eds) (2002) *Privatisierungsins titutionen in Mittel- und Osteuropa* (Berlin: Berlin Verlag Arno Spitz GmbH).
69. Concerning the promotion of participation by employed persons in profits and enterprise results (including equity participation), 92/443/EEC, Official Journal L 245, 26 August 1992, pp. 53–5.
70. It is merely a solemn declaration which should nonetheless be used as an aid to the interpretation of the provisions of the EC Treaty because it

reflects views and traditions common to the Member States and represents a declaration of basic principles which the EU and its Member States intend to respect.

71. In some countries, however, financial participation schemes have developed without specific tax incentives or when incentives have been reduced (Germany, Italy, the Netherlands, Canada). See V. Pérotin (2003) *Employee Participation in Profit and Ownership: A Review of the Issues and Evidence*, Working Paper, Social Affairs Series, European Parliament, Social Affairs Series, SOCI 109 EN, 01-2003.

72. Ibid., pp. 22–7.

73. European Commission (2003a), p. 17.

74. For a detailed technical description of the different mechanisms and schemes see Chapter 4 of this volume and M. Uvalić (1991). See also K. P. O'Kelly and A. Pendleton (2005) *Common Elements of an Adaptable Model Plan for Financial Participation in the European Union*, IAFP Working Paper, December.

75. See D. L. Kruse and J. R. Blasi (1995) *Employee Ownership, Employee Attitudes, and Firm Performance: A Review of the Evidence*, NBER Working Paper, Series 5277 (Cambridge, MA); D. C. Jones and T. Kato (1995) 'The Productivity Effects of Employee Stock Ownership Plans and Bonuses: Evidence from Japanese Panel Data', *The American Economic Review*, June, pp. 391–414.

76. Summarising OECD (1995) 'Profit-Sharing in OECD Countries', in OECD (ed.) *Employment Outlook* (Paris: OECD); M. Uvalić (1991), the experience so far suggests that cash-based schemes have had significantly greater incentive effects than share-based schemes.

77. See European Commission (2003b), p. 7.

78. J. Vanek (1965) 'Workers' Profit Participation, Unemployment, and the Keynesian Equilibrium', *Weltwirtschaftliches Archiv*, No. 2 was the first to argue that profit-sharing could have a positive macroeconomic effect on employment.

79. Positive: D. Vaughan-Whitehead (1992) *Interessement, Participation, Actionariat – Impacts Economiques dans l'Entreprise* (Paris: Economica); D. Kruse (1991) 'Profit-Sharing and Employment Variability: Micro-Economic Evidence on the Weitzman Theory', *Industrial and Labour Relations Review*, Vol. 44, April. Negative: S. Whadhwani and M. Wall (1990) 'The Effects of Profit-Sharing on Employment, Wages, Stock Returns and Productivity: Evidence from UK Micro-Data', *Economic Journal*, 100 (399), pp. 1–17.

80. The valuation of the shares before the acquisition may create unreasonable costs particularly in a small firm. This problem is exacerbated when the valuation is repeatedly necessary for different share acquisitions not occurring simultaneously.

81. See the Annex of the *Committee on Employment and Social Affairs* Report on the Commission communication 'on a framework for the promotion of employee financial participation', COM (2002) 364, 2002/2243 (INI); 'Models for Employee Participation in SMEs', PE 316 420.

82. A. Pendleton, J. Blasi, D. Kruse et al. (2002) *Theoretical Study on Stock Options in Small and Medium Enterprises*, Study for the European Commission (Manchester: Manchester Metropolitan University Business School); PriceWaterhouseCoopers (2002) *Employee Stock Options in the EU and the USA* (London: PriceWaterhouseCoopers).

83. S. Chang (1990) 'Employee Stock Ownership Plans and Shareholder Wealth: An Empirical Investigation', *Financial Management*, Spring, pp. 48–58; D. C. Jones and T. Kato (1995); H. E. Meihuizen (2000) *Productivity Effects of Employee Stock Ownership and Employee Stock Option Plans in Firms Listed on the Amsterdam Stock Exchanges: An Empirical Analysis*, Paper for the 10th Conference of the IAFEP, Trento, 6–8 July 2000; J. Sesil et al. (2000) *Sharing Ownership Via Employee Stock Ownership*, World Institute for Development Economics Research (WIDER) Discussion Paper 2001/25 (United Nations University).

84. An argument commonly used by German trade unions. See H. Tofaute (1998) 'Arbeitnehmerbeteiligung am Produktivkapital – Fortschreibung einer unendlichen Geschichte', *WSI Mitteilungen*, Issue No. 6, p. 376; D. Lipton and J. Sachs (1990) 'Privatisation in Eastern Europe: The Case of Poland', *Brookings Papers on Economic Activity*, 2.

85. In Germany the possibility of linking these 'Tariffonds' with the reform of the social security system was widely discussed. See *Die Zeit*, 10 December 1998.

86. As proposed for American ESOPs, see L. Kelso and P. H. Kelso (1991).

87. As defined in J. Shannahan and L. Hennessy (1998), p. 9.

88. If the P/E ratio is 5 and the interest rate is as low as 5 per cent, a standard seven-year level-principal loan amortisation schedule would require P/7 + P × 0.05 or almost a 20 per cent dividend in year one to service the loan.

89. For the USA, see C. Bachman and K. Butcher (2002) *ESOP Financing*, National Center for Employee Ownership Conference Paper (San Francisco, CA).

90. In a variation of the described loan structure, the lender often prefers to make the loan directly to the company, followed by a second 'mirror loan' from the company to the trust. The tax results will be the same as in the case of a direct loan to the trust. The principal repayments will still be deductible because the company has to make annual deductible payments to the trust in amounts sufficient to amortise the internal loan from the company to the trust. The amounts paid by the ESOP trustee to the company to amortise the internal loan will usually constitute tax-free loan repayments and can be used by the company to amortise the external bank loan. The 'mirror loan' structure provides the lender with a stronger security interest in the assets pledged to secure the loan. In the case of default the lender will be in a better position to defend against claims of fraudulent conveyance if it has taken collateral directly from the borrower rather than from a guarantor of the loan.

91. If local company law, as in the USA, or bylaws of the company requires this. In Ireland, for example, departing employees have no right to be bought out at market value.

92. The percentage of a company's free cash flow which will be required to service the repurchase liability on average over a period of years is fairly constant unless the multiple of the company's earnings (price/earnings ratio) alters dramatically. The average company will require cash equivalent to 7.5 per cent of the value of the allocated stock in the trust for repurchase liability purposes each year. This is equivalent to a 7.5 per cent dividend on the stock, but only on the stock already allocated to employee accounts in

the trust. See L. Lyon (1989) *The Repurchase Liability or the Phantom of the ESOP* (San Francisco, CA: Menke & Associates, Inc.), p. 4.

93. Thus the ESOP transaction should be modelled in advance to ascertain that the company can afford this amount of 'dividend'. Otherwise, there should be a limit on how large a percentage of the company's total stock may be acquired by the ESOP. A growing company may require almost all of its free cash flow to fund future growth, but a company growing this fast may well want to go public.

94. For US ESOPs, see D. Ackermann (2002).

95. See R. C. Bye (2002) 'The Case for COLI (Corporate-Owned Life Insurance) – Funding the Repurchase Obligation', Conference Paper, National Center for Employee Ownership, San Francisco, California.

96. Information provided by Menke & Associates, Inc., San Francisco, California. Costs are generally lower for smaller companies where the ongoing annual appraisals are generally around USD 5,000.

97. See E. Poutsma and H. van den Tillaart (1996) Financiele werknemersparticipatie in Nederland: tijd voor beleid! (The Hague: Nederlands Participatie Instituut). Set-up expenses are, however, usually tax deductible as, for example, in Ireland; see J. Shannahan and L. Hennessy (1998), p. 33.

98. European Commission (2003a), p. 52.

99. Council Regulation (EC) No. 2157/2001 of 8 October 2001 on the Statute for a European Company (SE); Official Journal, L 294/1.

100. As proposed in the report of the Committee on Employment and Social Affairs of 5 May 2003 (FINAL A5-0150/2003), pp. 11, 14 and expressed in the European Parliament Resolution of 5 June 2003 (P5-TA (2003) 0253), 31. IV; like the Council Directive 2001/86/EC of 8 October 2001, 'supplementing the Statute for a European company with regard to the involvement of employees' but with regard to financial participation.

101. Here it is the result of negotiations between employer and employee representatives.

102. European Commission (2003c) *Employee Stock Options, The Legal and Administrative Environment for Employee Stock Options in the EU* (Brussels: European Commission, Directorate-General Enterprise and Industry).

103. The general rules that (1) require that the acquisitions may not have the effect of reducing the net assets below the amount of the subscribed capital plus those reserves which may not be distributed under the law or the statutes and (2) require that only fully paid-up shares may be included in the transaction still apply across the board.

104. See Article L.225-259 to L.225-270 of the French Commercial Code: Employee shares collectively owned by paid personnel in a workers' commercial co operative.

105. See point 1.5 of the Presidency Conclusions of the Lisbon European Council (23–4 March 2000).

106. Commission communication seeking 'a framework for the promotion of employee financial participation', COM (2002) 364 Final, 5 July 2002, pp. 3, 10.

107. European Commission (2003a), p. 17.

108. The Commission-funded project, led by the author of this book, offers comprehensive empirical data on employee participation throughout the EU,

including its significance in economic practice, legal obstacles and future possibilities; the PEPPER IV Report is published in 2009.

109. On the transfer of small and medium-sized enterprises, 94/1069/EEC, with explanatory note, Official Journal No C 400, 31 December 1994, p. 1; reiterated in the Communication from the Commission on the transfer of small and medium-sized enterprises, Official Journal C 93, 28 March 1998.

110. One of the key areas defined in European Commission (2003b).

111. For a recent, comprehensive overview of the positive economic evidence (especially for ESOPs) see J. R. Blasi, D. Kruse and A. Bernstein (2003); they find an average increase of productivity level by about 4 per cent, of total shareholder returns by about 2 per cent and of profit levels by about 14 per cent compared with firms without PEPPER schemes.

112. For American ESOPs, see D. Ackermann (2002).

113. Theoretically, there is a temporary loss in the potential of the company caused by the obligation of the loan, since the borrowed funds used for the buyout otherwise might be used to finance further growth. It is unlikely, however, that a trade sale to an outsider, if at all possible, would trigger the same increase in productivity and profitability as a result of higher employee motivation.

114. The ESOP may also be used to buy out dissident shareholders.

115. Once the loan is paid off, of course, most companies make some arrangement for the presence of employee representatives on the plan committee.

116. 100 per cent buyouts are very difficult for most companies to finance without a significant part of capital from lenders who demand a very high rate of return (35–40 per cent). The costs for arranging the financing can amount to millions of Euros, which is certainly beyond the range of SMEs.

117. Implementing the Lisbon Community Programme for Growth and Jobs, on the Transfer of Businesses – Continuity through a New Beginning, 14 March 2006, COM (2006) 117 final.

118. Calculated by extrapolations from the final report of the BEST-project on the transfer of small and medium-sized enterprises, 2002, which estimated that the annual transfer potential for the EU-15 was 610,000 businesses. For example, the transfer volume of enterprises is estimated for Germany around 354,000 over the next five years (Institut für Mittelstandsforschung, Bonn, 2005), for France around 600,000 for the next decade (Vilain, La transmission des PME artisanales, commerciales, industrielles et de services, avis et rapport du conseil économique et social, 2004).

119. The volume of private equity transactions in Europe has been rising in recent years, with EUR 126 billion in 2005 and a new peak of EUR 178 billion in 2007; source: Incisive Financial Publishing, 2007.

120. Deutsche Bank Research (2007) 'Germany's Mittelstand – an endangered species? Focus on Business Succession', *Current Topics*, 387, 29 May 2007, p. 1, download available at http://www.dbresearch.de. See also PES Priorities for the EU Policy Agenda 2008, adopted at the Party of European Socialists Leaders' meeting on 21 June 2007, p. 3.

121. The part of LBOs in the total funds raised in Europe reached over 68 per cent in 2005. In contrast the amount of venture capital investments only

represents 5 per cent. See PSE Socialist Group in the European Parliament (2007) *Hedge Funds and Private Equity – A Critical Analysis*, p. 69.
122. The ESOP, invented in 1956, is the prototype leveraged buyout; the private equity form originated in the 1970s to use tax advantages that the US Congress had passed to encourage the ESOP.
123. Nevertheless, in the case of the ESOP, he may receive a little less because of the loss in interest caused by the duration of the multi-stage transaction.
124. In this example in the case of the ESOP the selling owner accepts 20 per cent of the price as a promissory note, while the Private Equity Fund raises 20 per cent by investment of the limited partners.
125. A Standard & Poors analysis of the big LBOs found that in 2004 they got 64 per cent of their invested capital back just after 29 months engagement in the target company, in 2005 – 27 per cent in just 20 months and in the first half of 2006 – 86 per cent in just 24 months. See PSE Socialist Group in the European Parliament (2007), p. 18.
126. Nevertheless, the average investor often obtains poor returns from investments in Private Equity Funds, potentially because of excessive fees. For a detailed analysis see L. Phalippou (2007) *Investing in Private Equity Funds: A Survey* (Amsterdam: The Research Foundation of CFA Institute).

# Part II  The Legal Background

# 2
# The Challenge: Functional Changes in Property Rights in Europe

*Herwig Roggemann and Jens Lowitzsch*

> *There is nothing which so generally strikes the imagination, and engages the affections of mankind, as the right of property.*
>
> William Blackstone, *Commentaries on the Laws of England*, 1793

## 2.1 Ownership in the welfare state and in post-socialist transformation

At the dawn of the eastward enlargement of the European Union, once again it becomes obvious that 'ownership is a historical, not a logical category'.[1] The Western model of the welfare state is in a severe crisis[2] and can no longer be maintained in its present form. At the same time, the Central and East European countries are trying various ways to integrate private ownership into the legal framework of a new post-socialist welfare state,[3] or are at least trying to lighten the social burden of transition to a market economy.[4] In this context, the role of property goes beyond the mere *functional control of men over legal objects and nature*; it assumes another dimension of property rights, that of *social integration* as an element of social stability, democracy, and economic justice.[5]

Furthermore, ownership, a fundamental legal institution in every developed economic society and legal community, has now taken a central place in the continuing privatisation processes in Europe. The (re-)introduction into law and economics of private ownership in Central and Eastern Europe, including ownership of land and the means of production, marks a point of no return in the privatisation process.[6] With the process of (re-)establishing private ownership in East and

Central European countries still underway, the discussion of the issue and its implications for legal, economic and tax policy in the Member States of the EU remain highly controversial.

## 2.2   Legal foundations of property

### 2.2.1   Functions of ownership

Property has both a legal and an economic dimension. The general assignment of liability and risks is one aspect of this duality. On the one hand, the economic essence of property is the owner's right to receive the income it earns.[7] On the other hand, private property has the economic function of both assessing and assigning economic risk and liability; it is the foundation of a credit system based on collateral. Property law not only provides the legal basis of a market economy and competition, it defines other economic categories: 'Property does not exist outside the economy, but it rather gives significance to all the terms/concepts which are meaningless in non-ownership economies.

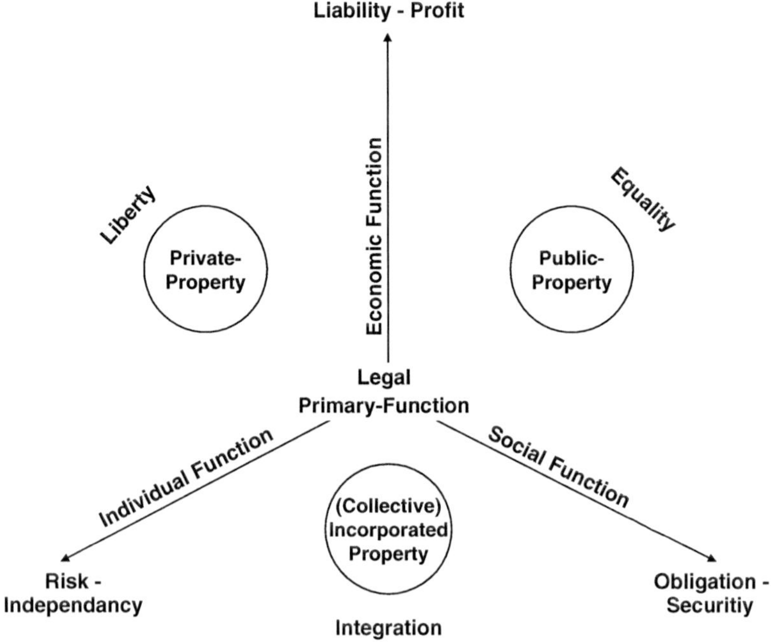


*Figure 2.1*   Functions of ownership.

This applies especially to interest, money and credit, but also to value, price, profit and market.'[8] Four legal functions of property may be distinguished:[9]

- the (primary) triple legal force of the model proprietor – to own, to use and to dispose exclusively;
- the right to receive the entire yield and to assume the liability and risks – the 'economic function';
- the integrational or 'social function'; and
- the guarantee of personal rights[10] and freedom,[11] the 'individual function'.

These legal functions of property give rise to forces that are in a permanent state of tension, confirming that property is a historically evolving category. The resulting force field can be expressed in the relation between freedom, equality and integration (see Figure 2.1). The legal institution of property thus works in three ways:

- As *private property*, it guarantees the owner his personal and economic freedom.
- As *public property*, it ensures a minimum level of equality of all citizens that are formally holding part of it.
- As *(collective) incorporated property* – in the form of public insurance institutions or joint-stock companies – it secures the individual as a part of the community and leverages, independently of the individual capacity, his integration in the civil society.

### 2.2.2   The changing content of property

The social functionality of property as developed in the jurisdiction of welfare states leads to a differentiation of the absolute concept of property. One can discern two lines of differentiation, each of which represents diminishing individual function and increasing social function.

**Increasing Social Relationship**

Owner as defined in civil law (personal property).

⇩

Owner as defined in civil law (land, houses, means of production).

⇩

Owner as defined in civil law (joint owner, partner, shareholder).

⇩

Non-owner as defined in civil law (occupant, user, tenant).

⇩

Non-owner (contract partner, employee).

⇩

Non-owner (interested party, neighbour, passer-by, co-user of nature).

⇩

Non-owner (rightful claimant, pensioner, unemployed person).

**Decreasing Relationship to Material Assets**

Home ownership (apartment ownership).

⇩

Land ownership.

⇩

Direct ownership of the means of production.

⇩

Ownership of the means of production mediated by company law.[12]

⇩

Valuable private legal positions.

⇩

Pension or other social entitlement under public law.

Within this system of functions, the law has a broad range of pro- and contra-arguments at its disposal for the solution of conflicts. The resulting compromises led a commentator on the United States Constitution to advance the extreme thesis that property rights themselves are fading away.[13]

### 2.2.3  Ownership and control of productive property

Property rights were also observed as failing in the relationship of ownership and the control of productive property, as the following quotations illustrate:

> In the most important sectors of our political economy, most individuals are in the process of being effectively separated from any discernible ownership relation to industrial property. That relation is tenuous enough when individuals are actual stockholders. It ceases to exist when the individual becomes a contract-claimant for the pension or other benefits he expects to receive through a trust fund or

other similar institution which holds legal title to the stock and other corporate securities making up its portfolio.[14]

And referring to the previous:

> This notion from the late 50's that ownership has been divorced from control of productive property today has become commonplace. The evidence is now before us that, with the advent of Pension Trusts, Mutual Funds and the large accumulation of corporate stock in the hands of Bank trustees, ownership itself as an operating reality is diminishing. We have reached a stage in the evolution of property – speaking only of productive property – where the individual is an owner because he possesses a piece of paper which says he is. The sole advantage left to the possessor of the paper, however, is the right, under certain circumstances, to receive income.[15]

Because of further economic differentiation, particularly the rise of the business corporation, the earlier simple forms of property acquisition and use by an owner or a holder have become inadequate. This has led to the evolution of forms of property, for example, share ownership, which are more abstract (see Figure 2.2). Equitable ownership, for example, leads to the solution that the *possessor* holds the right to (not abusively) use, possess and dispose. The formal owner, on the other hand, does not have the right of possession, but an abstract control right which is in no respect identical with the typical rights of a model owner.[16]

## 2.3   Ownership in European law

The legal rules of the European Union do not contain a binding concrete ownership constitution. This is still true of the ownership-related constitutional and political question of privatisation-socialisation (Article 222 EEC Treaty). However, the European Court of Human Rights (at Strasbourg) developed its own legal dogma of fundamental ownership protection, drawing on the European Convention on Human Rights of 1950, the rules of the treaty, and a comparison of national constitutions. The court's decisions have significant similarities with the (sometimes controversial) concept of the German Federal Constitutional Court, whereas some Western European constitutions do not acknowledge the legal categories defining content, limitations and social responsibility to the same extent. Most recently, the European Charter of Fundamental Rights has complemented and brought forward this substantial process.

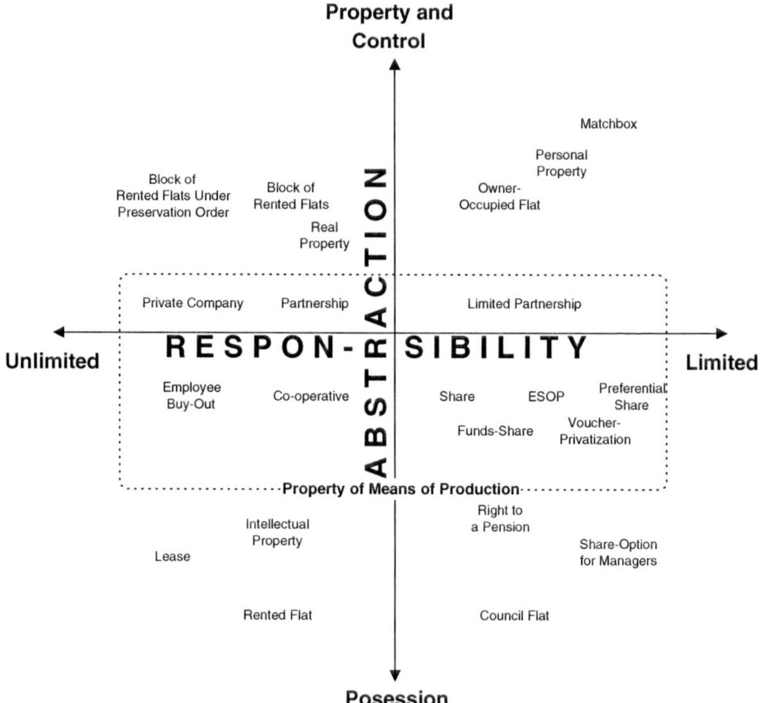



*Figure 2.2*   Differentiation of ownership according to level of abstraction and extent of responsibility.

### 2.3.1   European Community law in a narrower sense

Property law as European law was not included in the EEC Treaty. Article 222 states: 'This treaty does not interfere with the system of property ownership in the Member States.' Otherwise, the project of European integration would not have had a majority to begin with because of differences and variant traditions regarding the system of property ownership.[17] However, the whole logic of the treaties (limitation of national subsidies, freedom of services, freedom of goods traffic)[18] implicitly requires – despite state interventional tendencies (especially in agriculture) – an economic system which is based on a market economy and (at least also) on private property.[19] This is reflected in Article 4 (former 3a) of the EEC Treaty, included under the 'Maastricht Treaty' in 1992, establishing the 'basic principle of an open market society with free competition', which seems to acknowledge private ownership. Likewise

Article 44, where the 'freedom of acquisition and possession of real estate' enunciated in the context of the freedom of entrepreneurship clearly refers to private ownership.

Nevertheless, in accordance with Article 222 EEC Treaty, which expressly excludes legal and political jurisdiction over property from the competence of the EEC, the areas of authority developed in the secondary legislation of the European Community (Regulations and Directives) do not contain a specific ownership law. Because European ownership law is poorly developed, the national systems of ownership law differ to a great extent.

### 2.3.2   Ownership and European fundamental rights

A broader development took place in the area of fundamental rights. The foundation treaty, the 'Constitution of the European Community', does not contain a catalogue of fundamental rights.[20] However, the European Court of Justice developed European Community fundamental rights in the manner of English common law through its decisions in specific cases. The court drew on the main principles of freedom in the EEC Treaty, the regulations of the Convention and the constitutional traditions of the Member States. The work of the court is already approved by secondary legislation. After the Common Declarations of the Community's organs about fundamental rights from 1977[21] (soft law), Article F II (now Article 6 II) of the treaty now confirms that 'the community respects the fundamental rights [...] as they are guaranteed in the European Convention on Human Rights and as they result from the constitutions of the members as general principles of Community law.' This way, national courts and the European Court of Justice have enough means to control whether fundamental rights are respected or not. The standard of the European Community's fundamental rights is in permanent development.[22]

Furthermore, the concept of the Convention and interpretation by the European Court of Human Rights plays an important role in the development of the property function in the European legal system.[23] Article 1 of the additional protocol of ECHR from 1952 guarantees that property is respected. Expropriations are only licit in the public interest and may be done only by law. State regulations limiting the use of property for the general welfare remain unaffected. As in the German Federal Constitutional Court's ownership decisions, European courts must distinguish between expropriation limits on the one hand and rules for determination of limits on the other, according to their effect – use limitations do not establish a duty of compensation.[24] The integrational or 'social function' of ownership has also been recognised on a European level. The European Court of Human Rights interprets the Convention in such a way that the guarantee of property not only includes real rights, but also all legally acquired rights, including rights to incorporeal goods.[25]

Since the adoption of Article 17 of the European Charter of Fundamental Rights as part of the Treaty of Nice in 2001, the definition of the contents of ownership have become more precise.[26] At that time, the Charter, as a mere catalogue of policies, was not genuine *jus cogens* and thus had no *res judicata* effect. With the genesis of a European Constitution and the inclusion of the European Charter of Basic Rights as part of it, the Charter will become binding European Law.

## 2.4   The problem: Unequal distribution and concentration of capital

In the context of the current crisis of the welfare state, the challenge for the social function of ownership is the extremely unequal distribution of capital.[27] It is to be assumed that, as a result of this disproportion in the distribution of ownership, the market society will soon reach its limits. The thesis described in the equation 'ownership = freedom' is matched by the contrary equation 'non-ownership = non-freedom'. Despite this extremely important function of ownership for individual citizens, it seems equally unquestionable that at least a minimal role for the social functions of ownership must also be protected. The conflict over changes and cutbacks in the welfare state brings up the question of how to define the core minimum of social rights (pension, unemployment benefit, social aid) included in the ownership guarantee, which cannot be withdrawn by the legislature without violation of the Constitution.

Each individual's income and asset ownership are treated more or less differently in all developed market economies. All current industrial societies are still far from reaching the revolutionary ideal of a free and equal social system. This leads to two further questions:

- What are the barriers to establishing and setting up employee ownership in the EU Member States?
- Should there be limits to ownership concentration, and, if so, what should the legal means for implementing such limits be?

## 2.5   The German example

The Federal Republic of Germany (FRG) may serve to illustrate the problem of ownership distribution. The country was (as the FRG before unification in 1990) and remains one of the rich countries, even with its decline in wealth.[28] Despite rising national income in Germany over the past four decades since World War II ('explosion of wealth' because of a fourfold increase of per capita income),[29] income and asset differences increased along with social inequality. The asset differences are much larger than income differences. Concentration of assets, which can be defined as ownership concentration, is twice as large as income concentration. This development can be described as follows: 'The rich and wealthy in the FRG got richer and wealthier.'[30] Widely disputed statistics showed that one-tenth of the population owned half of overall assets in 1983. In this group, one per cent of the households owned 23 per cent of overall assets.[31] Another figure showed that about 74 per cent of domestic productive assets (excluding ownership by the state and foreign owners) was concentrated in the hands of 1.7 per cent of West German private households in 1966.[32] It is presumed that this high concentration remains stable or has even increased.[33]

This process of private ownership concentration in Germany has been accelerated by privatisation and (re-)privatisation in the new parts of Germany (the former German Democratic Republic).[34] Post-socialist (re-)privatisation in East Germany led to a transfer of ownership of productive capital. Nearly all middle-sized and large enterprises were transferred to West German or foreign owners. (Only about 10 per cent of such enterprises were transferred to foreign owners.)[35] Of the largest 50 enterprises privatised before 1994, 45 were transferred to West German owners, two to French owners and one to an Austrian owner. The Federal States Saxonia and Thuringia each received one enterprise. Former socialist state property was transferred to the local federal state.[36] The East German population became owners of newly privatised productive property only when small or medium sized enterprises were transferred by management buyout. However, this happened only in a few enterprises.

## Notes

1. See O. von Gierke (1889) *Die soziale Aufgabe des Privatrechts* (Berlin), p. 348.
2. In Germany this is exacerbated by the high and apparently long term budget deficit, which arose because of the extensive transfer of funds after the re-unification of Germany. The Bundesrechnungshof (Federal Court of

Financial Control) stated that this West–East transfer of capital reached the amount of EUR 325 billion in the first five years. Other authorities, such as the Ministry of the Treasury of North Rhine-Westphalia, estimate that the cost of unification totals EUR 500 billion.

3. Although embodied in the constitutions of several post-socialist states (for example, Poland, Croatia and Russia), the principle of the welfare state has been developed only partly or not at all; for the role and renaissance of private property in the post-socialist societies of Eastern and South-Eastern Europe, see H. Roggemann (1999b) 'Erster Teil: Einführung', in H. Roggemann (ed.) *Die Verfassungen Mittel- und Osteuropas* (Berlin: Berlin Verlag Arno Spitz GmbH), p. 98.

4. See W. Gärtner (1996), *Die Neugestaltung der Wirtschaftsverfassungen in Ostmitteleuropa* (Berlin: Berlin Verlag Arno Spitz GmbH).

5. Compare a recent study on the history of dogmatics and ideas on ownership and its historical relativity by D. Hecker (1990) *Eigentum als Sachherrschaft – Zur Genese und Kritik eines besonderen Herrschaftsanspruchs* (Paderborn and Munich: Schöningh), pp. 18, 204, 252.

6. For further remarks see H. Roggemann (ed.) (1996) *Eigentum in Osteuropa* (Berlin: Berlin Verlag Arno Spitz GmbH).

7. L. O. Kelso and M. J. Adler (1958) *The Capitalist Manifesto* (New York: Random House), p. 15; referring to Pollock v. Farmers' Loan & Trust Co., United States Supreme Court Reports, Vol. 157, 1895, p. 429: 'For what is the land but the profits thereof? … A devise of the rents and profits or of the income of lands passes the land itself both at law and in equity.'

8. See G. Heinsohn and O. Steiger (1997) *The Paradigm of Property, Interest and Money and its Application to European Economic Problems: Mass Unemployment, Monetary Union and Transformation*, IKSF Discussion Paper No. 10, July, p. 346; see also J. Hölscher (1996) *Bedingungen ökonomischer Entwicklung in Zentralosteuropa*, Vol. 3: Privatisierung und Privateigentum (Marburg: Metropolis), p. 109: 'Money and private property constitute the framework of categories for the market process, in which the accumulation is determined by the relation of interest rate and expected profit rate.'

9. See H. Roggemann (1993) 'Eigentumsordnung in Osteuropa', *Recht in Ost und West*, p. 321; H. Roggemann (ed.) (1996), pp. 29, 39.

10. '[P]roperty performs the function of maintaining independence, dignity and pluralism in society by creating zones within which the majority has to yield to the owner. Whim, caprice, irrational and "antisocial" activities are given the protection of law', Charles A. Reich (1964), *Yale Law Journal*, April.

11. 'In the main, it will be found that a power over a man's support is a power over his will', Alexander Hamilton (1788) *The Federalist Papers*, No. 73 in A. Hamilton et al. The Federalist II (New York: J. and A. McLean).

12. In this context see P. Badura (1994) 'Eigentum', in E. Benda, W. Maihofer and H.-J. Vogel (eds) *Handbuch des Verfassungsrechts*, 2nd edn (Berlin et al.: de Gruyter), § 10, p. 386: 'In large companies, the personal relation to individually exercised ownership rights is more or less weakened. [In this case] it is evident how much this economic property is related to society.'

13. See B. Schwartz (1965) *A Commentary on the Constitution of the United States*, Part II (New York and London: Macmillan), p. 229. Against this thesis also see H. Rittstieg (1976) *Eigentum als Verfassungsproblem – Zu Geschichte*

*und Gegenwart des bürgerlichen Verfassungsstaates*, 2nd edn (Darmstadt: Wissenschaftliche Buchgesellschaft), p. 24.

14. A. A. Berle, Jr. (1959) *Toward the Paraproprietal Society* (New York: The Twentieth Century Fund), p. 22.
15. L. O. Kelso (1960) *Lawyers, Economists and Property* (San Francisco, CA), p. 3.
16. Consequently, the legislature attempted to deal with the equitable ownership differently than with 'real' ownership (for example, in Germany) when passing the new insolvency code, leading to accusations of expropriation.
17. J. M. Thiel (1991) 'Grundrechtlicher Eigentumsschutz im EG-Recht', *Juristische Schulung*, p. 274, deals with the problem of whether Article 222 leaves only the organisation of ownership to the Member States or whether all ownership guarantees are excluded from EC control.
18. About interaction of ownership law and freedom of establishment, see R. Riegel (1986) 'Zur Bedeutung der Niederlassungsfreiheit im Europäischen Gemeinschaftsrecht', *Neue Juristische Wochenschrift*, p. 2999.
19. See B. Beutler, R. Bieber and J. Pipkorn (1993) *Die Europäische Union, Rechtsordnung und Politik*, 4th edn (Baden-Baden: Nomos), p. 63.
20. Efforts to enact them later failed; having the European Human Rights Convention ratified by the European Community/Union as an organisation was discussed, but not realised.
21. *Official Journal*, C 103/77, p. 1.
22. See summary by M. Schweitzer and W. Hummer (1993) *Europarecht*, 4th edn (Neuwied and Berlin: Metzner), p. 200. Sceptical about the possibility to define protection of fundamental rights on the basis of the European Human Rights Convention and constitutions is V. Skouris (1995) 'Werbung und Grundrechte in Europa', *Europäische Zeitschrift für Wirtschaftsrecht*, pp. 438–9.
23. See W. Peukert (1992) 'Zur Notwendigkeit der Beachtung des Grundsatzes des Vertrauensschutzes in der Rechtsprechung des Europäischen Gerichtshofes für Menschenrechte zu Eigentumsfragen', *Europäische Grundrechte-Zeitschrift*, Vol. 19.
24. See M. E. Villinger (1993) *Handbuch der Europäischen Menschenrechtskonvention unter besonderer Berücksichtigung der schweizerischen Rechtslage* (Zürich: Schulthess, Polygraph Verlag), p. 385.
25. See W. Skouris (1995), p. 441; M. E. Villinger (1993), p. 384.
26. Article 17, Right to Property, Paragraph 1. Everyone has the right to own, use, dispose of and bequeath his or her lawfully acquired possessions. No one may be deprived of his or her possessions, except in the public interest and in the cases and under the conditions provided for by law, subject to fair compensation being paid in good time for their loss. The use of property may be regulated by law in so far as is necessary for the general interest. Paragraph 2. Intellectual property shall be protected.
27. According to a 1997 survey, the wealthiest one million households in Germany possess much more property than the poorest 25 million households taken together. See *Die Woche*, 17 January 1997, p. 10.
28. See R. Geißler (1996) *Die Sozialstruktur Deutschlands*, 2nd edn (Opladen: Westdeutscher Verlag), p. 65, H. Schlomann (1993) in E. U. Huster (ed.) *Reichtum in Deutschland* (Frankfurt and New York: Springer), p. 54.
29. From 8,600 in 1950 to 36,000 in 1989, see R. Geißler (1996), p. 45.

30. See R. Geißler (1996), p. 61.
31. See H. Schlomann (1993), pp. 71, 73.
32. See W. Krelle, J. Schlunck and J. Siebke (1968) *Überbetriebliche Ertragsbeteiligung der Arbeitnehmer* (Tübingen: Mohr), pp. 72, 250.
33. See *Die Zeit*, No. 40, 23 September 2004, Economy 'Wo stehen die Reichen?' [How are the rich being?], and No. 34, August 2004, Economy 'Nur die Reichen werden reicher' [Only the rich get richer]; see also W. Krelle (1993) 'Wirtschaftswachstum und Vermögensverteilung' in Kirchenamt der Evangelischen Kirche in Deutschland (ed.) *Beteiligung am Produktiveigentum* (Hameln: Sponholtz), p. 37.
34. See G. Guttmann (1995) 'Geldvermögen und Schulden privater Haushalte Ende 1993', *Wirtschaft und Statistik*, p. 391; G. E. Zimmermann (1996) 'Neue Armut und neuer Reichtum: Zunehmende Polarisierung der materiellen Lebensbedingungen im vereinten Deutschland', *Gegenwartskunde*, 44, pp. 5, 14.
35. See J. Priewe (1994) 'Die Folgen der schnellen Privatisierung der Treuhandanstalt', Aus Politik und Zeitgeschichte, supplement of the weekly journal *Das Parlament*, B 43–44, pp. 21, 23.
36. See V. Offermann (1994) 'Die Entwicklung der Einkommen und Vermögen in den neuen Bundesländern seit 1990', in J. Zerche (ed.) *Vom sozialistischen Versorgungsstaat zum Sozialstaat Bundesrepublik* (Regensburg: Transfer-Verlag), p. 96; summary see R. Geißler (1996), p. 67.

# 3
# The Legal Framework for Implementing Financial Participation at the Supranational Level

*Jens Lowitzsch and Natalia Spitsa*

The diverse traditional national approaches to both participation in decision making and financial participation are a major impediment to change, as the controversy over European workers' councils has impressively demonstrated for more than 30 years. The same factors make it very difficult to reach a unanimous supranational compromise either in the Commission or in the Council.

## 3.1 The legislative process

The law of European Treaties in general permits majority vote decisions in a few cases, recently expanded by the Treaty of Nice. No less than 27 provisions have been changed completely or partly from unanimity to qualified majority voting, among them measures to facilitate freedom of movement for the citizens of the Union (Article 18 ECT) and industrial policy (Article 157 ECT). The so called 'co-decision procedure' (see Figure 3.1) has been extended to apply to seven provisions which are changed from unanimity to qualified majority voting (Articles 13, 62, 63, 65, 157, 159 and 191). Accordingly, most of the legislative measures which, after the Treaty of Nice, required a decision from the Council acting by qualified majority will now be decided by the 'co-decision procedure'.[1] In the field of social policy (Articles 42 and 137 ECT), despite maintaining the status quo, the Council, acting in unanimity, is empowered to make the co-decision procedure applicable to those areas still subject to the rule of unanimity.[2]

However, where taxation is concerned, Articles 93, 94 and 175 ECT, maintain the requirement of unanimity across the board (see Figure 3.2). This means that even though tax incentives are the most common way of leveraging financial participation schemes, a common European legal

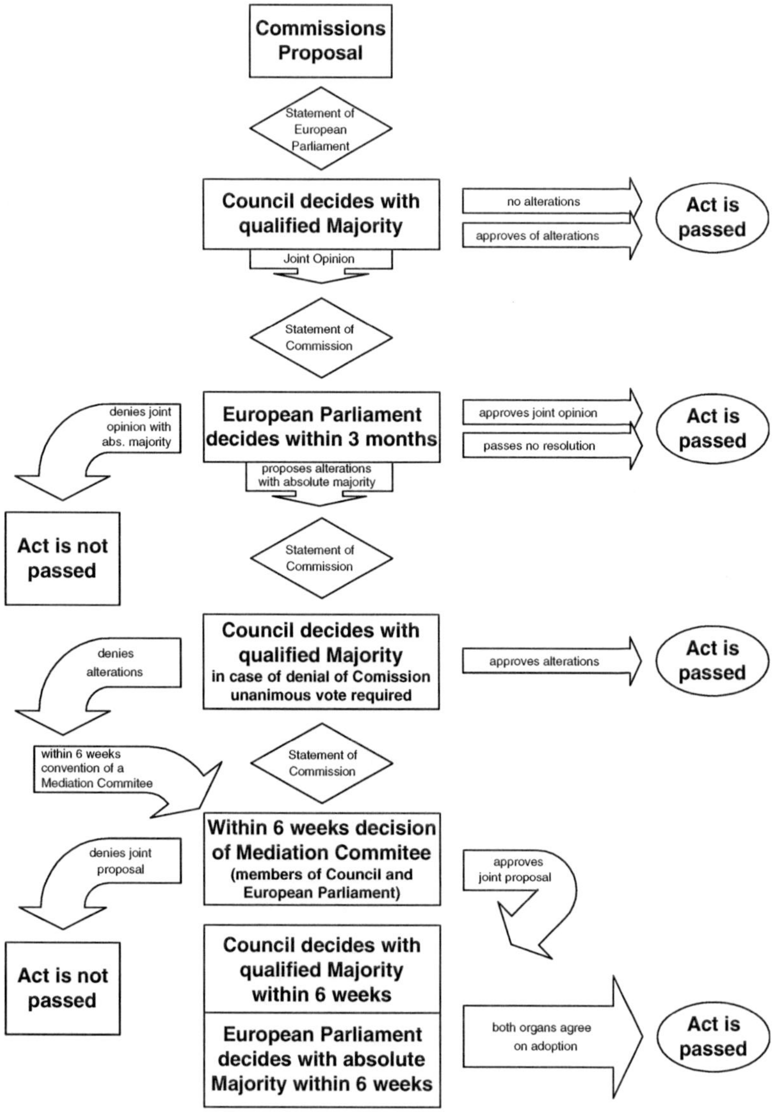

*Figure 3.1*   'Co-decision' procedure according to Article 251 ECT/Nice.

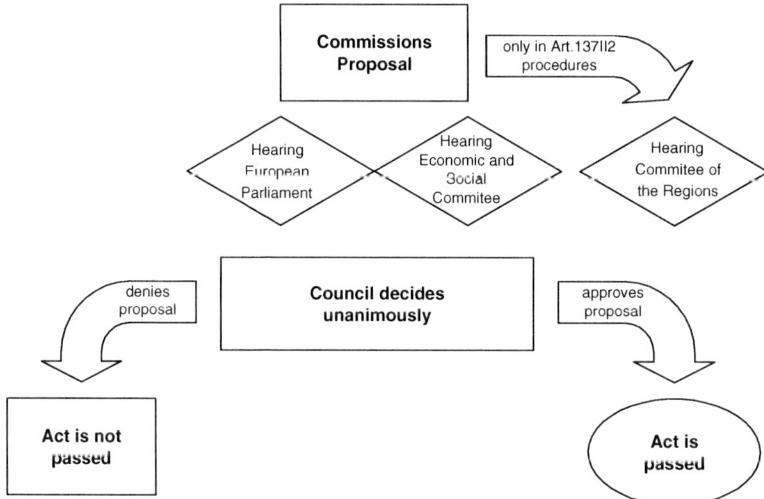


*Figure 3.2*  Legislative procedure according to Article 94 or 137 paragraph 2 (2) ECT requiring unanimous decision.

framework imposing such tax incentives would collide with the legislative tax sovereignty of nations.

## 3.2  Legal sources for employee participation at a European level

A European approach to the problem must provide a broad incentive system transcending the classical instruments of tax legislation. Establishing such schemes through legislation is of primary importance in order to give companies a clear framework for company decisions and actions.[3]

A legal foundation at the Directive level must therefore focus on 'majority vote' regulations to be successful. This is further necessary because the position of the governments in relation to the social partners, their role in society and their relation to each other varies significantly in the different membership countries.[4] Thus, a European regulation should allow a broad incentive system, one that provides different and flexible solutions corresponding to national situations. An adaptable scheme suitable for use throughout the European Union

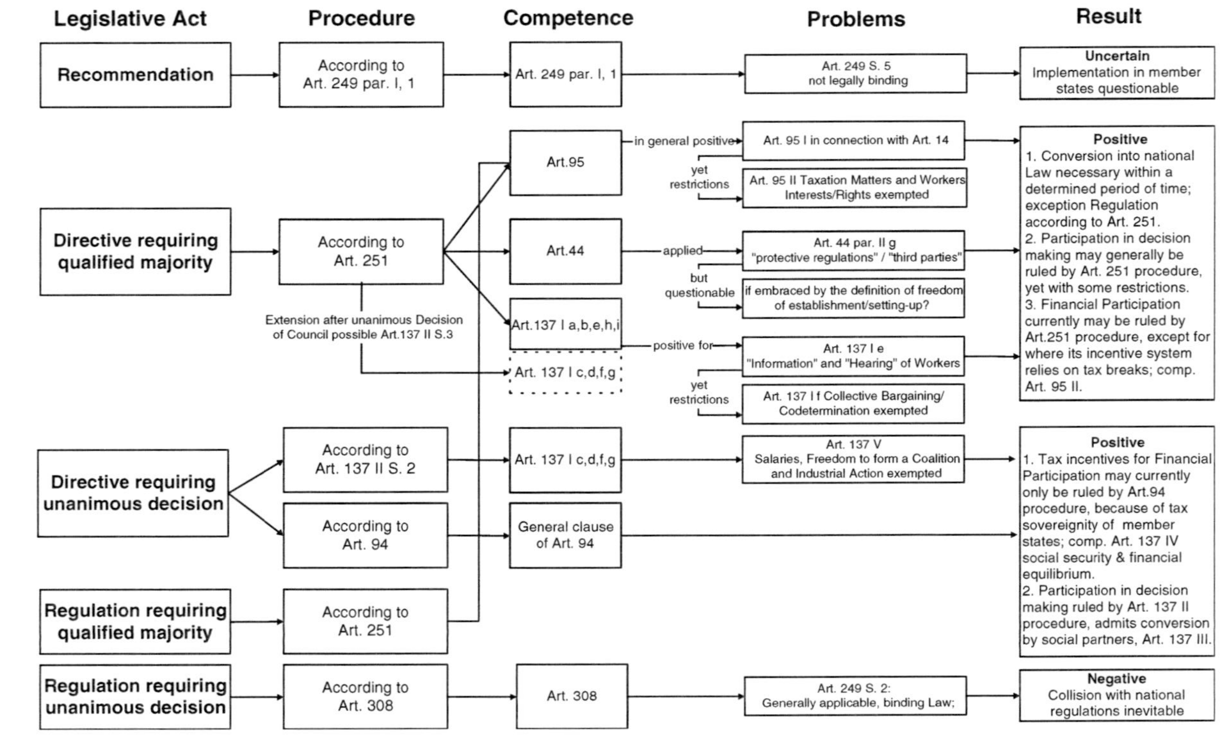



*Figure 3.3*  Legal sources for employee participation in the EU (ECT/Nice).

would collect the best practice of national legislation and customs and combine them in a single programme having alternative options.[5] The available legislative instruments, Recommendation, Directive and Regulation, with their advantages and disadvantages, are shown in Figure 3.3.

## 3.3   Dealing with tax incentives

### 3.3.1   The problem

At the national level, taxation can either inhibit or support the spread of employee financial participation. At the EU level, cross-border migration of employees partaking in financial participation plans, as well as the transfer of such plans by multinational companies to subsidiaries in different Member States, may involve problems caused by conflicting tax regimes.[6] Generally, attention is centred on tax incentives, often considered the state's main instrument for promoting employee financial participation. Tax incentives, however, are relative; they need to be analysed in the context of the general taxation system in the given country. National tax systems are not easily compared; it is even more difficult to compare taxation laws governing national financial participation schemes.[7] Moreover, compulsory social security contributions must be taken into account because they add substantially to the overall burden of state levies, especially on labour; also, in many countries, they influence the tax base of the main income taxes. A systematic overview of the situation in the EU-27 shows, on the one hand, the impact and, on the other hand, the limits of tax incentives in encouraging employee financial participation.[8]

The objectives in this chapter are as follows:

- To outline general systems of direct taxes as they affect employee financial participation in the EU. National tax systems will be classified as unfavourable, neutral or favourable for employee financial participation schemes.
- To review specific tax incentives for employee financial participation in order to determine whether they are a prerequisite for employee financial participation, and whether some tax incentives are more effective than others, irrespective of the country where they are offered.

Tax incentives can be considered efficient if the number of specific financial participation plans supported by these tax incentives increases immediately after the tax incentives have been introduced. However, historical data on such increases are currently available only for a few countries; therefore, the analysis of the efficiency of tax incentives in these countries will be presented only as an example.

### 3.3.2   General taxation of PEPPER schemes in the EU

The following direct taxes are relevant to employee financial participation:

- corporate income tax (CIT);
- personal income tax (PIT);
- taxes on dividends at shareholder level (special rates of personal income tax, 'investment tax', 'dividend tax', 'share income tax', and so on);
- taxes on sale of shares at shareholder level (special rates of personal income tax, capital gains tax, 'investment tax', and so on).

According to Article 3 paragraph 1 lit. h) ECT, an EU priority is to prevent the diversity of national tax systems from negatively affecting the development of the Common Market by harmonising national legal codes. As a special case of Article 3 paragraph 1 lit. h) ECT, Article 93 ECT stipulates that indirect taxes (VAT and excises) must be made consistent. Prompted by this provision, numerous directives have been issued and indirect taxation has already been harmonised to a great extent. However, there is no special provision on harmonisation of direct taxes.[9] Moreover, potential harmonisation in this area is restricted by Article 5 paragraph 2 ECT. On the one hand, the European Commission supports competition of direct taxes[10], regarding tax autonomy as the core component of state sovereignty, closely related to country-specific economic, social and cultural structures. On the other hand, it recognises the importance of preventing unfair tax competition, especially in the area of corporate taxation.[11] Because there is neither a legal basis nor political support for harmonisation of corporate tax rates, the European Commission currently favours the development of the Common Consolidated Corporate Tax Base (CCCTB).[12] However, even if the CCCTB should be introduced in all Member States, it will not apply to enterprises having no cross-border activities.[13]

Nevertheless, international tax competition is exerting considerable pressure, especially on corporate income tax rates, since the US tax reform of 1986. This is responsible for two persistent tendencies observable worldwide. Firstly, the tax burden has been shifted from direct to

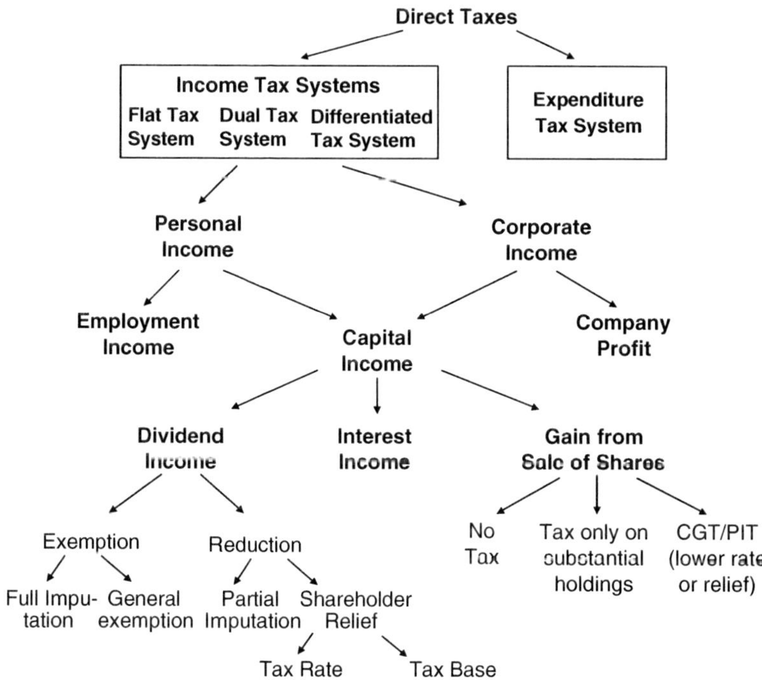


*Figure 3.4*   Direct taxes.

indirect taxes[14] (with some exceptions, for example, France), and from capital to labour.[15] Thus taxation of share-based plans may become more favourable over time than that of cash-based plans, because the tax burden on dividends and capital gains is lower than on employment income. Secondly, tax rates are lowered while the tax base is broadened.[16] Although this might lead to the abolition of specific tax incentives, it does not necessarily mean less favourable taxation: if the rates become sufficiently lower, this may compensate for the loss of tax incentives. The general characteristics of national systems of direct taxes are illustrated by Figure 3.4.

A common feature of all direct tax systems of EU member and candidate states is that only income and not expenditure is taxable.[17] Accordingly, as affecting the relationship between the respective tax burden on capital and labour, income tax systems can be divided into flat tax, dual tax and differentiated tax systems; all these systems have advantages and drawbacks from an economic standpoint and are currently present in different EU Member States. In a genuine flat tax system, represented by Romania and Slovakia, the tax burden falls equally on all sources of income, flat and relatively low, because the basic tax rate to which other tax rates are adapted is the tax on capital income. This system is generally equally favourable to all forms of employee financial participation. The same is true of tax systems that impose different tax rates on labour and capital income, but levy a flat personal income tax (Estonia, Latvia, Lithuania).[18] Dual tax systems represented, for example, by Sweden and Finland, are characterised by a highly progressive personal income tax as opposed to a flat tax on capital income. This combination is, theoretically, negative for cash-based profit-sharing and positive for share-based schemes. Most EU Member States have a differentiated tax system which generally favours employee share ownership if taxes on capital are flat and relatively low. As far as tax systems are concerned, no common tendencies can be observed. Taxation traditions and goals of EU Member States are different and none of the prevailing systems can be considered the best objectively.[19]

As far as the system of corporate income tax (taxation of dividends at the corporate and shareholder level) is concerned, no EU Member State provides relief for corporations, but many mitigate double taxation by providing relief for shareholders. Within the EU, classical, imputation, shareholder-relief and exemption systems are all represented. From the point of view of employee financial participation, classical systems (double taxation of dividend income; for example, Ireland, Latvia, Romania) are generally unfavourable.[20] Partial imputation generally leads to a higher tax burden at shareholder level than full imputation and shareholder-relief[21] and is, therefore, relatively unfavourable. Most countries currently offer shareholder-relief, but it is difficult to assess the effect on employee financial participation without comparing effective tax rates.[22] The best system for share-based plans is undoubtedly one that exempts dividend income from taxation by law (for example, Croatia, Cyprus, Estonia, Greece, Slovakia) or through full imputation (for example, Finland).

Taxation of capital gains from sale of shares is of great importance for employee share ownership. In this context, three concepts can be distinguished within the EU: exemption from taxation (for example, Belgium, Portugal, Cyprus, partially Bulgaria, Malta); taxation only on substantial holdings (defined differently in different countries, for example, Austria, Germany, Italy, Luxembourg, the Netherlands) and taxation by capital gains tax or by personal income tax at a lower (and usually flat) rate. Obviously, tax exemption is the most advantageous for employee financial participation. Taxation of substantial holdings is also favourable, because employee shareholdings are usually small. There is no common tendency for the taxation of capital gains.

Compulsory social security contributions[23] can either reduce the tax base of corporate and personal income tax or be calculated on after tax income (for example, Latvia). Otherwise, they impose an additional burden on gross income and are thus very unfavourable for cash-based profit-sharing, even when general taxes are low as in Slovakia. Further, social security contributions can be levied on capital income as in France (this would have had negative consequences for share-based schemes had France not introduced specific tax incentives). Generally, no common tendency in the development of social security is discernable, because in most countries contributions are connected to long-term insurance and thus are not as easily altered by the state as are taxes.

Tax and social security rates and deductions are interdependent within a national tax system, therefore each national system has to be analysed separately as a whole; details are presented in Table 3.1.

In the context of taxation, it is only relevant whether a financial participation scheme is cash-based or share-based and whether an 'intermediary entity'[24] is used as a vehicle. The same taxation rules apply to employee share ownership schemes and share-based profit-sharing schemes, both direct and deferred.

### 3.3.2.1 Employee share ownership

*3.3.2.1.1 Employee shares* The benefit in value from transfer of discounted shares is generally deemed employment income and correspondingly subject to full personal income tax and compulsory social security contributions at the employee level (see Figure 3.5). The employer company can generally deduct the discount as a personnel cost. However, valuation rules, especially for non-quoted shares, differ considerably between countries.[25] Taxation of dividends depends on the country-specific type of dividend treatment. Because there is no tax relief for the employing company in any EU Member State, full corporate tax generally is to be paid by the employer company on the entire profit, including the part to be distributed.[26]

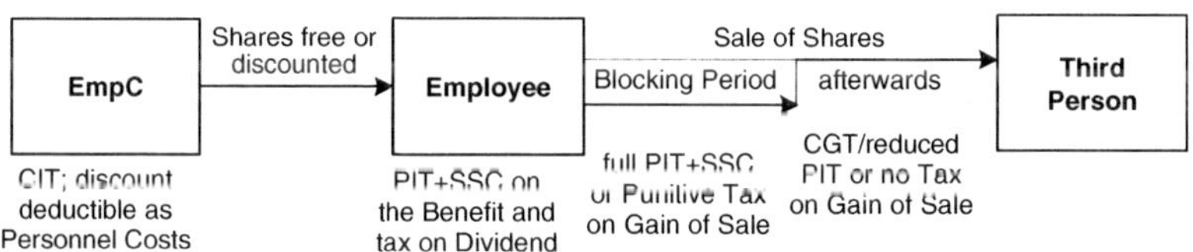



*Figure 3.5* Taxation of employee shares.

*Table 3.1*   General taxation and compulsory social security contributions

| Country | Type of dividend treatment | CIT[27] | Taxation of dividends at shareholder level[28] | Taxation of share sale at shareholder level[29] | PIT[30] | Compulsory SSC[31] |
|---|---|---|---|---|---|---|
| Belgium | Shareholder relief: reduced tax rate | 34% | 15% | Generally 0% | Progressive 25–50% central plus 0–9% sub-central; SSC deductible | Empl.: overall rate 13,07%<br>EmpC: overall rate 35% |
| Bulgaria | Shareholder relief: reduced tax rate | 10% | 7% | Shares of public companies listed at Bulgarian Stock Exchange 0% | Progressive 20–24% voluntary SSC deductible | Empl.: (cumulative) 12.43–25.74%<br>EmpC: (cumulative) 23.34–25.74% |
| Croatia | Dividend tax exemption for shareholders | 20% | 0% | 0% | Progressive 15–45% plus city surtaxes 0–18%; SSC deductible | Empl.: 20% to pension fund<br>EmpC: 17.2% to the health, unemployment, injury funds |
| Cyprus | Dividend tax exemption for shareholders | 10% | Generally 0% | Generally 0% | Progressive 20–30%; SSC deductible | Empl.: overall rate 6.3%<br>EmpC: overall rate 6.3% plus 2% to Social Cohesion Fund |

| Czech Republic | Shareholder relief: reduced tax rate | 24% | 15% withholding tax at source | General PIT for sale of shares within six months 28–43% | Progressive 12–32%; SSC deductible | Empl.: (cumulative) 12.5% EmpC: (cumulative) 35% |
|---|---|---|---|---|---|---|
| Denmark | Shareholder relief: reduced tax rate | 28% | 28% share income tax up to DKK 44,300, 43% above; not for professional traders | | Progressive 5–26.5% central plus 29–35% sub-central; ceiling 59% | Empl.: 8% labour market tax EmpC: 0% |
| Germany | Shareholder relief: reduced tax base | 38.7% | General PIT plus solidarity surcharge 5.5%; tax base reduced to 50% of the dividend income (half-income system); no SSC | 0% for small long-term holdings; for substantial share-holdings general PIT on difference between 50% of proceeds and 50% of acquisition costs | Progressive 15–45.4% plus solidarity surcharge 5.5%; limited by an absolute amount; pension and health care contributions partly deductible | Empl.: (average) 13–21.4% EmpC: (average) 20.5% Both limited by an absolute amount |
| Estonia | Tax exemption for shareholders; exemption of retained profits from corporate tax | 22% on distributed profits | 0% | General PIT | Flat 22%; mandatory SSC deductible | Empl.: contribution to the unemployment fund 0.6% EmpC: 'social tax' 33% plus contribution to the unemployment fund 0.3% |

(Continued)

*Table 3.1*   (Continued)

| Country | Type of dividend treatment | CIT[27] | Taxation of dividends at shareholder level[28] | Taxation of share sale at shareholder level[29] | PIT[30] | Compulsory SSC[31] |
|---|---|---|---|---|---|---|
| Greece | Dividend tax exemption for shareholders | 25% | 0% | Generally 0%; 20% on sale of shares of LLC or partnerships | Progressive 15–40%; SSC deductible | Empl.: 11.55% (16%) EmpC: 23.1% (28.06%); both limited by an absolute amount |
| Spain | Partial imputation | 32.5% | 15%; imputation credit | 15% if held more than one year, otherwise general PIT | 15–45% savings income deductible | Empl.: 16.35% EmpC: 30.6% |
| France | Partial imputation | 34.4% | general PIT with tax credit of 40% plus social levies (CRDS, CSG) – 11% | CGT 16%; on stock options 30–40% | Progressive 5.5–40% | Empl.: (cumulative) 10.6–17.8%; limited by an absolute amount EmpC: (aggregated) 29.72–34.22% |
| Hungary | Shareholder relief: reduced tax rate | 17.5% | 25% for dividends on up to 30% of equity; 35% above plus 14% health care contribution | 25%; on up to 30% of equity; 35% above | Progressive 18–36%; voluntary SSC deductible | Empl.: 17% limited by an absolute amount EmpC: 32 plus health care contribution |
| Ireland | Classical system | 12.5% | 20% | 20% | Progressive 20–42%; voluntary SSC deductible | Empl.: 2–6% EmpC: 8.5–10.75% |

| Italy | Shareholder relief: reduced tax base | 37.3% | General PIT; tax base reduced to 5% of dividend income; below 5% (or 2% of voting rights) 12.5% | 12.5% for small shareholdings; 27% on substantial; tax base reduced to 40% of gain | Progressive 23–43% plus surcharge 0.9–1.4%; SSC deductible | Empl.: (cumulative) 9.2–10.2% EmpC: (cumulative) 32.08% |
|---|---|---|---|---|---|---|
| Latvia | Classical system | 15% | General PIT | General PIT | Flat 25% | Empl.: overall rate 9% EmpC: overall rate 24.09%, both from after-tax income |
| Lithuania | Shareholder relief: reduced tax rate | 15% | 15% | Generally 15%; 0% if held more than one year and no substantial shareholding for last three years | Flat 27% | Empl.: 3% EmpC: 30.7% |
| Luxembourg | Shareholder relief: tax base reduced | 29.6% | 15%; tax base reduced to 50% of the dividend income | General PIT for short-term holdings; high allowance and half PIT rate for long-term holdings | Progressive 8–38% | Empl.: 11.8–14.05% EmpC: 13.15–20.75% |
| Malta | Full imputation | 35% | General PIT and tax credit for CIT | Stamp duty; shares quoted on Malta Stock Exchange tax exempt | Progressive 15-35% | Empl.: overall rate MTL 2.84–13.38 weekly EmpC: overall rate MTL 2.84–13.38 weekly |



(*Continued*)

*Table 3.1*   (Continued)

| Country | Type of dividend treatment | CIT[27] | Taxation of dividends at shareholder level[28] | Taxation of share sale at shareholder level[29] | PIT[30] | Compulsory SSC[31] |
|---|---|---|---|---|---|---|
| Netherlands | Shareholder relief: reduced tax rate | 25.5% | 15% for small, 25% for substantial holdings | 0% for small, 25% for substantial shareholdings | Progressive 33.65–52% | Empl.: 5.2–31.7% EmpC: 6.5–11.31% |
| Austria | Shareholder relief: reduced tax rate | 25% | 25%; optional: general PIT at a half rate; generally no SSC | 0% for small long-term holdings; for substantial shareholdings 25% | Progressive 23–50%; statutory and voluntary pension contributions partly deductible | Empl.: (cumulative) 16.85–17.2% EmpC: (cumulative) 20.5–20.7% deductible; both limited by an absolute amount |
| Poland | Shareholder relief: reduced tax rate | 19% | 19% | 19% | Progressive 19–40% | Empl.: average 22.2% EmpC: average 20.6% |
| Portugal | Partial imputation | 27.5% | 20%; imputation credit of 50% | Generally 10%; tax exemption if shares are held more than 12 months | Progressive 10.5–42% | Empl.: overall rate 11% EmpC: overall rate 23.75% |
| Romania | Classical system | 16% | Investment Tax 16% | Investment Tax 16%; 1% for long-term investment | Flat 16%; voluntary contributions to private pension funds deductible | Empl.: (cumulative) 17% EmpC: (cumulative) 30.35–31.35% |

| Slovakia | Dividend tax exemption for shareholders | 19% | 0% | General PIT | Flat 19% | Empl.: 13.4% EmpC: 28.4% |
| Slovenia | Shareholder relief: reduced tax rate | 23% | 20% | 0–20% according to the holding term | Progressive 16–41% contributions to private pension funds deductible | Empl.: 22,1% EmpC: 16.1% |
| Finland | Full imputation | 26% | Investment Tax 28%; generally no SSC | 28% | Progressive 9–32% central plus 18.46% (average) sub-central; SSC deductible | Empl.: (cumulative) 6.61–7.18%; EmpC: (cumulative) 20.69–32.69%; both limited by an absolute amount |
| Sweden | Shareholder relief: reduced tax rate | 28% | Individual Capital Income Tax 30% | 30% | Progressive 20–25% central plus 31.6% sub-central | Empl.: 7% EmpC: 32.28% |
| Turkey | Partial imputation | 20% | 15%; imputation credit of 50% | 0% if held more than four years, otherwise general PIT | Progressive 15–35% | Empl.: 15%; EmpC: 21.5% Both limited by an absolute amount |
| UK | Partial imputation | 30% | 10% up to the basic rate limit; 32.5% above; imputation credit | CGT 40%; taper relief | Progressive 10–40% | Empl.: overall rate 11% EmpC: overall rate 12.8% |

Abbreviations: CIT = corporation tax; PIT = personal income tax; CGT = capital gains tax; SSC = social security contributions; EmpC = employer company; Empl. = employee; IC = intermediary company.

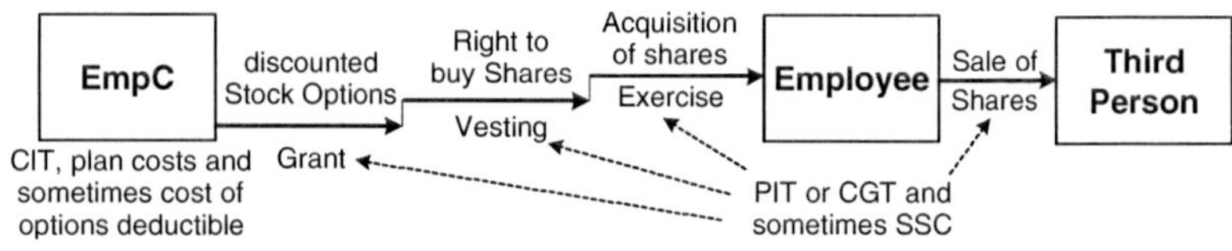


*Figure 3.6*  Taxation of stock options.

Different systems of dividend taxation at shareholder level are explained above. Taxation of gains from sale of shares depends on whether the shares are sold during or after the end of the blocking period. If the shares are sold during the blocking period, there are no major differences between EU countries: either full personal income tax and social security contributions or a special (high) punitive tax will be imposed. If the shares are sold after the end of the blocking period, taxation depends on the system of taxation of capital gains presented above. If there is no general exemption, or exemption for small shareholdings, other forms of tax relief usually apply.

*3.3.2.1.2  Stock options*   Taxation of employee stock options is complex owing to differences in the taxation moment and valuation methods which depend on the taxation moment. In most EU Member States, taxes are imposed at exercise; taxation at grant or optionally at grant or exercise, as well as taxation at sale of shares, are also practised (see Figure 3.6).

Upfront taxation at grant is connected with considerable risks, so that special tax relief such as reduced tax rate or tax base and exemption from social security contributions are necessary as compensation. Although it could be argued that stock option benefits should be considered as capital gains, it is deemed to be employment income in most EU Member States; as such it is usually charged as personal income tax and partly also subject to social security contributions. The employer

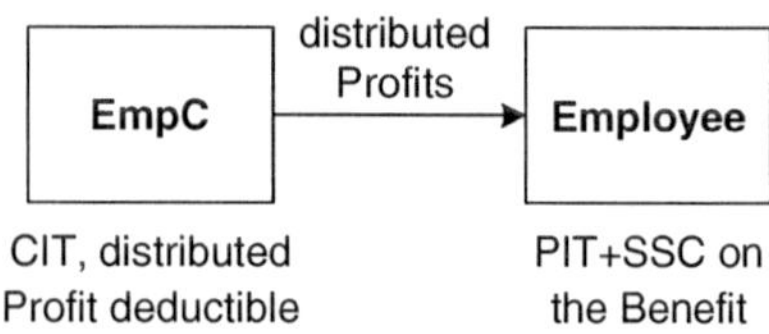


*Figure 3.7*  Taxation of profit-sharing.

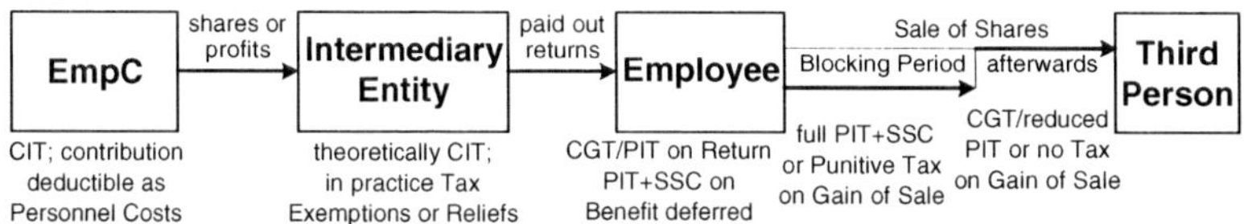


*Figure 3.8* Taxation of share ownership plans and profit-sharing plans using intermediary entities.

company can generally deduct setting up and operating costs of the plan as well as cost of options if the shares are repurchased (with the exception of, for example, Belgium). In some countries (for example, Denmark, Ireland, Luxembourg, Portugal), both the employer company and the employee are exempted from social security contributions.[32]

### 3.3.2.2   Profit-sharing

As far as cash-based profit-sharing is concerned, no major discrepancies exist between different EU Member States. Distributed profit is generally deductible for the employer company as a personnel cost (with the exception of Estonia, where it is instead subject to the tax on distributed profits), and it is subject to full personal income tax and social security contributions for the employees (see Figure 3.7). The same taxation rules as for employee share ownership apply to share-based profit-sharing (see 3.3.2.1.1).

### 3.3.2.3   Intermediary entities

Share ownership plans and profit-sharing plans using a vehicle for the holding of shares and the investment of accumulated funds exist in many varieties in different EU Member States, especially because of substantial differences in company law. However, there is a similar basic logic: the employer company can usually deduct contributions to the intermediary entity, as well as set up and operating costs, from the tax base of the corporate income tax; the intermediary entity is usually established in a tax-friendly form (see Figure 3.8). Taxation of employees would be the same as for simple share-based plans (see 3.3.2.1.1) if it were not for specific tax incentives (for example, deferred taxation of the benefit), which in most cases are granted.

### 3.3.3   Specific tax incentives for PEPPER schemes in the EU

Aside from specific tax incentives, most national taxation systems are more or less favourable to financial participation. The only tax system that actually hinders the development of financial participation is that of Estonia, owing to taxation of distributed profits at company level instead of general corporate income tax.[33] National taxation systems that exempt dividends and capital gains from taxation and social security contributions are especially advantageous to share-based schemes. Although details differ, generally in most countries the same taxes apply to similar plans so that the important difference is the general level of the tax burden of standard income taxes and compulsory social security contributions determined by tax rates and tax bases. As mentioned above, comparable effective rates cannot be calculated for all possible situations. Nevertheless, a substantial difference in tax rates implies a difference in tax burden. Thus it can be argued that low-tax countries generally have more favourable tax regimes for financial participation so that specific tax incentives are not necessary. The example of Ireland, however, shows that the government of a low-tax country can have a strong political interest in promoting employee financial participation; it can offer additional tax incentives even though the low level of general taxation limits their impact.[34] Therefore the different instruments used to create specific tax incentives are important. Incentives may take the different forms shown in Figure 3.9.

Tax rate reductions and exemptions, although most effective because they are based on law rather than arbitrary judgments of tax authorities, and confer the same advantages to all categories of income, are seldom used.[35] One reason for this neglect is that such tax incentives result in heavier losses of revenue; also, tax authorities have virtually

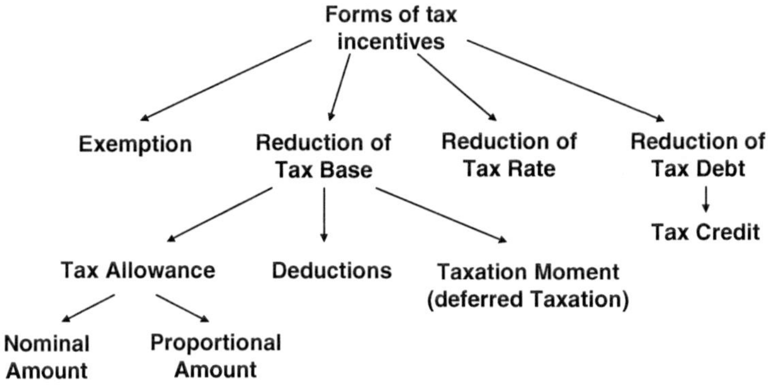


*Figure 3.9*   Forms of tax incentives.

no discretionary power over their use.[36] Deductions favour higher incomes under a progressive system of taxation, like the personal income tax in most EU Member States; tax credits (direct reduction of tax liability), on the other hand, are non-discriminatory and usually more valuable than an equivalent tax deduction or tax allowance.[37] Tax allowances benefit lower incomes whereas nominal tax allowances benefit the taxpayer less and therefore involve smaller revenue loss than would a proportional determination of the tax allowance. Deferred taxation favours share ownership schemes avoiding otherwise necessary additional liquidity at the moment of acquisition. Specific tax incentives for employee financial participation are currently in effect in 16 (mainly Western) countries out of the 29 Member States and candidate countries; these differ substantially in type and size. Details are presented in Table 3.2.

Although, at first impression, the table seems to suggest unbridgeable diversity, the analysis of the data leads to the conclusion that preconditions as well as forms of tax incentives are generally similar, but differ substantially in size. The table's columns correspond to the classification of employee financial participation forms in country profiles. However, as explained above, a different classification should be used for purposes of tax analysis: employee share ownership plans and share-based profit-sharing plans belong to the first category (with certain specific features of leveraged plans), stock option plans to the second category and cash-based profit-sharing plans to the third category.

### 3.3.3.1  Share-based plans

Tax incentives in most countries apply to non-leveraged share-based plans, share-ownership as well as profit-sharing. The most common pre-condition is a blocking period between one and seven years, the most common being five years (for example, Austria, Belgium, Denmark, France and Italy for some plans). A blocking period can be combined with an obligation to deposit shares with a bank. In leveraged share-based plans, shares must be deposited with an intermediary entity (intermediary company, fund or trust) and cannot be withdrawn within a certain period (up to ten years), which practically corresponds to the 'voluntary' blocking period in non-leveraged plans (for example, Austria, Finland, France, Ireland, UK). In some cases, tax incentives apply only if the primary plan is linked to a savings contract or scheme (for example, France, the Netherlands). In many countries, tax incentives apply only if the plan is broad-based (for example Austria, Denmark, Finland, Hungary, the Netherlands, Ireland, UK and France).

*Table 3.2*   Tax incentives for employee financial participation

| Country | | Employee | Employer Company |
|---|---|---|---|
| Austria | ESO | ES: Since 2001: Amount free of taxes and SSC up to EUR 1,453.46 annually, if five-year blocking period, plan broad-based, shares deposited with a domestic credit institution<br>SO: Since 1999: tax allowance (10% of the benefit per year, but not more than 50% of the total benefit tax-free) if options non-tradable, plan broad-based, value of underlying share at option grant not exceeding EUR 36,400 plus carry-forward of taxation for the remaining amount (taxation optionally at sale or at termination of employment, but at the latest at the end of the seventh year after grant) if options deposited with a domestic credit institution<br>IntE: Since 2001: up to EUR 1,453.46 annually CGT; if more PIT; no SSC | ES: Book value of transferred shares deductible as personnel costs<br>SO: Costs of share purchase or the amount not contributed to the equity in the case of capital increase deductible from CIT<br>IntE: payments to IntE and costs for IntE deductible from CIT; up to EUR 1,453.46 annually per capita tax-free; if more CGT; dividends on shares tax-free. |
| | PS | General: No<br>IntE: Do not exist | General: No<br>IntE: Do not exist |
| Belgium | ESO | ES: Since 2001: 15% tax on benefit, no SSC if two-five-year blocking period; tax base: quoted shares market value-costs, non-quoted shares purchase price-net asset value of shares; Sale of shares: tax-free up to 25% of equity; sale during blocking period 23.29% punitive tax<br>SO: Since 1999: taxation moment – at grant; taxation base: lump sum value = 15% of stock value at grant plus 1% for each year before exercise, value reduced by half (7.5% plus 0.5%) if options cannot be exercised within three years from grant, exercise period within ten years from grant, no guarantee against fall in value, strike price determined at option offer; no SSC<br>IntE: Do not exist | ES: Discount deductible from tax base of CIT<br>SO: Difference between market price of stock and exercise price of options deductible from tax base of CIT only if not EmpC, but a foreign company provides shares for employees at exercise and cross-charges the cost to EmpC<br>IntE: Do not exist |

| | | | |
|---|---|---|---|
| | PS | General: Since 2001: 15% tax for participation in the framework of an investment savings plan; 25% tax in other cases; but full SSC<br>IntE: Do not exist | General: No SSC<br>IntE: Do not exist |
| Denmark | ESO | ES: Since 1987 (broad-based plan): no PIT, no SSC on discount, if value does not exceed 10% of annual salary, five-year blocking period and shares deposited on trust with a bank<br>SO: (1) Broad-based plan (since 1987): no PIT, no SSC if value of options does not exceed 10% of annual salary and five-year blocking period; (2) Individual plan under § 7H (since 2003): no PIT, no SSC if value of options does not exceed 10% of annual salary or exercise price less than 15% lower than market price of underlying shares; (3) Individual plan under § 28: no incentives<br>IntE: Do not exist | ES: Discount deductible from tax base of CIT<br>SO: (1) Option costs deductible from tax base of CIT; (2) No; (3) Option costs deductible from tax base of CIT<br>IntE: Do not exist |
| | PS | General: (1) Broad-based plan (since 1987): up to DKK 8,000 tax-free if blocking period seven years and shares deposited on trust with a bank; (2) Individual plan under § 7H (since 2003): no PIT, no SSC on benefit if value does not exceed 10% of annual salary<br>IntE: Do not exist | General: (1) Costs of shares deductible from tax base of CIT; (2) No<br>IntE: Do not exist |
| Finland | ESO | ES: Since 1992: no PIT, no SSC on discount, if it does not exceed 10% and plan broad-based; Dividends: in public companies 30% tax-free; in private companies 100% tax-free if earnings per share less than 9% and the total amount less than EUR 90,000<br>SO: No<br>IntE: Do not exist | ES: Discount deductible from tax base of CIT<br>SO: No<br>IntE: Do not exist |

(Continued)

*Table 3.2*   (Continued)

| Country | | Employee | Employer Company |
|---|---|---|---|
| | PS | General: No<br>IntE: Since 1989/97: Personnel Funds no PIT, no SSC on 20% of pay-outs from the Fund, if five-year blocking period | General: No<br>IntE: EmpC: no CIT, no SSC on profits transferred to IntE;<br>IntE: earnings tax-free |
| France | ESO | ES: No<br>SO: No<br>IntE: Do not exist | ES: Training of employees on EFP: tax relief EUR 75 per hour and capita up to EUR 5,000 per company for two years (2007)<br>SO: No<br>IntE: Do not exist |
| | PS | General: Since 1986/94 (intéressement – gain-sharing): no SSC, but full PIT, if transferred immediately; tax incentives only if combined with savings funds (PEE, PPESV); Since 1967/86/94 (participation – profit-sharing): no PIT, no SSC, special flat tax of 7.6% on benefit if blocking period five years, the amount does not exceed 25% of gross salary up to EUR 14,592; returns tax-free if accumulated, 10% special flat tax if paid out during blocking period<br>IntE: Since 1986/94 (PEE – short-term savings plan): no PIT, no SSC, flat tax of 7.6% if blocking period five years and EmpC match does not exceed the ceiling; Since 2001: (PPESV – long-term savings plan): like short-term, but blocking period ten years; if EmpC match exceeds the ceiling for short-term, but is under the ceiling for long-term – flat tax of 8.2%; Returns: flat tax of 10% | General: Since 1986/94 (intéressement – gain-sharing): no SSC; tax incentives only if combined with savings funds (PEE, PPESV); Since 1967/86/94 (participation – profit-sharing): no CIT, no SSC, special flat tax of 7.6% on benefit if blocking period five years, the amount does not exceed 25% of gross salary up to EUR 14,592; returns tax-free if accumulated, 10% special flat tax if paid out during blocking period<br>IntE: Since 1986/94 (PEE – short-term savings plan): no CIT, no SSC, flat tax of 7.6% if blocking period five years and EmpC match does not exceed the ceiling; Since 2001: (PPESV – long-term savings plan): like short-term, but blocking period ten years; if EmpC match exceeds the ceiling for short-term, but is under the ceiling for long-term – flat tax of 8.2%; Returns: flat tax of 10% |

| | | | |
|---|---|---|---|
| Germany | ESO | ES: No PIT, no SSC on benefit, if not exceeding 50% of the share value and EUR 135 annually; savings bonus of 18% on investment up to EUR 400 annually if annual income up to EUR 17 900 and six-year blocking period<br>SO: No<br>IntE: Do not exist | ES: No<br>SO: No<br>IntE: Do not exist |
| | PS | General: No<br>IntE: Do not exist | General: No<br>IntE: Do not exist |
| Greece | ESO | ES: Since 1987: (only for JSC) no PIT, no SSC on benefit – if shares issued in a capital increase three-year blocking period; Dividends: tax on movable assets (10%)<br>SO: (1) Since 1999 'qualified plans': no PIT, no SSC at grant or exercise; (2) Since 1988 'non-qualified plans': gift tax can be applied instead of PIT at discretion of tax authorities<br>IntE: Do not exist | ES: Discount deductible from tax base of CIT, no SSC<br>SO: (1) No; (2) Costs of distributed shares deductible from tax base of CIT<br>IntE: Do not exist |
| | PS | General: (only for JSC, usually cash-based) no PIT, but SSC on benefit if not exceeding 25% of annual gross salary<br>IntE: Do not exist | General: Distributed amount deductible from tax base of CIT, but SSC<br>IntE: Do not exist |
| Hungary | ESO | ES: Since 2003 Approved Employee Securities Benefit Programme: no PIT and tax relief for voluntary insurance or benefit, if not exceeding HUF 50,000 annually and programme approved;<br>SO: Since 2003 Approved Employee Securities Benefit Programme: incentives as for ES<br>IntE: Since 1992 ESOP: no PIT on shares transferred via ESOP; contributions to ESOP deductible from tax base of PIT | ES: No<br>SO: No<br>IntE: Contributions to ESOP deductible from tax base of CIT |
| | PS | General No<br>IntE: Do not exist | General: No<br>IntE: Do not exist |

(Continued)

*Table 3.2* (Continued)

| Country | | Employee | Employer Company |
|---|---|---|---|
| Ireland | ESO | ES: (1) Purchase of new shares: at sale of shares no PIT, no SSC, only CGT on issue price, if full price paid, three-year blocking period and not exceeding lifetime ceiling of EUR 6,350; (2) Restricted Stock Scheme: deduction from tax base of PIT on benefit from 10% for one-year blocking period to 55% for five-year blocking period<br>SO: (1) Since 1999 SAYE: no PIT, no SSC at grant or exercise, if plan broad-based, SAYE contract with a bank for three, five or seven years, exercise price of shares up to 25% under the market value of underlying shares at option grant, plan approved by tax authorities; (2) Since 2001 APOS: no PIT, no SSC at grant or exercise, if plan broad-based, three-year blocking period, plan approved by tax authorities<br>IntE: ESOT enjoy incentives only if combined with APPS (see below) | ES: (1) No SSC; (2) No<br>SO: (1) No SSC; (2) No SSC<br>IntE: ESOT enjoy incentives only if combined with APPS (see below) |
| | PS | General: No<br>IntE: (1) Since 1986 APSS: no PIT, no SSC on benefit not exceeding EUR 12,700, if plan broad-based, three-year blocking period in trust, plan approved by tax authorities Sale of shares: CGT; sale during blocking period PIT at top rate on proceeds of sale less market value and CGT on increase in value; (2) Since 1997 ESOT: incentives only if combined with APSS trust | General: No<br>IntE: (1) Costs of setting up and operating the plan deductible from tax base of CIT, no SSC; (2) EmpC: incentives only if combined with APSS trust; IntE: no tax on dividends if dividends used for qualifying purposes |
| Italy | ESO | General: Sale gain taxed with 12.5 CGT instead of 40%<br>ES: Since 1999: no PIT, no SSC on benefit up to EUR 2,066; no SSC (since 2006) if three-year blocking period; in limited liabilitiy companies free share up to EUR 7,500 tax exempt | ES: Discount deductible from tax base of CIT<br>SO: No<br>IntE: Do not exist |

| | | | |
|---|---|---|---|
| | | SO: Since 1999: no PIT, no SSC up to EUR 2,066, if five-year blocking period between option grant and sale of shares, unless proceeds of the share sale invested in securities with the value equal to the difference of shares value at option grant minus share purchase price; PIT exemption abolished in 2008<br>IntE: Do not exist | |
| | PS | General: Since 2007: 23% deduction of PIT up to EUR 350 annually, no SSC<br>IntE: Do not exist | General: Since 1997/2007: 5% tax exemption for contributions distributed to employees, 25% deduction of SSC<br>IntE: Do not exist |
| Netherlands | ESO | ES: Since 1994, usually JSC: tax incentives only in combination with a savings plan – no PIT, no SSC, instead 15% flat tax, if plan broad-based, four-year blocking period, annual ceiling of the savings plan EUR 1,226<br>SO: No<br>IntE: Since 1994, usually LLC: regulation of tax incentives as for direct employee share ownership | ES: No<br>SO: No<br>IntE: No |
| | PS | General: Since 1994/2003: tax incentives only in combination with a savings plan – no PIT, no SSC, instead 15% flat tax, if plan broad-based, four-year blocking period, annual ceiling of the savings plan EUR 613<br>IntE: Do not exist | General: No<br>IntE: Do not exist |
| Portugal | ESO | ES: No<br>SO: No SSC<br>IntE: Do not exist | ES: No<br>SO: No SSC<br>IntE: Do not exist |
| | PS | General: Since 1969 (usually cash-based): no PIT, no SSC, if individual agreement concluded and effective<br>IntE: Do not exist | General: Profit distributed to employees deductible from tax base of CIT<br>IntE: Do not exist |

(Continued)

*Table 3.2*   (Continued)

| Country | | Employee | Employer Company |
|---|---|---|---|
| Slovenia | ESO | ES: Since 2008: 70% deduction from PIT on benefit not exceeding EUR 5,000 annually per employee, if one-year blocking period, 100% deduction, if three-year blocking period<br>SO: No<br>IntE: Do not exist | ES: Value of distributed shares deductible from tax base of CIT in the year, when the blocking period ends<br>SO: No<br>IntE: Do not exist |
| | PS | General: Since 2008 (for share-based PS): same as for ES<br>IntE: Do not exist | General: Same as ES<br>IntE: Do not exist |
| Spain | ESO | ES: (1) Since 2003: no PIT, no SSC on benefit up to EUR 12,000, if plan regular, each employee and his family own not more than 5% of equity capital, three-year blocking period; (2) Since 1997 Sociedades Laborales: no tax on company formation and tax credit of 99% on transfer tax, levies for notarial deeds on transfers to the company, debts, bonds and debenture bonds, if reserve for loss compensation 25% of annual profits<br>SO: 80% tax relief on up to 2× (annual medium wage × number of years before vesting), if vesting period not exceeding two years, options granted not annually, three years between option grant and share sale, plan broad-based<br>IntE: Do not exist | ES: No<br>SO: No<br>IntE: Do not exist |
| | PS | General: No<br>IntE: Do not exist | General: No<br>IntE: Do not exist |

| UK | ESO | ES: No | ES: No |
| --- | --- | --- | --- |
| | | SO: (1) Since 1980 SAYE: no PIT, no SSC at grant or exercise, if plan broad-based, exercise price of shares up to 20% under market value of underlying shares at option grant, SAYE contract with a bank, plan approved by tax authorities; (2) Since 1984/96 CSOP: no PIT, no SSC at grant or exercise, if value of outstanding options up to GBP 30,000 per employee, exercise price not lower than market value at grant, exercise period three to ten years after grant, plan approved by tax authorities; (3) Since 2000 EMI: no PIT, no SSC at grant or exercise, if value of options granted annually not exceeding GBP 100,000 per employee and GBP 3 million per company, tax authorities notified<br>IntE: Since 2000 SIP: no PIT, no SSC on benefit, if plan broad-based, 5 years blocking period in trust, value of shares up to GBP 3,000 (free shares), up to GBP 1,500 (partnership and dividend shares) annually per employee, plan approved by tax authorities; Sale of shares: no tax, no SSC if sold immediately after withdrawal | SO: (1)–(3) Costs of setting up and operating the plan; since 2003: costs of providing shares to the plan deductible from tax base of CIT, generally no SSC<br>IntE: Costs of setting up and operating the plan; since 2003: costs of providing shares to the plan deductible from tax base of CIT, generally no SSC |
| | PS | General: No<br>IntE: Do not exist | General: No<br>IntE: Do not exist |

*Abbreviations*: APOS = approved share option scheme; APSS = approved profit-sharing scheme; CIT = corporate income tax; CGT = capital gains tax; CSOP = company share option plan; EMI = enterprise management incentives; EmpC = employing company; ESOP = Employee Stock Ownership Plan; ESOT = Employee Share Ownership Trust; IE = intermediary entity; JSC = joint-stock company; LLC = limited liability companies; PIT = personal income tax; SAYE = Approved Savings-Related Share Option Scheme; SIP = share incentive plan; SSC = social security contributions.

However, some countries introduced broad-based as well as individual plans with partly different pre-conditions and tax incentives (for example Denmark). In some countries, where the plans are pre-defined in the law, approval of tax authorities is necessary (for example Hungary, Ireland, UK).

The most common form of tax incentives for employees on the benefit in share-based plans (excluding stock option plans) is an allowance of tax and social security contributions, but the absolute amount differs significantly, from EUR 135 per employee annually in Germany to EUR 12,700 in Ireland. In Finland and Denmark, where the amount is given as a percentage of annual salary, the allowance might be even higher (10 per cent in Denmark and in Finland for non-leveraged share ownership plans and 20 per cent in Finland for leveraged share-based profit-sharing). The tax-free amount in leveraged plans is often larger than in non-leveraged plans. Another possibility is a special, relatively low flat tax instead of personal income tax and social security contributions (for example, 15 per cent in Belgium, 7.6 per cent in France). In France, the special tax is imposed on the employees as well as on the employing companies. Relatively rare tax incentives for employees are deduction from the tax base of personal income tax (Ireland for restricted stock schemes, Slovenia for a short blocking period) and a savings bonus (Germany for very low incomes). Tax incentives on dividends are also applied quite seldom (for example, Finland, France), because taxation of dividends is always lower, and social security contributions are not levied. Because the employer companies usually can deduct the value of distributed shares as personnel costs under general taxation rules and are not subject to social security contributions on that amount, special incentives are not required. However, in France it was necessary to exempt the employer companies from social security contributions, which are usually imposed, and to introduce a special flat tax of 7.6 per cent on the benefit and of 10 per cent on the dividends, which also apply to employees. Specific tax incentives exist for intermediary entities in leveraged plans: all earnings (for example, Finland) or at least a certain amount of contributions and dividends (for example, Austria, Ireland, France, UK) are either tax exempt or levied by a special low tax.

### 3.3.3.2  Stock options

The greatest variety of tax incentives occur in connection with stock option plans. In addition, it is difficult to compare pre-conditions and incentive forms in different countries, because several stock option plans often exist in a single country. At a higher level of abstraction, the most common pre-conditions are blocking and exercise periods (for example, Belgium, UK, Ireland), restrictions on the difference between the market price of underlying shares and the exercise price (for example, Belgium, Denmark, Ireland, UK, Austria), the existence of a broad-based plan (for example, Austria, Denmark, Ireland, UK) and approval by the tax authorities (for example, Hungary, Ireland, UK). In the so-called SAYE plans in Ireland and UK, combination with a savings contract is required. As far as tax incentives for employer companies are concerned, eligibility often depends on whether the shares are to be purchased on the market or issued in the course of capital increase (for example, Austria, Greece).

The most common tax incentive forms for employees are an allowance of personal income tax and social security contributions, whereby the amounts are either the same as for shares, for example, Denmark, Hungary, or much higher, for example, CSOP (GBP 30,000) and EMI (GBP 100,000!) in the UK. Such forms as deferred taxation (for example Austria) or taxation at grant (for example Belgium) are country-specific. Tax incentives for employer companies are the deductibility of costs of share purchase or option costs from the tax base of the corporate income tax.

### 3.3.3.3   Cash-based profit-sharing

Only two countries (Greece and Portugal) have tax incentives for cash-based profit-sharing; in both cases these were introduced several decades ago. These tax incentives were obviously inefficient; the incidence of employee financial participation in Greece and Portugal is still the lowest among Western European countries. A possible reason for this inefficiency is restricted eligibility of – otherwise quite generous – tax incentives: in Portugal, tax incentives become applicable only on the basis of an individual contract limited in time; in Greece, tax incentives are applicable only to joint-stock companies.

### 3.3.4   Conclusions

Two general principles and several conclusions may be drawn from the combined data on tax incentives and the incidence of financial participation from the various countries.

- Tax incentives are not a prerequisite to financial participation. Financial participation schemes without tax incentives (for example, profit-sharing plans in Austria and Germany) sometimes have a higher incidence than those with tax incentives (for example, share ownership plans in Austria and Germany).[38] Therefore tax incentives are not to be considered a prerequisite to the development of financial participation. Furthermore, in low-tax countries (for example, Ireland), tax incentives are less important and, in any case, cannot be as large as in high-tax countries.[39]

- Tax incentives effectively promote the spread of financial participation.

  Countries with a long tradition of employee financial participation (for example, UK, France)[40] universally confirm this experience, but so do countries where tax incentives are quite recent (for example, Austria),[41] where a substantial increase has been observed, even though total numbers are still relatively low.

Firstly, tax incentives should (and in most countries actually do) target those taxes that constitute the heaviest burden in the national taxation system. Usually (with the exception of countries with flat tax systems which at present do not offer specific tax incentives) these are the progressive personal income tax and social security. Many countries therefore provide:

- exemptions from social security contributions for certain plans (for example, France, Belgium, UK, Ireland, Finland);
- levying a capital gains tax (for example, UK, for dividends Belgium);
- levying a special low tax (for example, France) in lieu of personal income tax; and
- tax allowances for personal income tax (for example, Austria, Finland, Ireland).

Secondly, tax incentives should be provided both for employees and the employer company, inasmuch as participation is voluntary for both parties in all EU Member States except France. However, this requirement is relative: in most countries the employer company has already been granted tax incentives in the form of deductions under general taxation law and only incentives for taxes involving the cost of shares and stock options are needed. In most countries, the only important incentive for the employer company is the exemption from social security contributions; this has actually been introduced in many countries (for example, France, Ireland, Finland, Belgium). The employee is usually more in need of direct incentives as the heaviest burden of progressive taxes falls on him or her.

Thirdly, even substantial tax incentives may prove inefficient when the pre-conditions of eligibility are too restrictive, complex or inflexible. This is the case (for example, in Greece) for cash-based profit-sharing and in Germany and Belgium for schemes of all types.[42] The flexibility problem can be solved, as in Ireland and the UK, by allowing the employer company to choose between less flexible approved schemes combined with substantial tax incentives and more flexible unapproved schemes combined with minor tax incentives. Another interesting approach was presented in the EC Report on Stock Options[43]: because direct taxes cannot be harmonised under the effective EU Treaty, as shown above, it might be reasonable to harmonise the pre-conditions for the application of tax incentives where they exist in a particular country. National legislators would be authorised to introduce additional national plans and to decide the size and the form of tax incentives for these as well as for those plans encompassing all of Europe. Harmonisation can only be accomplished if the existing pre-conditions in different EU Member States are at least comparable for all types of employee financial participation scheme, as is apparently the case for stock options. This comparison will be made in the forthcoming PEPPER IV Report.

Fourthly, some forms of tax incentives are more favourable for certain types of plans and lead to higher efficiency.

- For share ownership and stock options as far as benefit taxation is concerned: generous valuation rules combined with a favourable taxation moment (often linked to holding period), and, if possible, exemption from SSC both for the employer company and the employee.
- For dividends and sale of shares: a special tax rate or capital gains tax in lieu of personal income tax and, if necessary, exemption from SSC.
- For ESOPs and intermediary entities: exemptions from income tax on share acquisition[11] or on share sale if the profit is realised after a holding period or within a retirement programme; the company may qualify for tax relief on both interest and principal payments on the loan; sale of stock to an ESOP on a tax-deferred basis if the proceeds of the sale are reinvested in securities of other domestic corporations (tax-free rollover).
- For profit-sharing: a special tax rate in lieu of the progressive personal income tax as well as exemption from SSC for both the employer company and the employee.

However, the most effective forms of tax incentives do cause revenue losses. Therefore, efficiency should be weighed against the revenue requirements of each country independently. Should a government wish to introduce specific tax incentives, it might well begin with 'soft' tax incentives that do not cause substantial revenue losses, for example, tax allowances defined by nominal amount (as in Austria). Later, depending on revenue needs and the political climate, it may proceed to more effective measures: tax allowance as a proportional amount, deductions, tax credits, introduction of special low tax rates and, finally, full exemption from taxation.

Fifthly, despite the difficulty of their implementation at the European level (because of the exclusive jurisdiction of national legislation over tax law), tax incentives remain powerful tools for enhancing and broadening financial participation. This is especially true when they remain optional for the member countries and not subject to a unanimous vote of approval. Countries could voluntarily offer tax incentives singly or in groups. Such a step would create an increasingly favourable environment in which countries having an advanced tradition, such as France or the UK, would encourage emulation. Optional preferential treatment as part of the Building Block Approach requires distinguishing between profit-sharing schemes, share ownership schemes and Employee Stock Ownership Plans.

## Notes

1. The Intergovernmental Conference has not, however, extended the co-decision procedure (Article 251 ECT) to legislative measures which already come under the qualified majority rule (for example, in agricultural or trade policy).
2. This 'bridge' cannot, however, be used for social security.
3. See A. Pendleton et al. (2001), p. 9.
4. For example, the consensual continental contrasts with the Anglo-American confrontational model; likewise the strong position of the state in France contrasts with the powerful role of the German 'Tarifpartner' (collective bargaining parties, much like trade unions and employer associations).
5. Compare White and Case (2001), p. 4.
6. European Commission (2003a), p. 43 on obstacles to exportation.
7. For the comparison of general tax systems, different types of taxes, different systems of individual taxes, different tax rates, tax bases and taxation moments all must be considered. Tax rates are only comparable if effective tax rates are calculated. However, that is only possible for a specific tax and for a specific personal status and situation. Because most major direct taxes should be examined to determine their effect on employee financial participation plans, effective tax rates cannot be calculated for every possible status or situation.

8. Owing to the complexity of the issue, a discussion on comparability of individual country tax rates of EU Member States cannot be covered in this publication. For a more detailed discussion, see J. Lowitzsch, I. Hashi and R. Woodward (eds.), (Berlin 2009), the *PEPPER IV Report*.

9. Only more general provisions of Articles 94, 96 and 97 ECT on prevention of market distortions and, in cases of substantial discrimination, Article 87 ECT on prevention of state subsidies, Articles 39, 43, 49, 56 ECT (basic freedoms) and Article 12 ECT (general anti-discrimination provision) apply. However, these aim at non-discriminatory taxation of physical persons and legal entities from other EU Member States compared with domestic physical persons and legal entities and at prevention of double taxation. They do not lead to a higher degree of harmonisation.

10. See COM (1980), 139; H. Weber-Grellet (2005) *Europäisches Steuerrecht* (Munich: Beck), pp. 28, 152.

11. Whereas the issue of unfair tax competition was originally connected with such traditional tax havens as the Channel Islands and Monaco, it has gained even more importance with the accession of new Member States having generally much lower corporate and partially also personal income taxes than Western European EU Member States, except Ireland. See H. Weber-Grellet (2005), p. 163.

12. See COM (2001) 582 of 23 October 2001; COM (2003) 726 of 24 November 2003; CCCTB/WP/046 of 12 December 2006; COM (2007) 223 of 2 May 2007; the proposal, due in 2008, has not yet been completed, but it seems probable that the CCCTB could be introduced in several years. Seven Member States with relatively low tax rates are opposed to the idea, but no unanimous decision is required in this case. The EU Tax Commissioner declared that the initiative can, if necessary, be implemented by eight Member States through enhanced co-operation.

13. Moreover, the usefulness of this instrument for harmonisation of corporate taxation is considered questionable if no limits for corporate tax rates are set at the same time. See Bundesministerium der Finanzen (2007) 'Einheitliche Bemessungsgrundlage der Körperschaftssteuer in der Europäischen Union', *Monatsbericht des BMF*, April, p. 73.

14. See OECD (2005a) *Tax Policy Reform Conclusions* (Paris: OECD Centre for Tax Policy and Administration), p. 6.

15. See H. Weber-Grellet (2005), p. 30. There is no theoretical basis or empirical evidence for the assumption that the tax burden on capital should be lower than on labour, although the practice is based on it; see S. Ganghoff (2004) *Wer regiert in der Steuerpolitik?* (Frankfurt and New York: Campus), p. 35.

16. See OECD (2005a), p. 6.

17. However, Croatia has had an expenditure tax system from 1994 until 2000. For example, Bulgaria, Estonia and Hungary have an expenditure tax on fringe benefits payable by the employing company. The quite unusual Estonian corporation tax system (replacement of corporate income tax by the tax on distributed profits) could also be connected with the idea of expenditure tax.

18. These systems give more leeway to share ownership because tax rates on capital income are usually lower than those on labour. However, in practice, the advantage of flat tax systems may not be so substantial because

often relatively high compulsory social security contributions will be levied additionally.

19. Most Western European countries cannot introduce a flat tax system because of the potential loss of revenue, see for Italy OECD (2005b) *Tax Policy Reforms in Italy* (Paris: OECD Centre for Tax Policy and Administration), p. 4.

20. However, it depends on the personal income tax rate. For example, the income tax rates in Ireland, Latvia and Romania are relatively low.

21. See C. Spengel (2003) *Internationale Unternehmensbesteuerung in der Europäischen Union* (Düsseldorf: IDW-Verlag), p. 23.

22. Owing to globalisation of business and to the requirements of the EU law, there is a tendency to exchange imputation for shareholder relief systems. See C. Spengel (2003) p. 25.

23. Whether social security is levied as a tax, for example, as in Denmark and Estonia, or takes the form of social insurance contributions merely means that in the case of taxes there is no corresponding claim against a social insurance institution.

24. The generic term used for intermediary companies, funds with a separate legal personality and trusts (in common-law countries UK, Ireland and Malta), which accumulate distributed profits, hold, allocate and transfer shares, options or certificates of the employer company for employees, sometimes pay out dividends or returns, administrate dividends, and make investments.

25. The valuation of the same shares for the purpose of taxation of employees or employers may follow different rules and lead to different taxable amounts as in Austria. The moment of valuation of shares may also be different in different countries and lead to differences in value and in the tax base derived from it.

26. However, in one EU Member State, Estonia, corporate tax is replaced by the tax on distributed profits. This original system may have a positive economic effect on accumulation of funds, but it constitutes a strong disincentive for the employer company in relation to share-based employee participation plans as well as to cash-based profit-sharing.

27. Data on corporate tax for 2007 are presented in the report of the German Federal Ministry of Finance: Bundesministerium der Finanzen (2007), p. 68 (Table 1). The generic term 'corporate tax' includes in this context all central and sub-central statutory taxes and surcharges on corporation profits.

28. Data on dividend taxation from Deloitte (2007) International Tax and Business Guides, http://www.deloittetaxguides.com (database), accessed 20 July 2007.

29. Data on capital gains taxation from Deloitte (2007).

30. Data on personal income tax rates for 2006 are generally downloaded from European Union (2007a) European Commission, Directorate-General Taxes and Customs Union, 'Taxes in Europe' Database, http://ec.europa.eu/taxation_customs/taxinv, accessed 20 June 2007.

31. Data on social security contributions for 2006 are downloaded from the MISSOC database: European Union (2007b) European Commission, Directorate-General for Employment, Social Affairs and Equal Opportunities, Social Protection Systems in Member States (MISSOC), http://ec.europa.eu/employment_social/missoc/2006, accessed 20 June 2007.

32. For details, see European Commission (2003c), PriceWaterhouseCoopers (2002).
33. For this reason, it is contrary to the financial interests of the employing company to distribute profit to employees in cash-based profit-sharing schemes or as dividends to employees who have become shareholders. However, the Estonian tax system is to be changed in 2009 to comply with the EU Parent-Subsidiary Directive. See KPMG (2007) *Corporate and Indirect Tax Rate Survey 2007*, p. 15, http://www.kpmg.com/Global/IssuesAndInsights/ArticlesAndPublications/Pages/Corporate-Tax-Rate-Survey-2007.aspx, accessed 2 June 2009.
34. See Irish Department of Finance, TSG 98/12.
35. See C. Spengel (2003), p. 28.
36. To compensate for revenue losses caused by lowering the tax rate, either rates of other taxes are increased or the tax base is broadened. Thus a lower tax rate does not necessarily lower the total tax burden. It is not surprising that countries with low statutory tax rates like Ireland have fewer tax concessions than countries with high statutory tax rates like France, Italy and Spain. See C. Spengel (2003), p. 29.
37. However, more value for taxpayers means higher revenue losses for the state. In addition, tax credits generally cause higher tax administration costs. Recently, tax credit systems have been replaced by tax allowances in France and Italy. See K. Tipke and J. Lang (eds) (2005) *Steuerrecht*, 18th edn (Cologne: Schmidt), pp. 799, 802.
38. In Austria, only 8 per cent of enterprises and 6 per cent of the workforce participated in employee share ownership plans in 2005, tax incentives for which were introduced in 2001, whereas 25 per cent of enterprises operated profit-sharing plans without tax incentives; see R. Kronberger, H. Leitsmüller and A. Rauner (eds) (2007) *Mitarbeiterbeteiligung in Österreich* (Vienna: Linde Verlag), pp. 11, 17, 162. In Germany, 2.4 per cent of enterprises had an employee share ownership plan in 2001, supported by (marginal) tax incentives, whereas at the same time 8.7 per cent of enterprises operated profit-sharing plans without tax incentives; see S. Würz (ed.) (2003) *European Stock-Taking on Models of Employee Financial Participation, Results of Ten European Case Studies* (Wiesbaden), p. 59.
39. It should be noted that in countries that are considered low-tax, not all statutory taxes are necessarily low; the statement refers only to low statutory taxes. For example, in Ireland, corporate income tax is exceptionally low (12.5 per cent), whereas personal income tax is close to the EU average (20–42 per cent). Therefore, most tax incentives for employee financial participation in Ireland concern employees and not employer companies. The Irish Government declared that no tax relief that reduced the revenue from corporate income tax can be introduced because the low tax rate leaves very little leeway (Irish Department of Finance, TSG 98/12).
40. In France, legislation on voluntary employee financial participation without tax incentives of 1959 and even legislation on compulsory employee financial participation without tax incentives of 1967 did not lead to a significant number of plans in operation. Only in 1986, when the first tax incentives were introduced, did the number of plans increase rapidly; this upward tendency has been supported by the introduction of new tax

incentives; see S. Würz (ed.) (2003), p. 39. In the UK, although profit-sharing has existed since the nineteenth century and share ownership since the early 1950s, the number of plans remained small until the first tax incentives were introduced in 1978. Since then, the system of tax incentives and economic efficiency of incentives and plans are regularly reviewed by the government, and the number of plans is steadily increasing, especially revenue-approved plans; see S. Würz (ed.) (2003), p. 130; ifs School of Finance (2007) ifs ProShare, http://www.ifsproshare.org, accessed 20 July 2007.

41. In Austria, only 8 per cent of employee financial participation plans were implemented before first tax incentives were introduced in 1993, whereas 45 per cent of plans were introduced in four years after more substantial tax incentives became effective in 2001; see R. Kronberger, H. Leitsmüller and A. Rauner (eds) (2007), p. 32.

42. See European Commission (2003a), pp. 17, 24.

43. See European Commission (2003c), pp. 42, 43.

44. In Ireland this is the case only where the ESOP comprises an ESOT working in tandem with an Approved Profit-Sharing Scheme.

# 4
# Systematic Overview of Financial Participation

*Jens Lowitzsch and Axel Bormann*

## 4.1 Participation in property rights: Control and returns

There are two kinds of property rights inherent in employee participation: control, which is participation in decision making and returns, which is financial participation.[1] Whether a given scheme embraces participation in decision making depends on the prerogatives and rights that it confers upon employees. In employee share ownership, these rights are determined by whether ownership is direct or indirect, whether stock is held through an employee trust or co-operative, and whether voting rights and other forms of immaterial participation accompany ownership. In profit-sharing, there is no necessary link to any form of employee input into company decisions at any level. In practice, however, these schemes are often part of a package of participatory measures, including information and participation in control.

### 4.1.1 Participation in decision making

Employee participation in decision making generally takes two forms: entrepreneurial co-determination and co-determination within a going concern (see Figure 4.1).[2] Although the first is executed indirectly by representatives chosen by the employees, the latter can be either direct or indirect.

- Entrepreneurial co-determination usually concerns strategic, macro-level decision making in the firm. The best-known examples are the German 'Mitbestimmung',[3] with labour representatives occupying half of the seats on the company's supervisory board, co-operatives, and socialist labour self-management.[4]

121

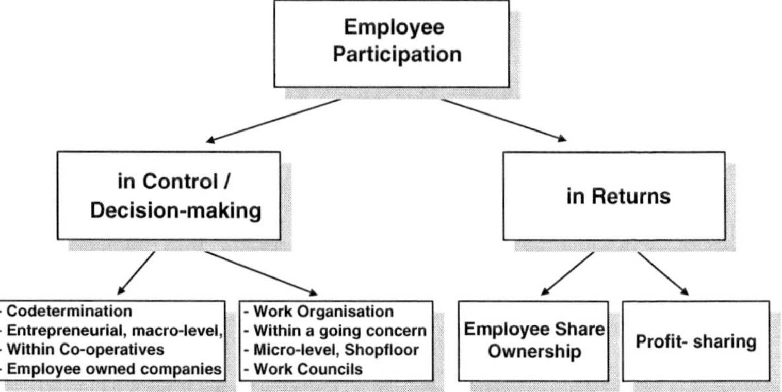


*Figure 4.1*  Participation in property rights: Control and returns.

- Co-determination within a going concern, on the other hand, consists of indirect participation through chosen representatives as well as direct participation by employees themselves. It usually involves shop-floor, micro-level decision making on social questions as well as on organisational matters. Familiar examples include workers' councils elected by employees (common in European countries like Germany[5] and more recently also found on a supranational level[6]) on the one hand, and Japanese quality circles[7] or Swedish autonomous work teams,[8] on the other.

### 4.1.2  Financial participation

For financial participation of employees, a distinction has to be made between profit-sharing (including gain-sharing) and employee share ownership (excluding executive stock options). The distinction is important because there are fundamental differences between the two (for example, in taxation). A third type of financial participation is through asset accumulation or employee savings plans which offer a vehicle to allocate and invest sums received in other schemes. Financial participation of employees is thus a form of remuneration, in addition to regular pay systems, that enables employees to participate in profits and enterprise results.[9] Although it can take a variety of forms, the most common are employee share ownership and profit-sharing, often in combination. Because this study is mainly concerned with financial participation, participation in decision making will only be referred to when relevant.

## 4.2   Employee Participation in Profits and Enterprise Results (PEPPER schemes)

The term 'financial participation' refers to all schemes that give workers, in addition to a fixed wage, a variable portion of income directly linked to profits or some other measure of enterprise performance.[10] The main feature of this bonus is that it is specifically linked to enterprise results and is not just a predetermined proportion of pay. There are two basic ways in which employers can distribute the financial results of improved enterprise performance to their employees: profit-sharing and employee share ownership.

### 4.2.1   Profit-sharing

In profit-sharing, part of an employee's remuneration is directly linked to the profits of the enterprise. Unlike individual incentives, this concept involves a collective scheme which generally applies to all employees. The formula, depending on the national scheme, may include profits, productivity and return.[11] Because profit-sharing schemes are related to measures of company performance in general, they are perhaps the most widespread form of financial participation.[12] The bonuses are normally paid in addition to the basic fixed wage, and provide a variable source of income.

Although profit-sharing bonuses can take several different forms, two main concepts[13] should be distinguished:

- Distribution on a deferred basis, commonly covered by the term 'deferred profit-sharing', with the bonus being:

  (a) invested in enterprise funds or frozen in special accounts for a specific period;
  (b) granted as several shares in the company, frozen in a fund for a certain period before employees are allowed to sell them (deferred share-based profit-sharing).

- Direct payment of profit-sharing bonuses to the workers in cash, usually referred to as 'cash-based profit-sharing'.

A related form of participation is the concept of gain-sharing, which is designed to provide variable pay, and usually to encourage employee involvement, by rewarding employees for improvements in individual and organisational performance. Gains, measured by a predetermined formula, are shared with employees, usually through cash bonuses. Gains constitute an addition to the basic salary paid to all employees, usually in order to reward individual or small unit performance. The formulas for measuring employee performance vary considerably; piece rates and productivity bonuses are most common, but other performance indicators may be used, such as profit, productivity, costs, sales, and so on.[14]

### 4.2.2 Employee share ownership

Employee share ownership is the second major form of financial participation. Funds can be raised either from the company or from employees. In the latter case, employees might voluntarily purchase company stock (thus acquiring equity) or they might lend money to the company or purchase company bonds (thereby increasing corporate debt).[15]

In the case of company equity, the shares are transferred directly or indirectly to employees, who may receive dividends and/or capital gains that accrue to company equity. Participation through the construction of a silent partnership or a usufructuary is rare, especially in the context of employee participation, and may result in both equity as well as corporate debt.[16]

Employee share ownership in practice – whether shares are held individually or under some form of trust – does not automatically entitle employee shareholders to have a say in the operation of the company.[17] Employees may be issued either non-voting stock or voting shares, but they have little or no control over the management of shares held in trust. Trustees may be appointed by management rather than elected by employees.

#### 4.2.2.1 *Direct purchase of shares/share savings plans*

The broadest spectrum of models is offered by share plans in which shares are distributed free or sold at market price (non-discounted) or under preferential conditions.[18] These preferential conditions can be sale at a discount rate (discounted stock purchase plan), sale at a lower price through forms of delayed payment (usually within a capital increase) or by a grant of priority in public offerings to all or a group of employees.[19] Finally, the purchase may be effected through periodic deductions from pay, with or without the employer's match or bonus. When the employer does contribute an (equal) amount in cash or shares, the plan is called a 'share savings plan'.

Other forms of direct purchase include producer co-operatives,[20] in which all the firm's shares are owned by its workforce, and employee buyouts, under which company shares are purchased exclusively by its individual workers.[21] For example, Poland implemented an employee buyout programme in the context of privatisation. It took the form of so-called leveraged lease buyouts (LLBOs).[22]

### 4.2.2.2   Broad-based stock options

Employee stock options,[23] unlike those granted to individual employees or small groups (especially managerial) to reward individual performance ('executive stock options'), are broad-based. The company grants employees options over shares, which entitle them to acquire shares in the company at a later date, but at a price fixed when the option was granted. The option has an expiration term and a vesting period starting with the grant date; it can take various forms, mainly depending on grant and exercise price.[24] The possibility of gains arising from upward movements in stock prices is the primary reward emanating from options. Unlike 'conventional' options, employee stock options as a rule cannot be traded, and the holder usually cannot hedge against the risk of declines in option value. Furthermore, employee stock options normally are subject to forfeiture before vesting should the employee voluntarily leave the firm.

### 4.2.2.3   Employee Stock Ownership Plans

In the United States,[25] the most popular form of workers' share ownership is the Employee Stock Ownership Plan (ESOP),[26] which has also been implemented in Europe[27] and Japan.[28] An ESOP usually involves a loan to an employee benefit trust, which acquires company stock and allocates it through periodic contributions to each employee's ESOP account. The loan may be serviced by payments from the company out of company profits, out of dividends paid on the stock held by the ESOP or (in rare instances) from employee salary reductions. There seems to be some confusion about amortising ESOP loans from the company's profits. Theoretically, it is the earnings of the ESOP shares that comprise the collateral for the loan; paid out, these are dividends, but because only ESOP participants receive this full pay-out of earnings they represent, in effect, a preferred dividend. When using the mirror loan approach (bank loan to company – company loan to trust), of course, the bank regards the entire asset base of the company as collateral for its loan, not merely the ESOP shares.[29]

### 4.2.2.4   Privatisation-related voucher/coupon schemes

In post-socialist countries, employee share ownership occurs in the form of shares that are distributed or sold to the workers of the company, or vouchers or coupons that are distributed to all citizens. Although the second option does not correspond strictly to the definition of financial participation, under which only the workers of the company should be involved, it can lead in practice to substantial employee share ownership.

Thus, for example, voucher privatisation in Slovenia, Poland and Croatia provided a way of creating employee ownership in conjunction with the privatisation process. Although the privatisation framework did not subsidise employee ownership by giving employees the right to acquire shares of their companies under favourable conditions, neither did it prevent employees from converting their vouchers into shares of the employer enterprise. Some companies did explicitly encourage employees to invest in their shares.[30]

### 4.2.3  Employee share ownership versus profit-sharing – Table 4.1

*Table 4.1*  Summary of differences between profit-sharing and employee share ownership

| Dimension | Profit-Sharing | Employee Share Ownership |
|---|---|---|
| Liquidity of benefit | Cash. Highly liquid (except when deferred) | Shares. Liquidity depends on presence of equity markets. |
| Immediacy of benefit (that is when employee can use it) | Immediate where profit share paid in cash, except where paid into company savings scheme or shares. | Deferred in most schemes (especially schemes where shares acquired at a future date), variable in privatisation schemes. Except dividends. |
| Link to profits | Direct link. Profit share usually directly linked to level or growth in profits. | Indirect link. Value of reward mainly linked to potential growth in share value, which is contingently related to profitability. |
| Link to performance period | Based on company performance in the most recent or current financial year. | Company performance after receipt of shares or grant of options usually most important for value of reward. |
| Accounting treatment | Treated as a wages item (though tax and social insurance exemptions may be available). Entered onto profit and loss account. | Separate from wages and salaries. A balance sheet item. 'Losses' to company from gains in value of options or discounts on share acquisition not usually recorded on profit and loss account. |

*Table 4.1* (Continued)

| Dimension | Profit-Sharing | Employee Share Ownership |
|---|---|---|
| Tax treatment | As wages item, subject to income tax and social insurance charges, although exemptions or reductions (for employee and employer) may be granted by statute. Company tax offset usually available to company. | As balance sheet item, share schemes per se do not attract tax concessions for the company (although direct financial support to employees to acquire shares may attract concessions). Employees usually liable to capital gains tax, not income tax, where schemes have statutory basis. |
| Employee risk | Risk that future payments may fluctuate in value. | Risk that current share holdings and options may fluctuate in value. |

*Source*: A. Pendleton et al. (2001) *Employee Share Ownership and Profit-Sharing in the European Union* (Dublin: European Foundation for the Improvement of Living and Working Conditions), p. 10.

## 4.3   Asset accumulation and employee savings plans

Asset accumulation and savings plans offer a vehicle to allocate and invest sums received as salary or as remuneration in collective schemes of financial participation. They allow employees to set aside a portion of their income in an account that is, in most cases, invested in stocks, bonds or other investment choices for a period before being made available to the employee. Additional individual contributions by employees are possible, and sometimes an employer contribution is received. To promote savings, governments in some countries (for example, Germany) match employee contributions. Although usually intended as a long-term savings programme, plans may allow for withdrawals or loans.

Commonly known as savings plans, incentive plans, or investment plans, these vehicles appear under a variety of names. They are most common in the USA, France, Germany and the Netherlands. In these countries, savings plans are usually defined contribution plans, following specific tax provisions. As a rule, the regulating legislation defines the maximum amount of both employee and employer contributions, eligibility criteria to prevent discrimination and the retention periods as preconditions for the tax exemption. The main objective of savings plans is asset formation – encouraging employees to save, while involving little risk for them.

## 4.4 Discussion: Pros and cons

### 4.4.1 Motivation, productivity and economic performance

Economic arguments for financial participation are based primarily on the improvement of motivation[31] and productivity.[32] The change from a rigid system of guaranteed wages in which rewards are independent of effort, to a system that provides workers with an income that is more directly linked to enterprise performance[33] is considered likely to lead to greater commitment, lower absenteeism and labour turnover, greater investment in firm-specific human capital and reduced intra-firm conflict.[34] If well designed, financial participation schemes influence the decision of future employees to join the company, while encouraging present employees to remain. In contrast to individual incentives, financial participation also promotes teamwork and a co-operative spirit, thereby facilitating improvements in work organisation and the adaptation of the labour force to new technologies. A truly effective productivity enhancement programme relies, of course, not only on the rewards available through a financial participation plan, but also on a well-designed informational campaign which instructs each employee on how they personally can most directly increase company profits and thus the stock price of their shares in the plan.

More sceptical theoretical appraisals of employee participation suggest that the individual incentives provided by financial participation are diluted by free-rider effects, particularly in larger organisations. This is because the gains from a productivity increase generated by one employee are shared among all employees who participate in a profit-sharing or stock ownership plan. Therefore, the argument goes, the positive productivity effects of financial participation will be wiped out in all but the smallest organisations. However, according to the findings of other theoretical and empirical studies,[35] these negative aspects are more than offset by the enhancement of co-operative behaviour and teamwork resulting from financial participation. Collective payment systems should provide an incentive to overcome rivalry at the workplace, and tend to encourage collaboration between individuals with a view to increasing effort and productivity.[36] A related argument holds that without a third party to monitor their effort, each member of a team of workers will try to shirk.[37] This, however, ignores the fact that workers are often much better equipped to monitor each other than is any third party.[38] For example, partnership arrangements with profit-sharing and mutual monitoring or self-monitoring can be viable in small teams. When the nature of work performed by individual workers makes monitoring costs prohibitively high, self-monitoring and participation are adopted frequently, for example, in many law firms.

Since the 1970s a rapid growth in employee ownership has been noted in Western countries, especially the United States,[39] West Germany,[40] Great Britain[41] and France.[42] Despite the initially rather sceptical attitude towards financial participation, the empirical research on this phenomenon has failed to prove a negative correlation between a firm's economic performance (profitability, productivity, and so on) and employee ownership. On the contrary[43], most recent results indicate a positive effect of employee share ownership.[44]

### 4.4.2   Economic growth and distributive effects: Binary economics

Louis Kelso's model of binary economics[45] strongly supports financial participation in the form of employee share ownership. Impacting such widespread issues as economic growth, income distribution and the democratisation of economic power, binary theory provides an alternative conception of market economics and private property. Louis Kelso and Patricia Hetter Kelso[46] believe that the problem of poverty might be better understood as the inevitable consequence of our closed, private property system, and that the appropriate remedy is to open this system so that growing numbers and eventually all individuals and families gain the effective right to acquire private capital on market principles. This solution recognises that physical capital – tools, machines, structures, processes – is an input factor on the production side of the free market, just as labour is. It recognises that things produce wealth and earn income just as people do. Instead of eliminating private property and thereby destroying the market economy (the formal Marxist way), non-owners should be encouraged to acquire income-producing property. Non-owners can thus be given the opportunity to participate in the economic success of the company for which they work not only as wage-earners, but also as shareholders.

### 4.4.3   Position of trade unions

Trade unions often fear the loss of power and influence in companies with substantial employee share ownership. Theoretical[47] and empirical[48] studies in Western countries have found no evidence for a negative correlation of financial participation and the position of trade unions. Rather than eliminating the need for unions, employee ownership expands the unions' role on the shop-floor, as well as at the entrepreneurial level. At the same time, employee ownership often expands the scope of collective bargaining agreements.[49] Although in transitional economies there seems to be a decline of trade union representation in companies after employee buyouts,[50] this decline appears more often to be linked to the change of the role of trade unions in these countries in general. In this context it should be stressed that it is the trade unions in transitional countries that are lobbying in favour of financial participation schemes.

### 4.4.4   Financial participation and participation in decision making

There appears to be a positive relationship between performance and direct employee participation in decision making.[51] Some recent findings[52] indicate that incentive effects of financial participation schemes are much greater when accompanied by greater worker participation in decision making. The implication is that co-owners can only be expected to make the changes necessary to attain greater productivity if they are given power to make the decisions that bring about those changes. Although financial participation may provide employees with the incentive for maximal involvement, direct participation gives them the tools to realise it. Often, to be sure, a long apprenticeship is needed before some employees begin to understand how their individual work influences profitability, whereas for those who aspire to participate in decision making at the management level, this period is correspondingly longer. The introduction of profit-sharing without a parallel development of workers' participation in decision making is neither practicable nor desirable.

In most employee share-ownership arrangements, there has been no significant transfer of decision making authority from management to employees. Depending on the structure of the plan, however, it is possible that management could lose some control as employees (and their representatives) gradually become more substantial shareholders. However, with the exception of distress buyout situations, where unions have at times taken an active role in establishing share ownership, it is almost always management that initiates and implements employee share ownership, hence preventing any loss of control by influencing the design of the scheme and its subsequent control and voting rights.

### 4.4.5   Failure rate of conventional and employee-owned companies

Although companies with financial participation schemes have generally outperformed their conventional competitors, there have been several highly publicised failures of enterprises in which the employees are majority shareholders.[53] A US study in 1995–6 surveyed all majority employee-owned firms that had failed over the past 25 years.[54] The research found no simple explanation for the failure of democratically controlled and operated ESOP or co-op enterprises. During the same period, poor management, compounded by the inability to master the market, were also responsible for the failure of thousands of conventionally run enterprises. This study found that financial participation and co-determination were positive rather than negative factors. No evidence could be found to support the hypotheses of confrontational labour relations or of newly assertive shareholder–employees. Almost all of the firms in the study had become totally uncompetitive and abandoned by the market by the time they were sold to the employees, in most cases to avert plant closure. All cited lack of capital, three quarters cited market problems, and over half cited production problems as causes of failure. The only deviation from conventionally run enterprises was found where workers accepted compensation concessions, but hesitated to lay people off. These cases were few. The dual corporate goals of making money while simultaneously preserving jobs were all too often the source of irregular business practices. The more important question is: why have so many enterprises acquired under similar circumstances not failed?

## Notes

1. See A. Ben-Ner and D. C. Jones (1995) 'Employee Participation, Ownership and Productivity: A Theoretical Framework', *Industrial Relations*, Vol. 34, No. 4, pp. 532–54.
2. See K.-R. Wagner (1995) 'Renaissance der Mitarbeiterbeteiligung', *Betriebsberater*, supplement to issue No. 7 of this journal; K.-R. Wagner (1993) *Management-Buyout: Führungskräftebeteiligung, Arbeitnehmerbeteiligung; Grundlagen – Modellhinweise – Neue Bundesländer – Rechtspolitik* (Neuwied, Kriftel and Berlin: Luchterhand).
3. See H. G. Nutzinger, U. Schasse and V. Teichert (1987) 'Mitbestimmung in zeitlicher Perspektive: Ergebnisse einer Fallstudie in einem Großbetrieb der Automobilindustrie' In F. R. FitzRoy and K. Kraft (eds) *Mitarbeiterbeteiligung und Mitbestimmung Im Unternehmen* (Berlin and New York: de Gruyter).
4. See N. Vučić (1972) 'Die sozio-ökonomische Lehre des Jugoslawischen Selbstverwaltungssozialismus', *Osteuropa*, Issue No. 6, p. 430.
5. See J. R. Cable and F. R. FitzRoy (1983) *Work Organisation, Incentives and Firm Performance: An Empirical Analysis of West German Metal Industries*, University of Warwick Mimeo Paper, presented at the 9th Meeting of the European Association for Research in Industrial Economics, 24–6 August 1983, Bergen, Norway.

6. Council Regulation (EC) No. 2157/2001 on the Statute for a European Company (or Societas Europaea, SE) and Council Directive 2001/86/EC supplementing the Statute for a European Company with regard to the involvement of employees adopted on 8 October 2001.
7. See S. Watanabe (1991) 'The Japanese Quality Control Circle: Why It Works', *International Labour Review*, Vol. 130, No. 1., pp. 64, 72–3; also H. Leibenstein (1987) *Inside the Firm* (Cambridge, MA).
8. Regarding the USA, see S. Cohen (1990) 'Autonomous work teams spread in the USA', *Associated Press*, 9 December 1990.
9. See M. Uvalić (1991); V. Pérotin and A. Robinson (1995) 'Profit-Sharing in OECD Countries', in OECD (ed.), *Employment Outlook* (Paris: OECD), pp. 139–69.
10. See H. J. Schneider and E. Zander (1990) *Erfolgs- und Kapitalbeteiligung der Mitarbeiter in Klein- und Mittelbetrieben,* 3rd ed. (Freiburg im Breisgau: Haufe), p. 20; compare with D. Vaughan-Whitehead (1995) *Workers' Financial Participation* (Geneva: International Labour Organization), p. 2, who includes gain-sharing in the definition of financial participation.
11. See H. J. Schneider and E. Zander (1990), pp. 20, 68.
12. A positive relationship was found by D. G. Blanchflower and A. J. Oswald (1998) 'Profit Related Pay: Prose Discovered?', *Economic Journal*, Vol. 98, and F. R. FitzRoy and K. Kraft (eds) (1987) 'Formen der Arbeitnehmer-Arbeitgeberkooperation und ihre Auswirkungen auf die Unternehmensleistung und Entlohnung', in F. R. FitzRoy and K. Kraft (eds) *Mitarbeiterbeteiligung und Mitbestimmung im Unternehmen* (Berlin and New York: de Gruyter).
13. See D. Vaughan-Whitehead (1995), and M. Uvalić (1991).
14. See D. Vaughan-Whitehead (1995), p. 2.
15. In the case of corporate debt, no share ownership is generated, and the revenue of the employees takes the form of interest and principal payments or only interest payments if a debt to equity swap is foreseen later. If employees are holding bonds from the company they receive dividends.
16. See K.-R. Wagner (1993).
17. In most in the USA and France (outside workers' co-operatives), employee share ownership is associated with little or no employee influence on entrepreneurial decisions. Even if they hold the largest block of shares, employee shareholders are not automatically represented on the board of directors. See V. Pérotin (2002) *Employee Participation in Profit and Ownership: A Review of the Issues and Evidence*, European Parliament, Social Affairs Series, SOCI 109 (Luxembourg: European Parliament, Directorate-General for Research), p. 8.
18. For example, in Great Britain, see UK Treasury Public Enquiry Unit (December 1998) *Consultation on Employee Share Ownership*; also G. Nuttall (January 1999) *Employee Ownership: UK Legal and Tax Aspects* (London: Field Fisher Waterhouse LLP). As to the 'method of choice' in Eastern Europe, see M. Weitzman (1991) 'How Not to Privatise', *Rivista di Politica Economica*, Vol. 81, No. 12.
19. See D. Vaughan-Whitehead (1995), p. 2.
20. For France, see J. Defourney, S. Estrin and D. C. Jones (1985) 'The Effects of Workers' Participation on Enterprise Performance: Empirical Evidence from French Co-operatives', *International Journal of Industrial Organisation*, Vol. 3, No. 2 (June). For Italy, see D. C. Jones and J. Svejnar (1985) 'Participation, Profit-Sharing, Worker Ownership and Efficiency in Italian Producer Co-operatives', *Economica*, Vol. 52, November issue.

21. Usually dominated by managers, especially in the US form of management-led buyouts.
22. See the studies by M. Jarosz (ed.) (1995), *Management-Employee Buyouts In Poland* (Warsaw: Instytut Studiow Politycznych, Polska Akademia Nauk), and M. Jarosz (ed.) (1996) *Polish Employee-Owned Companies in 1995* (Warsaw: Instytut Studiow Politycznych, Polska Akademia Nauk); also M. Jarosz (ed.) (2000) *Ten Years of Direct Privatisation* (Warsaw: Instytut Studiow Politycznych, Polska Akademia Nauk). For East Germany, where management buyouts were prevalent, see F. Barjak, G. Heimbold et al. (eds) (1996).
23. A. Pendleton, J. Blasi et al. (2002), PriceWaterhouseCoopers (2002).
24. S. Johnson and Y. Tian (2000) 'The Value of Incentive Effects of Non-Traditional Executive Stock Option Plans', *Journal of Financial Economics*, Vol. 57, pp. 3–34 distinguish six types: premium options, performance-vested options, re-priceable options, purchased options, reload options, and indexed options.
25. The scale of the phenomenon is summed up by J. R. Blasi (1988) *Employee Ownership: Revolution or Ripoff?* (Cambridge, MA: Ballinger Publishing Company), p. 2; compare also J. R. Blasi and D. L. Kruse (1991) *The New Owners: The Mass Emergence of Employee Ownership in Public Companies and What It Means to American Business* (New York: HarperCollins Publishers).
26. For American ESOPs, see L. Kelso and P. H. Kelso (1991).
27. For example, for the UK, see K. Walley and N. Wilson (ed.) (1992) *ESOPs: Their Role in Corporate Finance and Performance* (Hants: Macmillan), pp. 126–51; for Hungary, see B. Galgoczi and J. Hovorka (1998) *Employee Ownership in Hungary: The Role of Employers' and Workers' Organisations* (Geneva: International Labour Office).
28. See D. Jones and T. Kato (1995), pp. 391–414.
29. For American ESOPs, see D. Ackermann (2002).
30. For examples, see D. Vaughan-Whitehead and M. Uvalić (eds) (1997) *Privatisation Surprises in Transition Economies* (Cheltham: Edward Elgar).
31. See A. A. Buchko (1992) 'Employee Ownership, Attitudes and Turnover: An Empirical Asessment', *Human Relations*, Vol. 101, pp. 711–33.
32. M. Conte and J. Svejnar (1988) 'Productivity Effects of Worker Participation in Management, Profit-Sharing, Worker Ownership of Assets and Unionisation in US Firms', *International Journal of Industrial Organisation*, Vol. 6; compare also J. B. Say (1824) *Treaties on Political Economy; or the Production, Distribution and Consumption of Wealth*, Vol. I, Chapter XIV, On Production, Paris 1803, 2nd American edn, (Boston: Wells and Lilly, Court Street), p. 79.
33. An exception may be certain financial participation plans, such as employee savings plans, that are less directly linked to company performance.
34. H.-G. Guski and H. J. Schneider (1983) *Betriebliche Vermögensbeteiligung in der Bundesrepublik Deutschland, Teil II: Ergebnisse, Erfahrungen und Auswirkungen in der Praxis* (Cologne: Deutscher Instituts-Verlag); for Malta, see G. Kester (1980) *Transition to Workers' Self-Management: Its Dynamics in the Decolonising Economy of Malta* (The Hague: Spokesman Books for the Institute of Social Studies), pp. 171, 233–4. These results were confirmed in a recent analysis of Germany, France, Sweden and the UK by M. Festing et al. (1999) 'Financial Participation in Europe – Determants and Outcomes, *Economic and Industrial Democracy*, Vol. 20, pp. 295–329, based on data of the Cranfield Network on

European Human Resource (CRANET-E). However, M. Festing, et al. (1999) added that compared to profit-sharing the argument for employee ownership was not that straightforward.

35. See A. Pendleton, N. Wilson and M. Wright (1998) 'The Perception and Effects of Share Ownership: Empirical Evidence from Employee Buyouts', *British Journal of Industrial Relations*, Vol. 36 (1), March issue, pp. 99–123; J. Stack (1992) *The Great Game of Business: The Only Sensible Way to Run a Company* (New York: Doubleday).

36. Profit-sharing may work particularly well as a group incentive scheme in mass assembly plants where alienation is widespread and individual efforts cannot be effectively monitored. It may also be effective in highly skilled, diverse work teams in areas such as high technology production.

37. A. A. Alchian and H. Demsetz (1972) 'Production, Information Costs, and Economic Organisation', *American Economic Review*, Vol. 62, No. 5, December.

38. See H. Leibenstein (1987) *Inside the Firm* (Cambridge, MA: Harvard University Press), relating to the 'low effort conventions'.

39. See J. R. Blasi (1988), p. 2; compare also J. R. Blasi and D. L. Kruse (1991).

40. See H. Tofaute (1998); H.-G. Guski and H. J. Schneider (1986) *Betriebliche Vermögensbeteiligung: Eine Bestandsaufnahme* (Cologne: Deutscher Instituts-Verlag).

41. See UK Treasury Public Enquiry Unit (1998); also G. Nuttall (1999).

42. See *European Federation of Employee Share Ownership (EFES) News*, No. 1, September 1998; also Jean-Aymon Massie (1999) *Simplification du Plan Epargne Groupe – ELF*, 7th International Employee Ownership Conference, January 1999.

43. See D. Vaughan-Whitehead and M. Uvalić (eds) (1997), pp. 19, 20; K. Bradley, S. Estrin and S. Taylor (1990) 'Employee Ownership and Company Performance', *Industrial Relations*, Vol. 29 (3), pp. 385–402; M. Conte and J. Svejnar (1990) 'The Performance Effects of Employee Stock Ownership Plans' in A. Blinder (ed.) *Paying for Productivity: A Look at the Evidence*, (Washington, DC: Brookings Institution).

44. For a recent, comprehensive overview of the positive economic evidence (especially for ESOPs) see J. R. Blasi, D. Kruse and A. Bernstein (2003); they find an average increase of productivity level by about 4 per cent, of total shareholder returns by about 2 per cent and of profit levels by about 14 per cent compared with firms without PEPPER schemes.

45. First expressed in L. O. Kelso and M. J. Adler (1958); further developed and explicated in L. O. Kelso and P. Hetter (1967) *Two-Factor Theory: The Economics of Reality* (New York: Vintage Books, Random House).

46. See L. O. Kelso and P. H. Kelso (1991).

47. See R. Harbaugh (1993) *Equity-Sharing – Effects on Collective Bargaining Position of Trade Unions*, CERGE EI Working Paper (Prague: Charles University).

48. A. Pendleton, A. Robinson and N. Wilson (1995) 'Does Employee Ownership Weaken Trade Unions? Recent Evidence from the UK Bus Industry', *Economic and Industrial Democracy*, Vol. 16, No. 4, pp. 577–605.

49. See J. Logue et al. (1998) *Participatory Employee Ownership* (Kent, OH: Worker Ownership Institute), p. 109.

50. See H. Szóstkiewicz (1995) in M. Jarosz (ed.) *Management-Employee Buyouts in Poland* (Warsaw: Instytut Studiow Politycznych, Polska Akademia Nauk) and M. Jarosz (ed.) (1996); also M. Jarosz (ed.) (2000).

51. US General Accounting Office (1996) *Employee Stock Ownership Plans: Interim Report on a Survey and Related Economic Trends*, GAO/PEMD-86-4BR (Washington, DC: US General Accounting Office); US General Accounting Office (1986) *Employee Stock Ownership Plans: Benefits and Costs of ESOP Tax Incentives for Broadening Stock Ownership*, GAO-PEMD-87-8 (Washington, DC: US General Accounting Office); US General Accounting Office (1987) *Employee Stock Ownership Plans: Little Evidence of Effects on Corporate Performance*, GAO/PEMD-88-1 (Washington, DC: US General Accounting Office).

52. See D. Vaughan-Whitehead and M. Uvalić (eds) (1997), p. 20; also A. Pendleton, J. McDonald, A. Robinson and N. Wilson (1995) 'The Impact of Employee Stock Ownership Plans on Employee Participation and Industrial Democracy, *Human Resource Management Journal*, Vol. 5 (4), pp. 44–60.

53. See J. Logue et al. (1998), p. 123.

54. Conducted by W. Patton and J. Logue at the Ohio Employee Ownership Centre; see J. Logue et al. (1998), p. 125.

# 5
# The US ESOP as an Example of an Advanced Model

*John D. Menke, Stefan Hanisch and Jens Lowitzsch*

## 5.1 Historical background

For the first 100 years after the founding of the American republic, the USA was in fact a 'society of owners'. Ownership of a farm, ranch or small business was the norm rather than the exception. During the next 100 years, however, this situation changed radically with the coming of the industrial revolution and the eventual emergence and success of big business.

During the mid-1800s there was a legislative attempt to reverse the increasing tendency toward concentration of ownership through the enactment of the Homestead Act, which gave ownership of 160 acres of public land to any citizen who 'homesteaded' the land and made it productive through his own toil. By 1929, however, the concentration of corporate wealth and power again overpowered all other forms of ownership, leading to the Great Depression of 1929. During the next decade, the federal government attempted to restore purchasing power through massive measures of redistribution. These measures alleviated the symptoms, but did not cure the disease. Purchasing power was not fully restored until World War II created a whole new industry of defence contractors and small manufacturers.

After World War II, the US economy enjoyed two decades of prosperity before crashing again in 1974. In 1974, as in 1929, the US economy was again characterised by a high degree of concentration of ownership, by an abysmal lack of purchasing power, by extremely low rates of productivity, by violent confrontations between labour and management, and by a lack of capital for growth and expansion. Interest rates were at an all time high, and few banks were willing to lend in any event.

The stock market was at its lowest since 1929, and public offerings were non-existent.

Although stock bonus plans and profit-sharing plans that invest primarily in shares of company stock have existed since 1926, the first real Employee Stock Ownership Plan (ESOP) did not come into existence in the USA until San Francisco attorney Louis Kelso first designed a leveraged ESOP to buy out the founders of Peninsula Newspapers, Inc. in 1956. Between 1956 and 1986 the Kelso law firm went on to design ESOP buyouts for another 500 or so privately held companies. The ESOP concept was first codified[1] into law in the Employee Retirement Income Security Act of 1974 (ERISA).[2]

## 5.2   Foundations of the US Employee Stock Ownership Plan

The European policy makers' postulates are in line with the fundamental principles of the Employee Stock Ownership Plans developed by the Kelso firm in the United States, many of which have been legislatively implemented. The basic Kelso thesis is that every nation's capital assets must and can be broadly owned by its own citizens not collectively, but as the private property of individuals. Universal capital ownership is necessary because in a technologically advanced economy it is increasingly difficult and even impossible to attain a high standard of living solely through jobs and employment. People must supplement their wages and salaries with capital-sourced income – that is, interest and dividends – for everyone to participate in and enjoy the fruits of the private property, free market system.

ESOPs are retirement-type plans that qualify for special tax treatment. They operate through trusts established by the company to hold stock and other investments for the employees until the employee leaves the company. In return for significant tax benefits, companies must comply with a variety of rules to assure equitable treatment for plan participants. The benefits for the company include increased cash flow, tax savings and increased productivity from highly motivated workers. The main benefit for the employees is the ability to share in the company's success. Owing to the tax benefits, the administration of ESOPs is regulated, and under government supervision.

In an ESOP, the company, not the employee, funds the plans. Companies can fund these plans by contributing shares to the plans, contributing cash that the plans use to buy shares, or by having the plan borrow money to buy new or existing shares. If the plan borrows money to buy shares, the company repays the loan by making tax-deductible contributions to the plan to enable it to repay the loan. As the loan is repaid, several shares equal to the percentage of the loan repaid that year are released to employee accounts. If the plan does not borrow money, then as the shares or cash are contributed to the plan, the shares are allocated to individual employee accounts, usually based on relative compensation.

The ESOP is designed to build capital ownership into employees of a business in the course of efficiently financing its growth or other worthwhile corporate objectives, without touching employee pay cheques or savings. For employees, the ESOP is that constitutionally mandated missing link that gives them access to capital credit to buy the employer's capital stock and, without personal risk or liability, to pay for it from the pre-tax earnings of the assets underlying that stock. In other words, the ESOP equalises their access to capital credit with that of the already rich.

## 5.3   Structural changes needed to implement ESOPs and profit-sharing schemes

When the ESOP was proposed and adopted as part of the Employee Retirement Income Security Act of 1974 (ERISA), it was not as part of a grand new scheme of corporate finance (although the Kelso firm did succeed in getting language inserted into the Committee hearings that the 'ESOP is a tool of corporate finance'). Rather, it was proposed as a minor modification of the existing rules and regulations that applied to pension and profit-sharing plans. It was not initially blessed with any greater tax incentives or advantages than applied to qualified retirement plans such as pension plans and deferred profit-sharing plans. In effect, all that was proposed (and all that was initially adopted) was that deferred profit-sharing plans would be allowed to invest up to 100 per cent of their funds in shares of company stock, and that deferred profit-sharing plans would be allowed to borrow funds for purchasing shares of company stock.

To distinguish these new plans from deferred profit-sharing plans (which were not allowed to borrow money), these new plans were called ESOPs; they were also given an exemption from the fiduciary requirement of earning a 'fair rate of return' if the plan was designed to be invested 'primarily' in shares of company stock. The result was to create an entirely new kind of plan that enabled employees to become capital owners rather than mere recipients of profit-sharing funds. However, from a legislative and tax standpoint, the changes in the rules and regulations were minimal, and hardly anyone in Congress at the time recognised that the ESOP in effect converted employees into capital owners rather than mere beneficiaries of profit-sharing largess.

## 5.4   Key tax incentives for ESOPs

In addition to giving a potentially larger stake to employees, the ESOP also created a benefit for the existing owners. The ESOP created a new market for the existing owners to sell part or all of their stock to their employees through the ESOP. Before the invention of the ESOP, the only options available to owners desiring to exit the business were to sell their shares to the public in an initial public offering (IPO), sell their shares to a competitor or sell their shares back to the company itself. For most privately held companies, selling shares to the public in an IPO is not a viable option unless their company is in a high growth industry and has at least USD 100 million of annual revenues. For many companies, selling to a competitor is also not a viable option; because it usually means that the company will be downsized and merged out of separate existence. Selling shares back to the company itself also has a major disadvantage in that the sale will almost always have to be debt financed. The disadvantage of debt financing is that debt must be paid back with non-deductible dollars, which is prohibitively expensive in many cases.

All of these disadvantages are avoided when the owner sells his or her shares to an ESOP. With an ESOP, the shares are not sold to a competitor. Thus the firm continues its separate existence and its separate identity. With an ESOP, the purchase is usually debt financed, but the debt is paid back with tax-deductible dollars. Further, the ESOP can purchase the shares on a gradual basis so that the debt burden is not extensive at any given moment. For these reasons, as well as the fact that various studies confirmed that ESOPs were also effective in increasing employee motivation and productivity, ESOPs became increasingly prevalent during the ten-year period between 1974, when they were first codified, and 1984. In 1984, Congress determined that additional tax incentives were needed to further spur the growth and development of ESOPs. Consequently, the Tax Reform Act of 1984 added two key tax incentives for ESOPs.

The first new tax incentive was the so-called 'tax-free rollover' provision. Under this provision (§ 1042 of the Internal Revenue Code), if an ESOP acquires 30 per cent or more of the outstanding common stock of a regular corporation (now referred to as a 'C' corporation), the capital gains tax that the seller would ordinarily pay is deferred, provided that the seller purchases qualified replacement securities within 12 months of the sale. As long as the seller does not dispose of these replacement securities, the capital gains tax will be deferred indefinitely. If the seller subsequently dies, these qualified replacement securities receive a step-up in 'basis'. In this event, the capital gains tax is avoided completely. The second new tax incentive added by the Tax Reform Act of 1984 was the so-called 'deductible dividend'. Normally, any dividends paid by a corporation are not tax-deductible to the corporation. Under this new provision (§ 404(k) of the Internal Revenue Code), however, dividends paid on shares of company stock held by an ESOP are deductible to the corporation provided that these dividends are 'reasonable', and provided further that these dividends are used by the ESOP to repay an ESOP loan that was obtained to purchase shares of company stock. The purpose of this provision was to give companies even greater tax deductions in those cases where the company borrowed money to finance a purchase of company stock by the ESOP.

During the 20 years following the adoption of these two tax incentives, the number of ESOPs in the USA soared until the recession of 2002–3 slowed their growth. In the meantime, US corporate tax rates have changed to make the overall tax burden to corporate shareholders more favourable if the corporation is structured as an S corporation rather than as a C corporation. (An 'S' corporation is a corporation that is treated as a partnership for tax purposes, thus avoiding any taxation of profits at the corporate level.) Because the two special tax incentives for ESOPs only apply to C corporations, Congress realised that additional ESOP tax incentives would be needed for S corporations. Accordingly, the revisions that were made to § 1361 of the Internal Revenue Code in 2001 included an additional tax incentive for S corporation ESOPs. Under this tax incentive, any share of an S corporation's profits that is attributable to the ESOP as an S corporation shareholder will not be subject to the unrelated business income tax that is normally imposed on 'unrelated' earnings received by a qualified employee plan. Because the ESOP is otherwise a tax-exempt entity, this change means that the ESOP will be tax-exempt on all of its earnings, whether they are 'related' or 'unrelated'. The practical result of this change in the tax code is that in the case of an S corporation that is 100 per cent owned by its ESOP, 100 per cent of the earnings of the corporation will be exempt from any and all income taxation. In the three years since this change in the tax code, there has been a large increase in the number of S corporations that have become 100 per cent ESOP-owned.

## 5.5   The interim balance in 2007

As a result of the Kelso efforts, the ESOP is now a part of the social and economic fabric of corporate America. Over half of all the *Fortune 500* companies now sponsor ESOPs. Over 40 per cent of *Inc.* magazine's 100 fastest growing private companies now sponsor ESOPs. Now that ESOPs have existed in the USA for over 30 years (some ESOPs were put in place even before the 1974 legislation), there is a wealth of data to support the following conclusions

- ESOPs have been more successful than any other technique of corporate finance in extending the ownership of capital to people who would otherwise remain non-owners. As a result, there is a great deal more social stability, as well as less animosity, between capital owners and non-capital owners.
- ESOPs have, on average, provided a much higher level of retirement benefits than other types of pension and profit-sharing plan.
- ESOPs have helped to eliminate the 'us versus them' attitude in most ESOP companies. ESOPs have, in fact, brought about an unparalleled reign of labour–management peace and co-operation.
- ESOPs have been quite successful in increasing employee productivity and company profitability.
- ESOPs have been very successful in providing for business succession and continuity.

As of 2007, there were approximately 11,000 ESOPs in the USA, covering approximately 10 million employees. Most ESOPs are sponsored by privately held companies, of which about 3,500 are majority and about 2,000 100 per cent owned by the ESOP. According to a 2004 survey completed by the General Social Survey, out of 108 million people in the USA who work in the private sector, 21 per cent of employees own company stock, and the median value of the employees company stock ownership is over one-fifth of their annual pay. Employee stock ownership is widespread across all sectors of the American economy, ranging from nearly 60 per cent of employees in computer services to a low of 14 per cent in agriculture, mining and construction. Other sectors with a significant degree of employee ownership include utilities (55 per cent), durable manufacturing (30 per cent), non-durable manufacturing (30 per cent) and wholesale (23 per cent). Most ESOPs are sponsored by privately held companies.

## 5.6   Future prospects for ESOPs in the US

In May, 2007, Senator Blanche L. Lincoln introduced S. 1322, the ESOP Promotion and Improvement Act of 2007 in the US Senate. The bill's principal feature is a provision that would allow owners of S corporations to sell their shares to an ESOP under the same tax-free rollover provisions of § 1042 that currently apply to owners of C corporations. Although it is too early to predict whether this bill is likely to obtain passage by the US Congress, it is clear that several representatives in the US Senate and in the US House will continue to press for additional tax incentives to spur the further growth and utilisation of ESOPs. Also, as the US economy increasingly becomes more and more a 'service' economy, it would seem that the popularity of ESOPs will continue to grow, because service workers are more inclined to demand financial participation in the fruits of their own labour.

Two other recent developments are also likely to result in increased usage of ESOPs. First, globalisation and increased foreign competition have forced US companies to reduce employee wages and benefits to remain price competitive with foreign producers. As a result, US companies are increasingly eliminating all forms of guaranteed retirement benefits. For example, defined benefit pension plans and even regular deferred profit-sharing plans are almost extinct among privately held companies. Among privately held companies, 401(k) plans (which are funded largely by employee deferrals) and ESOPs are about the only types of retirement plan that still remain in vogue. Although a leveraged ESOP, like a defined benefit pension plan, requires a fixed contribution to repay the ESOP loan, this fact does not impede the adoption of ESOPs, because the ESOP provides double-duty dollars. That is, an ESOP enables the company to buy out the existing owners while providing employee benefits.

Second, among public company shareholders, the perception has developed that the high-tech bubble of the late 1990s was caused by overly incentivising top management with stock options. This perception has led the American Institute of Certified Public Accountants (AICPA) (the organisation that provides accounting standards for the accounting industry) to rule that stock option grants must be expensed on the company's income statement. As a result, many public companies are reducing or eliminating their stock option plans and are considering adopting ESOPs, which provide broad-based stock ownership for all employees, not just for the top management group.

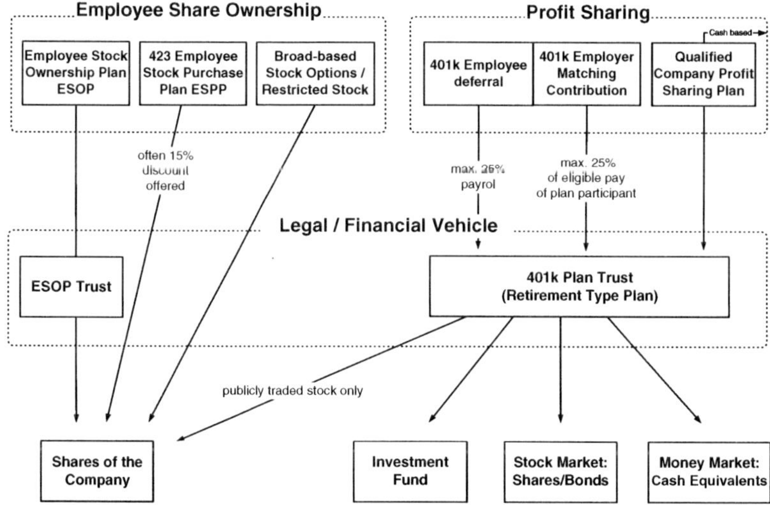



*Figure 5.1*   US system of financial participation.

## 5.7   Models of financial participation – The US and French systems

The American experience in institutionalising techniques for broadening the ownership of capital, valid in all of the 50 American states, provides a model for such a trans-jurisdictional framework. Moreover, the fundamental principles and structure of US financial participation (see Figure 5.1) are in line with the declared postulates of European policy makers. A comparison with the French model (see Figure 5.2) demonstrates that both systems are composed of the same basic elements that make up the Building Block Approach.

## 5.8   Four case studies

### 5.8.1   Market Contractors, Ltd. (Business Succession ESOP)

*5.8.1.1   The company*

The company was founded as a C corporation by a sole shareholder in 1978. Services include buildings, tenant improvements, remodels, re-imaging and fixture installations. The original market focus was the grocery industry, providing major remodel, fixturing and maintenance

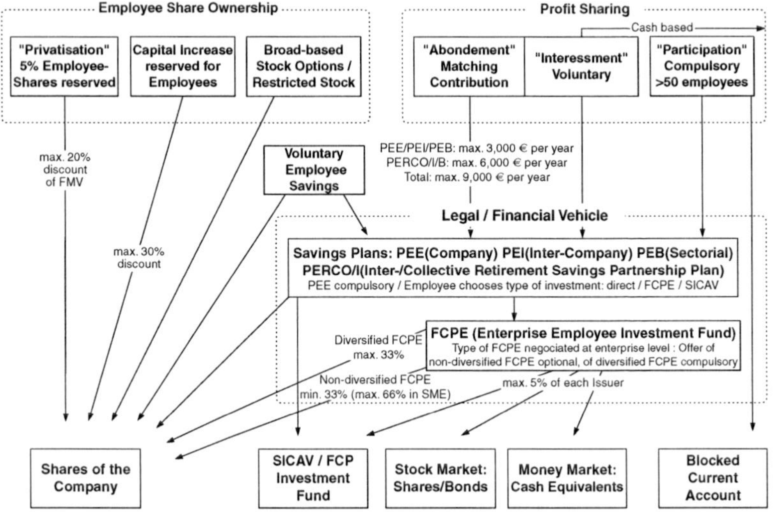



*Figure 5.2*   French system of financial participation.

services in Oregon and southwest Washington. Continuing growth has been achieved through the operation of a regional office in Portland and satellite locations in Seattle, Phoenix, Denver and Sacramento. Effectively the company has spread its base of operations to provide construction services in 13 Western US states. Its products and services have expanded to include casework and millwork. The client mix includes the following industries: banking/financial; medical/dental; retail; grocery; and restaurants. The company continues to base its growth on a wide diversity of trade disciplines and expertise, and a larger geographical market focus. An exclusive service offers corporate retailers and corporate franchisors a reliable, high-quality alternative to in-house resources for site development, facilities space planning management and construction management on a national scale. In 2006 the company had a turnover of USD 37,352,888 and pre-tax earnings of USD 1,867,644.

### 5.8.1.2   The plan

The Employee Stock Ownership Plan replaced a former Profit-Sharing Pension Plan; it originally became effective 1 November 1989, and was twice amended and restated, effective as of 1 November 1992 and

1 November 1999. In 2005, the ESOP owned 52.2 per cent of the company's shares. At that time, the company employed 148 people, 36 of whom were participants in the plan.

Originally, distributions of less than USD 3,500 were paid out in a lump sum after a five-year period of break in service. According to the 2000 amendment to the plan, amounts of less than USD 10,000 are distributed in a lump sum as soon as possible after termination. Also since then, the plan provides for distributions in five equal annual instalments after a five-year break in service. QDRO (qualified domestic relations order) distributions start as soon as possible after approval. Amounts less than USD 10,000 are to be paid in a lump sum; amounts of more than 10,000 in five equal annual instalments.

In 2006, a further 45 per cent of shares were sold to the ESOP, which finally owns 97.12 per cent of total shares. The value of the 45 per cent of shares was appraised at USD 9,338,220 (5× pre-tax earnings) or USD 54.34 per share.

### 5.8.1.3   Buying out the owner

Originally only 99 shares were issued. To facilitate share allocation in the ESOP, the company re-issued the shares, 159,840 shares replacing the original 99. The company was valued at USD 10 per share or USD 1,590,840.

In 1990, when the ESOP was installed, the company had just entered into a contract with a silent partner to purchase his interest. He held 48 shares or a little over 48 per cent of the company. The company borrowed money from the bank (USD 428,000) which was secured by 42,800 shares. The loan funds were used to cash out the silent partner and recapitalise the company. The original 42,800 shares were transferred to the ESOP as part of this transaction. Another 19,680 shares were contributed by the company to the ESOP. Finally, the ESOP owned 62,480 shares, of which 29,680 shares were still encumbered by the remaining balance of the bank loan of USD 296,800. The bank loan was paid down with USD 131,200 of the contribution in that year. So, in 1990, the sole shareholder owned 88,480 shares (55.36 per cent), the ESOP owned 62,480 shares (39.09 per cent), and two previous key employees owned 8,880 shares (5.55 per cent).

One key employee shareholder sold his 5,920 shares to the ESOP for USD 16 a share in 1996 (as of 31 October 1996, valuation). Also in 1996, many employees were asking to have more stock in the company instead of in Other Investments Account (OIA) funds because the company was performing better than OIA funds. So the company issued

10,000 new shares as a contribution valued at USD 19.50 per share or USD 195,000 for which the company took a tax deduction as a contribution. This brought the ESOP share in the company to 78,400 shares. In subsequent years, the ESOP purchased stock from the shareholders as follows: in 1997, 3,200 shares for USD 59,200 or USD 18.50 per share; in 2000, 3,076 shares for USD 100,031.52 or USD 32.52 per share, and again 708 shares for USD 23,024.16 or USD 32.52 per share; in 2001, 958 shares for USD 34,219.76 or USD 35.72 per share. The last purchase was financed by the company through a short-term loan to the ESOP. The sole shareholder sold 3,038 shares to the ESOP in 1999 for a price of USD 98,248.92 or USD 32.34 per share. In 2006, the company had 171,848 shares of its sole class of voting common stock issued and outstanding, 77,500 of which were owned by the sole shareholder. He sold all of these 77,500 shares to the ESOP for a total of USD 4,211,350 or USD 54.34 per share.

The ESOP paid USD 1,050,000 in cash, USD 500,000 of which were obtained from the OIA[3] of participants in the ESOP and USD 550,000 of which were borrowed by the company from the cash value of a certain life insurance policy owned by the company and loaned by the company to the ESOP in return for its promissory note (ESOP Company Note, interest rate 5.25 per cent). The ESOP will pay the principal of the ESOP Company Loan in 11 consecutive annual instalments of USD 50,000. The remaining unpaid principal balance of the ESOP Company Note falls due at the end of the 11-year period. In addition, the ESOP provided the seller with its promissory note in the amount of USD 3,161,350 for the balance of the purchase price (ESOP Seller Note, interest rate equal to the greater of the prime rate charged by the National Bank at its main branch in Portland, Oregon, less 1 per cent or the lowest long term applicable Federal rate applicable for purposes of Sec. 1274 IRC 1986, as amended). The ESOP will pay the principal of the ESOP Seller Loan in ten consecutive annual instalments of USD 105,378. The remaining unpaid principal balance of the ESOP Seller Note falls due at the end of the 10-year period.

### 5.8.1.4 *Average plan participant*

In 2005, the average plan participant (not including employees who were hired during the plan year or the majority shareholder of the company) was 44 years of age, had seven years of service and had been participating in the plan for seven years. His or her annual gross compensation amounted to USD 60,545. He or she has been vested 88 per cent of allocated shares. The total value of shares allocated to the account of the average plan participant has been USD 63,115; the value of vested shares is USD 60,161.

*5.8.1.4.1* Employee A (early participant)   Employee A was born in 1948. In 2005, he was 57 years old. He joined the company in 1989, 17 years ago, and has been participating in the plan for 16 years. His annual gross compensation amounts to USD 57,758. In 2005, shares in the total value of USD 201,423 have been allocated to his ESOP account. In accordance with his years of service, he has been vested 100 per cent. Thus, vested shares are valued at USD 201,423.

*5.8.1.4.2* Employee B (late participant)   Employee B was born in 1966. In 2005, he was 38 years old. He joined the company in 1998, seven years ago, and has been participating in the plan for six years. His annual gross compensation amounts to USD 49,940. As of 2005, his ESOP account had been allocated shares with a total value of USD 59,592. In accordance with his years of service, he has been vested 100 per cent. Thus, his total vested shares are valued at USD 60,161.

*5.8.1.4.3* Employee C (cashed-out)   Employee C was born in 1949. In 2005, he was 56 years old. He joined the company in 1991 and the plan in 1993. In 1998, after seven years of service and five years of participation in the plan, he retired. His final annual gross compensation amounted to USD 37,558. His ESOP account had accumulated shares to the total value of USD 43,105. He cashed out in four equal annual instalments to the amount of USD 10,776 each. In 2005, he received USD 10,776.

### 5.8.2   Stone Construction Equipment, Inc. (Business Succession ESOP)

*5.8.2.1   The Company*

The company is an S corporation and a national leader in the design, manufacture and marketing of light construction equipment. The more than 350 products designed and manufactured for worldwide distribution include: concrete and mortar mixers; power trowels; concrete and masonry saws; hand-held, walk-behind and ride-on dirt and asphalt compactors. The company was founded in 1967 and is located in Honeoye, New York, in an 150,000 square-foot facility. In 2007, the company ranks 43rd on the Rochester US TOP 100 list of fastest-growing private companies, a program of the Rochester Business Alliance and KPMG.

The company's book value at 31 December 2005 was USD 13,098,910, or USD 36.21 per share, based upon 361,787 shares of common stock outstanding. The company's average pre-tax earnings capacity for the financial years 2001–5 was in the range of USD 1,135,000 to USD 1,250,000. The sustainable EBITDA was estimated at USD 2,545,000 (its financial years 2001–5 weighted average EBITDA). The appraisal applied a guideline of a publicly traded company-based EBITDA multiple of 6.5×. The net shipments (sales) in the financial year 2005 amounted to USD 55,955,046. The present value of future pre-tax earnings capacity was estimated at USD 29,990,000.

### 5.8.2.2   The plan

The ESOP was originally installed on 1 January 1979, but was amended and restated effective twice, as of 1 January 1989 and 1 January 2001. Since 1995, several stock transactions have taken place each year, consisting of the issuance of restricted common stock to key management pursuant to an incentive stock option plan as well as the purchase of common stock into the company's treasury from terminating ESOP participants. Currently 221 (out of 249) employees participate in the plan.

The plan provides for lump sum distributions in case of death, disability or retirement during the following plan year. In the event that a participant's employment is terminated for these reasons, distribution of his or her plan benefit in excess of USD 1,000 shall start no later than one year after the close of the plan year in which the earliest of the following events occurs: normal/early retirement date, death, disability. Distribution of a participant's plan benefit attributable to employer securities acquired by the plan after 31 December 1986 will be made in a lump sum, as soon as administratively feasible, during the sixth plan year after the plan year in which the participant separated from service. If the total vested value of a participant's Corporate Savings Account (CSA) and OIA is USD 1,000 or less, distribution shall be made in a lump sum as soon as administratively possible after the participant terminates employment. Effective for all plan years beginning on or after 1 January 2005, the USD 1,000 limit was amended to USD 5,000.

As of 31 December 2005, the ESOP Trust owned 83 per cent or 361,787 of the company's outstanding common stock with a value of USD 16,740,000, or USD 46.27 per share. Twelve per cent of stock was still held by a second main shareholder and 5 per cent by other employees (owing to other retirement plans).

### 5.8.2.3   *Buying out the owner(s)*

The sole proprietor was born in 1940 and sold all of his stock to the ESOP before 1991 in order to start up a new business. In addition to the funds received from the sale of his stock, in 2005 he received an additional USD 42,179 from his 12-year participation in the ESOP. Altogether, between 1985 and 1995, the ESOP obtained 300,635 shares for a total value of about USD 6,000,000: 100,000 shares from outside investors for a total of USD 2,000,000, and 200,000 shares from the sole shareholder and his family for a total of USD 4,000,000.

In financial years 1983–4, the ESOP bought about 17 per cent of the outstanding stock (50,000 shares) at an average price of USD 19 per share. These transactions were financed out of operating cash flow. In the financial year 1985, the ESOP borrowed USD 1,000,000 from a bank and used the proceeds to buy stock from existing shareholders at USD 19 per share. In the financial year 1986, the ESOP borrowed USD 4,000,000 to purchase an additional 67 per cent of the outstanding stock (200,000) at USD 20 per share. In this transaction, the ESOP purchased all of the shares held by the founder and his family. This brought the ESOP to 100 per cent ownership. The loan was repaid over a ten-year term from 1986–96.

### 5.8.2.4   *Average plan participant*

In 2005, the average plan participant was 45 years of age, had 13 years of service and had been participating in the plan for 13 years. His or her annual gross compensation amounted to USD 54,605. The total value of shares allocated to his or her account was USD 52,095. He or she was vested 82.13 per cent of allocated shares having a value of USD 51,361.

*5.8.2.4.1   Employee A (early participant)*   Employee A was born in 1968. In 2005, he was 37 years old. He joined the company in 1988, 17 years ago, and has been participating in the plan for 17 years. His annual gross compensation is USD 44,545. As of 2005, shares with a total value of USD 8,368 have been allocated to his ESOP account. According to his years of service, he is 100 per cent vested. Thus, his vested shares are worth USD 58,368.

*5.8.2.4.2   Employee B (late participant)*   Employee B was born in 1953. In 2005, he was 52 years old. He joined the company in 1999, seven years ago, and has been a plan participant for seven years. His annual gross compensation amounts to USD 73,229. As of 2005, his ESOP account had accumulated a total value of USD 17,203. His years of service entitle him to 100 per cent vesting. Thus, his ESOP account is worth USD 17,203.

*5.8.2.4.3  Employee C (cashed-out)*  Employee C was born in 1953. In 2005, he was 52 years old. He joined the company in 1999 and the plan in 2000. In 2005, after six years of service and five years of participation in the plan, he terminated. His last annual gross compensation amounted to USD 31,843. He accumulated shares to the total value of USD 5,292. He cashed out with a lump sum of USD 4,234 after taxes.

### 5.8.3  Bad case: Golden Bear Packaging, Inc. (Business Succession ESOP)

#### 5.8.3.1  *The company*

The company was founded by two individuals in 1985 to act as a corrugated box converter that supplies printed cartons to electronics, food, and light- and heavy-industry clients within a 150-mile radius of the manufacturing facility. Throughout financial year 2001, a recessionary environment prevailed in the corrugated industry and it continued to plague the company in 2003. Management has taken steps to increase sales and cut costs and it appears that those efforts are beginning to pay off. With the debt load down to a manageable level, the company's survivability looks more promising. The fair market value (FMV) dropped from USD 3,949,000 or USD 1,583.65 per share in 1998 to USD 70,000 or USD 36.52 per share in 2002.

As of 31 December 2004, the fair market value of the company (on a minority interest basis) was appraised at USD 330,000 or USD 179.25 per share based upon 1841 shares outstanding. The company's book value at 31 December 2004 was USD −172,223. The company had an average pre-tax earnings capacity for the financial years 2000–4 in a range of USD −604,000 to USD 58,000. The adjusted EBITDA for the same period ranged from USD 327,000 to USD 217,000. The net shipments (sales) range from USD 7,864,000 to USD 4,004,000. The company is currently running at 30 per cent of its capacity and has a significant opportunity for growth.

#### 5.8.3.2  *The plan*

The company adopted a combined ESOP and 401(k) Plan which became on 1 January 1986, but has been amended and restated effective several times. As of 31 December 2005, the company had a total of 30 full-time employees (excluding executives). 26 of them are participating in the plan.

The plan provides for distributions in a lump sum in case of a participant's death, disability or retirement, not later than one year after the close of the plan year. In the event that a participant terminates employment for reasons other than death, disability or retirement, his or her vested plan benefit, if USD 3,500 or more, will be distributed in five equal annual instalments, starting not later than one year after the close of the third plan year following the plan year in which he or she terminates employment. Amounts of more than USD 500,000 shall be distributed in five equal annual instalments, plus one year (but not more than five additional years) for each USD 100,000 by which the plan benefit exceeds USD 500,000. If a participant's CSA or OIA are less than USD 3,500, distribution shall be made in a lump sum as soon as possible after the close of a plan year in which he or she incurs a one-year break in service.

During financial year 2002, the company acquired 484 shares from departing plan participants. During financial year 2004, the company repurchased and retired 76 shares from retiring ESOP participants. As of 31 December 2004, the ESOP owned 40.25 per cent or 741 out of 1,841 shares of the company's outstanding common stock. There was a financial year 2005 transaction in which the company repurchased 6.4 shares from the ESOP to remunerate a departing plan participant.

### 5.8.3.3   *Buying out the owner*

The ownership (2,500 shares) was originally shared between three shareholders to 56 per cent (1,400 shares), 40 per cent (1000 shares) and 4 per cent (100 shares). The 56 per cent shareholder sold his 1,400 shares to the ESOP in 1994 for USD 1,345,000. As of 31 December 2004, 54.32 per cent or 1,000 shares and 5.43 per cent or 100 shares were owned by the other two shareholders.

The transaction was financed by two loans of about USD 634,000 (so-called bridge loan) and USD 561,260 (altogether USD 1,195,000) given by the company to the ESOP in exchange for promissory notes and a contribution of the company about USD 150,000. The company borrowed USD 634,000 (term 90 days) and USD 561,260 (on a prime interest rate and a seven-year term) from a bank. After receiving cash payment for the 1,400 shares from the ESOP, the seller purchased a GE Bond as his Qualified Replacement Property (QRP) and margined against the bond in the amount of USD 634,000. The seller lent USD 634,000 to the company to repay the short-term bank loan. The company issued a promissory note to him for this amount.

### 5.8.3.4   *Average plan participant*

*5.8.3.4.1*   Employee A (early participant)   Employee A was born in 1950. In 2004, she was 54 years old. She has been employed at the company since 1991, for 14 years, and has been participating in the plan for 13 years, since 1992. Her annual gross compensation amounts to USD 49,394. In 2004, shares to the total value of USD 7,133 have been allocated to her ESOP account. In accordance with her years of service, she is vested 100 per cent. Thus, she has been vested shares to the value of USD 7,133.

*5.8.3.4.2*   Employee B (late participant)   Employee B was born in 1969. In 2004, she was 35 years old. She has been with the company for seven years, since 1998, and has been participating in the plan for six years, since 1999. Her annual gross compensation amounts to USD 34,680. In 2004, shares to the total value of USD 685 have been allocated to her ESOP account. In accordance with her years of service, she is vested 100 per cent. Thus, she has been vested shares to the value of USD 685.

*5.8.3.4.3*   Employee C (cashed-out before recession)   Employee C was born in 1972. In 2006, he was 34 years old. He joined the company in 1996 and the plan in 1997. In 2000, after five years of service and four years participation under the plan, he terminated. His last annual gross compensation amounted to USD 26,796. He accumulated shares to the total value of USD 4,678. He was vested 100 per cent and cashes out in five annual instalments at USD 936 during 2003–7.

*5.8.3.4.4*   Employee D (cashed-out during recession)   Employee D was born in 1971. In 2006, she was 35 years old. She joined the company in 1996 and the plan in 1998. She worked on a part-time basis from 2000. In 2001, after three years of service and four years participation under the plan, she terminated. Her last relevant (that is full-time) annual gross compensation amounted to USD 17,382 in the financial year 1999. She accumulated shares to the total value of USD 1,216, was vested 100 per cent and cashed out in 2006 with USD 1,216.

### 5.8.4   Bad case: Howland Electric & Electronic Wholesale Company, Inc.

*5.8.4.1*   *The company*

The company is a C corporation and primarily a wholesale electrical distributor carrying approximately 11,500 stock-keeping units. It produces inventory multiple lines but it also assists customers by providing free electrical design services which is unique among similar types of firms. The company was founded in 1952 as an equal partnership of three owners. In 1955, the company was incorporated.

The company has been suffering consistent loss for the last five years. Currently, the company is in liquidation and all of its assets are being sold. As of 31 December 2005, the fair market value of the company (on a minority interest basis) was appraised at USD 1,250,000 or USD 64.56 based upon 19,361.22 shares outstanding. The company's book value at 31 December 2005 was USD 637,519. The company had an average pre-tax earnings capacity for the financial years 2001–5 in a range of USD –164 to USD –101. The adjusted EBITDA for the same period ranged from USD –292 to USD –277. The net shipments (sales) range from USD 2,141 to USD 488,000.

### 5.8.4.2   *The plan*

The company had no plan for business succession. Selling the company to the ESOP was not an option because there was no capital apart from the value of the real estate. That is why, after the death of the owner, the company has come under liquidation. The bad performance of the company was also reflected in miscommunication between the ESOP advisory firm and the company. In the beginning, the ESOP was administered by other people. After the ESOP advisory firm took over the plan administration, there was a permanent problem in getting necessary data/information in time.

The plan provides for distributions in a lump sum up to USD 3,500 in case of a participant's death, disability or retirement, not later than one year after the close of the plan year. Amounts of more than USD 3,500 will be distributed in five substantially equal annual instalments. Amounts of more than USD 500,000 shall be distributed in five equal annual instalments, plus one year (but not more than five additional years) for each USD 100,000 by which the plan benefit exceeds USD 500,000. In the event that a participant terminates employment for reasons other than death, disability or retirement, his vested plan benefit, if USD 3,500 or more, will be distributed in five equal annual instalments, starting not later than one year after the close of the fifth plan year following the plan year in which he or she terminates employment. Amounts of more than USD 500,000 shall be distributed in five equal annual instalments, plus one year (but not more than five additional years) for each USD 100,000 by which the plan benefit exceeds USD 500,000. If a participant's CSA or OIA are less than USD 3,500, distribution shall be made in a lump sum as soon as possible after the close of a plan year in which he or she terminates employment.

As of 31 December 2005, the ESOP owned 23.82 per cent or 4,611.22 of the company's outstanding common stock. 76.18 per cent were attributed to the estate of the late sole shareholder. At the time, the number of employees dropped from 25 (when the ESOP started) to two employees (including one executive).

### 5.8.4.3   *Financing the ESOP transactions (as opposed to a succession ESOP)*

Two of the three shareholders passed away, so that the company had one remaining sole shareholder (14,750 shares) before the installation of the ESOP in 1993 (effective since 1 January 1992). This person passed away in 2002.

Newly issued stock was sold to the ESOP in three transactions. In the financial year 1992, the ESOP obtained 1,225.32 shares for a total of USD 113,134, or USD 92.33 per share. In the financial year 1993, the company conducted a partially leveraged employee buyout by selling 2,907.93 shares for USD 17,657.93, or USD 89.03 per share. The issuance of 673.01 new shares for USD 59,918 was financed by a bank loan which was repaid in 1994. In the financial year 1994 the company issued 5,137.24 new shares to the ESOP for USD 169,160. The purchase of 896.152 shares was financed by a bank loan which was repaid in 1995. During the financial years 1997–2000 shares were redeemed by the company from participants in the ESOP.

### 5.8.4.4   *Average plan participant*

**5.8.4.4.1   Employee A (early participant)**   Employee A was born in 1951. In 2004, he was 53 years old. He joined the company in 1990 and has been participating in the plan since its installation in 1992. He left the firm in 2004, after 14 years of service. His annual gross compensation amounted to USD 36,052. In 2004, shares to the total value of USD 21,609 had been allocated to his ESOP account. In accordance with his years of service, he is vested 100 per cent. Thus, he has been vested shares to the value of USD 21,609.

**5.8.4.4.2   Employee B (late participant)**   Employee B was born in 1962. In 2004, she was 42 years old. She has been with the company and has been participating in the plan for five years, since 2000. Her annual gross compensation amounted to USD 22,095. In 2004, shares to the total value of USD 399 had been allocated to her ESOP account.

In accordance with her years of service, she is vested 60 per cent. Thus, she has been vested shares to the value of USD 239.

*5.8.4.4.3*  Employee C (cashed-out)   Employee C was born in 1944. In 2005, she was 52 years old. She joined the company and the plan in 1994. In 1997, after three years of service and participation under the plan, she terminated. Her last annual gross compensation amounted to USD 28,250. She accumulated shares to the total value of USD 6151. She was vested 20 per cent and received distributed shares to the value of USD 1,230. She can use her 'put' option and sell these shares to the company.

## Notes

1. Because the tax code already authorised stock bonus plans and profit-sharing plans that were primarily invested in shares of company stock, Congress was persuaded to authorise leveraged ESOPs because leveraging the plan would allow the employees to acquire much larger equity stakes in their employers than they could otherwise acquire by buying stock on a year-by-year basis.
2. Before 1974 there was no explicit statutory authorisation for ESOPs. They were simply approved on a case-by-case basis by the Internal Revenue Service, based on certain existing regulations and revenue rulings that applied to stock bonus plans and profit-sharing plans.
3. Cash contributed to the ESOP that has not purchased company stock is allocated to each participant's OIA.

# Part III  Empirical Evidence and Country Information

# 6
# Benchmarking Financial Participation in the EU

*Iraj Hashi, Richard Woodward and Jens Lowitzsch*

## 6.1 Introduction: Assessing and benchmarking financial participation – The PEPPER IV Report[1]

The PEPPER IV Report is an interdisciplinary legal and economic comparative study. It provides a comparative assessment of financial participation in the EU-27 and in the candidate countries. It is based on coherent and thus, for the first time, comparable indicators.

### 6.1.1 Aims of the project and specific difficulties to be dealt with

The Report closed the gap between PEPPER I (1991, EU-12), PEPPER II (1997, EU-15) and PEPPER III (2006, ten new Member States and four candidate countries), and uses the benchmarking indicators developed by the Dublin Foundation in all 27 EU Member States and candidate countries. It consists of three complementary basic components that build on each other:

- description of the legal environment, fiscal or other incentives and links to participation in decision making with a specific focus on schemes for SMEs;
- benchmarking financial participation, that is, the scope and nature of financial participation schemes;
- comparative analysis of the national policies and characteristics that affect the environment for financial participation.

The final recommendations derived from the comparative analysis, best practice in the member countries and, in the context of the development of ESOPs, that in the United States. They set forth both a policy and a proposal for promoting financial participation at European and national levels.

The benchmarking exercise continues the projects 'Financial Participation of Employees in the New Member and Candidate Countries' and 'A European Platform for Financial Participation' (both successfully concluded), funded under the same budget line and building on the PEPPER Reports. It digests their results and data from previous studies (EWCS, Eiro, CRANET, EFES).[2] The purpose of the project is fourfold:

- to assess systematically similarities and compatibility of the laws and practices governing financial participation in the EU-27 and candidate countries;
- to close information gaps (that is, between PEPPER I, II and III) that currently prevent a full profiling of financial participation policy and practice;
- to discuss individual country's scores on the indicators against the background of comparable scores for the other EU Member States, providing a contextual frame of reference for each single profile;
- to further promote a common platform for financial participation within the European Union, in the context of comparative analysis.

An interdisciplinary conference, with key EU experts presenting preliminary project results, took place in October 2007 in Berlin; the PEPPER IV Report was presented in Brussels and in Strasbourg to the European Commission and Parliament in May 2008.

In 2004, the European Foundation for the Improvement of Working and Living Conditions (hereafter referred to as the European Foundation) commissioned a report that developed 16 specific indicators of financial participation policy and practice facilitating like-for-like comparisons of the financial participation situation in each Member State. The second stage of the process, to 'road test' these indicators, was undertaken in 2005. Although nine of the European Foundation's 16 benchmarking indicators were supported by existing data, seven of the measures were not supported at all. The benchmarking project addressed this data shortage, but not by undertaking a new study dedicated to financial participation; instead, as recommended by the pilot benchmarking study of Slovenia commissioned by the European Foundation, it referred to existing upgraded surveys (that is by the European Foundation's 'Eiro Comparative Study on Financial Participation in the New Member States', to whose questionnaire our team contributed input).

Furthermore, the Pilot Study by the European Foundation clearly demonstrated how the Foundation's nine supported indicators can be used to produce a partial profile (in the test case of Slovenia). To be independent of new EU-wide surveys, the work programme initially aimed at such a partial profile using those nine indicators. Including the results of the 'mini survey' of our project partners, additional indicators were added. For individual country's national sources (see Chapter 7) and 'blank spots' (in some cases for single countries and single indicators), our team provided the necessary supplementary information using our EU-wide network from the previous projects.

The Commission and Parliament identified transnational obstacles to the development of a European model for financial participation, which a High Level Group of Independent Experts had classified at the end of 2003. Our assessment of the legal environment investigates the possibilities for creating a European legal framework for financial participation. In so doing, the project, as recommended in PEPPER III, builds on the Building Block Approach to combine established schemes in a single programme with alternative options and to keep the different elements complementary.

### 6.1.2   The benchmarking indicators

#### 6.1.2.1   *Sources*

Any benchmarking exercise, especially one involving many countries, relies on the availability of comparable and consistent data. Although there are many studies on the impact of employee participation on firm performance,[3] there are very few sources of information on the availability and take-up of financial participation schemes across countries. Below we briefly present the main sources of information on financial participation schemes in European countries on which the discussion of this chapter and country reports are based. These sources are very different from each other and need careful interpretation.

(1)  CRANET Survey. This is a survey of companies with more than 200 employees[4] undertaken by the Cranfield School of Management (Cranfield University, UK) approximately every four or five years since 1992. It is largely a postal survey, sent to the Human Resources Departments of companies with the main aim of investigating the HR characteristics and practices of these companies. One section of the questionnaire is concerned with employees' remuneration and its components. In this section there are questions on whether the company offers any financial participation scheme

(specifically, share ownership, profit-sharing or stock option schemes) to various occupational groups of employees (management, professional and technical, administrative, and manual workers). In 2005, the survey covered 7914 companies in 32 EU and non-EU countries (the EU Member States and candidate countries not included were Ireland, Latvia, Lithuania, Luxembourg, Malta, Poland, Portugal, Romania and Croatia).[5] Because of the postal nature of the survey, the response rate is rather low (16 per cent in 2005). The CRANET sample is selected randomly from the population of companies with more than 200 employees and is designed to represent the size and sectoral distribution of companies in the population.[6] The companies included in the sample are selected separately in each round of the survey, thus the data are not in the form of a panel. To have a more complete picture of financial participation in all member and candidate countries of the European Union, we undertook mini-surveys in seven of the missing countries (Latvia, Lithuania, Malta, Poland, Portugal, Romania and Croatia).[7] The mini-surveys consisted of a smaller number of firms in each country and covered only those parts of the CRANET questionnaire related to remuneration and the general information about the company, thus were comparable to the CRANET survey.[8] It is essential to note that the CRANET survey does not indicate the incidence of financial participation schemes in companies but only their availability. Furthermore, for this research, we have been concerned with broad-based financial participation schemes (that is, schemes covering more than 50 per cent of employees) in private sector companies only, as profit-sharing or share ownership are largely not applicable to public sector organisations (which do not make 'profit' as such and do not always have shares to distribute to employees).

(ii) European Working Conditions Survey. This is a large-scale survey of working conditions across Europe undertaken by the European Foundation every four or five years to investigate a variety of factors influencing individuals working and living conditions. One section of the questionnaire deals with remuneration and sources of income, asking the respondent whether they receive any income in the form of profit-sharing or any income from the ownership of shares in the companies for which they work. Given that individual subjects may be employed, unemployed, self-employed or retired, the present survey is only concerned with the individuals who are in employment. The 2005 survey covered some 30,000 randomly selected individuals in 31 countries (including all EU and candidate countries as well as some non-EU countries). These surveys are conducted by face-to-face interviews and, consequently, the response rate is higher (48 per cent in 2005)[9]. As with the CRANET survey, only a small part of this investigation is related to financial participation. The previous round of this survey took place in two waves: in 2000 for the EU-15 and a few other European countries and in 2001 for the accession and candidate countries. Unlike the CRANET survey, which only shows the availability of financial participation schemes to employees, the EWCS represents the actual take-up of these schemes. However, the data apply to all employees, irrespective of the size of their companies. Given that respondents may be from any category of employee (managers, professionals, clerical or manual), it is not possible to identify whether any financial participation scheme is broad or narrow. Unlike the 2001 and the 2005 surveys, the 2000 round did not directly distinguish between employees of the public and private sector.[10]

(iii) European Federation of Employee Share Ownership (EFES) data. For many years, EFES has been collecting data on the scale of employee share-ownership in large companies in 29 European countries, including all 27 EU Member States. The population of this database consists of all listed companies with a market capitalisation of at least 200 million euros and large, non-listed employee-owned companies (those employing more than 100 people with employees owning more than 50 per cent of shares). The former group consists of 2270 companies and the latter of some 207 companies. The emphasis of this dataset is not on financial participation schemes in general but only on share ownership and only in large companies. Although the second group of companies do not include all the large, majority-owned companies, this group is only a small part (less than 10 per cent) of the total sample and does not change the overall picture significantly. In this benchmarking exercise, we use data from 2006 and 2007.

(iv) Country profiles based on various sources, including the PEPPER I, II and III Reports, the EIRO survey and our Project Expert Network in the field. These profiles of all 29 target countries (EU-27 plus Croatia and Turkey) cover developments in three areas: Evolution of Financial Participation Schemes, Social Partners' Attitudes, and Current Government Policy and Legal Framework.

To sum up, it is clear that the three sets datasets are not comparable to each other, as they refer to different indicators of financial participation. They should be seen as complementary, each highlighting a different feature of the development of employee financial participation. The diversity of these sources also emphasises the need for a new, comprehensive and consistent large-scale survey of employee participation across the whole of EU and candidate countries.

### 6.1.2.2   *The indicators and their link to the Commission principles*

Each of the benchmarking indicators selected complies with one of the essential principles of financial participation schemes set forth by the Commission in its communication seeking 'a framework for the promotion of employee financial participation'.[11] Needless to say, sufficient data were not available for all of the chosen indicators for screening.

Principle 1: Participation must be voluntary for both enterprises and
   employees.
   Indicator: Legislative and fiscal support for financial participation.
   The country profiles provide detailed information on whether specific legislation concerning financial participation exists and whether any tax relief is given. Furthermore, the overview of taxation systems and tax incentives distinguishes between incentives for firms and employees, on the one hand, and for profit-sharing and share schemes on the other.
Principle 2: Access to financial participation schemes should in principle be open to all employees (no discrimination against part-time workers or women).
   Indicators: The percentage of enterprises offering broad-based financial participation schemes to employees and the percentage of employees covered by such schemes.
   CRANET surveys measured this as the percentage of organisations offering financial participation to each of four occupational categories (managers and three non-managerial groups). In terms of the all-employees criterion, the assumption is that organisations that offer financial participation to a particular occupational group do so for all employees within that grade. Furthermore, CRANET surveys indicate the percentage share of each organisation's workforce falling into each occupational grade. Putting the two pieces of information together, it is possible to calculate the percentage of employees in each organisation who are offered financial participation.

Principle 3: Schemes should be set up and managed in a clear and comprehensible manner with emphasis on transparency for employees.
Indicator: Percentage of employees participating in financial participation.
The fourth EWCS asks whether the remuneration includes payments based on the overall performance of the company (profit-sharing scheme) and/or income from shares in the company the respondent works for.
Principle 4: Share ownership schemes will almost inevitably involve a certain complexity, and in this case it is important to provide adequate training for employees to enable them to assess the nature and particulars of the scheme in question.
Indicator: Countries with direct/indirect and consultative/delegative participation in decision making.
The country profiles give an overview of the different types of participation in decision making practised in different countries. Unfortunately, sufficient data for the screening of this indicator were not accessible. The available empirical evidence suggests that incentive effects of financial participation are much greater when accompanied by greater worker participation in decision making.
Principle 5: Rules on financial participation in companies should be based on a predefined formula clearly linked to enterprise results.
Indicators: Percentage of employees whose financial participation is calculated on a predefined formula and the percentage participating in regular, ongoing schemes.
The fourth EWCS asks whether payments are calculated on a predefined formula and whether these payments are received on a regular basis.
Principle 6: Unreasonable risks for employees must be avoided or, at the very least, employees must be warned of the risks of financial participation arising from fluctuations in income or from limited diversification of investments.
Indicator: European Employee Ownership Top 100 Index.
Sufficient empirical data for the screening of this indicator were not available. However, the information from the European Employee Ownership Top 100 Index allows an assessment of one dimension of risk through matching financial participation in quoted companies with their performance on the stock markets.
Principle 7: Schemes must be a complement to, not a substitute for, the existing pay system.

Indicator: Percentage of enterprises in which financial participation and regular salary are kept separate and distinct.

Sufficient empirical data for the screening of this indicator were not available.[12] Nevertheless, a good test for this indicator is to examine whether negotiations on the two issues take place separately and at different times; however, there is a danger of respondent bias (employers may be reluctant to give any information that could suggest salary substitution).

Principle 8: Financial participation schemes should be developed in a way that is compatible with worker mobility both internationally and between enterprises.

Indicator: Legislative and fiscal support for financial participation.

The country profiles look at specific financial participation schemes that are suitable for cross-border use. The overview of taxation systems and tax incentives provide complementary information about this dimension of financial participation.

## 6.2  Availability of financial participation schemes in EU companies

### 6.2.1  Percentage of firms offering broad-based FP to employees

We begin with a look at broad-based employee share ownership (ESO) plans on the basis of data from the CRANET survey of companies (supplemented with data we collected in an independent mini-survey). Figure 6.1 shows the percentages of companies with broad-based ESO and profit-sharing plans in 1999 and 2005 in 26 European countries (including six in which mini-surveys were conducted). As we see in Figure 6.1, between 1999 and 2005, ESOs grew in almost every country except the UK, and marginally in Spain and Finland (the weighted average for all countries grew from 11 to 18 per cent). If we look at the five leading countries in 2005 (with shares ranging from 33 to 40 per cent), we see that three of them (Poland, Bulgaria and Croatia) are transition countries (indeed, the absence of Slovenia in this group is surprising, as the country's privatisation programme generated a large amount of employee ownership); Denmark and France are the other two. The three lowest-ranked countries are Portugal, Turkey and Lithuania. Estonia is also one of the lowest-ranked countries, indicating the low incidence of ESO in the Baltic States generally. Spain and Portugal's low rankings also indicate the low level of coverage in the Iberian Peninsula. It is interesting that Denmark is far ahead of other two Nordic countries (Sweden and Finland), which might indicate a divergence of that country from at least some aspects of the 'Scandinavian model'. We note that Finland was ahead of Denmark on this measure in 1999, and that Denmark's leadership is thus a recent development owing to what seems to be extremely strong growth of ESO there in recent years. Finally, it is also interesting to note that Hungary, the Czech Republic and Slovenia have such similar levels of coverage (all are middle-ranked) in spite of the very different privatisation methods used in these countries. This is possibly an indicator of convergence of ownership structures in transition countries.

Figure 6.1 also shows how broad-based profit-sharing has developed between 1999 and 2005. Again, we generally see growth, except in the UK, the Czech Republic, and the lowest-ranked countries (Belgium, Bulgaria and Italy); the weighted average for all countries grew from 24 to 33 per cent. We also note a much wider range of results than in the case of ESO (for ESO, the proportion of firms offering a scheme ranges from 4 to 40 per cent; for profit-sharing from under 4 to over 92 per cent). It is not surprising that France is the leading country, far ahead of all others, as deferred profit-sharing is mandatory there.

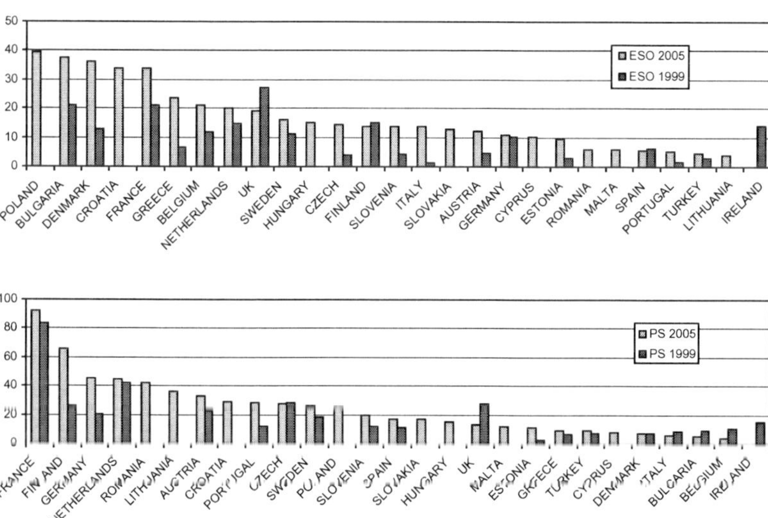


*Figure 6.1* Proportion of sample firms offering broad-based employee share ownership and profit-sharing schemes in European countries, 1999 and 2005 (in per cent).
*Source:* CRANET data and own survey (Croatia, Lithuania, Malta, Poland, Portugal, Romania – for 2007)

The second-ranked country is Finland. Germany, the Netherlands and Romania are similar, with coverage between 40 and 50 per cent. The lowest-ranked countries (with coverage under 10 per cent), in ascending order, are Belgium, Bulgaria, Italy, Denmark, Cyprus and Turkey.

It is interesting to note that two of the countries among the highest-ranked for ESO – Bulgaria and Denmark – are among the lowest-ranked for profit-sharing. This indicates that firms and countries choose ESO or profit-sharing for different reasons and do not see them as alternative forms of involving employees in the firm's business; thus, there is no correlation between the two schemes.

### 6.2.2   Financial participation schemes by size and sector

We are also interested in how employee financial participation might differ across firms with respect to firm size and sector of business activity.

The breakdown according to size is shown in Figures 6.2 and 6.3. The size categories can be described as medium (100–500 employees), large (501–1,000 employees) and very large (1,001 or more employees). For

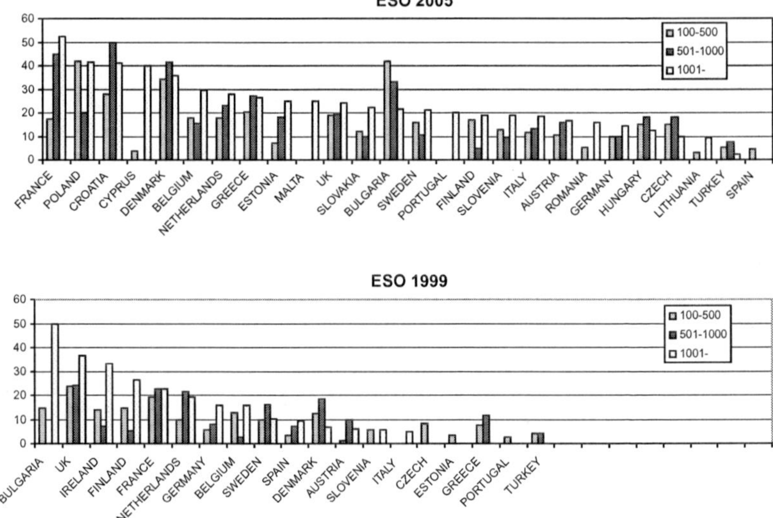

*Figure 6.2*  Percentage of firms in each size group offering employee share ownership schemes, 1999 and 2005.
Source: CRANET data and own survey (Croatia, Lithuania, Malta, Poland, Portugal, Romania – for 2007)

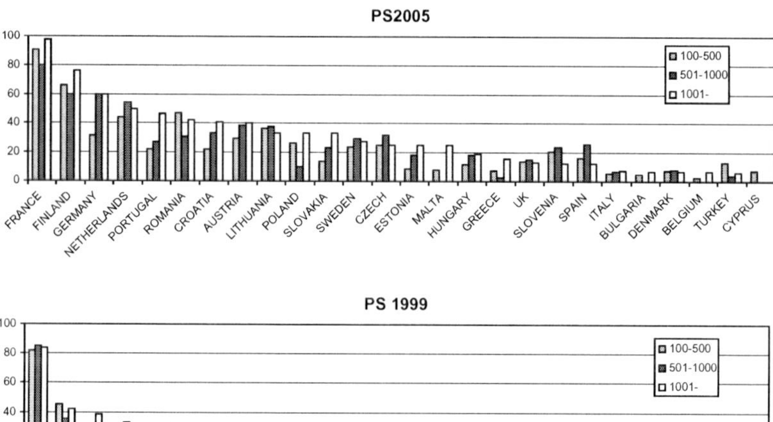

*Figure 6.3*   Percentage of firms in each size group offering profit-sharing schemes, 1999 and 2005.
*Source:* CRANET data and own survey (Croatia, Lithuania, Malta, Poland, Portugal, Romania – for 2007)

each country, we have calculated the proportion of firms in each size group offering a financial participation scheme. In general, it seems that both forms of employee participation are more prevalent in large and very large companies.

Figure 6.2 shows the data for ESO. Although the highest incidence is generally in the largest firms, we see notable exceptions in Croatia, Denmark, Greece, Hungary, the Czech Republic and Turkey, where the highest percentages of firms with ESO are found among large (but not the largest) firms, and in Bulgaria, where the medium-sized firms have the highest incidence of ESO. The situation was similar in 1999.

Figure 6.3 shows the data for profit-sharing. There is a much more even distribution across size classes here than for ESO, although again we see a prevalence (albeit a mild one) of the largest size firms. This situation appears to have changed little between 1999 and 2005.

In Figures 6.4 and 6.5 we present a sectoral breakdown of financial participation schemes, classifying firms into one of three main sectors: primary (agriculture and extractive industries), secondary (manufacturing) and tertiary (services). For 2005, we see a high average rate

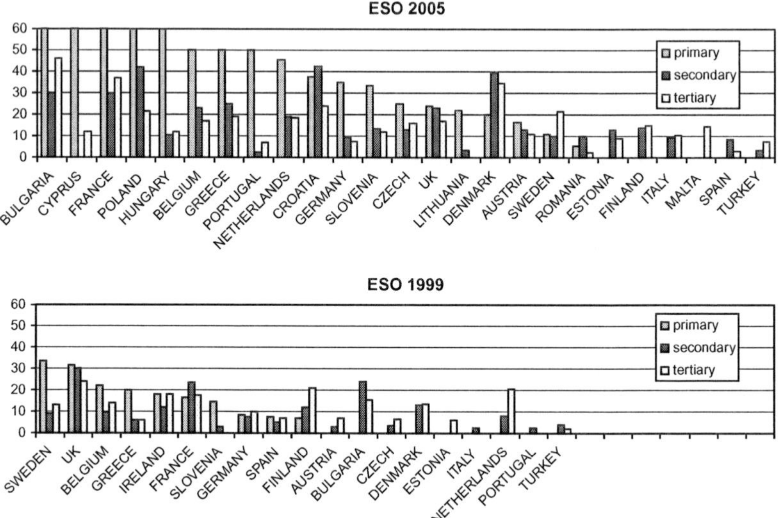



*Figure 6.4*  Percentage of firms in each sector offering employee share ownership schemes, 1999 and 2005.

*Source:* CRANET data and own survey (Croatia, Lithuania, Malta, Poland, Portugal, Romania – for 2007)

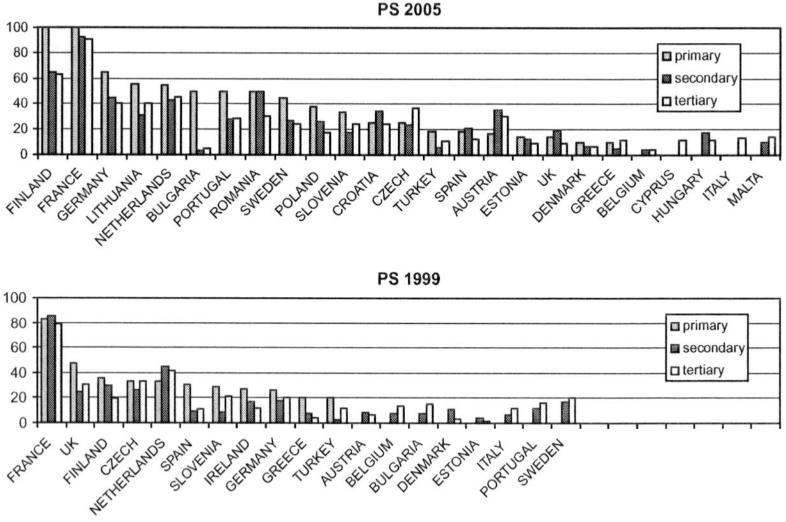



*Figure 6.5*  Percentage of firms in each sector offering profit-sharing schemes, 1999 and 2005.

*Source:* CRANET data and own survey (Croatia, Lithuania, Malta, Poland, Portugal, Romania – for 2007)

of incidence of both ESO and profit-sharing in the primary sector. However, this is mostly likely a statistical artefact due to the very small percentage of firms in the sample from that sector[13], and we see no such pattern for the 1999 data. The interesting differences would be between the manufacturing (secondary) and service (tertiary) sectors, in which the vast bulk of the workforce in a modern economy is found.

For ESO plans, based on the information contained in Figure 6.4, there is little differentiation between these two sectors (manufacturing and services) overall. In Poland and Croatia (countries for which we lack data for 1999), we see significantly more ESO plans in the secondary sector, whereas there is significantly more ESO plans in the tertiary sector in Bulgaria and Sweden[14]. In others, the tertiary and secondary sectors are close, with one of the two slightly higher than other, or virtually identical. In 1999, we see strong prevalence of ESO schemes in the secondary sector in France and Bulgaria, and strong prevalence in the tertiary sector in the Netherlands, Finland, Austria and Ireland. It is, however, difficult to say whether the changes between 1999 and 2005 reflect only changes in the sample or broader trends (especially given the generally much lower rates of incidence in 1999). It is perhaps worth noting the significant drops in the share of firms offering ESO schemes in all sectors in the UK (which can also be seen in Figure 6.1).

Figure 6.5 contains information on profit-sharing. Again, we generally observe the prevalence of profit-sharing schemes in primary sector firms. The number of countries with higher incidence in the secondary than the tertiary sector is roughly equal to that in which the situation is reversed. This was also largely the case in 1999, when overall incidence was lower across the board.

### 6.2.3   Percentage of employees covered[15]

Next, we consider the share of employees in the sample covered by ESO and profit-sharing plans. This is an indicator of the extent to which broad-based employee financial participation plans have been adopted in each country. We present the data on this indicator in Figure 6.6.

Looking at employee share ownership, we see that, as with the rise in the number of companies offering ESO plans, the coverage of employees by these plans is also growing in a large majority of countries (the weighted country average grew from 15 to 26 per cent between 1999 and 2005). The three leaders (with employee coverage averaging over 50 per cent) are the UK, France and Poland. There is a fairly long tail of low-ranked countries (with coverage averaging fewer than 10 per cent). In ascending order starting from lowest, these are: Spain, Lithuania, Hungary, Italy, the Czech Republic, Turkey, Estonia, Slovenia

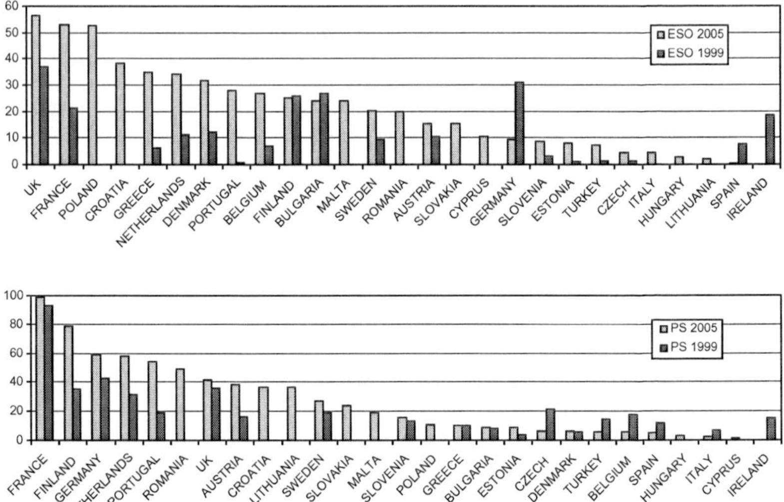


*Figure 6.6*   Proportion of employees covered by employee share ownership and profit-sharing schemes, 1999 and 2005 (in per cent).
*Source:* CRANET data and own survey (Croatia, Lithuania, Malta, Poland, Portugal, Romania – for 2007)

and Germany. Again, Slovenia's position here is surprising, given its privatisation history. It is also interesting to note that Portuguese companies seldom offer a plan, but those that do are large, with many employees (see Figure 6.2).

Turning to profit-sharing, we see growth, albeit slower and from a higher starting point (the weighted average for all countries rose from 30 to 37 per cent between 1999 and 2005). Here again we have a much wider range, from 100 per cent in France to under 1 per cent in Cyprus, and again we have a long tail of low-ranked countries. After France, other leading countries (with over 50 per cent) are (in descending order): Finland, Germany, the Netherlands and Portugal (Romania is just under 50 per cent).

### 6.2.4   Percentage of large (listed) firms with employee share plans

The EFES data cover Switzerland and Norway in addition to the 27 EU Member States; however, we ignore the Swiss and Norwegian figures in our discussion. The data on ESO in those companies presented in Figure 6.7 were gathered in 2007. On the basis of the data contained

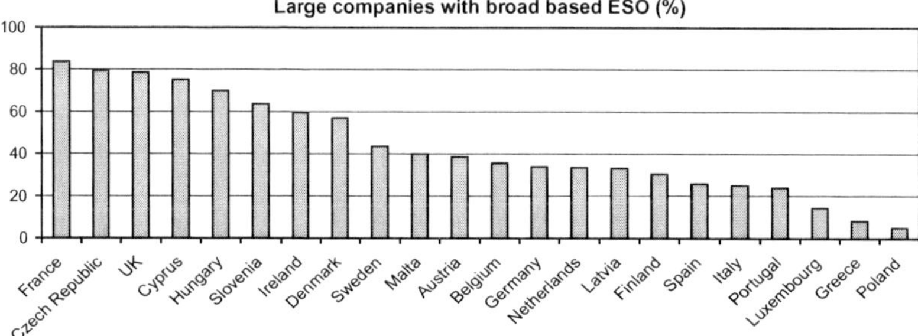


*Figure 6.7* Proportion of large EU companies with broad-based ESO schemes, 2007 (in per cent).
*Source:* EFES

therein, we arrive at a quite up-to-date picture of the actual incidence of broad-based ESO schemes in the largest European companies, which we can contrast with the picture emerging from the CRANET survey. (Note that five countries – Bulgaria, Estonia, Lithuania, Romania and Slovakia – have values of 0 per cent and are therefore not included in the figure.)

Although it is not surprising to find France, the UK and Ireland with high rates of incidence of broad-based ESO plans among large companies, the presence of the Czech Republic (represented by 34 companies in the sample), Cyprus (only four companies) and Hungary (20 companies) among the group of leaders is quite surprising. Denmark ranks high, which is consistent with the CRANET data, and so does Slovenia, which is what we expected, but did not find in the CRANET data. Poland and Bulgaria, which were leaders in the CRANET data, are in the rear here. (If the CRANET and mini-survey data for these countries are reasonably representative, this would indicate that ESO plans are concentrated in smaller and mid-sized companies in those countries, which would be quite unusual, although perhaps consistent with the Polish privatisation programme's emphasis on restricting management-employee buyouts to SMEs.) However, the relatively low positions of Romania and the Iberian and Baltic countries in the CRANET data are replicated here and thus seem to provide quite strong corroboration for the CRANET picture of those countries. The high ranking of Hungary and the Czech Republic here and their mid-level ranking in the CRANET data seem to indicate that something is happening with the dissemination of employee ownership in those two countries which has thus far eluded the attention of researchers, probably because of the low level of employee participation in the privatisation programmes of those countries. It would seem that, contrary to the experience of several other transition countries, the evolution of post-privatisation ownership structure has brought more, rather than less, employee ownership to those countries (possibly because of the policies of foreign investors).

## 6.3   Take-up rate of financial participation schemes in the workforce

### 6.3.1   Percentage of employees participating in FP schemes

The data from the EWCS survey presented in Figure 6.8 give us a picture of the actual extent of employee financial participation in the population of employed persons, as this is a survey of individuals rather than firms. As in the case of CRANET, it covers both ESO and profit-sharing schemes as well as the level of participation at two points in time (2000/01 and 2005), allowing us to draw some conclusions about the rate of diffusion of these schemes in recent years.[16]

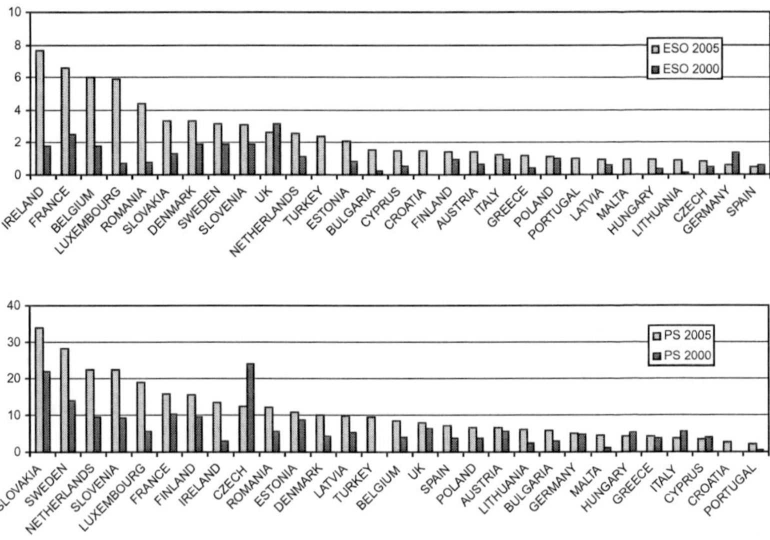


*Figure 6.8*   Proportion of employees involved in employee share ownership and profit-sharing schemes, 2000–5 (in per cent).
*Source:* EWCS

For ESO schemes, as in the case of the CRANET, we see growth in almost all countries (the weighted average for all countries rose from 1.3 per cent to 2.4 per cent). The exceptions were the UK, Germany and Spain (the UK and Spain saw declines in both the CRANET and EWCS surveys). The top countries (with participation rates over 5 per cent) were Ireland, France, Belgium and Luxembourg (France is the only one of these in both the CRANET and EWCS top country lists, although Ireland also does well in the EFES survey). The lowest-ranked countries (with participation rates under 1 per cent), in ascending order, were Spain, Germany, the Czech Republic, Lithuania, Hungary, Malta and Latvia (Spain and Lithuania ranked similarly low in both surveys; when we note that Portugal also has just over 1 per cent, we see these findings to be consistent with the earlier finding of a low incidence of ESO in the Baltic and Iberian countries[17]). We see strongly contrasting figures for Poland, which ranks highest in the mini-survey data and relatively low in the EWCS survey (and very low in the EFES survey).

Turning to profit-sharing schemes, again as in CRANET, we see a much higher incidence than in the case of ESO (for ESO, the 2005 weighted average for all countries was 2.4 per cent, for profit-sharing 9.1, and the range for ESO was 0.5–7.7, whereas for profit-sharing it was 2.1–33.9). As in CRANET, we see growth in almost all countries (the weighted average rose from 5.5 per cent to 9.1 per cent). The exceptions were the Czech Republic, Italy, Hungary and Cyprus (the Czech Republic and Italy saw declines in both CRANET and EWCS). The top countries (with participation rates of over 10 per cent), in descending order, were Slovakia, Sweden, the Netherlands, Slovenia, Luxembourg, France, Finland, Ireland, the Czech Republic, Romania, Estonia and Denmark (with France, the Netherlands, Finland and Romania ranking high in both the CRANET and EWCS surveys). The lowest-ranked countries (with participation rates under 5 per cent), in ascending order, were Portugal, Croatia, Cyprus, Italy, Greece, Hungary, Malta and Germany (Turkey, Cyprus, Greece and Italy ranked low in both CRANET and EWCS). The high ranking of Slovakia is very surprising, and we suspect that this may be due to the misunderstandings about the nature of profit-sharing schemes and the mistaken treatment of some bonuses as profit-sharing.

We also see high rates of ESO and profit-sharing for two countries for which recent CRANET data were not available: Luxembourg and Ireland. It must be remembered that the EWCS data do not distinguish broad and narrow schemes and, therefore, the high take-up rate of any scheme may only reflect the presence of share-based option schemes for management (which is likely to be the case in Luxembourg).

### 6.3.2   Percentage of employees participating in profit-sharing schemes with pre-defined formulas on a regular, ongoing basis

To refine our picture of profit-sharing, we wish to distinguish profit-sharing schemes run according to pre-defined formulas and providing payments to employees on a regular, ongoing basis from those that are dependent on the discretion of employees' superiors and thus do not provide any ex-ante incentives to employees to improve their performance at work. To do this, we present EWCS data for the year 2005 in Figure 6.9, showing the depth of profit-sharing schemes (that is, the percentage of the workforce participating in such schemes), of those that are run according to pre-defined formulas, and of those under which payments occur on a regular, ongoing basis. In all cases we see that profit-sharing schemes operating with high-powered incentives cover a smaller proportion of employees than those covered by schemes referred to (possibly incorrectly, namely Slovakia and Czech Republic) as profit-sharing. Using a strict definition of profit-sharing, we see that in the best cases approximately 20 per cent of the workforce is covered. Regardless of which of the three categories is used to rank the countries, there is little difference in the rankings.

The leading countries, independent of the category used to rank them, clearly include Sweden, the Netherlands, Finland, Luxembourg Slovakia, France, Ireland and Slovenia. At the rear are, equally as clearly, Croatia, Portugal, Hungary, Cyprus, Italy, Bulgaria, Greece and Lithuania. Given the similarity of results for more precisely defined types of profit-sharing and the general results presented in section 6.2.1, the comparison with the results from the CRANET survey and our mini-survey here is basically the same as it was there.

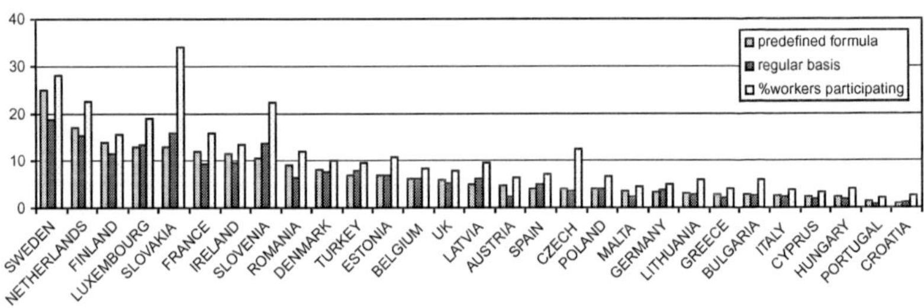



*Figure 6.9*   Profit-sharing in 2005: A closer look.
*Source:* EWCS

### 6.3.3   Percentage of employees holding shares in largest (listed) firms

Returning to the EFES survey of large European companies, we now consider the question of take-up of ESO schemes by employees: that is, how many employees have actually become owners as a result of the schemes. Figure 6.10 provides us with information on employee owners as a percentage of the total number of employees in the companies surveyed by EFES. For the entire sample, 26.17 per cent of the total workforce is actually participating in ESO plans (15.05 per cent for the 12 new EU Member States). We can, to some extent, compare this with the CRANET-based information on ESO coverage in Figure 6.2, although take-up is not the same thing as coverage.

Again, as in Figure 6.4, France leads, and Hungary and the UK also rank very highly (the leading positions of France and the UK are consistent with the CRANET information presented in Figure 6.6, though Hungary's high position here is in stark contrast to its low position there). Given the small number of Maltese and Luxembourg companies in the sample (five and seven respectively), the leading positions those two countries have here perhaps cannot be considered as representative (although the high ranking of Luxembourg is consistent with the EWCS survey results). Czech companies do not do as well for take-up as they do in offering schemes, and rank among the last countries here. In Denmark we see a similar discrepancy, though not as large as that in the Czech Republic (in Denmark's case this may be due to the rapid diffusion of ESO plans in very recent times, as noted in section 6.2.1: take-up may not have caught up with the rate of introduction of schemes). Not surprisingly, we again see Romania and the Baltic and Iberian countries in the rear (although Romania was mid-ranked in Figure 6.6).

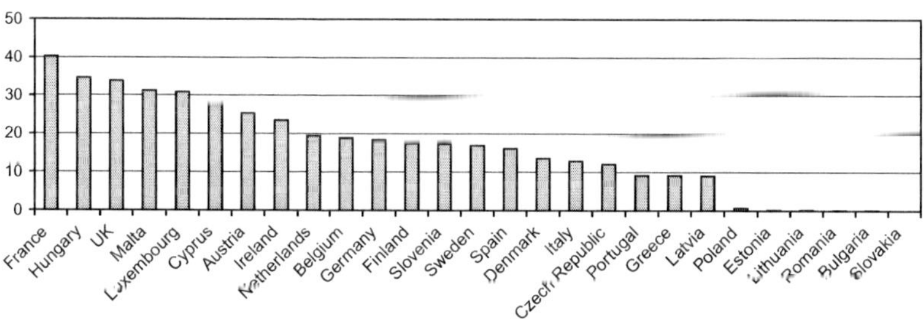


*Figure 6.10*   Proportion of employees participating in ESO schemes in large EU companies, 2007.
*Source:* EFES

## 6.4  Conclusions

Regardless of the data source used, the evidence presented here shows conclusively that Europe has seen extensive growth of employee financial participation in recent years. This is true for both profit-sharing and employee share ownership, although profit-sharing is more widespread than employee ownership (although Figure 6.9 suggests that the difference between the two may diminish or even disappear if we adopt a very strict definition of profit-sharing). The percentage of companies with financial participation schemes of various forms in operation is growing steadily almost everywhere in the European Union, and the percentage of company employees covered by, and taking up, these schemes is also increasing. On the other hand, on the basis of both company surveys (like those of CRANET and EFES) and surveys of individuals in the workforce (like the EWCS survey), it seems that financial participation has extended to a significant proportion of the working population in only a handful of countries. It is therefore clear that, although much has been accomplished, much remains to be done.

There are two other broad conclusions (leaving aside the recent members and candidate countries). First, the largest companies are more likely to offer their employees any financial participation scheme. And second, financial participation schemes are offered to, and have been taken up, on a larger scale by employees in the more developed EU countries – the UK, France, Scandinavian countries – and less so by the less developed members (Greece and Portugal). This implies that employers' recognition of the benefits of employee financial participation grows as economic development progresses and a country's GDP per capita rises.

Related to the above, the depth of financial participation schemes in most of the new members and candidate countries with a socialist past (the transition countries) is generally low. The ESO schemes, rooted in the privatisation programmes, have survived in some counties like Poland but gradually weakened in other countries in the process of secondary privatisation.

There are some discrepancies between data sources for certain countries; however, the overall picture is quite clear. Although for most individual countries it would be rather risky to make definitive assertions about the degree of advancement of dissemination of financial participation schemes on the basis of the data we have examined, we can identify what seem to be some regional trends. For example, we can state with a great deal of confidence that a few regions seem to be much less advanced in the dissemination of financial participation schemes than others, notably the Iberian Peninsula, the Baltic States, and the south-eastern corner of Europe (including Greece, Turkey and Cyprus). On the other hand, the data examined here seem to indicate that a West–East divide (that is, significant differences between the old EU-15 Member States on the one hand, and at least some of the ten post-communist states that have joined the EU since 2004) is less significant than one might have anticipated, or perhaps non-existent. There seems to be much more variation within those two groups than between them.

## Notes

1. We are grateful to Edvard Orlic, our research assistant, for his diligent and dedicated work.
2. EWCS: European Working Conditions Survey and Eiro Comparative Study on Financial Participation in the New Member States (both European Foundation for the Improvement of Working and Living Conditions); CRANET E: Cranfield Survey on International HRM (Cranfield School of Management); EFES: Employee Share Top 100 (European Federation of Employee Ownership).
3. These studies are usually concerned with individual or a small number of countries and use different methodologies in pursuing their objectives.
4. The 2000 Survey covered companies with 100 or more employees. The unit of investigation in CRANET is an 'organisation' or a 'business unit'. Although this may include a self-contained subsidiary of a larger company, in general it coincides with the boundaries of 'companies'. For the sake of simplicity, therefore, we refer to them as companies.
5. The number of companies in the countries of interest to this study was 5,214.
6. For more detailed information on the CRANET Survey, see CRANET (2005) and Pendleton et al. (2001).
7. Another survey is currently underway in Ireland (expected to produce comparable information). The mini-survey conducted in Latvia showed no financial participation scheme in any of 104 companies in the sample. Given the information from other sources (such as EWCS and various research papers), we believe this outcome is unrealistic, caused by a biased sample. As there was no time to repeat the exercise with a random sample, Latvia has been excluded from some of the tables. Luxembourg has been excluded from the benchmarking exercise altogether. Ireland was of course included in the 1999 CRANET.
8. The planned number of firms in each of these counties was 100 in larger and 50 in smaller counties, randomly selected. In practice, the total number of observations in these countries was 533 – in Malta, in particular, the number of firms interviewed was 17 (and for this reason, the information on Malta should be treated with caution). Furthermore, given that the number of large firms in some of these countries (Latvia, Lithuania, Malta, in particular) was small, firms with fewer than 200 employees were also included in the sample.

9. Of course, given that respondents either 'did not know' or 'refused to answer' some of the questions in the survey, the effective response rate was lower.
10. However, given that the surveys identify the sector of activity of the respondents, the gap between the 2000 and 2001 surveys has been reduced by the elimination of those respondents working in 'public services'.
11. COM (2002) 364 Final, 5 July 2002, pp. 3, 10.
12. The 2008 European Establishment Survey of the European Foundation for the Improvement of Working and Living Conditions is planned to include questions that could allow an assessment of this indicator.
13. If, for example, only two firms in a given country sample are agricultural and one is a dairy co-operative, we would have a 50 per cent rate for the primary sector.
14. This appears to be the case for Cyprus as well, but only because there are no secondary-sector companies in the Cypriot sample.
15. The questionnaire contains questions on the proportion of different categories of employees (managers, professionals, administrative and manual) to whom financial participation plans are offered and on the share of these different categories in the total workforce of the company. This allows us to calculate the number of employees in each company to whom financial participation plans are offered (and their share in the total number of employees in the sample for each country).
16. The earlier survey was done in two stages: EU-15 in 2000, and accession and other countries in 2001.
17. Although Estonia does better here than in the CRANET results.

# 7
# Country Profiles

*Jens Lowitzsch, Natalia Spitsa and Stefan Hanisch*

For each of the 29 countries (I–XXIX):
Evolution and diffusion of FP schemes.
General attitude (Social partners' attitudes and current government policy).
Legal and fiscal framework.
Share ownership.
Profit-Sharing.
Participation in decision making.

## I Belgium

Some forms of employee financial participation began to emerge at the end of the nineteenth century; the number of plans, however, remained very small, especially between 1945 and 1990. The Belgian government introduced its first incentives for employee share ownership in King's Arrest 'Monory-De Clerq' on 9 March 1982. These provisions were primarily intended to support the stock exchange in the wake of a financial crisis; among them was employee share ownership, submitted in a proposal by the Liberal Party. Still applicable, these provisions have proved efficient. Additional incentives were introduced in 1991 by the Law on Equity Capital Incentives. The Law on Incentives for Stock Options of 26 March 1999 and the Law on Promotion of Employee Financial Participation of 22 May 2001 followed. These last two laws introduced tax incentives for profit-sharing and employee share ownership schemes; however, the number of plans continues to be relatively small.[1] Approximately 10 per cent of large, primarily multinational companies in the financial sector had employee share ownership plans in 1999.[2] Stock option plans have become relatively widespread. More than 40 per cent of enterprises with more than 50 employees offered stock option plans in 2002.[3] Many of these, however, are limited to management.

## General attitude

Especially since the end of the 1990s, the government has supported employee financial participation, regarding it as a pillar of the social security system. However, legislative proposals have been introduced into Parliament since the beginning of the 1970s. These were mainly sponsored by the Liberal Party, although until 1999 the Socialist Party blocked all such proposals. At the end of the 1990s, the government announced a new employee financial participation promotion campaign intended to spread financial participation to 25 per cent of all employees. The employers' associations (for example, Federation of the Belgian Enterprises, National Federation of Small Firms and Traders) had given support to employee financial participation even earlier, seeking to influence the government through campaigns in the mass media which were obviously successful. The employers' associations, however, mainly favour financial participation only for executives and higher management. The trade unions (especially the largest, the Christian Unions – CSC/ACV, and the Socialist Unions – FGTB/ABVV) generally oppose any form of employee financial participation on the grounds that employees are powerless to influence competitiveness or profitability. To a certain extent, they do support employee share ownership plans not financed from the wages or salaries of employees.

## Legal and fiscal framework

The Law on Promotion of Employee Participation of 22 May 2001 regulates the procedure for establishing employee financial participation plans, especially cash-based and share-based profit-sharing. Terms and conditions prescribed by law (for example, rules for calculating length of employment, duration, mandatory or non-mandatory participation of employees, and blocking period) must be introduced by a collective agreement or, in companies without union representation, by a collective agreement or an act of accession.[4] For group-level plans, it is sufficient that the company which first proposed the plan within the group concludes the collective agreement and the other companies consult with their employee representatives. Moreover, the bodies representing employees must be informed of how the plan relates to the company's employment development and employment policies before the plan is introduced. Plans must include all employees, with the possible exception of employees with less than one year of service; different classes of employees may be treated differently under the plan if this is the industry-wide collective agreement or a Royal Decree. Plans are generally voluntary, unless the collective agreement or the act of accession provide otherwise. The size of the plan is limited by a double ceiling: the total annual amount of transfers under the plan cannot exceed 10 per cent of the payroll and 20 per cent of the annual profit after taxes.

*Share ownership*

Companies are allowed to acquire own shares up to 20 per cent of the equity capital for distribution among their own employees without decision of the general assembly (Article 620 paragraph 1 (2), 609 paragraph 1 (3) Law on companies (CL)). Shares acquired in this manner are not transferable for the period of five years (Article 609 paragraph 1 (4) CL). Furthermore, Article 329 paragraph 2 (1) CL allows companies to advance funds, make loans and provide security, with a view to acquisition of the company's shares by employees of the company within the limits of the value of distributable reserves, unless the company's net assets do not fall below the level of issued share capital. A discount is limited to 20 per cent of the share price (Article 609 paragraph 1 (3) CL.

Employees may be granted shares, share certificates or stock options under an employee share ownership plan. If the shares are held for two to five years, the special tax of 15 per cent on the benefit (if shares are transferred free or at a discount) applies. The blocking period terminates earlier if the employee is dismissed, resigns for serious cause, retires or dies, or if the plan shares are publicly offered, if control of the company has been changed by the transaction, or if the employee is transferred to a non-affiliated company under the collective agreement 32bis. Shares sold during the blocking period are subject to an additional punitive tax of 23.29 per cent. Stock option plans are governed by a special law.

*Share ownership plans.* If restricted stock is granted free, the benefit can be taxed at grant or, if ownership is transferred later,[3] at vesting. The tax base is the market value of publicly traded stock. If ownership is transferred later, the tax base is reduced to the market value less 20/120 (that is, 16.7 per cent) to compensate for market risk. On common stock granted free or at a discount, the taxable benefit corresponds to the fair market value of quoted shares or so-called net asset value[6] of non-quoted shares. For quoted shares the tax base can be reduced to 100/120 (that is, 83.33 per cent) under certain conditions.[7] The employer company can deduct the discount from the tax base of the corporate income tax if the stock is purchased and sold by a foreign company which charges the discount back to a Belgian company. If a Belgian company purchases and sells the stock, the deduction is subject to debate: if the discount is regarded as capital loss, it is not deductible; however, if it is regarded as personnel costs, it can be deductible. However, it is probable that the tax authorities will generally favour the more restrictive option.

*Stock option plans.* Stock option plans to which tax incentives apply are governed by the Law on Incentives for Stock Options of 26 May 1999. This law applies to stock options granted as of 1 January 1999. Stock options are taxed at grant. If the employee does not notify the tax authority within 60 days after grant, the option is considered refused.[8] Because employee stock options are usually not tradable, the tax base is generally a lump sum value equal to 15 per cent of the underlying stock value at grant plus 1 per cent for each year or part of the year beyond the initial five years from grant to expiration. The tax base can be reduced by half (that is, to 7.5 per cent plus 0.5 per cent for each year or part of the year) if options cannot be exercised until three years from the date of issue, the exercise period does not extend beyond the tenth year following the year of issue, the options are transferable only upon death of the employee, the underlying shares are of the employer company, its parent or grandparent company, no guarantee was issued by the employer company or an affiliated company against fall in value of the underlying share after its grant, and the strike price was determined at the time of offer. No compulsory social security contributions are to be paid on the lump sum benefit. The employer company can deduct the difference between the market value of the underlying stock and the exercise price of the option if the employee obtains shares from another company upon exercise and the costs are charged back to the Belgian company. Stock option plans and the prospectus must be approved by the Bank and Finance Commission before the introduction.

### Profit-sharing

Profit-sharing plans are usually cash-based. For small enterprises, defined in the Company Code, the so-called investments savings plan was introduced by the Law on Promotion of Employee Participation of 22 May 2001. Under these, an employee immediately loans their share of the annual profit to the company; the loan must be repaid within two to five years with interest. Tax incentives and pre-conditions for interruption of the blocking period for these plans are the same as for share ownership plans. All profit-sharing plans are subject to special tax rates on the attributed profit-share minus the general rate of the social security contribution: 15 per cent for investment savings plans and 25 per cent for other profit-sharing plans. The employer company cannot deduct the profit attributed to employees from its corporate income tax base.

*Participation in decision making*

Participation in decision making has no connection with financial participation; financial participation plans are specifically forbidden to extend existing decision making rights. However, the plan can only be introduced when a collective agreement or an act of accession and consultation with employees' representatives is prescribed for the remaining part of the plan so that terms and conditions are negotiated with employees' representatives; thus some elements of participation in decision making may be included in the financial participation plan.

## II   Bulgaria

The development of PEPPER schemes in Bulgaria has been influenced by both the historical commitment to a strong co-operative movement[9] and the special circumstances accompanying the transition to a market economy. The main form of employee financial participation became employee share ownership, with the voucher system being the preferred privatisation method at the beginning of transition in 1992–4. The proportion of enterprises privatised this way was low, about 4–5 per cent, with the management-employee buyout (MEBO) method gaining support from 1994 until 2000.[10] Close to half of the enterprises were privatised by insiders, but employee ownership has decreased over time. Although no data on the sales of shares by employees after privatisation are available, it can be fairly estimated that about 10 per cent of enterprises privatised by MEBO may still be under majority employee ownership. According to the Centre for Mass Privatisation, at the close of mass privatisation in 1998, shares were distributed as follows: 40.8 per cent state property; 6.4 per cent employees; 12.9 per cent individual shareholders, and 39.9 per cent privatisation funds. Later, however, these employees' shares were transferred to managers and outside owners. Profit sharing has developed only very recently, as the private sector has begun to stabilise and human capital has become a major factor in company success.

### General attitude

Three trade union organisations are recognised at the national level: the Confederation of Independent Trade Unions in Bulgaria (CITUB), the

Confederation of Labour Podkrepa, and Promiana. From early transition on, CITUB has been in favour of developing financial participation; its leader, Kastriot Petkov, has written books on the subject, including concrete proposals on helping workers get more involved in the capital, profits and decisions of their company. The transition period brought about a significant change in the power relationship between social partners. In the beginning, trade unions dominated the social dialogue. The end of the privatisation process, however, saw union power and influence drastically decrease. In recent years, the employers' associations have grown more powerful than trade unions. Until 2005, employers were represented by six national associations, which currently do not consider employee financial participation an important issue in either policy or practice.

The 39th Bulgarian Parliament, which vested power in the national government under Prime Minister Simeon Sakskoburggotski (2001–5), did show interest in questions relating to financial and decision making participation of employees. Under the guidance of Prof. Dr Ognyan Gerdzhikov, then President of Parliament, a comparative legal survey on national solutions within the European Union and some adjacent states was conducted. The survey, focussing on joint-stock companies, identified several national regulatory mechanisms and possibly contributed to the popularity of the ideas behind them. However, the survey resulted in no relevant act of law. The new government (as of 2005), under Prime Minister Sergey Stanishev, is sceptical of financial participation. Further, this issue has not been on the political agenda of Parliament, nor has any political party currently addressed it.

**Legal and fiscal framework**

Although no specific legal regulation applies to any PEPPER scheme, the legal framework provides neither incentives nor restrictions for employee financial participation.

*Share ownership*

*Privatisation (1992, 1997, abolished in 2002).* Under the Law on the Reorganisation and Privatisation of State and Municipal Enterprises of 7 May 1992 (LRP), employees with Bulgarian citizenship and permanent residency in Bulgaria before 2002 were entitled to preferential (free or discount) share acquisition. In voucher (mass) privatisation, each eligible individual could obtain free shares, with the total value of free shares distributed not exceeding 10 per cent of the nominal stock of the target entity. This privilege was abolished in 1998 when voucher privatisation was virtually abandoned. Under the stock-sales method, eligible individuals were entitled to acquire up to 20 per cent of the nominal stock at 50 per cent of the assessed price. This privilege was abolished in January 2002. The share acquisition itself had no tax relevance, subsequently, dividends received were subject to the general rule on dividend taxation. Furthermore, the LRP regulated the so-called MEBO company (rabotničesko-medidžǎrsko družestvo), a legal entity established by a minimum of 20–30 per cent of an enterprises employees for the sole purpose of participating in the privatisation process. A general incentive for a MEBO company was the permission to maintain stock of only 10 per cent of the minimum stock generally required for stock corporations or limited liability companies and the VAT exemption of the privatisation deal. Further incentives subject to specific conditions were a 100 per cent profit tax exemption for three years after privatisation and 50 per cent for the following two years, payment privileges, and immediate transfer of property in the case of enterprises of minor value. Thus, a MEBO company had significant advantages, especially an acquisition price about 36 per cent less than for other buyers, until these were abolished in March 2000.[11]

The effective Law on Privatisation and Post-Privatisation Control of 19 March 2002 (Article 7) states as a general principle of Privatisation Law the equality of privatisation candidates. The law gives no privileges based on the status of applicants. In particular, there are no provisions favouring employees. Current privatisation legislation negates the former LRP, which provided several preferential measures to facilitate employee participation. These were intended to narrow the social gap between capital owners and the labour force – a gap that the liberalisation of the Bulgarian economy opened during the post-communist era.

*Private companies.* The Commercial Law (CL) and company law in general contain no specific regulations pertaining to employee share ownership. In the absence of statutory regulation, therefore, certain general provisions will be examined here. There are no general squeeze-out or sell-out rules for the minority shareholders of a joint-stock company. However, the Law on Public Offers of Securities obliges a shareholder who has acquired 50 per cent of the stock of a public joint-stock company and wishes to keep this majority position to make an economically justifiable public offer to acquire the shares of the remaining shareholders (Article 149). The majority shareholder does not have the right to vote in the general assembly before that offer. This public offer is the only legitimate means of capital concentration available to a majority shareholder. Upon its expiration, he may acquire an additional

3 per cent of the stock per year. Also, where a shareholder of a limited liability company or a joint-stock company has voted against a mergers and acquisitions deal (Article 263c CL) or a joint-venture project (Article 126e Law on Public Offers of Securities), they have the right to have their shares bought by the company.

### Profit-sharing

Bulgarian employers do not usually link employee bonuses to the company's financial success. Although not forbidden, employers generally derive no benefits from such schemes under Bulgarian tax law. However, under Bulgarian law it is possible to offer profit-sharing contracts on an individual basis.[12] These may be cash-based or share-based.

### Participation in decision making

In most cases, employee ownership did not lead to participation in management. Currently, most employees are minority shareholders without notable influence. The rights of employees to participate in decision making under the Labour Code are extremely limited and have no significant influence on management. Although the workers' meeting composed of all employees of a given business once accounted for more than 20 sections[13] of the socialist version of the Labour Code, only two relevant provisions are currently in force. These empower the workers' meeting to choose between two or more drafts of a collective bargaining agreement when the trade union organisations at the enterprise level cannot agree on a single version (Article 51a paragraph 3 Labour Code). Also, the workers' meeting can decide the disposition of the company's social fund (Article 293 paragraph 1 Labour Code). The employer, however, is not obliged to establish such a fund. The CL provides that an employees' representative must be chosen in corporations[14] employing more than 50 persons. This representative must be given an advisory vote at the shareholders' meeting. The company is under no obligation to recognise more than one representative as its work force grows. Also, the number of employees has no effect on the form or the force of employee representation. Thus the CL establishes a model friendly to the employer.

## III   Croatia

Despite the fact that the economic and political system of Croatia, while a part of the former Yugoslavia, was based on employee participation for more than 40 years, its role today is relatively minor. Employee stock ownership created in the early stages of privatisation is steadily diminishing; the position of employees, previously strong, has weakened. By 1995, small shareholders owned (bought or subscribed to) about 20 per cent of the nominal value of the enterprises privatised during this first stage. During the second (1995–9) and third (1999–2002) stages of privatisation, support for employee participation ceased and employee ownership began to decline, falling to only 12 per cent in 1998; the decline continues up to the present moment, and there is little public support for measures that would reverse it. ESOP models, defined as any organised programme involving large numbers of employees as shareholders in the employer firm, is almost the only form of employee financial participation to be developed and to gain momentum after privatisation; still, ESOPs are rare and lack broad support. In a study from late 2003, 'organized programmes of larger involvement of employees in the enterprise ownership' were found in 9.4 per cent of enterprises (52 out of the 552 total surveyed).[15] Employees owned 10 per cent of shares in 68 per cent of enterprises reporting; in only 5 per cent of firms did employees own more than 90 per cent. Employees held a majority share (more than 50 per cent) in 12 per cent of enterprises.[16] Profit-sharing is rare; there is no mention of it in legislation, legal documents or collective agreements.

## General attitude

Trade unions had no part in the design of privatisation models, nor did they promote a stronger position for employees.[17] Not until the first two stages of privatisation had been completed did some unions and union leaders begin to advocate employee ownership as a means of privatising remaining state-owned assets, as well as for restructuring distressed enterprises, and to propose models for doing this. Employees are represented by numerous trade unions organised at different levels for various purposes. Employers, represented by the Croatian Association of Employers, have a stronger position in most issues involving the interests of employers and employees. The fact that employers are represented by a single organisation and employees by many only partly explains this disparity in power. On the issue of employee financial participation, employers and their organisation remain publicly non-committed, neither positively in favour nor adamantly opposed.

Croatian governments did not support employee privatisation beyond the first stage. Although this policy was entirely consistent with the ideological orientation of the right-wing governments in power during the first decade of transition, it is less easy to explain why the Social

Democratic governments, in office from 2000–4, made virtually no changes in the area of employee participation. Nor has the present government shown any serious intention of introducing measures to promote, or at least to regulate, employee financial participation. Some business spokesmen, representing firms that already have employee ownership in some form, have publicly advocated greater employee participation in the privatisation of the remaining state shares. They have also requested clearer regulation and support of existing schemes. Although these requests are currently being discussed, definitive feedback by either the government or political parties is still pending.

## Legal and fiscal framework

Employee financial participation is currently not explicitly regulated. Privatisation legislation in the past, however, has supported employee share ownership. Various schemes of financial participation, including profit-sharing and ESOPs,[18] occur in individual firms despite the absence of state regulation. Amendments to the Privatisation Law, now being drafted, are expected to bring ESOPs into the regulatory fold.

### *Share ownership*

*Privatisation (1991, 1996).* The Croatian Law on the Transformation of Enterprises Under Social Ownership 1991 (Transformation Law) gave employees, including managers and former employees, the right to buy shares at a discount proportional to their years of employment, starting at 20 per cent and adding 1 per cent for every working year up to a maximum of 60 per cent. Employees who paid for their shares in cash were given an additional discount of 10 per cent. Payment could also be made in instalments spread over five (later prolonged to 20) years. After having paid 5 per cent of the total price, the employee received all their discounted shares outright. Amendments to this Law in 1993 entitled employees to buy no more than 50 per cent of total shares with a value not to exceed one million EUR. One-third of the remaining shares were transferred to state pension funds and two-thirds to the state Privatisation Fund to be publicly tendered at market value.

After most enterprises had been privatised in 1996, a new act, the Privatisation Law, was adopted, which provided no special provisions or preferential conditions to employees.[19] The Transformation Law, however, was not repealed, and after 1996 some enterprises were still using it. In companies where small shareholders owned a significant amount of stock, so-called small shareholder associations were established. Although these did not take the form of registered associations and their membership was unstable, they did gain some influence in some enterprises because of a close relationship with trade unions.

Since privatisation was partly reversed in 1999, many shares of state enterprises still remain to be privatised. After the bankruptcy of 22.2 per cent of all privatised firms, the remaining assets were transferred back to the state Privatisation Fund. By 1999, 379,030 out of 641,152 sales contracts of employees who were buying discounted shares in instalments were in default. Recognising that the objectives of privatisation had not been achieved, a new law, the Law on Revision and Transformation and Privatisation, went into effect on 16 May 2005. The privatisation of 1556 enterprises was investigated under this law; procedural irregularities were discovered in all but 75.

*Private companies (2003).* According to Article 233 paragraph 2 of the new Company Law from 2003 (CL), a company can issue special employee stock with a value not exceeding 10 per cent of registered capital. Employee shares are non-voting until fully paid for. Furthermore, Article 313 CL stipulates a 'conditional capital increase' to fulfil the employee acquisition right. To facilitate employee acquisition, Article 234 CL exempts the company from the general prohibition against borrowing in order to acquire its own stock. This exemption is granted on condition that a reserve is created so as not to endanger equity capital by the sale of shares to employees. Because employees, including those who became shareholders during the course of privatisation, are usually minority shareholders, provisions protecting this class are also relevant.[20]

*Draft legislation (2006–7).* Amendments to the Privatisation Law are planned to provide several different schemes for selling shares to employees on preferential terms.[21] According to the present draft, the State Privatisation Fund would be authorised to sell shares to a joint-stock company on condition that the latter offer these shares to employees on the same or better terms. The ESOP model is an additional option. The management and employees of a joint-stock company could form a new ESOP limited liability company. The new company would take out a bank loan collateralised by the pledged shares and buy the shares from the Privatisation Fund in a single payment. If none of these schemes suit, the Privatisation Fund can sell shares directly to employees; shares thus acquired are voting shares. Enterprises that at the time of privatisation were not under social ownership but were administered by their managers and work force according to 'rights to administer' are a special case. They can transfer these rights back to the company, which, according to the draft, would increase the company's capitalisation. The new shares created would be assigned to the Privatisation Fund, which would then offer them for sale to those employees who were with the company at the time of privatisation. Although the draft was withdrawn from Parliament in 2007, it is still referred to in the ongoing discussion.

### Profit-sharing

There is no legal regulation of profit-sharing and hence no incentives. Although individual enterprises offer monetary incentives, especially to managers, bonuses are usually not linked to company profit. They are regarded as wage compensation and taxed accordingly.

### Participation in decision making

Employees of a private company employing at least 20 regular employees have the right to a voice in decisions that affect their economic and social rights and interests, under conditions and procedures prescribed by the Labour Law. Employees of such companies are entitled to elect one or more representatives to the employees' council by means of a free, direct and secret ballot. The function of the council is to protect and promote the interests of employees vis-à-vis the employer. If no employee's council has been established, the trade union assumes its powers. According to Article 158 Labour Law, at least one employee representative is to be a member of the supervisory board in companies employing an annual average of more than 200; also in companies that are public institutions, or in which the state owns at least 25 per cent of shares. It should be noted that this provision conflicts with a company law regulation on the establishment of a supervisory board.

## IV   Cyprus

Neither employee ownership nor profit-sharing have a significant extent in Cyprus. The country has developed financial institutions, with more than 50 per cent of households holding shares as financial assets, as well as a co-operative sector in which more than 50 per cent of the population are members. The industrial relations system is based largely on voluntary regulations that allow room for joint initiatives; it has at the same time a relatively high number of unions. Nevertheless, employee participation, either financial or in decision making, does not appear on the agenda of either the government or social partners.

### General attitude

The long tradition of tight regulation of financial markets, capital controls and limited financial assets available to households underwent change in the mid-1990s. A modern capital market has evolved through the Cyprus Stock Exchange, which officially launched operations in March 1996. Nevertheless, the boom and crisis of the Cyprus Stock Exchange left the public sceptical of the financial markets.[22] With respect to the average size of enterprises, in 2000 only 70 companies in Cyprus employed more than 250 employees.[23] Self-employment is a permanent feature, with self-employed persons accounting for 20 per cent of the active labour force.[24] Voluntarism has been developed through the Industrial Relations Code and operates through national tripartite bodies, among them the Labour Advisory Board, dealing with the main issues of industrial relations, and an equally important Economic Advisory Committee, dealing with economic policy issues.

Trade unions are mainly organised at the industry level and belong to strong federations or confederations, the most important being the Cyprus Workers Confederation (SEK, affiliated with the ETUC) the Pan-Cyprian Federation of Labour (PEO), and the Democratic Labour Federation (DEOK). Employers are also organised into industry- or branch-level associations, most of which are members of the Cyprus Employers' and Industrialists' Federation and the Cyprus Chamber of Commerce and Industry. During the 1990s, only SEK initiated a stance in favour of employee representatives' participation in decision making through participation of labour representatives at the board level of public and semi-public sector institutions and organisations; this effort met no success. Although the social partners shape the evolution of industrial relations, employee financial participation has not been an issue on their agendas.

Government economic policy in the past decade has not embraced the idea of financial participation of employees, favouring voluntary arrangements in industrial relations instead. The current government, which took office in February 2008 for a five-year mandate, is unlikely to usher in any changes in relation to this issue. The process of harmonising national and European law has recently led to debates concerning the evolution of the voluntary system of industrial relations, but issues of employee financial participation have been left untouched.

**Legal and fiscal framework**

The Cypriot legal system is based upon the same principles as those of the United Kingdom; all laws regulating business matters and procedures are based essentially on English common law.[25] The institutional and legal framework generally does not, at least intentionally, create incentives for the development of PEPPER schemes, but neither do they prevent it.

### Share ownership

Registered companies in Cyprus are mainly governed by the Cyprus Company's Law (CL), Chapter 113 of the Laws of Cyprus, as amended, which is identical to the UK's former Companies Act 1948. Under the CL, companies can be divided into companies limited by shares[26] and companies limited by guarantee.[27] There is no law in Cyprus on share option schemes for employees, but these may be included in private employment contracts or given to employees as part of an incentive scheme. The CL does not contain special rules on employee profit-sharing and contains only a mere notion of employee share ownership: The provisions of the Second Council Directive 77/91/EEC of 13 December 1976 were adopted by national legislation and specifically in the CL. Therefore, an exception to the general prohibition against acquiring its own stock, Article 57a CL permits a company to acquire its own shares without a special resolution of the general shareholders assembly if the shares are acquired for the purpose of being transferred to the company's employees or to the employees of an associate company. To facilitate the acquisition of shares by employees, Article 53 CL permits the company to advance funds, and make or secure loans, with a view to acquisition by employees of the company or employees of an associate company.

### Profit-sharing

There is no explicit law or regulation in the Cypriot legal system that prohibits companies from sharing profits with their employees. More generally, companies may agree to implement bonus schemes with their employees according to their performance or for percentages (commissions) according to the sales made by their department.

### Participation in decision making

The Companies Law does not contain any special provisions concerning employee participation in control and decision-making bodies in companies. In state and semi-state companies, where government has the prerogative of appointing the persons to serve on the administrative boards, it is customary that some high-level trade union officials from the largest unions are selected to serve as members. During the 1990s SEK supported participation of employees' representatives at the board level of public and semi-public sector institutions and organisations; this position, however, did not find wider support within the labour side. Yet, the implementation of Directive 2001/86/EC supplementing the Statute for a European Company with regard to the involvement of employees, as well as of Directive 2003/72/EC, supplementing the Statute for a European Co-operative Society with regard to the involvement of employees and of Directive 2005/56/EC, on cross-border mergers of limited liability companies have introduced provisions on employee participation in supervisory or administrative organs in line with the provisions of the aforementioned directives.[28] Laws implementing the Directives on Information and Consultation of employees and on European Works Councils provide for the right to information and consultation of employees' representatives in local and Community-wide establishments, respectively.[29] As the Cypriot system of employee representation is the single-channel system, there are no special elected works councils operating in Cyprus; rather information and consultation is conducted with trade union representatives. Information and consultation is also provided for under the provisions of the Industrial Relations Code in a range of cases, including when redundancies are to take place.[30] Though a non-legally binding document, this code has generally enjoyed a very high degree of compliance since its signing in 1977.

## V   Czech Republic

The country whose privatisation policy has granted by far the fewest concessions to insiders is the Czech Republic. Despite some tradition of both financial participation of employees and employee participation in decision making, the Czech privatisation framework did not include any special price reductions, credit arrangements or pre-emptive rights for employees. Czech policy opted for the voucher concept, with no specific schemes for employees. After the split with Slovakia in 1993, the corporate governance and enterprise structures were – and remain – unfavourable to employee participation in general. Out of 1,688 state enterprises privatised into joint-stock companies, 480 proposed and received approval to issue part of their shares as employee shares, but only 171 of these eventually gave shares to their employees. Employee share ownership remained insignificant, representing only 0.31 per cent of privatised assets. Under voucher privatisation, about 1.5 per cent of the total shares were allocated to employees. Currently, profit-sharing plans are rare; most are found in foreign companies. Of the existing, rather restrictive, regulations on employee share ownership and (share-based) profit-sharing, only the former have been implemented, although to a very limited extent.

## General attitude

Trade unions, for example ČMKOSs, do not actively promote employee participation, nor do they plan to do so in future. After the outcome of voucher privatisation, public confidence in share ownership and similar programmes is slight or non-existent. Trade unions see employee financial participation in the near future as extremely limited in both scale and scope. A similar view is held by the Czech Association of Employers/Entrepreneurs, SPČR: they have taken no official stand on employee participation models and neither have nor seek to acquire data on its practice by their members. Although participation in decision making – as part of the *acquis communautaire* – has been put on the agenda of tripartite negotiations, financial participation of employees has not. Today, employee participation is no longer a political issue; none of the democratic parliamentary political parties includes it in their programmes. It was last a political issue at the end of the 1990s, when Social Democratic Prime Minister Miloš Zeman tried to move employee financial participation forward on the agenda. Since then, politicians have remained silent on the issue.

## Legal and fiscal framework

Unlike some countries, the Czech legal framework contains no specific employee financial participation measure or regulation of any specific issue pertaining to PEPPER schemes. The only forms of corporate ownership the law makes available to employees are share acquisition and profit-sharing in joint-stock companies, and these only to a limited extent.

### Share ownership

*Privatisation (1990).* Mass privatisation made employee share ownership possible in principle. Each firm on the mass privatisation list had to submit a privatisation plan. This proposal could include any combination of available privatisation methods (for example, voucher scheme, domestic direct sale, foreign direct sale, public auction or tender, free transfer, or employee shares). It was possible for others besides firm management to submit a competing privatisation plan for all or part of each enterprise. The supervising ministry and the Ministry of Privatisation decided on the winning project (foreign sales had to be approved by the government). Finally, voucher privatisation itself provided an alternative way of creating employee ownership within the privatisation process. Nevertheless, in these programmes, a small proportion of shares was offered to and reserved for employees.

*Private companies (2000, 2004).* In 2000, Article 158 Commercial Code (CC) was revised in line with the *aquis communautaire* to abolish any type of special share; it also eliminated Employee Shares as a special type of share. Instead, from then on, joint-stock companies could amend to their articles of association to allow their employees to buy company shares at a discount. Previously issued Employee Shares had to be converted into regular shares by decision of the general shareholders assembly by January 2003. Since dissenting shareholders must be bought out in a public offering according to Article 186a paragraph 3 et seq. CC, employed shareholders were given the de facto opportunity to cash-out their shares. Acquisition of shares on preferential conditions according to Article 158 CC is limited to current or retired employees.

As an exception to the general prohibition against acquiring its own stock, Article 161a paragraph 3 CC, introduced in 2004, permits a company to acquire its own shares in order to sell them, in accordance with the articles of association, to employees of the company. In such cases the shares must be transferred on preferential conditions to the employees within 12 months of acquisition. If the transfer is not carried out within the stipulated period, Article 161c CC requires that the shares be sold or the share capital be decreased accordingly; if the company does not comply, a court can order its liquidation (Article 161c paragraph 2 CC). Furthermore, current legislation permits joint-stock companies to issue new shares granting employees favourable conditions in the context of so-called mixed capital increases; that is, the capital increase of a company issuing new stock financed by the company's own capital. According to Article 209a paragraph 3 CC, 50 per cent of the purchase price must be paid before the capital increase is registered in the commercial register, whereas the remaining 50 per cent may be paid for in instalments. According to Article 203 paragraph 3, 209 paragraph 2 lit. d) CC, shares issued to be acquired by employees shall not be considered a public offering, provided the designated employees shall have been identified in the decision of the general shareholders assembly on the capital increase.

To facilitate the acquisition of shares by employees, the legislation further permits the company to fully pay for the stock acquired by its own employees. The restrictions on the preferential conditions for the purchase of shares by employees are enumerated in Article 158 paragraph 2 CC. As in the previous regulation, the overall value of the granted discount for the issued shares may not exceed 5 per cent of the enterprise's equity capital and must be covered by the company's own resources. In addition, Article 161e paragraph 3 CC contains a regulation excepting a company from the general prohibition against leveraging the acquisition of its own stock if these shares are to be sold, in accordance with the articles of association, to its own employees. Thus share acquisition by the employees of a particular company may be leveraged by the company's discounting the purchase price within the aforementioned limits, by credit financing, by providing collateral or by a combination of these three preferential methods.

### Profit-sharing

Nothing in the Czech legal system prohibits profit-sharing. The only explicit regulation is Article 178 paragraph 4 of the CC, which states that in accordance with the articles of association employees may be entitled to a share of company profit (cash-based profit-sharing). According to Article 158 CC, the articles of association may also stipulate that profits allocated to employees be used exclusively to purchase shares on preferential conditions or to offset the discount granted to employees for this purpose (share-based profit-sharing). Share-based profit-sharing is also mentioned in the context of capital increases. A capital increase generally requires the approval of the general shareholders assembly. However, Article 210 CC, in accordance with the articles of association, assumes that this decision will be delegated to the management board. Article 210 paragraph 4 CC regulates a capital increase by the issuance of shares to be transferred on preferential terms to employees. It emphasises that this option is especially suitable in cases where the general shareholders assembly has previously directed that profits allocated to employees be used exclusively to purchase these shares. These benefits are all taxable at the progressive personal income rate of 15 per cent to 32 per cent. Therefore as personal income rises, the incentive to provide additional benefits progressively decreases. Benefits from profit-sharing, for example, may be as much as 17 per cent less than the same amount in dividends paid to shareholders.

### Participation in decision making

Article 200 CC requires joint-stock companies with more than 50 employees to have one-third of its supervisory board composed of employee-delegated members. There are no special rules on employee participation in decision making with respect to PEPPER schemes or privatisation matters. According to Law No. 1/1992 Sb. on Wages, Remuneration for Work Readiness and Average Earnings, as amended, among the negotiable issues in collective bargaining agreements are the amount of and the conditions for providing incentive wages (bonuses, rewards, and so on), which includes participation in company profits. The main structure for representing employees at the workplace is the local trade union group, which needs only three individuals to set it up. Until 2001 this was the only structure; since then it has been possible to set up a works council in companies with more than 25 employees where there is no trade union organisation and where at least one-third of the workforce requests such a body. Nevertheless, most companies have no representation at all. The most important level of collective bargaining in the Czech Republic is at the company level, although in many companies bargaining does not occur. Industry-level agreements cover some industries, and following legal changes in 2005 these can again be extended more widely.

## VI   Denmark

Employee financial participation began to be discussed at the end of the 1950s, in connection with an ideological debate on the concept of economic democracy and in response to the Swedish Wage-Earner Fund model. In 1987, the Liberal Conservative Government introduced the first tax incentives for certain forms of broad, voluntary, share-based plans at the enterprise level. Many firms implemented these plans with success. However, the issue of financial participation then disappeared from the political agenda, remaining dormant until the beginning of the new century. In 2003, several new individual share-based plans as well as stock option plans were added. In 2005, these new plans were amended, in response to problems that had emerged in practice. All plans are based on employee shares or stock options.

The Tax Ministry now regularly reports to Parliament on the progress of employee share ownership. According to the 2005 report, the number of employees participating in the various plans and the corresponding asset values were as follows: broad share-based profit-sharing, 10,000 employees, DKK 163 million; broad profit-sharing based on stock options, 1,000 employees, DKK 10 million; individual stock option plan without limitations, 4,047 employees, DKK 388 million. According to the 2006 report, the newly introduced individual profit-sharing plans based on shares and stock options covered 1,326 employee participants in 77 enterprises. It should be noted that these numbers reflect the 'flow': that is, the number of additional plan participants/shares in the respective year. Data in absolute numbers were presented by the trade union Dansk Metal for 1999: an estimated 160,000 employees were shareholders in their companies, while 13 per cent of companies in high-growth industries and 25 per cent of all IT companies operated a share-based plan for their employees.

## General attitude

In the 1960s and 1970s, the Danish Trade Unions Federation and the Social Democratic Party submitted several proposals for compulsory collective funds, national and regional, in response to the Wage-Earner Fund (the Meidner Plan) of Sweden. These proposals were strongly opposed by both the Danish Employers Federation and the parties of the central and right political spectrum; they preferred tax incentives for voluntary plans at the enterprise level. At the same time the government wanted to introduce additional tax incentives for existing schemes, but failed to get its draft law through Parliament.

Employee financial participation remained a highly controversial political issue until the late 1980s. During the 1990s, little attention was paid to financial participation by either the government or social partners. Since the beginning of the present decade, the government has actively supported employee financial participation by introducing and adopting new individual share-based plans. Trade unions have been reported to be rather indifferent, whereas employers' associations seem to be sceptical and reluctant to an extension of employee participation in general.

## Legal and fiscal framework

The following employee financial participation plans are currently regulated: broad-based share-based profit-sharing plans, including stock options; broad-based share ownership plans; individual share-based profit-sharing plans, including stock options, and individual stock option plans without limitations.

### *Share ownership*

Companies are allowed to acquire own shares up to 10 per cent of the subscribed capital for distribution among their own employees within an 18-month period (Article 48 paragraph 1 (1), 2 Law on Public Companies – PCL). The acquisition of shares shall only be made to the extent that the company's equity capital exceeds the amount which cannot be allocated as dividend, following an acquisition of shares; the share capital less own shares held must amount to not less than DKK 500,000 (Article 48 paragraph 4 PCL). Furthermore, the company is entitled to advance funds, make loans and provide security, with a view to acquisition of the company's shares by employees of the company under a qualified stock purchase plan (Article 115a paragraph 2 PCL), unless the shareholders' equity of the company would fall below the amount which may not be distributed as dividend (Article 115a paragraph 2 (2) PCL). The articles of association may authorise the board of directors to issue new and bonus shares to the employees of the company or any subsidiary; authorisation to this effect may be granted for one or more periods of up to five years each (Article 37 paragraph 1 PCL).

*Employee shares.* Under the broad-based share ownership plan connected with tax incentives (§ 7A Tax Assessment Law), shares of the employer company can be offered at discount to all employees; special rules may apply according to length of employment, working hours or seniority. The plan may not include management (for example, members of the supervisory board). If the reduced price is paid in full at appropriation, the value of the shares does not exceed 10 per cent of the annual salary, and the shares are placed under bank trusteeship for five years, the employee is only liable to share income tax at sale while the employer company can deduct its costs from its corporate income tax base.

*Stock option plan.* The stock option plan under § 28 Tax Assessment Law is individual and may include members of the supervisory board. The number of options under this plan has no limits. However, it must be filed with the tax authorities. The employee is taxed at exercise of the option on the difference between the market price and the purchase price and again at the time of sale with the share income tax. The employer company can deduct the options cost from its corporate income tax base.

### Profit-sharing

*Broad, share-based.* These plans, linked to tax incentives (§ 7A Tax Assessment Law), introduced in 1987, are based on share or stock options. They must include all employees, although special rules may pertain to length of employment, working hours or seniority; they must exclude management, for example members of the supervisory board. The plan must be approved by the tax authorities. If free shares are allotted within the plan, no tax need be paid by the employee at grant on total share values not exceeding DKK 8,000 (2006), and shares are placed in trust with a bank subject to a blocking period of seven years. In the case of stock options, the employee pays no tax at grant or exercise if the value does not exceed 10 per cent of annual salary and the shares are placed in trust with a bank for a blocking period of five years. According to the 2005 amendment, the obligation of the employee to return shares to the issuing company under certain circumstances is not an obstacle to tax exemption. In both cases, general taxation rules in force at the time the shares are sold apply: if the income from sale of shares does not exceed DKK 44,300 (2006), the tax rate is 28 per cent; otherwise 43 per cent. The employer company can deduct from its corporate income tax base the value of shares or options transferred to employees.

*Individual, share-based.* First introduced in 2003 under § 7H Tax Assessment Law, these plans are based on shares and/or stock options. Only employees are eligible, and members of the supervisory board are excluded. The employer company and the employee must conclude an agreement that is to be endorsed by an auditor or attorney and submitted to the tax authorities. Only common stock can be allocated. The value of shares may not exceed 10 per cent of annual salary. The value of stock options should not exceed 10 per cent of the annual salary or the exercise price should be less than 15 per cent lower than the market price of underlying shares. This means that an employee is eligible for tax incentives if he acquires shares under the 10 per cent rule and, additionally, stock options under the 15 per cent rule, but not stock options under both rules. If the above pre-conditions are fulfilled, the employee is exempted from personal income tax and social security contributions at grant or exercise and is only liable to the share income tax at sale according to general taxation rules. However, the employer company cannot deduct costs from the tax base of the corporate income tax.

*Cash-based.* Plans are independent of tax incentives; their incidence is reputedly low.

### Participation in decision making

No direct connection exists between participation in decision making and employee financial participation. Financial participation plans are specifically enjoined from extending the existing rights in connection with participation in decision making. Financial participation is generally not a part of collective bargaining agreements.

## VII   Germany

Despite a long-standing tradition and the general acknowledgement of the positive effects on both productivity and job creation, employee financial participation is not widespread. Traditionally, German schemes focus on defined contribution savings plans with a total capital allocated much higher than that of all employee share plans; with regards to financial participation, the combination of share ownership plans with these savings plans may be considered typical. Germany's lower standing compared with other countries and a recent decrease in employee share ownership may be attributed to insufficient government support. Another reason is the traditional scepticism of both trade unions and employers' associations towards employee financial participation.

Since 2007, several government officials as well as representatives of major political parties declared that employee financial participation should be better promoted in the future. Nevertheless, resulting from the substantial differences that divide the two member parties of the Grand Coalition the new 'Law on Capital Participation of Employees' which came into force in April 2009 merely increased existing insignificant fiscal incentives. Under the new Law and the 3rd Law on Asset Participation including previous provisions[31] these are only offered for employee share ownership, whereas profit-sharing is not supported by any tax incentives.

Although profit-sharing enjoys no tax incentives, it is more widespread than share ownership. In 2001, 8.7 per cent of enterprises were reported to have profit-sharing schemes, and 2.4 per cent share ownership schemes.[32] In 2005, profit-sharing plans were operated by 9 per cent of enterprises according to the IAB company survey[33] and by 11 per cent according to the BISS project;[34] share ownership plans were implemented by 2 per cent of enterprises according to the IAB survey and by 3 per cent of enterprises according to the BISS survey. In 2006, 620 joint-stock companies maintained share ownership plans for 1,423,000 employees, and 250 limited liability companies for 8,000 employees; 17,000 employees of co-operatives had membership status (AGP/GIZ of 1 January 2007). According to the IAB company survey, profit-sharing plans are prevailingly implemented in companies with more than 500 employees (one-third of all such companies) and in the mining, utilities, banking and insurance sectors (one-quarter of all companies in the above sectors), whereas no relevant difference between the sectors exists as far as employee share ownership is concerned. Additionally, financial participation is much more widespread in Western German than in Eastern German companies, and in foreign companies located in Germany rather than in German-owned companies.

## General attitude

Regardless of periodical discussions of the topic during the past 50 years, until recently, the attitude of the government and social partners towards employee financial participation has been – with some exceptions – generally indifferent or negative. After Federal President Horst Köhler endorsed employee financial participation in 2007, in response to his speech, Federal Chancellor Angela Merkel and several politicians of the Grand Coalition announced to improve the legal framework. Nevertheless, the concepts of the members of the Grand Coalition remained contradicting[35] and – with new Law on Capital Participation of Employees that passed parliament on 23 January 2009 – resulted in a modest compromise leaving far behind previous ambitious plans for reform.

Trade unions continue to exercise strong political power through workers' co-determination, despite declining union membership. With some exceptions, most Unions fear decentralisation and de-solidarisation of the wage policy along with a general loss of power. As an argument against profit-sharing, they cite the risk that employers could calculate a decrease in the amount of profit to the detriment of employees. Employee share ownership, they argue further, imposes on employees the risk of losing both jobs and share income. Profit-dependent wage components are usually accepted only as auxiliary earnings in good times, while participation in loss is refused. Employee share ownership as a partial substitute for wages or in combination with wage reductions is generally rejected. Recently the employers' associations have paid more attention to employee financial participation. They generally favour voluntary company-level plans and share plans over profit-sharing.

## Legal and fiscal framework

German legislation permits both share ownership and profit-sharing, whereas no fiscal or other incentives are available for the latter. Asset formation or savings plans offer a vehicle to allocate and invest sums received as salary or as remuneration in financial participation schemes. In this context, share schemes can be combined with such savings plans and, to promote asset formation of employees, the employee contributions may be matched by the state. The 2009 Law on Capital Participation of Employees did not change the incentive system under § 19a of the Income Tax Law and the 5th Law on Asset Formation, but merely increased the amounts, percentages and income ceilings: with regard to an employer allowance, the ceiling of the value of the tax-free benefit from free or reduced shares from EUR 135 to EUR 360 annually; the absolute limit of the savings bonus matching employee investments of up to 400 EUR of 18–20 per cent (that is, a maximum bonus of EUR 80 annually compared with a maximum of EUR 72 previously); and the income ceiling for eligibility of the bonus from EUR 17,900 to EUR

20,000 annually, which is still exceptionally low. As previously a blocking period of six years applies.

*Share ownership*

Share ownership is mostly practiced in joint-stock companies (Aktiengesellschaft) owing to special features of German company law. In commercial partnerships (OHG, KG), the concept of co-ownership and thus co-entrepreneurship on the on hand and the inflexible transferability of the legal position of a partner on the other preclude the development of employee share ownership. In limited liability companies (GmbH), employee share ownership is rare because of specific legal obstacles, for example, the relatively strong position of a shareholder compared with management and the transfer of share ownership only by notarial deed. However, a partnership that serves to facilitate employee financial participation in a limited liability company and holds a share of this limited liability company as its sole asset (holding-GbR), is not required to make a notarial deed to transfer its shares.[36]

*Employee Shares.* In joint-stock companies, stock can be distributed to employees in connection with the acquisition of the firm's own shares or with a capital increase. With regard to the acquisition of the firm's own shares with a view to the transfer to its (former) employees or employees of affiliated firms (§ 71 para. 1 (8) JSCL), a decision of the General Assembly is not necessary provided the shares are transferred within 12 months; a prerequisite is a reserve fund for own shares to be established without reducing equity capital or reserve funds (§ 71 paragraph 2 sentence 2 JSCL, § 272 paragraph 4 CC). The company may advance funds, make loans or provide security to facilitate the acquisition of the shares by the employees (*financial assistance*, § 71a paragraph 1 sentence 2 JSCL). With regard to capital increase, the law provides for a conditional capital increase (§§ 192 et seq. Law on Joint-Stock Companies – JSCL) and a capital increase by authorized capital (§§ 202 et seq. JSCL). In both cases a General Assembly's decision is necessary and the nominal amount restricted to 50 per cent, the amount of shares or stock options to 10 per cent of equity capital (§ 192 paragraph 3 sentence 1). In the latter case, the board of directors is authorized by the general meeting to increase capital up to a certain nominal value. Such an authorization, however, must be intended in the company statute. The general meeting's decision to authorize the board requires a majority of three-quarters of the decision-making stock capital (§ 202 paragraph 2 JSCL). If an employee receives stock from the employer company under their employment contract free of charge or at a reduced price, the difference between the market value and the subscription price is regarded as a part of their salary. However, the benefit is exempt from taxes and social security contributions with a maximum of 360 EUR in a calendar year (§ 19a paragraph 1 Income Tax Law).[37] Proceeds from the share sale are not taxed if the period between the date of acquisition and sale is more than one year (§ 23 paragraph 1 (2) Income Tax Law).

*Stock options.* These are more common as executive schemes, but broad-based schemes exist. The decision to adopt a stock option plan as part of a capital increase (see above §§ 192 et seq. and §§ 202 et seq. JSCL) must contain a description of the allocation scheme (§ 193 para. 2 (2) JSCL). The plan itself must determine the strike price per share (§ 193 paragraph 2 (3) JSCL). In lieu of the strike price, the decision can state the basis for the calculation of the price. Details on the blocking period and vesting period shall be included in the decision on capital increase (§ 193 paragraph 2 (4) JSCL). The law stipulates a blocking period of at least two years.

*Special Fund for Employee Participation.* Introduced by the 2009 Law on Capital Participation of Employees primarily for SMEs these funds are governed by the Investment Law. They pool voluntary employee savings, including savings bonuses as well as capital participation shares offered by participating companies to their employees, and re-invest them in these companies and in the capital markets. The funds may be set up at branch level in co-operation with employers association and/or

*Table 7.1* Composition of the special fund for employee participation: Limitations for certain types of assets/issuers in per cent of total value of the Special Fund

| minimum 60 per cent | | maximum 40 per cent |
|---|---|---|
| qualified assets of enterprises that grant their employees contributions in order to acquire shares in the Special Fund | | qualified assets of other enterprises/ other investments |
| maximum 20 per cent of a single enterprise/group | | |
| up to 100 per cent | maximum 25 per cent | maximum 5 per cent of each issuer/ investment fund: |
| • listed securities<br>• selected financial instruments<br>• non-bonded loan-claims | • non-bonded holdings<br>• non-listed securities | • listed securities<br>• blocked current account<br>• money market: cash equivalents<br>• investment shares<br>• derivatives |

trade unions and have to invest 60 per cent of their assets in the employer companies (see Table 7.1). Although a company may apply for re-investment, it has no claim to actually receive financing from the fund.

The model has yet to be accepted by the market and it is uncertain whether there will be enough interested companies and fund management firms.

### Profit-sharing

Profit-sharing, although not legally regulated or supported by tax incentives, is believed to be more widespread than employee share ownership. The statistical evidence on this issue might result from unclear definitions, e.g., that indirect financial participation (for example, employee loans, participation certificates and debenture bonds) is considered as profit-sharing. The only genuine form of profit-sharing practised more commonly is cash based profit-sharing within a bonus plan, which partly connects the share amount to the annual profit of the enterprise and partly to the individual performance of the employee.

### Participation in decision making

Co-determination and participation rights of employees through their representatives are traditionally well developed under German labour law. Employees (and to a certain extent trade unions) are represented in the supervisory board, and the workers' council protects the rights of employees at the level of the individual undertaking. There is no direct connection between participation in decision making and financial participation of employees in the sense that financial participation plans would automatically extend existing rights pertaining to decision making.

An employee shareholder enjoys mandatory rights (right to control, right of participation, right to demand information). Examples of these rights are the right of a shareholder in a limited liability company (GmbH) to inspect and demand information pursuant to § 51a of the Law on Limited Liability Companies, and the right of the stockholder in a joint-stock company (AG) to demand information at the general meeting pursuant to § 131 of the Law on Joint-Stock Companies.

## VIII  Estonia

Employee financial participation has made little progress in Estonia. PEPPER schemes did not develop during the period of independence between the two world wars or under the Soviet regime. Although employee participation in decision making had some role in state enterprises during the Soviet era, it was later dismissed as a relic of that system. Employee ownership was briefly popular as a tool for privatising publicly owned assets in the early stages of privatisation, but turned out to be a temporary expedient. Neither was employee financial participation considered relevant to the solution of employment and social problems. In 1995, 29 per cent of employees were estimated to be owners in 1995; by January 1997, this figure had fallen to around 25 per cent.[38] In January 2005, out of a sample of 722 firms, 19 (2.63 per cent) were (partly) employee-owned with a share ownership ranging from 20 per cent to 100 per cent.[39] Profit-sharing is rare in Estonia, but other forms of monetary incentive schemes are used in more than 50 per cent of cases.[40] Some information on profit-sharing in Estonia was found in the Estonian management survey (1997/98), with only 13 instances or 5.9 per cent being reported out of a sample of 220 firms.

**General attitude**

Currently, social partners are represented by the Confederation of Estonian Trade Unions and the Estonian Employers' Confederation. They do not have equal power; the trade unions traditionally are the weaker party. Recent debates between social partners on employee participation were triggered by the necessity to transform the *aquis communautaire* into Estonian law. The government is waiting for a trade union initiative, but the trade unions are in no hurry to comply. PEPPER schemes have not been on Parliament's political agenda. Only one political party has addressed this issue: the Social Democratic Party. These circumstances make it unlikely that Estonia will adopt new legal regulations on employee participation soon.

**Legal and fiscal framework**

No specific legislation on any PEPPER scheme in Estonia exists at present. The legal framework neither creates nor prevents incentives for the development of PEPPER schemes.

*Share ownership*

*Privatisation (1990, abolished in 1993).* Semi-private forms of business ownership ('people's enterprises' and leased enterprises) introduced in the early stage of privatisation under Soviet law (and later legalised under Estonian law), in particular leased enterprises, are assumed to have been a major source of employee ownership in Estonia. In the privatisation of small and medium-sized enterprises, employees were given a pre-emptive right to buy the enterprise at the initial price. By

1993, when all privileges were abolished, small enterprise privatisation was almost complete; an estimated 80 per cent of enterprises had been taken over by insiders. The privatisation programme for large enterprises was finally adopted in 1993. Following the German Treuhand model, it contained no preferential rights for employees. Employee ownership of shares in enterprises purchased during privatisation is decreasing. Enterprises in the energy sector, as well as public utilities, are still partly state-owned; they could be put up for sale in the future. The current Privatisation Law offers no privileges to employees or other potential buyers. The few privileges employees had under Estonian law were abolished as early as 1993.[41]

*Private companies.* Estonian commercial law contains no special rules on profit-sharing or on employee share ownership with respect to acquisition, limitations on the number of shares or issuance of employee stock for any specific undertaking; general rules therefore apply. Some employees still hold shares purchased during privatisation and thus have the rights attached to these securities according the Commercial Code (CC) and Securities Market Law (SML). Because employees who became shareholders often acquired minority shares in newly founded limited liability companies and joint-stock companies during early privatisation, provisions about the rights of minority shareholders and shares acquired during this period are important.[42] If securities issued by a company are offered solely to its employees or managers, the prospectus need not be made public and registered (§ 17 paragraph 1 (2) SML). Consequently employees and management are not entitled to compensation pursuant to § 25 SML on losses resulting from the volatility of acquired securities.[43] Furthermore, if a company provides investment services solely to its employees and management, it does not have to be registered as an investment firm (§ 42 paragraph 1 SML). Thus it can conduct investment activities without a licence (§§ 48 et seq. SML). It is not obliged to report transactions (§ 91 SML) or to have additional reserve and risk funds (§§ 93 et seq. SML), nor are there additional requirements for managers (§ 79 SML).

### Profit-sharing

Special legislation on profit-sharing with regard to employees does not exist; therefore, there are neither direct incentives nor direct restrictions. For employees it is preferable to receive distributed profits under a corresponding scheme rather than as wages/salaries because they do not have to pay income tax on profits or dividends. Nevertheless, the resident company pays income tax at the rate of 22 per cent on distributed profits (§ 18 paragraph 1, 4 ITL), whether the distribution is monetary or non-monetary (§ 50 ITL); this is a disincentive for profit-sharing.

*Participation in decision making*

Although Estonian company law is so strongly influenced by German law that rulings by German courts can be used to interpret provisions of the Estonian CC, special rules on the participation of employees in management and decision making contained in a special German law (Betrieb sverfassungsgesetz) were not considered by the Estonian law-makers. If employees are also shareholders, they have voting rights in each company form, although they generally have no influence on resolutions of the general meeting because they are, in most cases, minority shareholders.

## IX   Greece

The first tax incentives for employee financial participation plans were introduced as early as 1974. Legislation broadened tax incentives in 1980 and 1987. Currently in place are special regulatory laws and tax incentives covering cash-based profit-sharing, employee share ownership and certain types of stock option plans. Although employee financial participation plans are still not widespread, they have been on the increase since the beginning of the current decade, especially executive stock option plans. Thirteen per cent of companies listed on the Athens Stock Exchange offered stock option plans in 2007, mainly to executives. Thirty thousand persons (1.8 per cent of employees) participated in these plans.[44]

The EU High Level Group of Independent Experts[45] found that the limited spread of employee financial participation plans, despite tax incentives, was attributable to the complexity and restrictions of the regulations. Tax incentives are indeed restricted to joint-stock companies (anonimes etairies). However, the number of such companies in Greece is quite high (16,767 companies in 2007), with most being SMEs. The complexity of the regulations arises from the fact that the provisions on tax incentives are dispersed through many different pieces of legislation. Another important factor inhibiting the spread of employee financial participation is the reluctant attitude of social partners at the company level, although social partners at the national level view the issue more positively.

### General attitude

The government generally supports PEPPER schemes by initiating and implementing tax incentives for specific types of plans. Employers' associations were not initially interested in employee financial participation. Trade unions (that is, the General Confederation of Greek Workers and public sector unions), originally strongly opposed, have accepted financial participation since the beginning of the 1990s. Attitudes of both social partners have become more favourable since the beginning of the present decade. Facilitation of PEPPER schemes has been on the national collective bargaining agenda. In the current round of collective bargaining (2008), both social partners made facilitation of employee financial partnership an issue to be included in the agreement. However, this agreement requires government ratification to become applicable at the company level.

**Legal and fiscal framework**

Special legislation, including tax incentives, exists for cash-based profit-sharing, employee share ownership and stock option plans.

*Share ownership*

Both share ownership and stock option plans enjoy tax incentives under certain conditions.

*Share ownership plans.* Since 1987, joint-stock companies have been allowed to acquire their own shares in order to distribute them to employees. If these shares are purchased on the public market, up to 10 per cent of equity capital can be distributed; the distribution must be made within 12 months. If the shares for distribution are to be issued in the course of a capital increase, up to 20 per cent of the annual profit can be distributed; the shares must be blocked for three years unless the general meeting provides otherwise. If these pre-conditions are satisfied, the employee is not subject to either personal income tax or social security contributions on the benefit, but is liable to the tax on movable assets (10 per cent) on dividend or interest payments. The employer company can deduct the distributed amount from the tax base of the corporate income tax. According to the Circular of the Ministry of Finance of 2000, gift tax applies to the employee's benefit rather than personal income tax. When the shares are sold, only the transfer tax is applicable; companies often offer shares to employees at a reduced price to overcome opposition to privatisation.

*Stock option plans.* Stock option plans are divided into qualified plans under the Law 2971/1999 and non-qualified plans under the Presidential Decree 30/1988. In qualified plans, the shares to satisfy the claims of option owners at exercise are issued in a qualified capital increase whereby the number of shares should not exceed one-tenth of shares already outstanding. In such plans, employees are not subject to taxation at grant or exercise or liable for social security contributions; the employer company, however, cannot deduct the cost of the shares. In non-qualified plans, shares to satisfy the claims of option owners at exercise are purchased on the public market. Under these plans, employees are generally subject to personal income tax and social security contributions, but the local tax office can levy a gift tax instead of the personal income tax if 'the benefit derived exceeded the proper measure'. The employer company can deduct the value of distributed shares as personnel costs. Because there has been a substantial increase in the number of executive stock option plans since the year 2000 and the benefit of the executives usually exceeded 50 per cent, the government is considering much higher tax rates (40 per cent) in such cases.

### Profit-sharing

Profit-sharing plans are predominantly cash-based and linked to tax incentives. The company is allowed to distribute 15 per cent of annual net profits to employees. Each employee can receive up to 25 per cent of annual gross salary as their profit-share. The company must submit a list of beneficiaries, with amounts payable to each individual employee, to the workers' council within one month of approval by the general meeting. However, it must be noted that only a few companies have workers' councils; when they exist, they must be informed, but their approval is not required. In practice, no case is known where this pre-condition became a problem. If these pre-conditions are met, the employee is exempt from income tax, but subject to social security contributions on the profit-share amount. Profit-sharing distributions are exempt from the corporate income tax, but social security contributions are not.

### Participation in decision making

There is no direct connection between participation in decision making and financial participation of employees. In particular, financial participation plans cannot extend existing rights for participation in decision making. The employees in the 'socialised sector' (for example, public utilities and transport), where two levels of employee representation are compulsory for companies under state control (representative assembly of social control setting broad policy objectives: one-third employees, one-third board of directors, one-third elected by employees) might have influenced the introduction and design of financial participation plans but did not choose to do so.

# X   Spain

Employee financial participation in Spain typically takes two forms: Workers' Companies (Sociedades Laborales), which combine employee share ownership with decision-making rights, and profit-sharing. In recent years the number of Workers' Companies and of their employees (approximately 20,000 enterprises in 2007, employing 125,000 workers) have shown steady growth at higher rates[46] than conventional companies, indicating the success of this form of financial participation. Profit-sharing plans are mainly cash-based. According to a Ministry of Labour and Social Affairs survey in 2006, 18.8 per cent of private sector employees participate in some kind of profit-sharing in their workplace.[47] There are relatively few employee share ownership and stock option plans; these are mainly found in large multinational companies and often limited to the executives. Tax incentives for share purchase plans, however, introduced in 2003, could encourage employee share ownership to spread.

## General attitude

Under the Spanish Constitution, the government is obliged to take an active role in facilitating access of employees to ownership of productive assets. Both major political parties (the right wing PP and the left wing PSOE) are in favour of the concept of Workers' Companies (Sociedades Laborales). The present government supported employee financial participation with tax incentives for Workers' Companies and employee share ownership schemes. The employers' associations are careful not to promote plans limited to executives only, as in the past stock options adversely affected the financial markets, caused political friction and left a negative image generally. Nevertheless, they do not actively support broad-based plans. Trade unions accept financial participation plans only if they are on top of regular wages. Associations that lobby to protect the advantages gained by companies practicing financial participation exist at both the regional and firm levels (for example, MCC, CONFESAL, CEPES, Federaciones de Cooperativas). In 2008 (responding to a proposal by CONFESAL), a modification of the Law on Workers' Companies to eliminate some restrictive prerequisites, thereby making this type of firm more like a normal firm with standard labour relations, is under consideration.

## Legal and fiscal framework

Workers' companies are governed by the Law on Workers' Companies of 1986, substantially amended in 1997. There is no special regulation pertaining to profit-sharing.

*Share ownership*

Companies are allowed to acquire own shares for distribution among their employees (also for exercising of stock options) up to 10 per cent of their equity capital (Article 75 paragraph 1.1, 2 Law on Stock Corporations – SCL), under the conditions determined in Article 75 paragraph 1–4, 76 paragraph 1 SCL. Furthermore they are entitled to advance funds, make loans and provide security, with a view to acquisition of the company's shares by employees of the company (Article 81 paragraph 2 SCL).

Workers' companies constitute the typically Spanish form of employee share ownership. In addition, some listed companies implement stock option plans (although often for executives only), whereas in non-listed companies share purchase plans are practised. Most recently, tax incentives for employee share ownership and stock option plans with regard to income tax liability were introduced by the Law on Stock Ownership Incentives 46/02 of 18 December 2002, effective 1 January 2003.

*Workers' companies (Sociedadas Laborales).* These can be founded as a workers' company or become a workers' company by changing their corporate form. Since 1997, there have been two forms: Sociedad Anónima Laboral (SAL), with minimum equity capital of EUR 60,000; and Sociedad Limitada Laboral (SLL), with minimum equity capital of EUR 3000. The majority of shares must be held by the employees, but individual employees may not hold more than one-third of the capital. The articles of association must contain regulations on transfer of shares when an employee shareholder leaves the company. Each workers' company must establish a special fund for the compensation of losses amounting to 20 per cent of its profits (compulsory 10 per cent for normal companies and additional 10 per cent for workers' companies). The remaining 80 per cent of the profits can be distributed between the members of the workers' company or attributed to a voluntary reserve to increase the company's own capital and thus the value of its shares. If the compensation fund amounts to 25 per cent of annual profits the company benefits from a 99 per cent tax exemption from capital transfer tax (this affects primarily acquisitions of real estate by the workers' company). Persons who wish to join a workers' company have the possibility of receiving the unemployment security payments they are entitled to as a single flat payment (instead of monthly payments for the duration of unemployment) conditional on contributing the sums to the capital of the workers' company. Furthermore, workers' companies are exempted from taxes in connection with company formation and capital increases and have a tax credit of 99 per cent of taxes connected with transfer of shares to employees, notarial deeds on transfers to the company, notarial deeds on bond debts and debenture bonds. These incentives only apply to the setting up of the workers' company (that is, they do not affect personal income tax liability, and so on). The Law on Workers' Companies details special labour regulations (for example, on allocation of working time between employee shareholders and other employees). The federal Labour Ministry and municipalities exercise control over the workers' co-operatives.

*Share ownership plans (share purchase plans).* These have enjoyed tax incentives under certain conditions since 1996, which were specified in law RD 214/1999 and extended in 2003. Shares are excluded from income tax assessment under the following conditions: (1) the market value of the benefit at the time of acquisition does not exceed EUR 12,000 per annum; (2) shares are offered within the framework of a regular compensation plan (but not necessarily of a broad-based plan); (3) each employee and their family members own not more than 5 per cent of the equity capital; and (4) the shares are blocked for three years, tax incentives apply. Shares given to employees under these circumstances will not be considered as payments in kind.[48] No tax incentives apply to dividends, but at sale of shares a flat tax of 15 per cent instead of the personal income tax is imposed on the employee. Furthermore, for New Company Limited Partnership (SLNE), a mechanism providing an incentive for employee savings to acquire shares or holdings in the employing company, a 'company savings account' was introduced in 2003.[49]

*Stock option plans.* These are also linked to tax incentives as of 2003. If the vesting period does not exceed two years and options are not granted annually, a 40 per cent personal income tax allowance (limited by the annual medium wage determined by law multiplied by the number of years before vesting) applies. If the shares cannot be sold within three years after the option grant and the plan includes all employees on equal terms, the amount of the tax allowance and the ceiling are doubled. Approximately 40 listed companies operated stock option plans in 2003.[50]

### Profit-sharing

Since the 1994 reform of the labour market Law 11/1994 mentions the use of bonuses connected to the results and situation of the enterprise. Both cash-based and share-based profit sharing plans are found, but cash-based profit-sharing prevails. In many cases, profit-sharing plans contain financial indicators as well as performance-related indicators, so that they cannot be considered as genuine profit-sharing plans. Some share-based plans ('performance shares') are linked to financial indicators, such as BPA, RTA, and so on. Stock appreciation rights, that is, payment in cash or transfer of shares connected to the increase in the share value at the end of a determined period, are sometimes granted, but rarely.

### Participation in decision making

Employee share ownership in Workers' Companies is directly linked to participation in decision making. The board of directors cannot decide on liquidation, capital increase or reduction, or board composition without general assembly consent. Each member of the workers' company has the right to be a candidate for election to the governing bodies of the company. In other plans, there is no direct connection between participation in decision making and employee financial participation; in particular, financial participation plans cannot extend the existing rights pertaining to participation in decision making.

## XI  France

France has a relatively long tradition of employee financial participation, especially different forms of profit-sharing and collective savings plans. The first profit-sharing plans (so-called intéressement) were introduced in 1959, but they did not become widespread until substantial tax incentives were introduced and restrictions abolished in 1986. A second type of profit-sharing plan (participation) introduced in 1967 was compulsory for all companies with more than 100 employees, a number reduced to 50 employees in 1986. Additionally in 1967, tax incentives were introduced for profit-sharing and the first short-term savings plans (Plan d'Epargne d'Enterprise (PEE)) were adopted. Important improvements were enacted in 1994 for all types of plan. The most recent employee financial participation plan is the long-term savings plan (Plan d'Epargne-Retraite Collectif (PERCO), introduced as Plan Partenarial d'Epargne Salarial Volontaire (PPESV) in 2001 and renamed in 2003) designed to facilitate voluntary savings for retirement. Stock option plans were first introduced only for listed domestic companies in 1970 and extended to unlisted and foreign companies in 1987. Although the taxation of these plans became more favourable in 1996, they are still prevailingly used by executives and seldom broad-based.

Currently, four basic plans are the most common: voluntary profit-sharing (intéressement), compulsory profit-sharing (participation), short-term savings plans (Plan d'Epargne d'Enterprise (PEE)) and long-term savings plans (Plan d'Epargne Retraite Collectif (PERCO)). Whereas 'participation' is compulsory for all companies with 50 or more employees, the other plans are voluntary. All these plans are traditionally classified as profit-sharing plans, although 'intéressement' can be linked to indicators other than profit or to non-financial indicators and savings plans are more a financial vehicle for profit-sharing than genuine profit-sharing plans. The traditional classification is followed here but with the above reservations. Shares can be transferred to employees directly for free or at a discount, but distinctive share ownership plans are seldom. Employee share ownership generally emerges from profit-sharing plans when profit-shares, employee earnings or employers' matching amounts are invested in company shares. For this reason, statistical data are only available for profit-sharing plans (which have to be registered with the Ministry of Labour) and not for employee share ownership.

According to the data of the Association Francaise de Gestion (AFG), two-thirds of large companies operated profit-sharing plans with 10.3 million beneficiaries in 2006. In this year, the total amount of funds allocated in profit-sharing plans was EUR 12.9 billion, of which EUR 5.8 billion were held in 'participation' profit-sharing plans, EUR 2.5 billion in 'intéressement' profit-sharing plans, EUR 2.9 billion were voluntary payments of employees and EUR 1.7 billion were matching payments by the employing company to PEE and PERCO. The cumulative value of assets (including funds invested in 2006, value of the remaining assets and capital gains from these assets) was EUR 82.4 billion, which is 19 per cent more than in 2005. In 2006, 52 per cent of assets from funds were invested in company shares, so it seems that employee share ownership is increasing, although the share of employees in most companies is still less than 3 per cent.

**General Attitude**

Successive governments have been developing employee financial participation schemes for the past 40 years. Legislation had to become more complex to prevent discrimination of lower ranking employees in relation to management on the one hand, and to prevent employee abuse of these schemes to avoid taxes on the other. The main political goals are more equal distribution of wealth through participation in enterprise results, enhancing purchase power and solving social security problems, especially pensions.

The employers' associations support voluntary plans as these allow more flexibility in the planning of labour costs; they strongly oppose compulsory schemes, although they are compelled to implement them. Employers also support the development of savings plans and advocate the view that these should be closely connected to pension plans and even replace them. The trade unions generally support all schemes that do not lead to a reduction of cash pay. If employee assets are to be invested, the trade unions advocate diversification on the grounds of less risk rather than investment in the employer company's shares. They oppose using the savings plans to reduce or replace pensions.

## Legal and fiscal framework

The major employee financial participation plans 'intéressement' profit-sharing, 'participation' profit-sharing, short term savings plans (Plan d'Epargne d'Enterprise (PEE)) and long-term savings plans (Plan d'Epargne-Retraite Collectif (PERCO))[51] were introduced by various laws (that is, Law on Profit Sharing of 1959, Law on Compulsory Profit Sharing of 1967, Law on Employee Savings Plans of 1967) which have been amended many times, most recently by the Law of 31 December 2006 and the Law of 4 December 2008. Irrespective of the type of plan, an employee starting to work for the company must be informed of the plans in operation and the pre-conditions of participation. Company training of employees on financial participation issues is linked to tax incentives. The tax relief for the employer company is EUR 75 for one hour training of the employee, but not more than EUR 5,000 per company for two years.

As confirmed by the 2006 amendment, plans have to be approved by the Ministry of Labour before introduction. If the state authority submits no objections within four months of submission of the agreement by the employer company, the plan is deemed approved. However, this provision does not protect the employer company, should the competent state authority contest the plan implementation.

### Share ownership

As explained above, no special share ownership plans are common; share ownership is generally acquired by profit-sharing plans. However, it is possible to transfer free shares to employees; since 2006 such transfers are without a holding period and with a vesting period of four years. In short-term savings plans it is possible to offer employees to subscribe to a capital increasing at a subscription price with up to 20 per cent discount of the fair market value using their savings and company matching contributions. In privatisation, 5 per cent of shares are reserved for employees and can be offered at a discount of up to 20 per cent of fair market value.

*Profit-sharing*

As explained above, all major plans are broadly regarded as profit-sharing plans. An employee may participate in different types of plan at the same time if several plans are offered by the company. The combination of different plans is advantageous from the viewpoint of taxation and, therefore, quite common. Profit-sharing accumulations can be transferred to PEE or PERCO as well as – for profit-sharing only – to a special blocked account in the companies' accountancy. Since 2006, it is prescribed by law that the company must introduce PEE if it operates a profit-sharing plan (participation) and must introduce PERCO if it has been operating PEE for more than five years.

"Participation" profit-sharing plans are compulsory; the other three plans are voluntary. Profit-sharing, both 'intéressement' and 'participation', as well as PERCO can be introduced only on the basis of an agreement with employee representatives, whereas PEE may also be based on a unilateral decision of the employer company. All plans must be broad-based (that is, apply to all employees, with the exception of those with less than three months of service). A blocking period of five years (profit-sharing, PEE) or until retirement (PERCO) is compulsory and linked to substantial tax incentives, which generally include exemption from personal income tax and social security contributions and imposition of special social contributions of 7.6 per cent for both employees and the employer company and on returns of 10 per cent. The blocking period expires under certain personal circumstances of employees (death, disability, cessation of employment, insolvency, marriage, birth of a third child, divorce while keeping custody of at least one child, purchase of a principal residence, founding or acquisition of an enterprise by the employee).

Invested employee earnings and matching amounts of the employer company must be, and employee profit-shares can be, transferred to mutual funds (FCPE), usually managed by assets management firms, which are branches of banks or insurance companies that invest the assets in shares or bonds of the employer company or of several different companies. FCPEs are usually at enterprise level (whereas special rules apply to SMEs), they may be either diversified or non diversified (see Tables 7.2 and 7.3), and although the company must offer the former the latter is optional. If the employer company is not listed, the FCPE is obliged to invest one-third of assets in marketable shares or bonds, unless the company buys back 10 per cent of its own shares or all assets belong to employees planning to participate in a leveraged buy-out. After the blocking period expires, the accumulated assets are paid out as a lump sum (all plans) or an annuity (only PEE and PERCO).

*Table 7.2*   Composition of the Diversified FCPE: Limitations for certain types of assets/issuers in per cent of total value of the FCPE

| maximum 33 per cent | minimum 66 per cent |
|---|---|
| (0 per cent for multi-non-listed SME fund) | (100 per cent for multi-non-listed SME fund) |
| qualified assets of enterprise/ group that grant their employees contributions in order to acquire shares in the FCPE | other qualified assets/investments:<br>• maximum 5 per cent of each issuer/investment fund<br>• maximum 10 per cent of diversified investment fund investing in employer company |

*Table 7.3*   Composition of the Non-Diversified FCPE: Limitations for certain types of asset/issuer in per cent of total value of the FCPE

| 33–100 per cent | maximum 66 per cent |
|---|---|
| (maximum 66 per cent for non-listed SME fund) | (minimum 33 per cent for non-listed SME fund) |
| qualified assets of enterprise/ group that grant their employees contributions in order to acquire shares in the FCPE | other qualified assets/investments maximum 5 per cent of each issuer/ investment fund |

In the following, individual plans are presented.

*Compulsory Profit-Sharing (participation).* This is compulsory in all companies with 50 or more employees, although voluntary in smaller companies. However, not all such companies have introduced profit-sharing plans in practice, especially if they cannot pay the minimum amount of profit-share due to plan participants according to the compulsory formula given the financial results. The compulsory formula for the special profit-sharing reserve is as follows: $0.5 \times$ (net profit − 5 per cent of share capital) $\times$ total wage bill/value added. In addition, an additional bonus (the so-called 'working dividend') can be paid according to the general rules of the company's profit-sharing plan if profits are substantially higher than expected. The maximum annual amount per employee is equivalent to 75 per cent of the annual ceiling for the calculation of social contributions, for example, for 2009 EUR 25,731. The plan can be introduced on the basis of an agreement with the trade unions, with the workers' council or with the approval of a two-thirds majority of employees. Since 2006, profit-sharing became a compulsory part of collective agreements of the economic sectors which then may be applied to individual companies on a voluntary basis. Since the 2008 amendment, each year employees may opt to have their profit-share paid out for the current year. If they do not, their profit-share is automatically deferred and, during the blocking period, transferred either to a special blocked account in the accountancy of the company (CCB) or to a mutual fund (FCPE). If deferred, the benefit is exempted from personal income tax and regular social security contributions; a 2 per cent social tax for employers and a flat social contribution of 7.5 per cent plus 0.5 per cent (total 8 per cent) on 97 per cent of the employee's contributions apply instead. The interest or returns are subject to a special social contribution of 10 per cent and, if paid out during the blocking period, income tax (if the interest or returns are accumulated, they are exempt from income taxation).

*Voluntary Profit-sharing (intéressement).* This is voluntary and its formula is free. It can be linked to indicators other than profit, such as reduction of losses, fewer work injuries or other performance related indicators, but it is usually based on financial indicators. The maximum amount is the same as for the profit-sharing plan. It is introduced by a three-year agreement with the trade unions or the workers' council, which is not automatically renewable, or on the basis of approval by two-thirds of all employees. The amount normally is paid out to the employee immediately and is then exempt from social security contributions (except the special flat social contribution of 7.5 per cent), but subject to full personal income tax. However, if the profit-share is invested for more than five years in a company savings plan (PEE) or until retirement in a long-term savings plans (PERCO) income tax exemption applies and the fiscal treatment is as described above.

*Savings plans (PEE, PERCO).* These are voluntary and their formula is free. The holding period is five years for PEE and until retirement for PERCO. An employee can transfer part of their earnings and/or their profit-share up to a ceiling of the total amount of 25 per cent of their gross earnings to the savings plan. The company is entitled (but not obliged) to match the employee contribution with an amount up to three times higher. The maximum matching amount (abondement) was originally expressed in absolute figures, but, since 2006, it has been expressed as a proportion of the annual social security ceiling. The maximum matching amount is higher for the investment in company shares than for diversified investment, and higher for PERCO (about Euro 6,000) than for PEE (about Euro 3,000) and may reach up to circa Euro 9,000 cumulative. The matching amount is generally exempted from personal income tax and social security contributions, but is subject to a special social contribution of 7.5 per cent. However, the amount of the matching contribution exceeding the ceiling for PEE in PERCO is subject to an 8.2 per cent flat tax, and the amount exceeding the ceiling for PERCO is subject to full personal income tax and social security contributions for the employee and the employer company. As above, the tax on interest and returns is a flat tax of 10 per cent. After the blocking period expires, the amount may remain in the PEE/PERCO with the same fiscal advantages, can be paid as a lump sum or an annuity or invested elsewhere, for example. In large companies, leveraged savings plans are frequent; furthermore, employees can use an interest free bank loan to purchase up to ten times more shares than with their own earnings against a share in capital gains.

*Participation in decision making*

Most major employee financial participation plans can be introduced only on the basis of an agreement with the trade unions or the workers' council, so that employee representatives generally participate in negotiations on the design of the plans. In addition, the workers' council is usually consulted before the agreement is signed and informed of the implementation of profit-sharing plans, both 'intéressement' and 'participation'. For savings plans, a special supervisory body elected by the workers' council must be consulted and informed. Mutual funds are managed by a supervisory board consisting of one-half employee representatives, elected by the workers' council for two years, and one-half employer representatives. If the assets are invested in company shares, the chairman must be an employee representative. In practice, this body is inefficient, because the management decisions are taken at face value by the bank or insurance company and generally accepted by the supervisory board. If employees own more than 3 per cent of the equity capital of a listed company, they must have at least one representative on the company board who must be elected. The mandate of the representative ends upon cessation of employment. All companies have to amend their statutes accordingly at the first extraordinary meeting after the publication of the law. However, this provision does not play a major role in practice, because employees have a larger share in a very small number of companies.

## XII   Hungary

Employee ownership has been the main form of financial participation in Hungary. It has been variously structured to include employee acquisition of state assets on preferential terms during the first wave of privatisation, employee share ownership as a part of external privatisation, long-term incentive plans and stock options. In the first stages of privatisation, the most prevalent form of employee ownership was the Hungarian Employee Share Ownership Programme, modelled on the US ESOP. Although briefly popular as a quick expedient for getting assets into the hands of company employees, now that privatisation is over, the number of ESOP companies is declining. Except for the Approved Employee Securities Benefit Programme, introduced by tax laws in 2003, the other PEPPER schemes, including profit-sharing, are found only to a limited extent. Having little support in official economic policy, they are not formally registered or reported. As for profit-sharing, according to Hewitt Associates,[52] eight out of ten Hungarian enterprises use short-term incentives that go beyond the simple sales premium. Of these, 20 per cent use profit-sharing; most (67 per cent) base profit-shares on the employee's status in the hierarchy, but many (23 per cent) set other criteria as well. According to the survey, however, only 10 per cent of employees entitled to a profit-share actually receive one.

## General attitude

Trade unions at the national level actively promoted employee ownership in various forms. Local trade unions, however, often took a surprisingly passive stand, declaring their interest in employee buyouts but taking no role in organising the procedure. Other local trade unions actively lobbied for preferential shares and ESOP buyouts. In addition to influencing privatisation decisions, unions usually had at least one of their leaders as a member of the organising committee and the ESOP trust. Employees and their trade union representatives regarded the ESOP and other buyout schemes as tools for preserving jobs. Since the end of privatisation in 1998, lobbyists have fought, so far with little success, to gain political support and financial incentives for extending the use of ESOPs beyond the privatisation process, and to make use of this technique in cases of liquidation. Another important effort of lobbyists was to amend ESOP and tax laws to protect existing ESOPs from an unfavourable economic environment. To summarise, Hungary has no focused policy on employee ownership. Although political parties on both left and right declare their commitment in the past as well as most recently, the principle has yet to be translated into economic policy.

## Legal and fiscal framework

The legal framework of employee financial participation includes both profit-sharing and employee share ownership. However, no specific legal or tax incentives for profit-sharing are granted either to employer or employee. Company law explicitly regulates employee shares, including stock options. Recently an Approved Employee Securities Benefit Programme with specific incentives has been introduced.

*Share ownership*

*Employee privatisation on preferential terms (1991, 1995, 2007).* The Privatisation Law of 1991 contained various preferential privatisation techniques. In 1995 a new Law on Privatisation, still in force, reduced some allowances for employees, but offered at the same time new forms and techniques: that is, privatisation on deferred terms, employee privatisation on preferential terms, Egzisztencia credit and ESOPs.[53] In 2007 the Law on Privatisation was superseded by the Law on State Property[54] which, however, preserved the described incentive system. Privatisation offers three financial techniques for acquiring employee ownership on preferential terms: (1) price reduction, (2) purchase by instalment and (3) purchase on credit. Thus a discount of up to 150 per cent of the annual minimum salary is possible. However, the nominal value of shares thus acquired may not exceed 15 per cent of the company's registered capital nor the discount granted exceed 50 per cent of the purchase price. In the event of paying the discounted price in instalments, except if sold within the framework of an ESOP (see below), a down-payment of 15 per cent is required in cash, upon which payment of the remainder may be deferred for a period of up to three years at the prevailing interest rate charged on public debts. Further, Hungarian citizens may take up to 50 per cent of the property that they wish to acquire, up to a maximum of HUF 50 million, as an Egisztencia credit, regardless of the number of buyers.[55]

*Employee stock ownership programme (1992, 2003, 2007).* In Hungary the US ESOP system strongly influenced the law regulating the establishment and functioning of ESOPs.[56] Basically, the Hungarian ESOP followed the American trust model. However, there is a major difference between the two systems: whereas the Hungarian ESOP is a privatisation vehicle with the organisation ceasing to exist as soon as all the securities are paid for and their ownership transferred to the employees, the US ESOP continues to administer the securities of employees.[57] The Hungarian ESOP is an independent legal entity; so-called privatisation and non-privatisation ESOPs exist. In the case of the former, the ESOP buys the property of the State Property Agency or of municipalities; there are incentives attached to this form. In the latter case, shares or business shares not at the disposal of the State Property Agency are sold, for example, already existing securities or securities issued in connection with capital increase. The only difference between the two forms is that there are no specific incentives encouraging companies or employees to establish non-privatisation ESOPs. If the employees decide that the ESOP should remain in place, regulations for the period after repayment (for example, rules for marketing shares) must be developed.[58] The ESOP is fully liable for its obligations. Members of the ESOP are not liable for its debts except for the securities already allocated to them. Until the shares are transferred to the plan participants, the ESOP owns the shares. As for the exercise of property rights, participants have voting rights in proportion to their registered shares, but only up to a maximum of 5 per cent of the property acquired by the ESOP.

Tax exemptions for privatisation ESOPs allow the company to offer tax allowances for property sold to the ESOP as prescribed by the Corporate Tax Law. Accordingly, the company may deduct up to 20 per cent of the amount paid to the ESOP from its tax base. ESOPs were not subject to corporate profit tax until 31 December 1996. However, after that date, the income of ESOP falls under the rules of the Law on Corporate Tax and Dividend Tax, and, accordingly, 16 per cent tax is paid on their taxable income.[59] According to Personal Income Tax Law, securities transferred from the company to employees are tax-free since they are not considered income; however, when the employee sells these shares, the proceeds are taxed at the capital gain rate of 20 per cent.[60]

*Private companies (1988).* Employees' shares, first introduced by the Law on Business Associations of 1988, still exist under the current law. They are registered shares and can be issued free of charge or at a reduced price in accordance with the provisions of the articles of association of the joint-stock company, for example, in the context of a Long-Term Incentive Plan or a broad-based Stock Option Plan. Employees' shares may be issued in conjunction with a simultaneous share capital increase of the joint-stock company, up to a maximum of 15 per cent of the increased share capital. A joint-stock company may pass a resolution entitling employee held shares to dividends from after-tax profits to be distributed among shareholders before the shares belonging to other categories or classes of shares, but following shares granting preferred dividends. In the event the employee dies or terminates their employment, except in the case of retirement, their heir or the employer has the right to transfer the employee's shares to other company employees within six months.[61] The employer company can distribute them free or at a discounted price, making this form of financial participation very attractive to employees. However, this form of share acquisition enjoys no tax incentives. Since 1 January 2003, income received in the form of securities is no longer regarded as an allowance in kind.[62] Thus, in the case of employees' shares, the difference between the purchase price and the sale price is subject to personal income tax.

*Approved Employee Securities Benefit Programme (2003).* At the beginning of 2003, new legislation[63] came into effect allowing companies to set up state-recognised, tax-qualified stock plans. The organiser of an Employee Securities Benefit Programme has to submit an application for its recognition to the Ministry of Finance, which informs the relevant tax authorities of its decision. To be approved, the programme must comply with certain proscribed conditions, for example, only securities issued by the applicant company or by its majority shareholder may be offered in the programme; statutory threshold levels of at least 10 per cent employee participation and a management share of less than 25 per cent representing less than 50 per cent of total share value. At the time of sale, the employee is taxed on the spread between exercise price and sale price. This capital gain is taxed at 20 per cent, separately from other income.[64] Companies have no withholding or reporting obligations in connection with employee stock option or purchase plans. The first HUF 500,000 of the shares that have met vesting requirements are not taxable at exercise or vesting. Any shares deemed non-qualified are taxed as normal employment income (progressive scale from 18 to 38 per cent). Vested shares must be held in a security account overseen by a trustee during an obligatory three-year vesting period which ends on 31 December of the second year after the securities have been acquired. At the end of the vesting period, employee shareholders enjoy the same rights as any other shareholder of the same class. The most recent amendment of the Law on Personal Income Tax (Act LXI of 2006) stipulates that gains of all share purchases and similar transactions should be added up in the given tax year and that in calculating the tax base, instead of the nominal value at the time of allocating the share option, the actual value at the time of purchase is the relevant number, not the nominal value at the time of allocation. At the same time, according to the interpretation of the officers at the Ministry of Finance, the amendment abolished the blocking period.

### Profit-sharing

Except for Article 5 of the Labour Code, stating that an employer may grant any benefit to its employees if it is provided in a non-discriminatory manner, no regulations exist. There are neither tax allowances nor other incentives for profit-sharing; any kind of benefit paid to employees falls under the Personal Income Tax Law and there is no allowance for employers.

*Participation in decision making*

Employee representatives make up one-third of the supervisory board in companies with more than 200 employees. In companies with more than 200 employees having a two-tier board system (both a supervisory and a management board), the works council has the right to nominate one-third of the members of the supervisory board. In companies with a single-tier board system (only a board of directors), employee participation at the board level must be regulated by an agreement between the works council and the company. This is a new development (before the 2006 legislation only two-tier board structures were possible), and it represents a potential weakening of employee representation at the board level, because there are no minimum requirements. Furthermore, Article 42 of the Law on State Property requires, that before adopting a decision about the sale of an enterprise under majority state ownership, the employees' representatives must be informed about any possible opportunities about the acquisition of ownership by the employees. Workplace representation in Hungary is provided by both local trade unions and (since 1992) elected works councils, with the balance between the two varying over time. After legal amendments initiated by the socialist government elected in 2002, only the union has the right to negotiate collective agreements.

# XIII   Ireland

Although employee financial participation has been discussed in Ireland since the mid-1970s, not until 1982 was the first tax incentivised plan introduced (Approved Profit-sharing Scheme – APSS). Additional tax incentives came in 1986. During the tax reform of 1997, additional plans (Approved Savings-Related Share Option Scheme – SAYE; Employee Share Ownership Trust – ESOT) were added. In 2001 another plan (Approved Share Option Scheme – APOS) was approved.

There are now six share-based plans linked to tax incentives – the four approved schemes enumerated above plus the purchase of new shares and restricted stock schemes. In addition there is an unapproved stock option plan. According to statistics provided by the Irish Business and Employers Confederation (IBEC), in 2002 there were in operation 400 APSS plans, 15 APOS plans and 90 SAYE plans with 140,000 employees. Whereas the number of new schemes declined after 2001, it has been increasing again since 2004. In 2008, 10 per cent of the private sector workforce (estimated 135,000 employees) participated in 500 APSS schemes according to the Irish ProShare Association Revenue Review of APSS. Although there were only 125 SAYE plans in 2008, they seem to be the most popular judging by the number of participating employees. Many companies combine several approved plans and operate unapproved ones (no statistics are available). Most plans are found in listed multinational companies.

## General attitude

Employee financial participation, especially share ownership, has been supported by successive governments, as a means of aligning the interests of employees with employers and making retirement more secure. However, it has not been linked with pension policy so far. Employee Financial Involvement (EFI) is addressed in national economic programmes and in national wage agreements, but is regulated only by local collective agreements or by in-house agreements.

Since the beginning of the 1980s, the Irish Business and Employers' Confederation (IBEC) has supported tax-efficient share schemes and regard them as a key element in recruiting and retaining personnel, but only if they remain voluntary. The Irish ProShare Association, which promotes and conducts research on employee financial participation, was founded by IBEC. Trade unions also support those financial participation plans that provide explicit financial rewards as well as a sense of participation. Representatives of both employers and trade unions support partnership initiatives at the enterprise level.

## Legal and fiscal framework

Employee financial participation plans fall into two categories: either they are approved or unapproved. Plans introduced under the annual finance acts and approved by and registered with the Inland Revenue enjoy tax advantages as well as exemption from PRSI (compulsory social security contributions), which especially benefit employees. Unapproved plans may be designed and introduced at the employer company's discretion but receive no specific tax advantages. Approved plans must be designed in accord with legal specifications whereas unapproved plans enjoy more flexibility. Under current legislation, all approved plans (and typically unapproved plans as well) are share-based, including profit-sharing, share ownership and stock option plans. Tax incentives for approved plans are governed by the Taxes Consolidation Act of 1997, as amended (Part 17, Schedules 11, 12, 12A, 12B and 12C).

Unapproved plans are used for granting shares or options to individual employees, where the company does not operate an approved scheme or where the company wishes to award shares in excess of the amount that can attract favourable tax treatment or in contravention of the rules of any of the approved schemes. Unapproved plans are usually combined with approved plans.

*Share ownership*

Companies are generally allowed to acquire own shares (Section 211 paragraph 1 Companies Act 1990 – CA 1990). The prohibition of insider dealing shall not prevent a person from acquiring securities in a company pursuant to an employee profit-sharing scheme (Section 110 paragraph 1 lit. b) CA 1990). Money and loans can be provided by the company to facilitate the acquisition of shares under an employees' share scheme designed to enable present and former employees of the firm and members of their families to acquire shares in the firm or other firms in the same group (Section 60 paragraph 13 lit. b) and c) CA 1963).

An approved share ownership plan (purchase of new shares) as well as three stock option plans (SAYE, APOS and restricted stock) are supported by tax incentives. There is also an unapproved stock option plan that exempts employees from PRSI contributions but imposes the full personal income tax at exercise.

*Share ownership plans.* In the purchase of new shares, if employees pay full price for newly issued shares and hold them for three years, the subscription cost (subject to a lifetime ceiling of 6,350 EUR as of 2006) is exempt from both personal income taxes and PRSI. A capital gains tax is based on the issue price. The employer company is also exempt from PRSI. In a Restricted Stock Scheme, participants are given a future interest in shares, subject to certain restrictions. On shares held for at least one year, the employee may deduct a specific percentage of the benefit from the personal income tax base (from 10 per cent for one year to 55 per cent for more than five years).

*Approved Stock Option Plans.* The Approved Savings-Related Share Option Scheme (SAYE), introduced by the Finance Act of 1999, is currently the most popular plan judging by the number of participants relative to the number of companies operating such schemes. It must be open to all employees on similar terms, with possible exception of employees with less than three years of service. The plan is structured as follows: the employee makes a save-as-you-earn (SAYE) contract with a bank, agreeing to save a specified monthly amount (EUR 12 to 500) through deductions from after-tax remuneration for a period of three or five years service,[65] while the employer corporation grants him share options for the maximum number of shares their SAYE savings will be able to buy at the exercise price. The SAYE contract always includes a tax-free bonus to be awarded at completion, the amount depending on the term. The exercise price may be up to 25 per cent lower than the market value of the shares at the time of grant. At maturity of the SAYE contract, the employee may choose to exercise the option, selling or retaining the shares, or to receive the savings and bonus in cash. These requirements fulfilled, the employee is exempt from the personal income tax at the time of grant or exercise; the capital gains tax, however, is levied at the time of sale. Neither the employee nor employer must pay PRSI.

The *Approved Share Option Scheme (APOS)* was introduced in the Finance Act of 2001. Eligibility requirements are the same as for the share option scheme described above. It is further required that at least 70 per cent of options are transferred to the broad-based plan; shares may not be sold within three years of grant. These requirements fulfilled, the employee is exempt from the personal income tax at grant or exercise; at sale, the capital gains tax must be paid on the difference between proceeds and option price. Neither the employer company nor the employee is liable for PRSI.

### Profit-sharing

The oldest form of financial participation is the approved profit-sharing, introduced in 1982. It is a share-based leveraged profit-sharing plan. Cash-based and/or direct share-based profit-sharing plans are also possible, but have no tax advantages. Individual gain-sharing based on performance-related indicators, promoted by the government since 2000, may be more widespread than cash-based profit-sharing.

*Approved Profit-Sharing Scheme (APSS)*. The APSS must apply to all employees on similar terms, with the possible exception of those having less than three years service. Any shares allocated under APSS cannot be subject to restrictions other than those that apply to all shares of the same class. An exception to the general rule on restrictions exists, when the company's articles of association require an employee or director to dispose of their shares on leaving the company.[66] Employee shares are held in trust and cannot be withdrawn for two years; not until the third year do tax incentives apply. The trust must allocate the shares to the employees within 18 months and subsequently is not held liable for the tax on dividends. Employee benefits of up to EUR 12,700 (2006) are exempt from both income taxes and PRSI contributions. If the shares are sold during the blocking period, the employee is liable to personal income tax on the lesser amount of the market value of the shares or the proceeds of sale. Shares sold after the blocking period are subject only to the capital gains tax.

Subsidiary schemes to APSS are the 'relinquished salary' scheme, where the employee is allowed to deduct up to 7.5 per cent of their base pre-tax salary to increase their share-based profit-sharing, and the employer matching scheme (so-called BOGOF, that is, buy-one get-one-free), where the employee buys shares with their after-tax income and the employer matches their purchases. The employing company can deduct costs of setting up and operation of the plan and costs of providing shares to employees, and it is not liable to PRSI.

*Employee Stock Ownership Trust (ESOT)*. Since 1997 the APSS has been allowed to combine with an ESOT, similar to the American Employee Stock Ownership Plan (ESOP). In contrast to the APSS trust, the ESOT is empowered to hold shares for 20 years; it may also borrow funds and sell shares. The trust pays no tax on dividends used for specified purposes (for example, acquiring shares, repaying loans, and so on). Shares transferred to the ESOT must be common shares, fully paid for and irredeemable. There are three types of trust structure permitted: single trustee; majority of trustees are employees; and equal employee/company representation plus an independent trustee. On shares not transferred directly to employees but first to the APSS trust, tax incentives for APSS apply. The ESOT is not subject to capital gains tax on disposal of shares provided the proceeds are used for specified purposes. The ESOT was widely used for privatisation of state-owned enterprise. Usually 14.9 per cent of the equity capital of the company undergoing privatisation was accumulated in the ESOT for employees. Shares were typically acquired by a combination of loans and a direct state grant, in exchange for productivity concessions and the agreement of trade unions to privatise. A well-known example is the Eircom ESOP, whereby the employees own 35 per cent of the shares through an ESOT which has a representative on the board of the now privatised company.

### Participation in decision making

Participation in decision making and financial participation have no direct connection, nor can existing decision making rights be extended by a financial participation plan. General provisions of labour law, such as equal pay and prohibition of discrimination, also apply. Employee representatives in Ireland's single-tier boards are only found in the state-owned sector, where they normally account for a third of the total. Privatisation has cut the number of companies covered and the process is continuing. There is no statutory system for workplace representation in Ireland. Those who work in unionised workplaces – about half of the entire workforce – have representation through the union. New procedures have been introduced as a result of the EU directive on information and consultation, but they may not make much difference. National pay pacts have provided a framework for bargaining in Ireland since 1987. Agreed between the unions, employers and government, they are not legally binding, but have been widely observed.

## XIV   Italy

Financial participation in Italy has emerged particularly since the mid-1980s, with the development of firm level bargaining agreements. This development took place at a time when companies were restructuring their production processes and redesigning human resource management; labour unions, seeking more power and legitimacy, saw to it that workers had an important role in shaping these agreements at the company level.

The most important form of employee financial participation used to be profit-sharing but recently employee ownership has been catching up. The Italian privatisation process, implemented on a large scale since the 1990s, had no significant impact on employee ownership. Workers co-operatives, on the other hand, have significant importance in the commercial sector, as well as a long historical tradition. Tax incentives for employee financial participation were introduced in the late 1990s; unlike in most other countries they regard also smaller firms, i.e., limited liability companies.

### General Attitude

Under the Tripartite Agreement of 1993,[67] new rules on decentralised bargaining and income policy were adopted. Although this had a positive effect on the introduction of PEPPER schemes, corresponding tax incentives for promoting employee financial participation were not introduced until 1997; the emphasis as placed on achieving macro-economic benefits through linking pay to performance, especially to check wage inflation. Promoting a new environment of participation at the micro-economic level was less relevant. It is difficult to evaluate what impact the bargaining rules of the 1993 agreement had on the spread of employee financial participation in Italy; regularly published official data on the incidence of these plans is lacking. Recently, however, a renewed interest in this issue has stimulated new proposals to make compensation schemes more flexible and to increase tax incentives. This government initiative, supported by both, unions and employers' representatives, confirmed by Law No. 126/2008 was extended in the 2009 budget.

Trade unions and employer representatives alike have mixed views of financial participation. Trade unions agree in principle on the positive effects of profit-sharing but are divided over employee share ownership schemes. Of the major trade unions, CISL is in favour of share schemes, regarding them as a means to expand participation in decision making; UIL, on the other hand, believes it not the function of trade unions to promote share ownership. CGIL, however, is traditionally opposed to share schemes; its position is that employee financial participation is better realised through special complementary funds (Fondi di previdenza complementare). Employer associations are similarly divided. Confindustria wants to leave the matter entirely to individual enterprises without taking a stand. The organisations representing SMEs (Confartigianato, Confcommercio) are more open to financial participation if it takes the form of funds to promote regional development of SMEs.

In summary, the political situation in Italy is in a state of evolution. All political parties agree on introducing fiscal incentives (namely, tax reduction) to encourage company-level agreements linking increases in remuneration to increased productivity. This principle was mentioned in the tripartite agreement of 23 July 2007; although not yet implemented, it is expected to decrease the tax burden on remuneration made in the form of profit-sharing. Despite increased interest in this subject, other kinds of participation, for example, employee shareholding, do not have the unanimous support of employer associations and trade unions.

## Legal and Fiscal Framework

Although Art. 47 Italian Constitution recognises the right of workers to have access to share investments in the main production industries, legislative support of employee financial participation is comparatively underdeveloped.[68] Special legislation, including tax incentives, exists for profit-sharing, employee share ownership and stock option plans.

### Share Ownership

Pursuant to the Law No. 262 of 28 December 2005, quoted companies that intend to provide share or stock-option plans to employees, directors or consultants need the approval by the shareholder meeting; they also must communicate information on the plan to both Consob (the Italian Securities and Exchange Commission) and to the public. In general the sale gain is taxed with 12.5 CGT instead of 40% provided that the transfer regards less than 2% of the votes or 5% of the capital in quoted companies or respectively less than 20% of the votes or 25% of the capital in non-quoted companies; in cases of losses the amount can be carried forward as a tax credit.

*Share plans* – The Italian Civil Code (hereinafter referred to as CC) regulates discounted employee shares in joint-stock companies with a holding period of 3-5 years.[69] According to Art. 2441 CC, the preemptive right of shareholders can be suspended for up to 25 per cent of newly issued shares by majority vote of the general assembly if these shares are to be transferred to employees; for more than 25 per cent, majority shareholder vote is required. To facilitate the acquisition of shares by employees, the law permits a company to advance funds and to make and secure loans, with a view to acquisition by employees of the company, conditional that this 'financial assistance' is within the limits of distributable reserves (Art. 2358 CC). Furthermore, Articles 2349 and 2351 CC permit the issuing of special Employee Shares in capital increases with specific rules for form, tradability and rights (see below Part 3, XIV.2b). Since 1999 pursuant to Decree Law 505/99 free shares are not considered income and are exempted from personal income tax and social security contributions up to a threshold of Euro 2,066. According to Art. 51 of the Income Tax Law (hereinafter referred to as ITL), the tax exemption is linked to a blocking period of three years. However, no blocking period has to be observed if the shares are transferred *ex lege* (decision of the Tax Agency No. 97 of 25 July 2005).

*Privatisation* – Pursuant to § 381 Law No. 266 of 23 December 2005, the by-laws of companies in which the State has a significant ownership position may foresee special financial instruments or categories of shares, to be offered free to all shareholders, or in the case of specific shareholders for the payment of compensation in order to facilitate the privatisation process.

*Stock option plans* – Specific rules regarding stock option plans were introduced in 1997 under Art. 48 para. 2 lit. g) and g-bis) ITL as amended by the Decree Law 314/97. Decree Law 505/99 exempted the increase in value between grant and exercise of the option from social security contributions and personal income tax with new conditions for the tax exemption introduced by Decree Law No. 262 of 3 October 2006 (the so-called Financial Law converted into Law No. 286/2006): (1) minimum vesting period of three years from when they are assigned; (2) at the moment when the employee exercises the option or the share is accrued, the company is listed on the market;[70] (3) a minimum holding period of five years from date of exercise, for shares representing the difference between the value of the shares at grant and the amount provided by the employee. Nevertheless the exemption from PIT was cancelled by Decree Law No. 112/2008 and Law No. 113/2008.

*Limited liability companies (SRL)* – While a share in a SRL transferred as remuneration is subject to corporate income tax at company level, a free share is exempt from tax and social security contributions up to an amount of Euro 7.500 (2009) with the notary fees borne by the employer.

### Profit-Sharing

Rules for profit-sharing (quote di salario legate agli obiettivi di reddi-tività/produdutivita) are determined by collective bargaining at the firm level. Tax incentives for profit-sharing were introduced by the Decree Law No. 67 of March 1997 allowing a partial tax exemption for employ-ers' contributions up to one per cent of the payroll, this percentage was subsequently increased to 3 per cent.[71] Further, a ten per cent 'compul-sory solidarity contribution', substituting for the general social security contribution, was introduced. Although the new Law No. 247/2007 increased the tax exemption for employer contributions to a maximum of 5%, the Inter-ministerial decree of 7 May 2008 set a ceiling of 3%. The employer benefits from a 25% reduction in social security contri-butions. The employee is exempted from social security contributions, which the state covers in order not to reduce the initial contribution. The ceiling of the annual maximum value of the bonus rose from Euro 3.000 to Euro 6.000 with the income ceiling for eligibility for incentives fixed at Euro 35,900 annually.

### Participation in Decision-Making

Employee financial participation is generally not linked to the exten-sion of the existing participation rights in decision-making. A rare exemption is Art. 2351 CC. it stipulates that shareholders of specific Employee Shares can be granted the right to nominate a representative to the management or supervisory board under the company's articles of association. Nevertheless, Art. 2351, introduced with the 2003 reform of the Civil Code has not been used to date. Although Art. 46 of the Italian Constitution recognises the right of workers to 'co-operate in the running of the companies in a manner and within the limits defined by the law', this regulation was never transformed in special laws.

However, Law No. 300/70 guarantees the freedom of trade unions and the right to be represented. The so-called Intesa Quadro between the major trade unions CGIL, CISL and UIL of 1 March 1991 introduces an organ of union representatives (RSU, rappresentanze sindacali unitarie) which may be set up in any company with more than 15 employees and has the right to represent workers, for example in collective bargaining. Information rights (for example, about investment, planning, production, forecasts, technological changes) and consultation rights (for example, on internal work rules and the working environment) are defined in collective bargaining contracts. The recent transposition of the European Directives on Information and Consultation rights (Decree Law 25/2007) into national law extends and strengthens the effectiveness of these rights in all companies employing more than 50 employees.

## XV   Latvia

Employee financial participation in Latvia may be summarised as poorly developed and on the decline. During the transition period, privatisation shaped the environment for employee financial participation and influenced the current state of employee share ownership and profit-sharing. However, the transition process only resulted in a low level of employee financial participation. By the end of 1998, shares with the nominal value of LVL 27 million, amounting to 13.56 per cent of total shares, had been sold for vouchers to 25,611 employees and former employees of the companies, amounting to 13.56 per cent of the shares. During the period 1997–9, employee and former employee ownership decreased by 19.2 per cent and 23.3 per cent.[72] Profit-sharing is reported in only 7 per cent of 167 enterprises responding to a 1997 management survey, but five out of 28 enterprises had majority employee ownership.

### General attitude

Trade unions are quite weak; the current rate of unionisation in Latvia is 18 per cent. The Free Trade Union Confederation of Latvia (FTUC) is the biggest non-governmental organisation in Latvia; it protects the interests of employees who are trade union members at branch and inter-branch levels, and represents 25 organisations. Financial participation of employees is currently not on the trade unions' agenda. Employers are represented by the Latvian Employer's Confederation (LEC), which considers the issue of financial participation of employees is outside the Confederation's area of expertise. The government is not concerned with employee financial participation; its priority is employment. The Ministry of Social Affairs concentrates its activities on solving problems related to increases in the minimum wage and unemployment allowances. Nor is employee participation on the political agenda of Parliament. Recently, however, political parties and policymakers have shown a growing interest in this issue.

## Legal and fiscal framework

Both employee share ownership and profit-sharing are found in Latvian companies and are directly or indirectly regulated by legislation. Although there is no special legal regulation of profit-sharing, several pieces of legislation relate to employee share ownership. Regulation in this area has not been systematic, so existing legislation partly creates incentives and partly inhibits these schemes.

### Share ownership

*Privatisation.* Small privatisation started in November 1991 in accordance with the Law on the Privatisation of Objects of Trade, Catering and Services. Local privatisation commissions decided the privatisation method, initial price, and so on. Potential privatisation methods were sale to employees, auctions to a selected group, open auctions, and sale to a selected buyer. Buyers had to be Latvian citizens or to have been residents of Latvia for at least 16 years.[73] Large privatisation of state-owned property and land was and still is being done by the Latvian Privatisation Agency. Although in an advanced stage, the privatisation process is not yet completed, so that it remains possible for employees to acquire shares under the Law on the Privatisation of Objects owned by the state or a municipality and the Law on the Reorganisation of State and Municipal Enterprises in Corporations (RL). Shares of state-owned corporations can be sold to employees, in the course of privatisation, at a price even lower than the nominal value of such shares. However, the shares to be sold to the employees cannot exceed 20 per cent of the share capital of the particular company (Article 57 RL). If municipal objects are privatised by restructuring, the privatisation plan must contain a clause stating how many shares will be sold to employees, as well as the discount if such is applicable according to law (Article 40 paragraph 2 (5) RL). The 20 per cent limit on employee share privatisation seems to be a limitation of rights rather than an entitlement, because there is no clear legal obligation to offer any shares whatsoever to employees in a particular privatisation case.

*State or municipal owned companies (2001).* According to the Law on State and Municipal Corporations, the government of Latvia or the respective municipal authority decides in which state or municipal company employee shares can be issued (Article 68 paragraph 1, 2). Employee shares can only be owned by employees and board members. If employment is terminated, or the board member leaves office, the employee's shares are transferred back to the company. This is one of the exceptions when a company is allowed to acquire its own stock (Article 70). Employee stock acquired by the company must be transferred to employees within six months. Shares not transferred within the prescribed time period will be cancelled and the share capital decreased accordingly (Article 71 paragraph 1, 2).

*Private companies (2004).* For a limited liability company, there are no special legal regulations on employee share ownership so general rules apply. By contrast, a joint-stock company may issue shares that can be acquired by employees in the broad sense, that is, including managers (Article 255 paragraph 1 Commercial Law (CL)). Employee stock shall be issued only on account of the net profit of the company, and the total value of employee stock should not exceed 10 per cent of the registered company's equity capital (Article 255 paragraph 4 CL). Another limitation of employee stock is the requirement that the company's own capital not become less than the registered capital (Article 255 paragraph 5 CL). No voting right and right to liquidation quotas are attached to employee stock issued according to Article 255 CL.[74] Such stocks can be freely sold if the articles of association do not provide otherwise (Article 255 paragraph 7 CL).

### Profit-sharing

There are no legal limitations or regulations pertaining to profit-sharing. Salaries may be made dependent upon company profit and benefits may be provided in the form of premiums or in other forms directly linked to the profits of a particular company. However, all other benefits are subject to a personal income tax of 25 per cent. This reduces the incentive to provide additional benefits since the benefits of profit-sharing are 25 per cent less than they would be on dividends paid to employee shareholders; dividends are not subject to tax.

### Participation in decision making

There is no statutory employee representation at the board level in Latvia. The main form of workplace representation in Latvia is through the unions, but since the revised Labour Law (LL) came into effect on

1 June 2002, it has also been possible to elect 'authorised employee representatives' (Article 10 paragraph 1 LL). Both are involved in information and consultation and both can be involved in collective bargaining, although non-union representatives can only negotiate if there is no union (see Article 18 paragraph 1 LL). The employer shall consult with employee representatives on issues that may affect the interests of employees, in particular decisions which may substantially affect work remuneration, working conditions and employment (Article 11 paragraph 1 (2) LL).

## XVI   Lithuania

After Lithuania regained independence, employee ownership was used to implement privatisation. In the initial stage 1991–5, employee buy-outs at a discount, combined with the extensive use of vouchers by employees and leasing with the option to buy, resulted in a high percentage of employee majority ownership. By 1994, fewer than 5 per cent of privatised firms in the programme implementing the Law on the Initial Privatisation of State-owned Property (LIPSP) had no employee ownership, whereas the percentage of enterprises where employees had taken over most of the privatised assets increased from 3 per cent in 1991–2, to 65 per cent in 1993 and 92 per cent in 1994–5 (Privatisation Department at the Ministry of Economics). Because most of the preferential rights of employees were abolished in 1995, employee ownership began to decline, and ownership is now mainly in the hands of management and outsiders.[75] No data are available on profit-sharing. At present in Lithuania, financial participation tends to be viewed as an incentive for motivating managers, initiated by managers and current owners of companies.

### General attitude

Trade unions are organised through the Lithuanian Trade Union Solidarumas, the Lithuanian Labour Federation and the Lithuanian Trade Union Confederation, the last being the largest and strongest union with more than 120,000 members. In the early stage of transition, unions promoted employee ownership and actively contributed to place EO on the Lithuanian privatisation agenda. The general objective of trade unions is higher wages for employees while associating employee ownership with an increase in company profitability. Although no particular actions concerning employee financial participation are currently on the Confederation's agenda, this issue could garner support if any industrial trade union made a proposal. Employers are organised within the Lithuanian Confederation of Industrialists, which actively promotes the interests of large businesses and in the Lithuanian Employers' Confederation; the question of employee financial participation has not been addressed by either of them. Although the former has no official position on this issue, it supports initiatives of individual enterprises. Recently, employers have been paying more attention to employee motivation, for example, through financial incentives; this interest is prompted by the emigration of skilled workers, a growing problem. The coalition parties that came into power in 2004, including the Social Democrats (LSDP), the New Union (Social Liberals) and the newly established Labour party (DP), do not mention financial participation in their official programmes. Their focus is on increasing social guarantees and reducing poverty and unemployment.

## Legal and fiscal framework

Employee financial participation is only slightly regulated. Current legal regulations neither contain special provisions on PEPPER schemes nor provide companies with incentives to introduce them.

### Share ownership

*Privatisation (1991, abolished 1995, 1997).* The first stage of privatisation started when the Law on the Initial Privatisation of State-Owned Property of 1991 with the agent of the rapid privatisation in Lithuania being the voucher scheme.[76] Employees had the opportunity to buy a certain percentage of shares in the first round of auctions at lower rates before most of the remaining shares were sold in public offerings in later rounds. The percentage of shares available for employees was increased from 10 per cent in 1991 to 30 per cent in 1992 and to 50 per cent after the former Communist Party came into power in early 1993. The additional 20 per cent shares reserved for employees after 1993 did not initially include voting rights; later the general meeting could convert these shares into regular voting shares. The second stage of privatisation was based upon a new Law on Privatisation of State-owned and Municipal Property of 4 July 1995 which aimed at the sale of residual shares and some of the very large companies, including public utilities and infrastructure enterprises and abolished Vouchers; only cash privatisation was permissible. The third Law on Privatisation, still effective, was adopted on 11 April 1997. Privatisation of most enterprises in Lithuania is now complete. However, privatisation is still possible and the respective legal regulations are still in force.[77] The current Law on

Privatisation contains no significant preferential rights for employees in the privatisation process. However, if shares are privatised by public tender, employees can be offered up to 5 per cent of the state-owned shares at par value. This provision does not apply to enterprises under state control or to enterprises in which employees have already acquired shares of their employer enterprises under other laws (Article 16 paragraph 3). If shares are offered at a public tender or by direct negotiation, the final payment can be postponed for five years in the case of employees (Article 20 paragraph 3).

*Private companies (1995, 2003).* In the course of capital increase, corporations (joint-stock companies as well as limited liability companies) can issue employee shares after all shares subscribed at the time of incorporation have been paid for (Article 43 Law on Companies,[78] (CL)). The CL sets no maximum percentage on these new employee shares. They are to be distributed among all employees wishing to purchase them, except for management (Article 43 paragraph 2 CL). A restriction period of not longer than three years must be determined within which employee shares can be sold only to other employees (Article 43 paragraph 3 CL). During this period employee shares are not only of limited tradability, but also non-voting (Article 43 paragraph 3 (3) CL), although employee shares are ordinary shares (Article 43 paragraph 1 (1) CL). Article 43 paragraph 5 CL stipulates that an employee must pay for subscribed employee shares before the restriction period for the transfer of shares expires. The first payment should be made in cash within a short period; further instalments can be deducted from the employee's salary upon application of the employee. The corporation may not exact pressure on employees to force them to purchase shares or to pay for shares by salary deductions (Article 43 paragraph 4 CL). After the restriction period for the transfer of shares expires, employee shares become ordinary shares and can be sold to third parties not company employees (Article 43 paragraph 3 CL). Because most employees are minority shareholders, provisions on the protection of minority shareholders apply.

### Profit-sharing

There are no specific regulations on sharing profits with employees. Because companies pay income tax on dividends, this is viewed as an expensive method of profit distribution; therefore priority is given to share buyback schemes. Employee monetary incentive schemes used in companies include payments of premiums and bonuses, in some cases related to company turnover and profits. Bonuses have tax advantages, because they are not double taxed as dividends are (firstly at corporate profit tax rate, secondly at income tax rate), but taxed only as income for individuals (33 per cent).

*Participation in decision making*

According to the Labour Code[79] (LC), employees may be represented and protected by trade unions or by work councils (Article 19 paragraph 1 LC).[80] The work council should include representatives of all employees. A trade union, however, can be established by a small number of employees in an enterprise. The power to negotiate with the employer has been vested in trade unions (see Articles 19 paragraph 1; 21 paragraph 2; 60 paragraph 4 LC). Trade unions are active in only a few private enterprises; but the special law on work councils (Article 21 paragraph 1 LC) has not yet been adopted, so that in practice no work councils can be established. As a result, conditions favour the creation of trade unions and an expansion of their activities.

## XVII   Luxembourg

Few employee financial participation plans exist, and these are mainly in multinational companies in the financial sector. Presumably the most common form is cash-based profit-sharing; the data, however, are unreliable in  that the widely used bonus plans ('gratification') are generally unrelated to profits or other financial indicators and therefore are not genuine profit-sharing plans. Share ownership and stock option plans are few and very seldom broad-based.

According to a recent cross-country study, the percentage of enterprises offering various forms of financial participation plans in 2005 was as follows: employee share ownership plans, 3.9 per cent, and profit-sharing plans, 13.7 per cent (EWCS). Approximately 25 per cent of companies offered stock option plans in 2003.[81] Note that these figures include executive plans.

### General attitude

Government interest in employee financial participation dates from the beginning of the 1990s. At that time, policymakers were especially advocating voluntary profit-sharing, with the proviso that it should not be made a part of collective agreements. Nevertheless, no concrete policy measures were adopted, and in recent years the issue has not been broached. Employers' associations (organised in the Union des Entreprises Luxembourgeois, UEL) were generally opposed to financial participation schemes, preferring other flexible pay models; however, they have not recently taken a position. The two major trade unions, the Onofhängege Gewerkschaftsbond Lëtzebuerg (OGBL) and the Lëtzebuerger Chrëschtleche Gewerkschaftsbond (LCGB), were sceptical about employee financial participation, fearing loss of control over the collective bargaining process. Nevertheless, some collective agreements have included elements of profit-sharing.

## Legal and fiscal framework

No special legislation or tax incentives exist for any form of employee financial participation.

### Share ownership

Companies can acquire own shares up to 10 per cent of the subscribed capital for distribution among their own employees or employees without decision of the general assembly (Article 49-2 paragraph 3 Law on Commercial Societies – CSL). Companies are allowed to advance funds, make loans and provide security, with a view to acquisition of the company's shares by employees of the company, unless the net assets of the company would fall below the amount of the subscribed capital, plus the reserves (Article 49-6 paragraph 2 CSL).

Broad-based share ownership and stock option plans, if any, exist in very few large multinational companies. There is no special legislation on these types of plans. Stock option plans can be divided into potential options (not tradable at grant) and tradable options (tradable at grant). Tradable options for employees are very rare. The employee is subject to personal income tax at exercise, but exempt from social security contributions. The employing company can deduct the costs of the plan and is exempt from social security contributions.

### Profit-sharing

Cash-based profit-sharing is supposed to be the most common form. This is difficult to distinguish, however, from the commonly practised bonus plan (gratification), which is unrelated to financial indicators. Nevertheless, incidental evidence suggests that sometimes collective agreements link this 'gratification' to company profits. Because collective agreements, except for those declared binding for subsidiaries, are not public, it is difficult to quantify this phenomenon. An exception is the collective agreement for the banking sector. We may conclude that genuine cash-based profit-sharing plans, especially broad-based ones, will be very rare.

*Participation in decision making*

There is no direct connection between participation in decision making and financial participation of employees; in particular, financial participation plans cannot extend existing rights pertaining to participation in decision making. In companies with compulsory employee representation on the board (pursuant to Article L. 426-1 Labour Code, in state companies and companies with more than 1000 employees), employee representatives may initiate and influence the design of financial participation plans.

## XVIII   Malta

Despite a strong historical link to the United Kingdom, the source of much of the law on companies and employment, in practice employee financial participation is not well developed in Malta, being neither well diffused nor enjoying much political support. The ramifications of the nationalisation programme in the 1970s and the privatisation drive of the 1990s had the unintended consequences of introducing employee financial participation in some larger firms first. However, privatisation cannot be said to have been auspicious for workers' participation. The largest schemes in operation at two previous state-owned enterprises are share ownership schemes; profit-sharing is rare. Most of the firms that operate financial participation schemes have a unionised work force with trade union support.

### General attitude

The government policies that actually triggered the largest PEPPER schemes in practice were not focused upon employee financial participation but produced it rather as a side effect. Between 1971 and 1987 the newly elected government of the Malta Labour Party (MLP) embarked upon a programme of nationalisation as part of the de-colonialisation process, seven years after attaining political independence. The banking sector, at that time dominated by two major banks, was one of the nationalisation targets. The winding up of a 'widow and orphans' fund in operation in these banks before nationalisation resulted in the creation of several shares for the employees of one of these banks. The privatisation programme of 1990 adopted by the Nationalist Party (NP), in power since 1987, also had the unintended consequence of introducing employee financial participation schemes in the banking sector. Reversing the process of nationalisation begun by the previous administration, the government divested itself of several entities in which it was a majority shareholder. A side effect of this privatisation process was the creation of a trust fund for the benefit of employees in one of the banks.

Despite the social partners' apparent lack of enthusiasm, trade unions have supported all the schemes that were proposed, putting them into practice and actively participating in their administration. With no collective bargaining at the sectoral level, it is easier for Maltese trade unions to support such schemes in practice. The most active trade union in this area is the Malta Union of Bank Employees. This arises from the fact that the two major banks, where the union is heavily represented, were the targets of both the aforementioned nationalisation and privatisation programmes. The general trade unions, that is, the General Workers Union, the island's largest union, and the Union of United Workers, were also involved in prolonged discussions with the Government about the introduction and implementation of a public sector scheme which gave employees the opportunity to set up co-operatives and submit tenders for work contracts. PEPPER schemes have never been prominently featured on the agendas of the two major political parties. The present NP government, although rather passive, is not adverse to financial participation.

**Legal and fiscal framework**

Maltese law tends to refer to employee participation schemes indirectly; it tacitly recognises that Maltese firms may put such schemes in place (by private or collective agreements), rather than establishing a formal framework for their establishment or creating any significant fiscal or other incentives. However, Maltese law does provide a legal instrument for ESOPs, namely the trust vehicle. Tax incentives for financial participation schemes are few.

*Share ownership*

*Privatisation (1990).* The privatisation drive which the Nationalist Party embarked upon in the early 1990s resulted in a share ownership scheme being put into place for the employees of two formerly parastatal entities[82] which were partly privatised.[83] However, these schemes had no statutory basis; they were set up and regulated by private agreements (both individual contracts and collective agreements) between the newly privatised companies and their employees. Interestingly, the statutes of two as yet un-privatised utility providers, the Enemalta Corporation[84] and the Water Services Corporation,[85] explicitly permit the 'establishment, by the Corporation [...] of schemes or incentives related to productivity or performance'.

*Private Companies (2004)*. There is no statutory framework for either share ownership or share option schemes. Maltese law does not regulate the exact conditions under which share option schemes may be offered. It is left to individual companies to create their own schemes based on general company and civil law principles. Provided a company is empowered by its memorandum and articles of association to implement employee financial participation schemes, employers wishing to adopt one of the two types of schemes can enter into private or collective agreements with their employees, setting out the scope, terms and conditions. Where the employer company is itself the issuer of the shares to be offered to its employees, it is not considered to be providing an investment service subject to the Investment Services Act 1994 (IS Act).

Shares must be allocated to employees in accordance with the general rules set forth in the Companies Act 1995 (CA). As a general rule, the CA prohibits a company from acquiring its own shares (Article 105 paragraph 1 CA) or the shares of its parent company (Article 110 paragraph 1 (a) CA), or providing financial assistance for the purchase of either (Article 110 paragraph 1 lit. (b) CA). However, Article 106 paragraph 4 CA and Article 110 paragraph 2 CA make an exception to this general rule allowing a company to both acquire its own shares or those of its parent and to provide financial assistance in order to facilitate the acquisition of shares by or for its own employees or the employees of a company of the same group.

It should also be noted that the CA generally allows companies to offer their shares at a discount or pay a commission to anyone subscribing or agreeing to subscribe to company shares. This may also apply where shares are offered to employees at a discount in a corporate share ownership scheme. In this context the CA does not differentiate between discounted shares offered to employees or to third parties.[86] Tax law, on the other hand, offers no significant tax incentives for these schemes. As for stock options, it offers certain minor incentives. Under the Fringe Benefit Rules issued under the Income Tax Act,[87] share options are taxable only upon exercise.[88]

*Employee Stock Ownership Plans (ESOPs)*. Maltese law contains no specific legislation on ESOPs. Recent trust legislation,[89] inspired by Jersey legislation, has seamlessly integrated the UK common law concept of trusts into Maltese law. A trust can take many forms, and although the concept originated in the UK, trusts are not exclusive to countries that follow the common law tradition. One of these civil law countries is Malta which, through the Trusts and Trustees Act 1988, as amended in 2004 (Trusts Act), allows Maltese individuals and companies both to found and be a beneficiary in trusts regulated by Maltese law. The Trusts Act does in fact contain an explicit reference to 'employee benefit or retirement schemes or arrangements' as forming the basis of a trust. Although traditionally used for hedge funds, the 'Collective Investment Scheme' (CIS) may also be the basis for an ESOP.[90] For the taxation of ESOPs that fall within the definition of CISs, unfortunately the Income Tax Act 1948 does not distinguish between exempted and non-exempted CISs; therefore the income from CIS ESOPs will be taxable at the normal rate. For taxation purposes, a CIS is treated as a prescribed fund. Investment income, as defined in the Income Tax Act 1948, which is received by a prescribed fund, is subject to a withholding tax of 15 per cent on bank interest and 10 per cent on investment income from other sources. Other income and capital gains remain exempt for prescribed funds. When Maltese resident participants of the CIS (the employees) redeem, liquidate or cancel their units in the CIS, they are not subject to a second withholding tax.

### Profit-sharing

Maltese employment law considers profit-sharing arrangements between employers and employees as forming part of the employee's wage. Maltese labour legislation also recognises service contracts in which remuneration is solely in the form of a commission or a share of the employer's profits,[91] although these are rarely found in practice. This treatment as a 'wage' implies that any share of the profits will be computed with the employee's salary for the imposition of income tax.

### Participation in decision making

There are no general statutory arrangements for board-level representation in Malta. Employee representatives in companies at board level are only found in the state-owned and recently privatised sector, and even here they are becoming less common. In Malta it is the union, provided it is recognised (that is, the employer agrees to negotiate with it), that normally represents the employee at workplace the level. Although EU directives have led to new arrangements for non-unionised employees, these do not seem to have been implemented to any extent. Legislation in 2006, requiring the setting up of information and consultation structures, applies to companies with 150 or more employees from January 2006, and to companies with 100 or more employees from March 2007. From March 2008 on, it applies to companies with 50 or more employees. The key level for collective bargaining is the company level. There is also protection for those not covered by collective bargaining through a series of wage orders for specific industries that set minimum terms.

## XIX   Netherlands

Employee financial participation schemes were introduced in the 1950s on behalf of expatriate executives from the United States. Many plans, especially share ownership and stock option plans, are still limited to top management. Savings plans combined with profit-sharing or employee share ownership plans, generally broad-based, have been implemented since the 1970s. The combination of profit-sharing and share ownership plans with savings plans is most common in the Netherlands and thus may be considered typical.

A long-term study of the development of employee financial participation from 1996 to 2001 found that the number of enterprises with employee financial participation schemes more than doubled during that time period, from 4 per cent to 9 per cent. Although these figures include executive plans, a trend could be observed: executive plans had decreased in number, whereas broad-based plans had increased.[92] Profit-sharing plans showed only a 5 per cent rise during the same period. The assumption was that this form of financial participation had peaked.

More recently, a study of employee financial participation in companies listed on the Amsterdam Stock Exchange showed that 62.5 per cent of AEX companies offered such plans.[93] Stock option plans, offered by 41.7 per cent of the AEX companies, were the most popular. These figures, however, also include executive plans. New nationwide statistics on various kinds of employee financial participation plans are currently being prepared by the Netherlands Participatie Institut, but as of May 2009 they had not been published.

### General attitude

Employers' associations traditionally backed only the management model; recently, however, they have begun also to favour broad-based plans for reasons pertaining to employee motivation. Ordinarily there is no connection between share ownership and business form. An exception is the small family enterprise whose owners generally oppose employee share ownership because they fear loss of control. Trade unions, which generally have been opposed to employee financial participation, recently have declared their support for broad-based plans on condition that no substitution for regular remuneration will be required. In 2001, the trade unions began a discussion on whether profit-sharing and broad-based stock option plans should be included in collective bargaining agreements. This proposal, however, has not been accepted.

The government has given little support to employee financial participation of late, having concluded that such plans, especially the most prevalent limited to executives only, do not contribute to a more equitable distribution of wealth.

## Legal and fiscal framework

When combined with savings plans, profit-sharing or employee share ownership plans benefit specific tax incentives; for this reason this combination is the most typical form of employee financial participation. In 1994, legislation on deferred profit-sharing, cash-based profit-sharing and stock options was enacted.

### Share ownership

Companies are entitled to acquire own shares up to 10 per cent of the subscribed capital for distribution among their own employees or employees of a firm group without decision of the general assembly, if the articles of association provide so, within an 18-month period (Article 98 paragraph 4, 5 Civil Code (CC)). The equity capital reduced by the acquisition price shall not fall below the amount paid for the shares plus reserve funds (Article 98 paragraph 2, 3 CC). Article 98c paragraph 2 CC allows companies to advance funds, make loans and provide security, with a view to acquisition of the company's shares by employees of the company or employees of a firm group, with certain restrictions for closed joint-stock companies.

*Share ownership plans.* Although public companies (Namloze Venootschap) may transfer shares directly, limited companies (Besloten Venootschap) must use an intermediary because share transfer for them can be made only by means of a notarial deed. The intermediary chosen for this purpose is usually a foundation (Stichting Administratie Kantoor, SAK). It owns the employee shares, exercises voting rights and transfers depository receipts of shares to the employee shareholders. Other business forms can also be used as intermediaries. Tax incentives do not apply to share ownership not combined with a savings plan. Under a savings plan, an employee may save from his pre-tax salary a legally specified maximum amount (EUR 613 in 2008). However, if savings are converted into shares, the annual maximum allowance is doubled (EUR 1,226 in 2008).

*Stock option plans.* These were originally limited to executives, but there has been an increase in the number of broad-based plans since the beginning of the 1990s. Options may be conditional (for example, subject to a vesting period or a performance-related proviso) or they may be unconditional (that is, tradable at grant). Specific rules regarding the moment of taxation introduced in 2001[94] and respective tax incentives were recently abolished so that taxes are now to be paid at exercise only.

### Profit-sharing

Profit-sharing is found in both cash-based and share-based forms. Since 2003, tax incentives for profit-sharing plans depend on their being combined with a savings plan. The general rules governing savings plans and corresponding tax incentives, discussed under share ownership above, also apply to profit-sharing plans. Additionally, under plans that include at least 75 per cent of employees, with employee shares being held in the savings plan for four years, a 15 per cent flat tax is paid at exit in lieu of personal income tax and social security contribution. Under certain circumstances, the four-year blocking period is waived (for example, if the employee buys a principal residence, starts a new business, or takes a sabbatical or educational leave of absence).

### Participation in decision making

There is no direct connection between participation in decision making and employee financial participation. The latter plans are specifically enjoined from extending those participation rights already in force. Moreover, employee financial participation is generally not a part of collective agreements. Companies with a workers' council (compulsory in all firms with more than 100 employees) must obtain council approval for any amendments made in the 'system of remuneration'; broad-based employee financial participation plans are regarded as a part of this system. However, no approval of the workers' council is required in the case of 'discretionary plans', that is, plans restricted to management only.

## XX   Austria

The total number of financial participation plans, although still relatively small, has increased significantly since 2001 in response to the introduction of tax incentives. Only 8 per cent of plans currently active were established before 1990; 48 per cent date between 1990 and 2000, and 45 per cent after 2000.[95]

Recent measures promoting employee financial participation focus on share ownership. Currently 8 per cent of enterprises, mostly listed joint-stock companies, have introduced employee share ownership plans; through these, 160,000 individuals, or 6 per cent of the Austrian work force, own an average of 5 per cent or less of shares in their employer firms.[96] Leveraged employee ownership plans (similar to ESOPs), using different forms of foundations as a vehicle, were introduced in connection with privatisation.

Stock option plans, generally not broad-based, have been implemented in 1 per cent of enterprises. Profit-sharing plans are found in 25 per cent of enterprises, mostly small and medium-sized trade companies.[97]

## General attitude

By the end of the 1990s, the government had become more supportive of employee financial participation. Behind this change in attitude were such factors as increasing competition with Eastern European economies, promotion of employee participation by the EU, and impending privatisation of several large state-owned companies (for example, voestalpine AG, Vienna Airport, Saline AG, AMAG, AUA, OMV). Both the trade unions and employers' associations strongly support employee financial participation and co-operate with each other in this area.

After tax incentives were introduced in 2001, the Federal Workers' Chamber (BAK) and the Austrian Economic Chamber (WKÖ), in co-operation with the University for Applied Science Wiener Neustadt, conducted a study (2005) of the effects of financial participation on enterprise results and employee attitudes in individual companies. This study found that 80 per cent of employer companies and workers' councils in firms which have employee financial participation plans are satisfied with the results, whereas 71 per cent of enterprises without such plans would introduce them if the legal framework were improved.[98] In their proposals for reforming the legal framework, representatives of both employers and employees focus in part on the same issues: introduction of tax incentives for employee participants of profit-sharing schemes, higher tax incentives for participants in employee share ownership schemes and more incentives to encourage small and middle-sized companies to introduce employee ownership schemes, especially leveraged ones similar to the ESOP.

The only controversial issue is whether employee financial participation should include a role in decision making. Trade unions are critical of models that subject employees to risk, as with non-voting employee shares, without granting corresponding rights; they also object to schemes that benefit only management, for example, stock options.

Because labour law already requires employee participation in decision making, this issue only affects small enterprises without workers' councils.

## Legal and fiscal framework

The incidence of various models of employee financial participation depends on the business form. Share ownership plans have been introduced in the following: quoted joint-stock companies (AG), 45 per cent; co-operatives (Genossenschaft), foundations (Stiftung), registered associations (eingetragener Verein), 50 per cent; limited liability companies (GmbH), 6 per cent; they do not exist in partnerships (OHG, KG, OEG, KEG, GbR).[99] An absolute obstacle to employee share ownership in partnerships is the institute of co-ownership under the Austrian company law; this institute is typical of Germanic legal systems.

Other obstacles to the spread of employee share ownership plans in limited liability companies include the strong position shareholders enjoy compared with management, the transfer of share ownership only by notarial deed, and the absolute prohibition against a company acquiring its own shares.

Employee share ownership is based on a direct participation model in 21 per cent of enterprises.[100] Leveraged models are relatively rare owing to high costs and complex administration; they are found in large publicly quoted joint-stock companies, especially those created by privatisation.

The Law on Capital Market Offensive of 5 January 2001 introduced tax incentives for employee share ownership schemes by amending the Income Tax Law (ITL) and the Capital Tax Law (CTL). Profit-sharing plans are found in every third limited liability company and every second private joint-stock company.[101]

*Share ownership*

Employee share ownership plans are mainly based on direct share transfer. However, leveraged share ownership plans and stock option plans have become more widespread since 2001.

*Direct share ownership plans.* A joint-stock company is generally prohibited from acquiring its own stock, but this does not apply to employee shares (§ 65 paragraph 1 No. 4 Law on Joint-Stock Companies (JSCL)). A resolution of the general meeting is required to introduce such employee shares. The resolution remains in effect for 18 months. Transfer of shares to employees in connection with a capital increase, excluding pre-emptive rights of existing shareholders, is possible if the resolution of the general meeting on the capital increase makes this exclusion (§§ 65 paragraph 2a, 153 paragraph 5 JSCL). No period for the transfer of shares to employees is specified in the JSCL, but this transfer must take place immediately after issue to comply with company law. Current and retired employees of the employer company and of affiliated companies may participate in an employee share ownership plan (§ 15 JSCL). The definition of affiliated companies was extended in 2005: companies affiliated within the economic sector under the company law and companies that are members of an association in liability (according to § 30, paragraph 2a of the Federal Law on Competition) are also deemed to be affiliated. A blocking period for the transfer of employee shares is not prescribed, but shares are usually held for at least five years for tax purposes. Pursuant to § 3 paragraph 1 No. 15(b) ITL and § 49 paragraph 3 No. 18(c) of the Law on Social Security Contributions, a tax and social security allowance of up to EUR 1,460 applies to the benefit from the transfer of discounted shares if the shares are held for at least five years, the plan is broad-based and shares are held by the employees but deposited with a domestic credit institution or a fiduciary that administrates the shares and exercises voting rights according to the employee's instructions. This tax allowance applies only to current employees of a domestic or foreign employing company or an affiliated company. The employer company is also exempted from the obligation to pay social security contributions in this case. The employers' associations, trade unions and the legal literature all object that the tax allowance is too low and advocate an increase of up to EUR 5000. Taxation of dividends on employee shares depends on the economic ownership. If the employee has the economic ownership of shares, the capital yields tax or, upon application of the employee, half of the personal income tax, is imposed (dividends on shares of foreign companies are always taxed at half of the personal income tax) (§ 37 paragraph 4 ITL). If the employee is not the owner (for example, if the employing company may buy the shares back at will or if the shares must be returned at termination of the employment contract), full personal income tax and social security contributions are imposed.

*Leveraged share ownership plans.* By the Law on Capital Market Offensive of 5 January 2001, the ITL was amended also in relation to the taxation of private foundations. Because of prospective privatisation of large state companies, a model for 'strategic ownership' of employees had to be developed. An already-existing business form, the private foundation, was chosen to serve as the vehicle of the leveraged employee share ownership plans. Whereas many large privatised enterprises use a private foundation under the Law on Private Foundations as an intermediary company (for example voestalpine AG, Saline AG, AMAG), some use a new form 'employee participation foundation' (Belegschaftsbeteiligung-sstiftung) defined in § 4 paragraph 11 No. 1(c), ITL (for example, Vienna Airport).[102] The foundation holds and purchases the shares, exercises voting rights and transfers returns to the employees.[103] In contrast to direct employee share ownership plans, the beneficiaries of leveraged plans enjoying tax concessions can also be retired employees and family members (spouses, children) of employees. A foundation can only be used for shares of domestic companies; the definition of affiliated companies in connection with the foundation was not extended in 2005. The value of its own shares or money for purchasing shares transferred to the foundation as well as the costs of establishing and operating the foundation can be deducted from the tax base of the corporate income tax by the employer company. The foundation distributes the amount of contribution by the employer company over nine financial years, and EUR 1,460 per employee per annum is tax-free (§ 13 paragraph 1 last sentence CTL). Dividends on shares held by the foundation are also tax exempt (§ 10 paragraph 1 CTL). However, the capital gains tax is imposed on contributions used for administration. The employee pays capital gains tax on returns transferred by the foundation of up to EUR 1,460 and full personal income tax, but no social security contributions on the amount in excess thereof.

*Stock option plans.* Stock option plans are generally limited to management. Executive officers and members of the management bodies of joint-stock companies are allowed to acquire shares through stock options if the shares constitute not more than 20 per cent of equity capital (§ 159 paragraph 5 JSCL). However, a few broad-based stock option plans are also found. Taxation of stock options for employees depends on economic ownership. At the time economic ownership is transferred, the shares become taxable. The criteria for economic ownership are the relationship and tradability of options. According to § 3 paragraph 1 No. 15(c) ITL, 10 per cent in one year and 50 per cent of the difference between the value of the underlying share at exercise of the option and the value of the underlying share at grant of the option are tax exempt if certain pre-conditions are met: the options must be non-tradable, the plan must be broad-based and the value of the underlying shares at grant must not exceed EUR 36,400. If options are deposited with a domestic credit institution or with a fiduciary, taxation of the remaining amount can be deferred until the acquired share is sold or the employment contract terminated, up to the seventh year after the option grant. The employer company can deduct the cost of shares.

*Profit-sharing*

Although there are no tax incentives, profit-sharing schemes are relatively widespread, especially in small corporations. Most are cash-based and take into consideration such factors as turnover, EBIT, cash flow, and so on, alone or in combination, and not necessarily balance sheet profit.[104] A profit-sharing plan may be introduced through a collective agreement, an in-house agreement, or an employment contract. However, an in-house agreement can regulate the pre-conditions, factors, calculation methods and form of payment (§ 97 paragraph 1 line 16 Law on Employment Contracts (LEC)) only if the factor to which the plan refers also considers the expenditure of the enterprise.[105] A plan not regulated by an in-house agreement is usually based on individual employment contracts whose content is not restricted in this respect. A participating employee is entitled to examine the basis of his share calculation in the books (§ 14 Law on Employees). If the plan originates in a collective agreement, the workers' council is also entitled to examine the calculation basis, but not documents on individual wage payments (§ 89 LEC).

*Participation in decision making*

Under labour law, co-determination and participation rights of employees through their representatives are traditionally well developed. Employees send members to the supervisory board (§ 110 paragraph 1, 5 LEC) and are represented by the workers' council. There is generally no direct connection between participation in decision making and financial participation of employees; in particular, financial participation plans cannot extend existing rights in connection with participation in decision making. However, the employees in their capacity as shareholders can take substantial influence on important decisions of the general meeting (for example exercise the squeeze-out right) and be represented in the supervisory council if their cumulative share is at least 10 per cent. Certain aspects of financial participation plans can be regulated by a collective agreement and/or an in-house agreement; in this case, employees' representatives participate in negotiations and decisions. The following rights of the workers' council can be connected to financial participation: right to information (§§ 91, 92 LEC), right to consultation in the case of operational changes (§ 109 LEC), and right to demand elimination of faults (in this context all circumstances of financial participation detrimental to employees; see § 90 paragraph 1 LEC). Only 17 per cent of enterprises operating financial participation plans indicated problems in connection with decision making.[106] In general, problems arise only in small enterprises that do not have a workers' council.

# XXI   Poland

The most significant form of employee financial participation in Poland today is employee ownership. Poland's privatisation programme was characterised by significant incentives for employee participation, especially in firms privatised by leasing and transformed into so-called employee companies (spółki pracownicze). Ownership structures in these companies have, on the whole, been relatively stable, with non-managerial employees retaining, on average, a significant portion of enterprise shares. Research conducted in the late 1990s from a sample of 110 employee-leased companies privatised between 1990 and 1996 showed that on average the share of non-managerial employees in ownership decreased from 58.7 per cent immediately after privatisation to 31.5 per cent in 1999. Approximately 32 per cent of leasing-privatised firms were still majority-owned by non-managerial employees by mid-1999. Over time, more and more shares were also found in the hands of outsiders (probably largely because of retention of shares by people whose employment relationship with the firm ceased for whatever reason), while the presence of strategic outside investors (including foreign investors) had begun to be felt in a minority of firms by the end of the last decade.[107] Less significant forms of minority employee share ownership emerged from privatisation methods other than leasing. Insiders possessed only 12.7 per cent of shares at the beginning of 1998, and this fell to 11.4 per cent two years later. Although, all current forms of financial participation may also be used in employee compensation schemes outside privatisation, there are no tax incentives to encourage this.

### General attitude

No interest in further development of PEPPER schemes can be observed either in political or trade union circles. For PEPPER schemes and other forms of workers' participation, the positions of trade unions like Solidarność were and still are inconsistent and often ambiguous. Institutions created to support employee-owned firms in Poland include the Union for Employee Ownership (Unia Własności Pracowniczej), the

All-Poland Chamber of Employee-Owned Companies (Ogólnopolska Izba Gospodarcza Spółek Pracowniczych) in Poznań, and the Gdańsk Employee Ownership Bank (Bank Własności Pracowniczej SA w Gdańsku); however, their role in employee-led privatisation in Poland was very limited. As of early 1996, the Union for Employee Ownership, founded in the autumn of 1990, had only 76 member firms, some of which were still state-owned.

Clearly, since the mid-1990s, the main, openly declared objective of privatisation policy has been to maximise revenues; therefore, all but the smallest state enterprises are to be privatised by commercial methods, despite the fact that employee-owned firms were often the most successful. Moreover, policymakers have encouraged enterprises being commercially privatised to seek outside investors; for this purpose, a clause was included in the 1996 Privatisation Law requiring at least 20 per cent of the shares of a leasing firm to be purchased by persons not employed by the firm. One hundred per cent management–employee buyouts were thus made difficult. Policymakers provided no incentives for the extension of employee financial participation other than through privatisation schemes.

## Legal and fiscal framework

In Poland the legal framework provides various forms of PEPPER schemes, embracing on the one hand share ownership and profit-sharing, and on the other the private sector as well as enterprises undergoing privatisation. However, no incentives have been provided by policymakers for the extension of PEPPER schemes. All forms of participation are available for use in employee compensation schemes, although there are no tax incentives to do so.

### Share ownership

*Employee companies (1990, 1996).* So-called Employee Companies emerged from leveraged lease buyout (LLBO) privatisation. This is one form of so-called liquidation privatisation introduced in 1990, which, according to Article 39 of the Law on Commercialisation and Privatisation (PrivL.[108]) since 1997 requires the following: relatively good financial and market conditions; no requirement for substantial investment to modernise, replace, develop equipment, and so on; a yearly turnover of a maximum of EUR 6 million; a maximum of EUR 2 million of equity consisting of two enterprise funds; and willingness of management and employees to assume the financial risk involved in undertaking a common investment (including third parties). A newly established private company concludes an agreement with the State Treasury to lease the assets of the state enterprise for a maximum period of 15 years.[109] The interest payment was set at 30 per cent (75 per cent of 40 per cent) if the central bank refinance rate exceeded 40 per cent; in 1993 this was lowered to 50 per cent of the refinance rate.[110] Moreover, a leased company can apply to its founding organ for a reduction of interest payments owed as a result of postponements during the first two years of the leasing period if its investment expenditures out of profits amount to at least 50 per cent of its net profit. Finally, the corporate income tax law allows firms to include the interest portion of their lease payments as costs, thus reducing their tax liability. The new privatisation law in 1996 additionally leveraged the financial lease contracts in order to enhance the credit-worthiness of employee-leased firms applying for bank loans. Article 52 PrivL makes it possible for full ownership to be acquired before the end of the contract if one-third of total leasing rates have been paid, provided the balance sheet for the second business year of the company has been approved. If more than half of the total leasing rates have been paid, the blocking period is cut in half. Because of conditions on the Polish credit-market, this regulation has become very important in practice.[111]

*Employee shares in capital privatisation (1990, 1997).* According to Articles 36 et seq. of the new PrivL, which came into force in early 1997, employees can acquire 15 per cent of shares for free, with the restriction that these shares be exempt from free trade for two years, and for three years in the case of employees elected to the management board. Generally, they are required to enter their claim six months before the company is registering because the right expires otherwise; the right is also good for six months after sale of the first share. Shares are allocated in groups made up according to length of employment in the enterprise. The total value of allocated shares under these claims may not exceed the sum of the average salary in the public sector for 18 months, multiplied by the number of employees acquiring shares. This rule applies not only to commercialised companies undergoing capital privatisation and those included in the Mass Privatisation Programme, it was also extended to include 15 per cent employee participation in a 'direct privatisation' transaction involving sale of an enterprise as a going concern, as well as in kind contributions of an enterprise (Article 48 paragraph 3, Article 49 paragraph 4 PrivL). The only other exception is commercialisation through debt-to-equity swaps.

*Private companies (2003).* In an exception from the general prohibition against acquiring its own stock, Article 362 paragraph 1 of the

Commercial Companies Code (CCC) permits a company to acquire its own shares in order to offer them to current employees, retired employees of the company or employees of an affiliated company contingent upon a business relationship of at least three years.[112] In this case, Article 393 No 6 CCC requires a decision by the general shareholders assembly and Article 363 paragraph 3 CCC states that the shares shall be transferred to the employees within 12 of acquisition. Acquisition of the company's own shares in this case is subject to the provisions that the total nominal share value may not exceed the value of 10 per cent of the enterprise's equity capital, and that the purchase price, together with the transaction cost, may not be higher than the reserve set aside from the company's own profits (Article 348 paragraph 1 CCC).[113] Additionally, under current legislation, joint-stock companies may issue new shares to be transferred to employees in the context of so-called conditional capital increases, with Article 448 paragraph 2 No. 2 CCC expressly referring to the possibility of transferring shares to employees to satisfy previously acquired claims from profit-sharing. A prerequisite to this form of capital increase is that the employees are identified in the decision made by the general shareholders assembly on the capital increase.[114] A companion regulation is Article 442 paragraph 1 CCC, which stipulates the possibility of capital increases financed by the company's own capital, referring to Article 348 paragraph 1 CCC about reserves made from the company's own profits. To facilitate the acquisition of shares by employees, under Article 345 paragraph 2 of the CCC, the legislature has made an exception to the general prohibition against leveraging acquisition of its own stock. Thus, conditional upon the creation of a corresponding reserve (Article 348 paragraph 1 CCC), the company may advance funds, make loans and provide security to expedite the acquisition of its stock by its own employees or those of an affiliated company.

*Stock options*. Employees may receive stock options, regular or on a privileged basis (at below-par prices or free of charge), although there is no specific regulation to this effect.

*Pre-emptive Right of Purchase of an Enterprise under Insolvency Law (2003)*. The Insolvency and Reorganisation Law (IRL) of 2003, a completely new version of Polish insolvency law,[115] provides a contingent possibility for setting up employee companies in the context of a liquidation procedure. If the sale of the debtor's business as one or several functioning units is impossible, then each asset is to be auctioned publicly by the administrator, under supervision of the judge-commissioner. If assets are not sold at a public auction or the judge-commissioner does not accept the offer, he can order a second auction, or can determine the minimum price and conditions of sale and allow the administrator to find a purchaser or to sell assets free of procedural restrictions (to be approved by the creditors' committee). In this case, a commercial company founded by at least half of the debtor enterprise's employees and with the participation of the Treasury has a pre-emptive right of purchase of the enterprise or functioning enterprise units (Article 324 IRL).

### Profit-sharing

The possibility of implementing profit-sharing as a form of remuneration in addition to wage systems and directly linked to enterprise profits is stipulated in Article 347 paragraph 3 and 348 paragraph 1 CCC for joint-stock companies (tantiema).[116] Furthermore, as already mentioned, share-based profit-sharing is regulated in the context of conditional capital increases under Article 448 CCC, which mentions the possibility of transferring shares to employees, especially in cases where they have acquired claims from profit-sharing. The general type of scheme linked to enterprise results is referred to in Polish as a 'bonus' but has no legal foundations. Other practices currently sanctioned by law are compensation forms linked to an employee's individual results (gain-sharing); these are not generally linked to enterprise results and thus do not constitute a PEPPER scheme.[117]

### Participation in decision making

Co-determination at the strategic level takes the form of obligatory representation of employees on the supervisory boards of commercialised companies of, initially, two-fifths of the members and, from the moment the state ceases to own 100 per cent of the shares, one-third (Article 14 PrivL). Furthermore Articles 11, 12, 60 PrivL provide a detailed procedure for the election and qualification of representatives, whereas Article 15 PrivL protects their employment contract for the duration of their term and the year following. A new feature in the context of 'social compensation' is the participation of an employee representative on the executive boards of privatised enterprises employing more than 500 employees (Article 16 PrivL). Outside privatisation, development of participation in decision making has been very limited, even in companies where employees have significant share accounts. Poland is still dominated by an elitist and managerial corporate culture that minimises opportunities for participation. Almost all progress made in the area of participation in decision making in Poland may be attributed to the European Union.

Although the development of both direct and indirect (representational) employee participation in decision making in employee-owned companies seems rather low, there are signs that some potential for genuine employee involvement could be latent in these firms. In many Polish employee-owned companies, for example, no dividends have been paid out, even after two or three years as a private firm, because of decisions to plough back profits into investment or to not pay dividends until the lease is paid off. That employee shareholders can be convinced to vote in favour of such 'austerity' plans is evidence that the entrepreneurial attitudes characteristic of genuine ownership and participation may be present among the work forces of certain employee-owned companies.

## XXII   Portugal

No tradition of employee financial participation has emerged in Portugal for historical and economic reasons. The Portuguese economy is still based on small companies under continuous family ownership; these owners are reluctant to grant participation rights to employees. Moreover, flexibility in employment and labour costs as well as relatively low unemployment have been achieved independently. Employee share ownership and stock option plans were promoted in connection with privatisation in the 1990s after the French example. However, this did not lead to any substantial increase in employee share ownership because a significant number of employees, before the share transfer, had signed contracts waiving their rights and agreeing to sell their shares immediately after the end of the blocking period. Currently, only a few plans are operated by large multinational companies primarily in the financial and insurance sector; most of these are cash-based profit-sharing plans; however, single cases of employee share ownership as well as stock option plans do occur (for example, Siemens, EDP, Portugal Telecom, Cimpor).

### General attitude

The government is indifferent to employee financial participation. Nor are employers' associations interested because wage flexibility has been achieved by other means. Initially, the trade unions were suspicious of financial participation, but they have changed their attitude since 1988 and now try to promote it. However, this is true only of independent trade unions, for example SIMA (Sindicato das Industrias Metalurgicas e Afins), which has proposed to include financial participation in collective agreements. The largest trade unions, UGT (Uniao Geral de Trabalhadores) and CGTP (Confederacao Geral de Trabalhadores), generally do not support such initiatives.

## Legal and fiscal framework

A few financial participation plans are operated primarily by large companies in the financial and insurance sector; many of these plans are limited to executives. Cash-based profit-sharing schemes predominate.

### Share ownership

Under Portuguese legislation, companies are generally allowed to acquire own shares (Article 316 paragraph 1, 317 Commercial Societies Code (CSC)). Furthermore they are allowed to advance funds, make loans and provide security, with a view to acquisition of the company's shares by employees of the company or employees of affiliated firms, unless the liquid assets of the company would fall below the sum of the subscribed capital plus non-distributable reserves (Article 322 paragraph 2 CSC). The general assembly may limit or abolish pre-emptive right of shareholders for 'social reasons' (Article 460 paragraph 2 CSC).

The number of share ownership and stock option plans is very small, executive plans included. The existing plans are purported to be modelled on similar plans in the UK and Ireland.

*Share ownership plans.* Share ownership plans were used on a larger scale in the privatisation process between 1989 and 1998. According to Articles 10 and 12 of the Framework Privatisation Law of 1990, a certain percentage of the capital reserved for acquisition or subscription had to be reserved for current employees and, if employed by the company for more than three years and not dismissed as a result of a disciplinary proceeding, for former employees as well; the blocking period was for two years. As to privatisation of individual companies, special laws containing specific conditions (for example, the relation of pre-emption rights of employees to pre-emption rights of other individuals), in compliance with the Framework Privatisation Law, were enacted. The employees had to pay a certain price determined by the Minister of Finance. On shares held for at least two years, gains in share value were not taxed. In addition, employees enjoyed tax incentives if they purchased shares offered for public sale by the state; they could deduct up to 30 per cent of total taxable income, up to a fixed amount.

*Stock option plans.* Stock option plans are often limited to executives. Because the total number of stock option plans, including executive plans, is very small, the number of broad based stock option plans will probably be fewer than ten. There are no special rules on taxation of stock options in financial participation plans for employees; employee stock options, like other types of stock option, are subject to the personal income tax at the time exercised, and no social security contributions need to be paid.

*Profit-sharing*

Both cash-based and share-based profit-sharing schemes exist, with the percentage of cash-based profit-sharing schemes being much higher. Profits allocated to employees are usually transferred immediately, but under certain conditions can be blocked for one to two years. Conditions are determined at the company level. Since 1969, the profit-share of the employee has not been treated as remuneration, exempting employees from personal income taxes and social security contributions on this amount (Article 261 Labour Code). However, the profit-share must be based on an individual agreement covering a specific period; otherwise it will be fully taxable. The employer company can deduct distributed profit transferred to the employees.

*Participation in decision making*

No direct connection exists between participation in decision making and employee financial participation; in particular, financial participation plans may not extend the existing rights in connection with participation in decision making. Financial participation is not a part of collective agreements, although the trade unions have proposed including such schemes on several occasions. Employee representation on the executive and supervisory boards is prescribed by law in certain public companies, but not often implemented in practice. Although consultations on financial participation plans are not compulsory, they sometimes take place, especially in the case of profit-sharing plans, to improve the design.

# XXIII   Romania

Employee financial participation in Romania is a relatively new idea, as distinguished from various pseudo-schemes attempted under the communist regime. PEPPER schemes emerged during early stage privatisation; at that time voucher privatisation and insider privatisation through an ESOP-like scheme were the two main privatisation methods. The most prevalent form is employee share ownership, mainly through ESOP-like schemes. It is estimated that by the end of 1998, over a third of all industrial firms in the State Ownership Fund had undergone ESOP privatisation, with an average employee ownership of 65 per cent and a median of 71 per cent; in addition, ESOP participants made up the largest owner group in one-quarter of Romanian privatised firms, making this method the country's most important tool for state ownership divestment.[118] Nevertheless, after more than ten years of transition, only 40 per cent of large enterprises and about two-thirds of medium-size enterprises have been privatised. The number of state-owned or state-controlled firms in Romania remains larger than that total in the other Central and Eastern European countries combined.[119]

Since 2001 cash-based profit-sharing, known as 'The Fund of Employee Profit Participation', has been compulsory in companies and in autonomous bodies where the state is the sole or majority owner. At a national level, net profits directly paid to employees in 2003 were about 2.2 per cent on average, whereas 70.3 per cent was distributed from salary funds, including premiums and benefits.[120] Although the number of profit-sharing firms is still limited, their number is gradually increasing.

**General attitude**

Although employees are represented by a considerable number of large trade-union confederations, employers' associations – 11 of them registered – are even more fragmented. In privatisation of utilities and the oil and gas industry, employees often have purchased shares through trade unions, because the unions, being very strong in these sectors, have substantial influence, including the right to appoint at least one member to the boards of administration. In some cases (for example, the sale of 8 per cent of the social capital of the PETROM Company, representing a total value of about EUR 200 million) the trade unions tried to have the relevant law amended to make employees' associations controlled by the trade unions become the purchasers of the offered shares rather than individual employees. Such cases illustrate that the interests of trade unions and their legal representatives are not necessarily in line with the interests of individual employees, and that sometimes trade unions try to achieve their goals at the expense of employees' rights. Trade unions have a very strong position in the tripartite council (National Social and Economic Council), which also includes the government and the employers' associations. Employers' associations have not yet addressed the issue of financial participation of employees. However, according to Article 104 of the Collective Labour Contract concluded at the national level for the years 2007–10, employers and trade unions committed to mutual information about changes in the property form of their companies and to sustain the participation of employees' associations in their privatisation. Well-known examples of ESOP associations founded in 2008 are that of SC Oltchim MBO gathering 2000 employees from OLTCHIM SA – more than half of the number of total employees – and that in Electrica SA acquiring 10 per cent of the employer company.

At present, employee financial participation of is of little interest to either the government or political parties. The last significant commitment by policymakers was in 2001 when the aforementioned compulsory cash-based profit-sharing scheme, The Fund of Employee Profit Participation, was introduced. Only one aspect of financial participation of employees is currently being addressed by the government: the sale of minority shares to employees in public enterprises now in the process of privatisation. These include utilities (or the so-called Régies autonomes), oil and gas, banks, as well as state companies. However, because economic privatisation policy was recently changed to favour sales to strategic outside investors, including foreign investors, government support is expected to decline. In some of these privatisation cases, trade unionists and representatives of political parties are suspected of engaging in insider deals and corrupt practices at the expense of employees; therefore the general public has little confidence in government support of employee financial participation.

## Legal and fiscal framework

Romanian law lacks a systematic legal framework for regulating employee financial participation. However, several laws passed in conjunction with the privatisation process influenced the extent to which the concept of employee financial participation has spread, with mass privatisation and an ESOP scheme being the major forms. The only legal regulations of profit-sharing concern a compulsory scheme in (majority) state-owned companies to which National Labour Collective Agreements apply.

### Share ownership

*Privatisation (1991, 1995, 1999).* The Romanian Privatisation Law 58/1991 decreed that 30 per cent of shares be free shares transferred under alternate privatisation methods, mainly through vouchers and contained regulations on preferential treatment for employees and management in the sale of shares through the national Privatisation Agency. According to Article 48 of Law 58/1991, employees (including management) of the relevant enterprise had a pre-emptive right to purchase the offered shares on preferential terms. In a fixed price sale, the 'insider share price' had to be 10 per cent lower than the public price; in the case of a sale by competitive bidding, the insider offer had to be accepted by the Privatisation Agency as long as the offered price was not lower than 90 per cent of the highest public bid. This preferential treatment was extended to the direct sale procedure, where the insider offer had to be accepted by the Privatisation Agency in the event of an equal negotiation offer from other interested parties. The 30 per cent quota was reaffirmed by Law 55/1995 on the Acceleration of the Privatisation Process; the privatisation agency compiling a list of suitable enterprises issued the so-called 'nominal value vouchers for privatisation' to be distributed among the resident population that had not made full use of their property vouchers received according to Law 58/1991. This new law contained the first real incentive for employee financial participation in voucher privatisation. Although members of the public who owned the nominal value vouchers could exchange their vouchers only for shares of companies chosen from the privatisation agency's list of suitable enterprises, Article 5 offered employees, former employees (pensioners or the unemployed) and managers the same opportunity to acquire shares of non-listed companies.

*Employee Stock Ownership Plans (1992, 1994, 1997, 2002).* ESOP associations stem from Rule 1/1992 on the Standard Procedure for the Privatisation of Small Enterprises by the Sale of Shares in force as of January 1993. Although focused on the privatisation of so-called 'small enterprises' with not more than 50 employees, this regulation defines insider privatisation through an ESOP-like scheme implemented by means of direct negotiations with interested employees and managers as the standard privatisation procedure. However, the shares were not acquired directly by participating employees but by an incorporated association of share owners ruled by Law 77/1994, allowing employees and the management of partly or fully state-owned enterprises earmarked for full or partial privatisation to establish ESOP associations.[121] Until 2002, only one ESOP association could be established in each enterprise to be privatised, eliminating the possibility of competition between associations over the purchase of one specific enterprise. Membership in the ESOP association, although voluntary, was a precondition for making use of the advantages and rights. The law prescribes that a minimum of 30 per cent of the total number of employees and management staff must participate in establishing the ESOP association. The employing enterprise is obliged to disclose all relevant commercial and financial information to the association's founding committee; it must also bear the costs of a preliminary feasibility study. The ESOP association buys and administers the shares for its members. Membership is open to employees with open-ended labour contracts for at least half-time employment (since 2002 also to fixed-term employees and to pensioners), to members of the management of the employer company and former employees, both unemployed and pensioners.

The association's main decision making body is the general meeting in which each member has one vote. The general meeting adopts the ESOP association's articles of association, which must contain strict rules on the distribution of shares purchased. With the share not being acquired directly by employees and management, but the intermediary ESOP association, with an autonomous legal personality, participation in decision making therefore depends upon the decision-making procedure within the association and how members' decisions are transmitted to the shareholders' meeting. The ESOP association may also purchase shares on behalf of individual members. In this case the shares are distributed directly to and administered by the members themselves once they fully pay for the shares either with cash or privatisation vouchers. The main advantage of buying shares through the ESOP association is the use of the credit offered either by the Privatisation Agency itself or by external banks. Shares bought under the name of the association are not vested directly to individual members, but retained by the association until they are entirely paid for, serving as credit securities during this period. ESOP associations' members have pre-emptive rights to the unvested shares, based on length of employment, firm position and salary. If the members do not exercise their pre-emptive rights, these shares may be distributed to new employees. When all shares are distributed to its members, the association must be dissolved. Law 77/1994 additionally offers preferential instalment options[122] for shares purchased by ESOP associations. This involves a low advance payment, complemented by a minimum repayment period of five years and a maximum interest rate of 10 per cent per year. Given the high inflation rate that pertained during the 1990s, this interest rate limit turned out to be remarkably advantageous.

*Private companies*. The legal framework established by Romanian company law is defined by Law 31/1990 on companies, republished in 2004. Romania has only made partial use of the tools/exceptions offered by the Second Council Directive 77/91/EEC of 13 December 1976 to promote employee financial participation by corporate legislation. Regarding permission to acquire the companies' own shares for its employees, Article 103 Law on Companies offers an exception to the restrictive general rule for such transfer which requires extraordinary decision of the shareholders' meeting in the case of the acquisition of shares for the employees of the company. The second exception is Article 106 paragraph 2 Law on Companies: that is, the encouragement of share acquisitions by employees by permission to advance funds and to make or secure loans for this purpose.

*Profit-sharing*

In 2001 the government passed Ordinance 64/2001,[123] covering state or municipal enterprises whose legal form is prescribed by Law 31/1990 on Trading Companies, with the state as single or majority owner, or in a specific legal structure which is still widely used by public utilities (regiă autonoma, governed by specific regulations). The ordinance regulates the details of profit distribution, such as reserve funds, payouts to owners and the coverage of losses from previous years. In Article 1 lit. e), the ordinance also contains a provision that sets the maximum payout rate for employee profit-sharing at 10 per cent of the overall profit of the enterprise (10 per cent in the case of companies, or 5 per cent in the case of autonomous bodies, depending upon employees' performance and contribution to the financial results).[124] There is no current provision for a minimum rate; it should be noted that the number of state firms actually making a profit is still low. Nevertheless, Ordinance 64/2001 is one of the few laws expressly dealing with the issue of employee profit-sharing. Against the background of the pronounced encouragement of ESOP privatisation schemes, profit-sharing in companies privatised through this method should be widespread, as a side effect of share ownership. Because ESOP privatisation policy particularly favoured the sale of smaller enterprises to employees and management, profit-sharing schemes should be over-represented in the sector of small and medium-sized firms.

*Participation in decision making*

Although legislation before 1990 emphasised employee participation in decision making excessively, the privatisation laws passed since 1990 have contained no special regulations on this issue. The notion of employees' co-determination, as in German law, was not introduced. Company law does not provide any legal means for the privileged participation of employees in decision making. However, it does contain various provisions protecting the interests of minority shareholders. The new Labour Code of 2003, and the nationwide collective agreement with trade unions for the period 2007–2010, contain regulations for some compulsory consultation procedures if management is planning any changes in labour conditions.

## XXIV  Slovakia

Despite political declarations in the mid-1990s, PEPPER schemes have made little progress in Slovakia, while financial participation remains marginal. The environment for employee participation has been generally more favourable than in the Czech Republic owing to a major difference in the privatisation plan of Slovakia revised after the split from Czechoslovakia in December 1992. Starting with a focused policy favouring the voucher scheme, the new government switched to traditional privatisation methods – trade sales in particular but also insider privatisation – in its second privatisation wave. The populist government in the mid-1990s used employee shares in conjunction with managerial types of privatisation to facilitate property transfer to members of their party. However, the subsequent reformist government abolished this system; from 1998 onwards, the Dzurinda government focused on revenue-oriented privatisation of the remaining state enterprises, which included telecommunications, gas utilities and large banks. The private ownership structure that emerged from this point is totally dominated by external or managerial ownership.

### General attitude

The general attitudes towards employee participation, current and past, can be summed up as 'unsuitable for Slovak economics'. External ownership is the preferred form of ownership; no incentives to encourage other forms or employee participation are provided. A survey of past and recent literature on enterprise sector development and corporate governance in Slovakia reveals no professional or public interest in employee participation. Moreover, there is no mention of insider shares; at best, managerial ownership and buyouts are dealt with. In general, attitudes toward employee participation are similar to those in the Czech Republic.

Trade unions overall also seem indifferent. The only document on the website of the Confederation of Trade Unions of the Slovak Republic that mentions employee shares is concerned with social dialogue, not shares as a form of corporate governance; the reference is merely casual, with no apparent implication. Today, political parties seem to ignore this issue, except for the Communist party, which explicitly mentions employee shares in a 1994 programme that has not since been modified. Based upon partly anecdotal evidence, we conclude that the probability that employee shares will become a focal issue of government economic policy in the near future is low; the subject seems of interest only to the far left of the political spectrum and of no concern to trade unions, government or the general public. High unemployment may be the explanation.

## Legal and fiscal framework

Under present Slovak law, which is similar to the Czech Republic, there is no specific employee financial participation programme or any particular law or regulation pertaining to any specific PEPPER scheme. The only form of employee participation in the ownership structure of corporations covered by general laws has been a few regulations on the acquisition of shares by employees and profit-sharing in joint-stock companies.

### Share ownership

*Privatisation (1995, abolished 1996).* The Slovak Republic National Council Act No. 192/1995 was the basic legal act that accelerated direct sales primarily, while subsidising domestic entrepreneurs and enabling them to participate in the privatisation process under favourable conditions. Direct sales were to be used to compel employee ownership, obliging the transferee either to issue employee shares that accounted for 10 per cent of the companies' equity capital, or to enable employees to acquire at least a one-third[125] stake in the transferees' equity. Instalment payments scheduled for five to ten years, with the first instalment at about 20 per cent of the purchase price, were foreseen to offset the domestic financial capital shortage.

*Private companies (1989, 2001, 2004).* In 2001 the concept of genuine employee shares as a special type of share was abolished in favour of an option allowing joint-stock companies to include rules in their statutes that allow their employees to buy company shares at a discount. According to § 768c paragraph 17 Commercial Code (CC), previously issued employee shares had to be converted into regular shares by a decision of the general shareholders assembly by January 2004. In case the conversion requirement was not met, § 768c paragraph 14 CC stipulates the possibility of liquidation of the company by court decision. Section 204 paragraph 4 CC introduced the possibility of employees acquiring shares on preferential conditions to replace employee shares. The general prohibition against a company acquiring its own stock, regulated in §§ 161a and 161f CC, is in principle an obstacle to the introduction of employee shares. However, the corporate charter can permit (pursuant to the rules laid down in § 161a paragraph 2 lit. a) CC, introduced in 2004) a company to acquire its own stock for the purpose of transfer to its employees; such shares must be transferred within 12 months of acquisition by the company. Under current legislation, joint-stock companies may issue new shares that grant employees favourable conditions in the context of so-called mixed capital increases (according to § 209a paragraph 1 CC): that is, the capital increase of a company issuing new stock financed by the company's own capital. According to § 204 paragraph 4, the general shareholders assembly can authorise the offer of a certain number of those shares to employees at a lower price than the offering price, with the difference paid from the company's own resources.

To facilitate share acquisition by employees, legislation allows a company to fully pay for the stock acquired by its employees. Section 204 paragraph 4 CC states that a prerequisite to the preferential conditions for the purchase of shares by employees is that the overall value of the granted discount for the issued shares has to be covered by the company's own resources. The terms will be decided by the general shareholders meeting. In the case of the mixed capital increase previously mentioned, applying § 204 paragraph 2 CC, and in analogy to § 209a paragraph 3, 5 CC, the total discount may amount to 70 per cent of the share price provided that the remaining 30 per cent is paid by the employees at the moment of the transaction, unless the down-payment for the acquisition is financed otherwise. In fact, § 161e paragraph 2 CC, introduced in 2004, contains an additional regulation permitting the company an exception to the general prohibition against leveraging the acquisition of own its stock, to facilitate the acquisition of shares by its employees. The company may make loans to employees for the purpose of acquiring newly issued shares or to buy them from third persons; it is also to guarantee such loans from third persons provided that this does not endanger the company's own funds. Thus a company may enable its employees to acquire company shares by discounting the purchase price, by providing credit and financing, by acting as guarantor or by a combination of all three preferential conditions.

*Profit-sharing*

Nothing in the Slovak legal system prohibits companies from sharing profits with their employees. The only explicit regulation is provided in § 178 paragraph 4 CC, which states that, in accordance with the corporate charter, employees may be entitled to a share in the company's profits (cash-based profit-sharing). Either the corporate charter or the general shareholders meeting may also stipulate that profits allocated to the employees be used exclusively to purchase shares on preferential conditions, or to make up the discount granted to employees in such a purchase (share-based profit-sharing). Further, share-based profit-sharing is mentioned in the context of capital increases. As a rule, a capital increase requires the decision of the general shareholders assembly, but § 210 CC, in accordance with the corporate charter, allows delegation to the management board. Section 210 paragraph 4 CC regulates a capital increase through issuance of the shares to be transferred to employees on preferential conditions. This possibility is especially emphasised in the case where the general shareholders assembly has previously decided that the part of the profits that it allocates to employees is used exclusively to purchase these shares. All those benefits will be subject to personal income tax of 19 per cent.

### Participation in decision making

According to § 200 CC, joint-stock companies (similar remnant as in the Czech case owing to common initial conditions) with more than 50 employees must have one-third representation of employee-delegated members on the supervisory board. There are no special rules for participation of employees in decision making for PEPPER schemes or privatisation matters. For employee shareholding, the general rules of the Commercial Code concerning shareholders rights apply.[126]

## XXV   Slovenia

Slovenia has a long tradition of employee participation, starting with employee self-management in the 1950s. The strong tradition of employee involvement in corporate affairs is reflected in both the Slovenian model of privatisation and in the development of Slovenian company law. Furthermore, in contrast to other Eastern European countries, Slovenia has retained relatively strong political support for the financial participation of employees up to the present time, with draft laws being presented in 1997, 2002 and 2005. Although Parliament did not pass any of the draft laws, supporters of financial participation have established associations to promote a legal framework. Their efforts finally led to success: on 29 February 2008, the Law on Employee Share Ownership and Financial Participation was adopted by the Parliament.

Damijan et al. (2004)[127] reported that insider ownership decreased by more than 10 per cent in the period 1998–2002 (from 38.52 per cent to 26.17 per cent). The number of firms predominantly owned by employees (managers excluded) declined from 74 to 26. Of these firms, 10 per cent had no employee owners; in 25 per cent employees held less than 5 per cent of shares, whereas in half of the sample, the aggregate level of employee ownership did not exceed 18.4 per cent. There were only 25 per cent of firms in the sample with employee ownership exceeding 40 per cent of firm capital. By contrast, profit-sharing schemes are rare. Kanjuo-Mrčela (2002)[128] found that only about 7 per cent of the 41 largest Slovenian firms had actually constituted a 'fund of own shares' to remunerate their employees. About 32 per cent of the firms introduced the possibility of employee profit-sharing in their articles of association. This possibility, however, often remains unexploited (in 22 per cent of firms in the sample).

### General attitude

Debates over the establishment and continuance of employee ownership and other forms of financial participation began in the early 1990s. In 1995 a group of enterprise representatives, union representatives, journalists and academics established the DEZAP (Employee Ownership Association). DEZAP's main task is to encourage employee ownership in Slovenia — its inception, growth and effectiveness. In pursuit of these objectives, the Association promotes the adoption of suitable legislation on employee ownership, provides professional assistance to, and training and education of, employee owners, develops networks of employee-owned firms, and promotes co-operation with other firms and international organisations. A similar organisation, the Association of Works Councils (Studio Participatis), currently consisting of 100 members, supports all forms of employee participation.[129] Trade unions, however, have varying views. For example, they opposed the 1997 profit-sharing law because it linked the introduction of profit-sharing with wage concessions, a connection that explained why the law as rejected. Finally, the promotion of employee financial participation, for example, by tax allowances, is one of the stated objectives of the Slovenian Association of Managers for 2005 (Združenje Manager).[130]

Tax issues were the main obstacle to the adoption of the Law on Employee Financial Participation in 1997. In October 2002 the Slovenian Economic Ministry established an expert group to prepare the regulations on employee share ownership and other forms of financial participation. A new draft Law on Employee Financial Participation, submitted to Parliament by the Social Democrats in 2005, was rejected. These draft laws made employee financial participation plans compulsory; consequently employer groups strongly opposed these laws, all of which were proposed by centre-left governments. The 2006 draft law, however, was prepared by the first centre-right government in co-operation with the social partners and agreed upon in the Economic Social Council in December 2007. This draft law was adopted by the Parliament on 29 February 2008.

## Legal and fiscal framework

The new Law of 29 February 2008, which took effect in April 2008, regulates share ownership and share-based profit-sharing plans (though not stock option plans) and offers strong tax incentives for the schemes eligible. However, the Ministry of Finance has yet to issue the Order authorising these incentives. When the Order is issued, interested companies will be obliged to register with the Ministry to become eligible for tax incentives. However, privatisation law, on the basis of which employee ownership first emerged in Slovenia, and general company law contain regulations with regard to financial participation.

### Share ownership

*Privatisation (1993, 1997).* Privatisation was introduced by the Law on Ownership Transformation of 1992[131] (LOT), which authorised the sale of companies and social capital to workers or third parties, and defined a special form of workers' participation in social capital. Companies under social ownership were transformed[132] into corporations and issued shares in the amount of the value of the social capital. The shares could be distributed or sold internally, sold to outsiders, or assets sold to outsiders. The LOT provided for the mandatory distribution of 40 per cent of the social capital to different funds (10 per cent to the Pension Fund, 10 per cent to the Restitution fund[133] and 20 per cent to the Development Fund for subsequent sale to Privatisation Investment Funds). The firms were then entitled to distribute (in exchange for employee vouchers) up to 20 per cent of ordinary shares among current and former employees, including retired employees. Registered shares obtained by workers could not be transferred for a period of two years after the issue date, except as an inheritance. In practice, however, employees found ways to sell their shares before this period was up, and many sold them immediately.

Furthermore, companies had discretion over the allocation of the remaining 40 per cent of their capital (after the distribution of 40 per cent to various funds and 20 per cent to inside owners); they could either sell to insiders (internal buyouts) or outsiders (outside privatisation). In an internal buyout, workers could buy shares with the profits of the companies owned by participants in the internal sale programme, as well as with their salaries or other sources. The workers could also obtain a part of the shares to satisfy salary claims or other legitimate claims against the company. Further, the option of the so-called one-fifth company model was introduced to support employee participation in ownership. For privatisation purposes, Slovenian citizens were granted vouchers; the value of vouchers granted to each individual depended upon the length of employment (Article 31 LOT). Vouchers could be used to obtain shares in the employer company within the limitations of internal distribution (the initial 20 per cent), to obtain shares of Privatisation Investment Funds, to purchase shares of other companies privatised by public sale, and to purchase shares or other property of the Republic of Slovenia and state-owned companies offered to the public in return for vouchers (in the last case, vouchers could not be freely traded).

Certain measures were taken to preserve employee ownership after privatisation, beginning with the two year restriction on trading shares gained from internal distribution (respectively four years for the case of an internal buyout). To prevent decline in employee ownership, some firms decided to limit trading by internal acts, namely through 'shareholder agreements' prohibiting the sale of employee shares to outsiders and providing for employee representation of employees in the firm's decision-making process. However, shareholder agreements proved easy to abandon and difficult to administer.[134] Upon the proposition of DEZAP, the Slovenian Chamber of Commerce and the Association of Free Trade Unions, an amendment was introduced to the Takeover Law of 1997; this provided for the possibility of an institutional organisation of inside owners in the firm's Workers Associations and exempted them from public bids (Article 81). By the amendment to the Take-Over Law, Worker Associations became professional proxy organisations and, as such, had to act in accordance with the Takeover Law (Article 298) and the provisions of the Company Law.[135] The earlier laws regulating transformation and privatisation, although not abolished, are no longer in practice because privatisation is generally complete.

*Private companies (2004, 2008).* The transposition of the Second Council Directive 77/91/EEC of 13 December 1976 into Slovenian CL 2004 allowed companies to buy their own shares up to 10 per cent of the subscribed capital for distribution to their own employees and employees of associated companies within a one-year period (Article 240 CL). This provision applies to both joint-stock companies and limited liability companies; tradability is unrestricted for shares thus acquired. Furthermore, Article 241 CA allows companies to advance funds, make loans and provide security for the acquisition of company shares by their own employees or employees of an associate company. Pursuant to Article 318 CL, part of the profit can be distributed to employees in the form of new shares if the general meeting so decides.

Under the new Law of 29 February 2008, employees are granted a 70 per cent tax relief on distributed shares held for one year, and a 100 per cent tax relief on shares held three years, up to an annual maximum of 5,000 EUR. In addition, no social security contributions are imposed on the benefit. In the original draft law, only employees covered by collective agreements, that is, with the exception of management and other key personnel under individual contract, were eligible for tax incentives. However, the version of the Law finally adopted includes all personnel categories, but only for a limited amount. The annual amount for financial participation may not exceed 20 per cent of company profit or 10 per cent of the employees' total gross salary. The employer company may deduct the value of distributed shares from the corporate income tax base.

*Profit-sharing (1993, 1993)*

The new Law of 29 February 2008 also applies to share-based but not cash-based profit-sharing. The rules of the Law explained in the section on share ownership also apply to share-based profit-sharing. Further, general provisions of company law may also apply. In Article 228, the new CL of 1993 regulates the use of net profit. This profit must primarily be used for covering losses and creating legal and statutory reserves. The remaining net profit not exceeding 50 per cent may be used for other reserves; if the articles of association so provide, a part may be distributed to employees and members of the management and supervisory boards.[136] These matters are decided by the general meeting in determining distribution of profit. In summary, the CL makes profit-sharing possible provided that there is enough profit to cover losses, legal and statutory reserves, that the articles of association allow some use of profits for employees, and that the general meeting approves the decision.[137] The participation amount is usually determined as a percentage of the annual profit of the company.

*Participation in decision making*

Article 75 of the Constitution specifies the terms and conditions of employee participation in management. It was implemented by the special Law on Workers' Participation in Management of 1993[138], which regulates workers' participation in the management of economic units regardless of ownership form, including co-operatives.[139] According to this law, workers may participate in management by submitting initiatives, by demanding information, by consultations with their employer, and by participation in decision making, including the right to reject employers' decisions. In particular, workers are entitled to nominate from one-third to a half of supervisory board members and, in firms with more than 500 employees, one member of the management board. Because employees who obtained shares in the course of privatisation are as a rule minority shareholders, special provisions of the CL on the protection of minority shareholders apply. These special rights relate to the general meeting, the right to information, the right to examine the books and the right to lodge a complaint against the decisions of the general meeting. On the other hand, these rights do not include the right to replace management.

## XXVI   Finland

Personnel Funds are the only form of financial participation to enjoy fiscal incentives and the support of the social partners. In 1989, the Council of State appointed a committee to find new forms of co-operation for enhancing economic democracy, competitiveness and productivity. A draft law in 1987[140] proposed voluntary Personnel Funds as a key element. The funds were to encourage efficiency at the company level, 'innovations' at all levels, and a balanced division of decision making and responsibilities. The law, enacted in 1989 (814/1989), immediately attracted great attention. Most of the funds in place today were established then. A total of 82 funds have been established between 1990 and April 2007, of which 28 have been closed down.

There are now 54 operating Personnel Funds with about 126,000 members covering over 5 per cent of the workforce. It is not clear why the number of funds is not higher. The Ministry of Labour made a study (1999) of the funds that had closed down. In 10 companies out of 13 the closure was due to changes in the company structure, for example mergers and acquisitions. Another cause was a shift towards performance-related pay (two cases in the forest industry). Since the recession in the mid-1990s only a few funds have been established each year; recently their popularity has increased though. Interest in Personnel Funds has recently grown; in 2005 eight new funds were registered, more than in any other year since 1991.

**General attitude**

Until recently, Personnel Funds were the only subject discussed by the social partners. Personnel funds were promoted by employees' associations (for example, Central Organisation of Finnish Trade Unions – SAK, the Finnish Confederation of Salaried Employees – STTK, and the Confederation of Unions for Professional and Managerial Staff – AKAVA) and employers' associations (for example, Confederation of Finnish Industries – EK, Commission for Local Authority Employers – KT, and the State Employer's Office) as well as the government.[141]

However, the interest in financial participation is growing; social partners improve organisational and pay flexibility; the current government and social partners regard Personnel Funds as a good instrument for achieving flexibility. At present these parties are discussing methods to facilitate and promote the use of Personnel Funds. Current incentives for employees and employers do not seem to enhance their use as much as intended though.

Options and share ownership are not viewed as proper subjects for collective bargaining. Some employees' associations would like profit-sharing or performance-based pay to be subject to collective wage bargaining negotiations. The employers' associations think that the companies should have the flexibility to unilaterally decide whether such pay forms should be used.

**Legal and fiscal framework**

*Share ownership*

Companies are generally allowed to acquire own shares (Chapter 7 on Law on Joint-Stock Companies (624/2006)). Furthermore the company is entitled to advance funds, make loans and provide security, with a view to acquisition of the company's shares by employees (Chapter 4 § 12c Law on Joint-Stock Companies (624/2006)).

Personnel Funds may sometimes be considered to be employee ownership when fund assets are invested in the company. Here, however, they are defined as profit-sharing.

*Employee shares.* Companies may transfer shares to employees at a favourable price. The benefit is tax-free if the discount is up to 10 per cent below the current price and most employees have access to the plan (§ 66 paragraph 1 Income Tax Law). Thirty per cent of dividends from public companies are tax-free, and 70 per cent are taxed as capital income. The company withholds 19 per cent in tax from payments to the employees; employees can deduct this tax from the personal income tax base. Dividends of private companies are tax-free if earnings per share are less than 9 per cent and the total amount of earnings does not exceed EUR 90,000; otherwise, they are taxed as dividends of public companies.

*Stock options*.[142] The first stock option plans in publicly traded companies in Finland were launched in 1987. A large increase was observed between 1998 and 2000, when the stock market was at record highs. Most option schemes are used in publicly traded companies and in companies that are preparing for initial public offering. The schemes are either broad-based or selective. Broad-based schemes include all employees or at least the majority, while selected schemes are mostly for the management. Broad-based schemes became popular in 1998–2000, but their popularity has waned. The Law on Joint-Stock Companies (624/2006) requires companies to report all relevant conditions and changes in their stock option schemes to shareholders. Generally in Finland stock options are either given free or in exchange for a loan to the company which is usually to be repaid in one to three years. Options typically can be exercised two to four years after grant. The exercise period may extend from a few months to a few years. The share price is usually set to correspond to the price at the time of grant. Stock options are taxed as earned income. The employer pays social security contributions.

### Profit-sharing

*Personnel Funds.* Personnel funds have been the most frequent form of employee financial participation since 1990. The Law on Personnel Funds (814/1989) was issued 15 September 1989 and amended several times thereafter. The Personnel Funds are deferred profit-sharing plans allowing investment in the equity of the employer company and thus involving an element of employee share ownership.[143] Annual payments to the fund should be (at least up to 50 per cent) accumulated from company profits. The employer retains the right to choose the criteria for profit-related payments, but these must be fixed, typically a year in advance.[144] The funds are established on the basis of company-level agreements, prerequisite is that a company has at least 30 employees.[145] The law requires all employees to be included in the plan; only senior management may be excluded. A Personnel Fund is registered with the Ministry of Labour and is a legal entity in its own right. However, it may engage only in the activities determined by the Personnel Funds Law (814/1989). The funds invest their assets either in shares of the employer company or other companies, in investment funds, bonds or bank accounts. These investments multiply the financial returns of the employees beyond company profits.

The assets in the Personnel Fund are allotted to individual accounts. The shares are generally distributed to employees either in relation to base pay or to hours worked. Individual accounts are blocked for the first five years of participation. After that, a member can withdraw up to 15 per cent of the value of his accumulated fund share. At retirement, the employee is entitled to withdraw the value of the fund share either immediately or in instalments within four years. The law requires the fund to provide each employee with information about his account at least once a year by letter. Personnel funds enjoy several tax advantages. For employees, 20 per cent of the payouts from the fund are tax-free (§ 65 of the Income Tax Law). The fund pays no taxes on its earnings (§ 20 Income Tax Law). The employer company is not liable to social security contributions, and can deduct profits contributed to the fund as professional expenses from the corporate tax base (§ 8 Corporate Tax Law). Since 1999, amendment 344/99 has also allowed the funds to be established in civil service departments and in state-owned companies. In lieu of profit, the government offices use measures of performance. In 2000 (amendment 1145/99), the law was changed to allow employees to withdraw their share in cash if it is permitted by Personnel Fund regulations. Internationalisation and globalisation led to a change that also allowed Finnish international companies to extend profit-sharing plans, including Personnel Funds, to its subsidiaries abroad (amendment 499/2002).

Even though Finnish Personnel Funds were inspired by Swedish Wage-Earner Funds and US employee stock ownership plans, important differences exist between these schemes. Neither ESOPs nor Wage-Earner Funds (WEFs) are profit-sharing schemes. In ESOPs, the trust acquires shares with borrowed capital, and in WEFs with the government assistance.[146] Whereas Personnel Funds typically distribute their shareholdings quite widely and invest in other securities, employee share ownership plans invest only in their own firm. The main difference between Personnel Funds and Wage-Earner Funds is that the former are completely voluntary and operate at the level of the firm, whereas the latter operated at the national level for the benefit of the entire workforce. In the design of Finnish Personnel Funds, the employers explicitly wanted to avoid the Swedish obligatory model.

*Performance-related pay.* Neither legislation nor incentives for performance-related pay exist. Performance-related pay may be paid from company profit or from budgeted money or it may be a mixture of both. Plans may be related both to individual (gain-sharing) performance as well as collective performance (profit-sharing). Of those employees belonging through the employer to the Confederation of Finnish Industries (EK), 52 per cent participate in some performance-related pay scheme. This concerns about 500,000 employees. Performance-related pay that is other than a Personnel Fund is used in one-third of the companies. EK estimate that in the whole private sector (also not members) 46 per cent of employees joined performance-related pay schemes. There are differences between sectors and personnel groups. The pay schemes usually cover the whole workforce, but they may cover only a part of the workforce. PRP was more common in the industry sector (69 per cent) than in the service sector (44 per cent) or building sector (40 per cent).

### Participation in decision making

Financial participation is generally not linked to the extension of participation in decision making. Although wage increases are subject to collective agreement, companies may adopt profit-sharing and other performance-based payments independently without negotiations.[147] However, financial participation in form of Personnel Funds, which is the most common form in Finland, requires the consent of two-thirds of employees to establish or to dissolve a fund pursuant to § 9 Personnel Funds Law (814/1989).[148] Co-determination, employees' representation on the supervisory board, is prescribed in the Law 725/1990 (Finnish companies) and in 758/2004 (Societas Europaea and European Co-operatives). In companies with more than 150 employees, the employees have a right to elect representatives in the company management, that is one-quarter of the members of – depending on the company type – the supervisory board, the board of directors or management groups. There are no data available for how many companies have employees in the supervisory board.

## XXVII  Sweden

There is no specific system for direct promotion of employees' financial participation in profits or shares in Sweden, despite the fact that discussions about financial participation, namely Wage-Earner Funds, started in Sweden at the beginning of the 1960s. The Law on Wage-Earner Funds was enacted in 1983,[149] whereby most of their assets were placed in shares of large companies. The obligation to make contributions to the funds was abolished in 1990.[150] There are no common definitions of different pay systems in Sweden, which makes comparisons difficult. There are no statistics on how many companies use financial participation. In Sweden, there is no particular national promotion for financial participation. One of the main thoughts behind the taxation reform in the late 1990s was that all different sources of work income should be handled in the same way, and therefore there is no income tax relief for the employees.

Profit-Sharing Foundations are used, but the extent is unknown because they are not registered with any authority. Performance-based pay is used in several companies and the collective agreements leave place for them. Performance-based pay is based both on collective and individual results. It is not possible to distinguish how many of these plans actually are profit-sharing plans. One study shows that 19 per cent of the employees were involved in broad-based profit-sharing plans and 12 per cent in broad-based share ownership plans in 1998, and that the number seems to have increased since.[151] The Swedish Trade Union Confederation's studies show large differences between different groups. In 1998, profit-sharing was most common among younger employees in the private sector with a full-time job and highly paid men working in the industry sector.

### General attitude

Employers' associations regard financial participation as a good method of attaining increased flexibility in labour costs, depending on the success of individual firms. Because trade unions fear that financial participation will become a part of basic remuneration and affect regular rises in pay, their view is neutral and sometimes negative. In practice, financial participation remains a local issue, whereas the national associations are more concerned with the taxation issues of financial participation as they affect their respective constituencies, for example for employers the Confederation of Swedish Enterprises and for employees the Landsorganisationen (LO), the Swedish Confederation of Professional Associations (SACO) and the Swedish Trade Union Confederation (TCO). Government has little interest in financial participation and engages in no direct promotion. The government view is that employment income from different sources should be taxed at the same rate. The history of Wage-Earner Funds may still affect the debate on financial participation.

## Legal and fiscal framework

### Share ownership

Companies are generally allowed to acquire own shares (Chapter 11 Swedish Company Act 2005:551 (SCA)). Furthermore they are entitled to advance funds, make loans and provide security, with a view to acquisition of the company's shares by employees of the company or employees of the firm group, their spouse and children (Chapter 21 §§ 6, 16 paragraph 2 (2) SCA). Not less than half of the company's employees shall be covered, and the advance or loan shall be repaid within five years (Chapter 21 § 6 SCA).

*Employee shares.* The employer may offer stock purchase programmes to the employees at a discount price, but no incentives are available. Employees pay income tax on the difference between the discount and the market price, whereas the employer pays social security contributions at the time of grant if the grant price is below market. Future gains are taxed as capital income.

*Stock options.* Stock option programmes became more common in Sweden during the 1990s. One of the reasons was that generally tax is paid on capital income, which is lower than that on income of employment. Nevertheless, employee stock options are not considered as financial instruments, and thus taxation is not as favourable as for other options. The employer has no contributions at time of grant; social security contributions are paid at time of exercise.[152] Likewise, employees are not taxed at time of grant. At the time of exercise the difference between the market price and the exercise price of the shares is taxed as income of employment and social security contributions are due; future gains are taxed as capital income (§ 12 Income Tax Law 1999:1299). Employee stock options usually have the following characteristics: they are only available to employees within a company or group, granted for free with an exercise period of five to ten years and are not portable if the employee leaves the company.

### Profit-sharing

Cash-based profit-sharing exists but remains unregulated by law. No incentives exist for cash bonuses. No statistics on profit-sharing are available.

*Profit-Sharing Foundations.* Although legally possible since 1962 (Law 1962:381), the first Profit-Sharing Foundations in Sweden were established a decade later. A Profit-Sharing Foundation is an entity for the benefit of employees, to which the employer company contributes a percentage of company profit and which is governed in accordance with legally defined principles. If the company decides to create a Profit-Sharing Foundation, the employees, often through union representatives, establish the foundation and determine its charter, including the provision on how the contributions are to be invested. In listed companies, the assets are often partly invested in company shares.

A Profit-Sharing Foundation must fulfil certain requirements under the Law 1990/659. Employer contributions should represent a reward to employees for improving their performance. At least one-third of the employees must participate. Profit-sharing contributions are to be vested for at least three years. Terms and conditions must equally apply to all participants. When the foundation is terminated, its assets must be distributed directly to the employee participants, not to the company. The purpose of the foundation is to administer the allocated assets according to specific directions of its charter.

Employer contributions to the foundation were once exempt from social security contributions and payroll tax (1992–7). This probably influenced the number of new funds. Today the employer pays a payroll tax of 24.26 per cent on contributions at the time they are made (§ 25 Law 1996/97:21) in lieu of a social security contribution of 32.28 per cent which is paid on wages. No tax incentives are given to employees; they pay taxes on income attributed to employment service at the time their trust accounts are distributed. The foundation pays capital tax 1.5 per cent on its assets (§ 20 of the Law on Governmental Capital Tax 1997/323).

The purpose of a Profit-Sharing Foundation is to motivate employees, to increase both their identification with the firm and their efforts to make it more profitable. Because there is no systematic registration of Profit-Sharing Foundations, it is impossible to know the extent of use or number. The most famous Profit-Sharing Foundation in Sweden is that of Handelsbanken, called Oktogonen, enacted in 1973. Every year since then, except for 1992, Handelsbanken has contributed a part of its profit to the foundation. Shares are divided equally among employees, and the employee collects their payments at the age of 60. The foundation was Handelsbanken's largest shareholder in 2004, owning 10.1 per cent of the voting shares and 9.6 per cent of the capital. One-third of foundation assets was invested in Handelsbanken shares, and the remainder was invested in the shares of publicly traded companies.

*Participation in decision making*

Employee financial participation is not connected to participation in decision making. The extensive co-determination, representation and consultation rights of employees, mainly through trade union representatives, are governed by the Law on Board Representation (1987:1245) and the Law on Co-determination at Work (MBL 1976:580). The Act on Board Representation gives the local trade union the right to appoint two representatives to the board of directors if the company has at least 25 employees. If the company has at least 1000 employees and operates in several industries or business sectors, the trade union has the right to appoint three board representatives. Under the Act on Co-determination at Work, all important matters about the relation between employer and employees' organisations shall be determined by negotiation. The employee is always represented by the trade union organisation, which has the right to negotiate. In the case of the employer, the right of negotiation may be exercised either by an employers' organisation or by the individual employer.

## XXVIII   Turkey

On the whole, financial participation of employees has played a limited role in Turkey. Share ownership schemes have been implemented mostly in the context of privatisation and in multinational companies, whereas profit-sharing is found in private companies. Employees of many privatised enterprises have become share owners, with incentives such as discounts, payment by instalments and loans being used. Anecdotal evidence has been found for the presence of ESOP-like schemes based upon associations and foundations that hold the shares of the employer firm (for example, Adana Kağı Torba Sanayii T.A.Ş. and Teletaş Telekominikasyon Endüstri Ticaret A.Ş.) on behalf of employees, who acquire shares from contributions of company profit. The legal framework contains no special regulations for PEPPER schemes and some even inhibit their further development, although reforms of the Commercial Code are underway. Except for the tax deductibility of employers' contributions and specific tax-exempt associations and foundations, there are no direct incentives for setting up PEPPER schemes.

According to a 2007 study of corporate governance in publicly traded Turkish companies, 3 4 per cent have employee share ownership programmes, and 15 per cent have employee pension funds and other funds or foundations for retirement or unemployment insurance. More than 20 per cent of the companies have profit-sharing, though no distinction is made between broad-based schemes and those restricted to management (board members).[153]

## General attitude

Employee financial participation is not currently an issue for trade unions; their positions are inconsistent, probably because of lack of knowledge about the schemes available. Their attitude, however, can be described as generally positive, considering that, if the government would establish a consistent legal framework, employee ownership could benefit not only employees, but also the economy. On a national level, employees are represented by the Confederation of Rights of Turkish Workers' Trade Unions (Hak İş), the Confederation of Turkish Workers' Trade Unions (Türk İş) as well as the Confederation of Revolutionary Workers' Trade Unions (DISK). During the discussion of the tax reform of 1968, the Conservative Hak İş had a more positive attitude towards employee participation than the Türk İş. Employers, generally, present themselves as opposed to employee participation, in particular to participation in decision making and employee ownership, and most collective agreements are influenced by this attitude. They are, primarily, represented by the Turkish Industrialists' and Businessmen' Association (TÜSİAD) as well as by the Turkish Confederation of Employers' Associations (TİSK). However, according to a report of the TÜSİAD, participation of employees in privatisation is considered a positive factor in broadening income distribution and avoiding labour disputes.[154] According to a survey conducted by the Capital Markets Board of Turkey in 2004[155] among the companies listed at the Istanbul Stock Exchange (ISE), 56 per cent of the responding companies were in favour of employee participation in the management of the company. Employee participation has been discussed by academics, politicians and trade unions since the tax reform of 1968.

The 58th Government (Justice and Development Party), in its instant action plan of 2002, encouraged Turkish citizens working abroad to invest their savings in the privatisation of Turkish enterprises. According to the party programme, the intention was for companies subject to privatisation to be primarily offered to employees, along with certain other target groups. Accordingly, the Privatisation Law was amended by Law No. 4971 in 2003 to stipulate that employees can participate in privatisations conducted by public offers.

**Legal and fiscal framework**

Employee financial participation is covered by different laws; the recognised forms are profit-sharing, stock options and, to a limited extent, employee share ownership. Legislation permits employee share ownership in joint-stock companies during privatisation and in private companies through setting up welfare funds and mutual assistance funds for their employees' benefit. Except for tax deductibility on employers' contributions to special tax-exempt associations and foundations, there are no direct incentives for PEPPER schemes.

*Share ownership*

*Privatisation (1984, 1994, 2003)* – The privatisation programme in Turkey was initiated in 1983. Privileges for employees in connection with privatisation were introduced by Decree No. 18514 of the Public Participation Fund of 13 September 1984, regulating administration, usage and other issues. This decree allowed employees as well as the local citizenry to be included in the case of share sales.[156] According to Decision No. 54 of the Housing Development and Public Participation Board of 30 April 1987, shares of enterprises to be privatised should primarily be offered to employees, local residents and Turkish citizens working abroad. Pursuant to Article 18 of the Privatisation Law,[157] privatisation could be conducted by sale, lease, the granting of operational rights, the establishment of property rights other than ownership, profit-sharing and other legal dispositions depending upon the nature of the business. In the context of a share deal, the sale of shares to employees is expressly regulated and, depending upon the privatisation decision in each individual case, employees may be entitled to purchase shares at a discount and/or in instalments. Furthermore, Law No. 4971 of 15 August 2003 amended some laws and the decree law on the establishment and duties of the General Directorate of the National Lottery Administration, amending Article 7 of the Privatisation Law to stipulate that employees can participate in privatisations conducted by public offer. In this context the possibility of granting credit to employees from funds of foundations set up by the employer company (see below ESOPs) according to Articles 468 and 469 of the Turkish Commercial Code[158] (CC) is important. Thus, acquisition on preferential terms, such as deferred payment in instalments, credit from established foundations and discounted prices, are among the possible incentives stipulated by privatisation legislation to leverage employee ownership in privatisation.

*Private companies (2003).* Turkish commercial law does not contain special rules for any business form on employee share ownership about share acquisition, limitation of the number of shares or the issuance of employee stock; therefore general rules apply. Nevertheless, the Corporate Governance Principles of June 2003, which are recommended by the Capital Market Board for adoption by individual listed companies, do promote PEPPER schemes. Generally, corporations are not allowed to acquire their own stock (Article 329 CC) and, unlike regulations in other countries, exceptions from this general rule do not include special rules on employees' shares.[159] Thus, even if freely disposable equity of the amount necessary for this purpose is available, Article 329 CC is an obstacle to all schemes that enable employees to acquire shares if part of the price or the whole price of the stocks is paid for by the company (for example, acquisition below market price, free shares, premium, bonus, and so on). However, there is no restriction on offering shares to employees on favourable conditions in the course of a capital increase provided the price is not lower than the nominal value (Article 286 CC). Furthermore, according to Article 14/A of the Capital Market Law, if the company's articles of association permit, publicly held joint-stock corporations may issue and offer to the public preferred non-voting shares. A foreign multinational company wishing to implement a financial participation plan for employees working in a subsidiary or companies of the same group in Turkey in accordance with the rules of the home country must register the plan with the Capital Markets Board of Turkey, which will evaluate the application and approve or reject it. The sale should be conducted through an intermediary institution, for example a bank, special financial institution or brokerage house.

*Employee Stock Ownership Plans (ESOP).* Although genuine ESOPs have not been implemented in Turkey, ESOP-like schemes have been found. These are based upon associations or foundations which collectively hold the employer firm's shares on behalf of employees, with the employer company making contributions from company profits to facilitate their acquisition. Pursuant to Article 468 paragraph 1 CC, funds allocated for assistance to employees shall be set aside from the property of the company, and a foundation can be set up in accordance with the provisions of the civil law with the funds serving as its assets.[160] As such, welfare funds or mutual assistance funds created for the benefit of employees are allocated to the foundation (or association), which in turn can invest in the stocks or other securities of the founding company. Thus the provisions of Articles 468 paragraph 1 and 469 paragraph 3 CC make it possible to overcome the constraints of Article 329 CC, which prohibits a company from acquiring its own shares. Further, the foundation deed may provide that the property of the foundation shall consist of a debt to the company, making it possible to finance the acquisition of shares by employees on credit. According to Article 469 paragraph 3 CC, even if the articles of association contain no specific provision, the general assembly can decide to set aside funds to establish assistance funds for employees. After setting up a foundation or other organisation for the benefit of employees, the founder company can provide resources either from profits on the basis of a general assembly resolution or from optional reserves for social purposes. As a rule, allocations are to be regulated by the provisions on assistance funds in the articles of association. Employers' contributions to foundations (associations, and so on) that have been granted tax exemption by the Council of Ministers are tax deductible up to a maximum of 5 per cent of the current year's profit. Employees can also make individual contributions.

*Profit-sharing*

Article 323 of the Code of Obligations authorises any agreement that grants a share in profit to employees in addition to their basic fixed wage. In publicly held joint-stock companies, this may apply only if authorised by the articles of association (Article 7 of a Communiqué of the Capital Markets Board of Turkey,[161] (DivComm)). Joint-stock companies must retain 10 per cent of the net profit each year as a reserve until it equals 20 per cent of the capital ('first allocation', Article 466 paragraph 1 CC). If dividends to shareholders exceed 5 per cent of the annual profit or if profit is not distributed as an entitlement from holding shares, for example, to employees, foundations or company management, then an additional 10 per cent of the amount of profit to be distributed must be retained as a 'second allocation'. Joint-stock corporations with shares not traded on the stock exchange are required to distribute the first dividend principally in cash. However, companies not exempt from independent auditing[162] can distribute the first dividend in cash and/or in the form of bonus shares (share-based profit-sharing). Corporations that partly or wholly prefer to distribute the first dividend in the form of share-based profit-sharing are required to obtain shareholder approval. Dividends of shareholders who did not exercise this right or who had no opportunity to do so are paid in cash. In cases of making donations or distributing profit-shares to foundations (see foundations discussed earlier in the ESOP section) another Communiqué of the Capital Markets Board of Turkey[163] further requires that these payments should not result in 'inconsistent' transactions;[164] that information on the donations needs to be given to shareholders at the general assembly; and that all necessary information must be disclosed and published in the ISE Daily Bulletin.[165]

*Participation in decision making*

Turkish companies are not required to include employees in the corporate governance process, and there is no obligatory regulation on participation of employees in the management of the company. However, roughly one-third of traded companies do have a programme for the participation of employees in management.[166] The Capital Markets Board of Turkey Principles recommends that companies establish mechanisms and models to encourage stakeholders' participation in management, while giving priority to employees but without hindrance to company operations.

## XXIX   United Kingdom

Profit-sharing plans first appeared in the UK at the end of the 19th century, and employee share ownership plans were introduced in the 1950s. These plans, however, remained small in number until the introduction of tax incentives in 1978. Approximately 5,000 companies currently maintain employee financial participation schemes approved by the Inland Revenue.[167] With the abolition of the last approved profit-sharing plan (Profit-Related Pay – PRP, or Approved Profit-Sharing Scheme – APS) in 2002, the remaining approved plans, as well as numerous unapproved plans, are all share-based.

Approved plans operated in a 2006 breakdown as follows: Share Incentive Plans (SIP) – 830 (IR tax cost GBP 320 million); Savings-Related Share Option Schemes (SRSO), Sharesave or SAYE Schemes – 960 with approximately two million employees (IR tax cost GBP 412 million); Company Share Option Plans (CSOP) – 3,030 but with many fewer employees than SRSO (IR tax cost GBP 205 million), and Enterprise Management Incentives (EMI) – 2,570 with 27,000 employees (IT tax cost GBP 170 million).[168]

Many companies combine several approved plans and operate unapproved plans (no statistics available). Because approved plans are based on long-term holding and withdrawals that are not reported to HM Revenue and Customs, it is impossible to determine the exact number of employees participating in plans at a given moment.

## General attitude

Successive governments have committed themselves to supporting employee financial participation plans and promoting widespread share ownership for reasons both ideological and pragmatic. These include making enterprise more democratic, developing financial markets and fostering social welfare. The present government, with the London Stock Exchange and a consortium of major companies, were the original founders of ifsProShare. This is an independent organisation that promotes wider share ownership and financial education. It still plays an important role in promoting the interests of companies having financial participation plans, disseminating information on best practices and consulting with companies interested in setting up such plans.

The Confederacy of British Industry (CBI) and other employers' organisations generally support the employee participation plans proposed by the government, especially employee share ownership plans, but they have also criticised some approved plans for lack of flexibility. The government responded to this criticism by introducing the more flexible Share Incentive Plan. The CBI also set up a special task force to discover why employee shareholding has been declining since the 1990s. The government used these research findings to design new employee financial plans to reverse this decline.

Trade unions over the years have taken a dim view of employee financial participation on the grounds that it would undermine the traditional collective bargaining process. This was their reason for strong past opposition to Profit-Related Pay Schemes. Recently, however, they have changed their attitude. The Trades Union Congress (TUC) has declared itself in support of employee financial participation schemes that are broad-based, and if both employees and employee representatives are consulted before introduction. Recently some trade unions have themselves proposed new schemes of financial participation.

## Legal and fiscal framework

All employee financial participation plans fall into one of two catego ries: approved by the Inland Revenue or not approved. Plans introduced under the annual Finance Acts must be approved by and registered with Inland Revenue; they enjoy substantial tax and NIC exemptions, enumerated in the Income and Corporation Taxes Acts, especially for employees. Unapproved plans may be introduced at the employer's discretion, but receive no special tax incentives. Approved plans must conform to law; unapproved plans are more flexible. Under current legislation, all approved plans (and typical unapproved ones as well) are employee share ownership plans. Unapproved plans are used for granting shares, options or cash equivalents that exceed legal maximums to individual employees or to employees who are not UK tax subjects. Unapproved plans are usually combined with approved plans. It is also possible to design a hybrid model containing provisions both approved and unapproved.

*Share ownership*

Companies are generally allowed to acquire own shares (Section 143 paragraph 3 lit. a), 162 paragraph 1 Companies Act 1985 – CA 1990). Money and loans can be provided by the company to facilitate the acquisition of shares under an employees' share scheme designed to enable present and former employees of the firm and members of their families to acquire shares in the firm or other firms in the same group (Section 153 paragraph 4 lit. b), c); 153 (bb) (i); 743 CA 1985).

Share ownership plans may be approved or unapproved. Under current legislation there are four approved plans: one direct share ownership plan, with several modifications, SIP and three stock option plans (SRSO, CSOP and EMI). SIP and SRSO are broad-based, whereas CSOP and EMI may be restricted. Although not regulated, some forms of unapproved schemes are quite widespread: Long-Term Incentive Plans (LTIP), restricted Shares Plans and Unapproved Option Plans. Whereas LTIP and Restricted Shares Plans are predominantly confined to executives, Unapproved Option Plans are often broad-based complements to an approved plan. The following section will cover only approved plans.

Inland Revenue Approved Share Ownership Plan – The Share Incentive Plan (SIP) was introduced under the Finance Act of 2000 to replace the PRP on which it is partly modelled. Several possible modifications make it more flexible than earlier plans; also longer holding periods discourage tax evasion. The employer company sets up a trust to serve as an intermediary in allocating shares to employees. The share may be allocated without cost (Free Shares), at a discount, or at full price (Partnership Shares); also the employer may match the employee's partnership shares (Matching Shares). Dividends paid on all shares may be reinvested in additional shares (Dividend Shares). Each plan modification is subject to specific requirements that, if met, confer substantial tax advantages on both employees and the employer company. These generally take the form of exemption from both the personal income tax and national insurance contributions. The plan must include all employees, with the possible exclusion of those employed less than 18 months, and the same general provisions must apply to all participants. Tax exemptions are valid for all versions of the plan after the shares have been held for five years, or earlier if the employee terminates his employment on account of injury, disability, redundancy, retirement or death; also if transferred under the Transfer of Undertaking (Protecting of Employment) Regulations of 1981, or on the employer company ceasing to be an associated company. Shares sold immediately after withdrawal are exempt from a capital gains tax. Regulations specific to each plan are as follows.

*Free Shares* cannot be withdrawn from the trust during a holding period of three to five years. However, if the employee withdraws the shares or their employment ceases between the third and fifth year for reasons other than above, personal income tax and national security contributions are payable on the lesser of market value on the award date and the market value on the withdrawal or cessation date. If the employment ceases for other than the stated reasons before the end of the three-year holding period, full personal income tax and national security contributions are imposed. An employee share in the plan is limited to GBP 3,000 per annum.

*Partnership Shares* are purchased by the trust from a part of the employee's pre-tax remuneration according to the employee's agreement with the employer company. The shares are purchased either within 30 days of pay deduction or at the end of a specified accumulation period of up to 12 months. If the latter, the share price is the lowest market price of the period. An employee is limited to GBP 1,500 per annum. After the five-year holding period or termination of employment for the given reasons, the employee is exempted from personal income tax, and the employer exempt from national security contributions. However, the employee is only exempted from paying national security contributions if his total earnings fall below the ceiling on national security contributions. If the employee withdraws the shares or his employment ends for a reason other than those stated between the third and fifth year, personal income tax and national security contributions are exacted on the lesser of the amount of the employee contributions for purchase and the market value of shares on the date of withdrawal or cessation.

*Matching Shares* can be offered by the employer company up to two Matching Shares for each partnership share. These are allocated to the employee on the same day as partnership shares are acquired. The holding period is the same for Matching Shares as for Free Shares.

Up to GBP 1,500 of dividends per annum can be used to purchase Dividend Shares. The general holding period for Dividend Shares is three years. If these shares are withdrawn or employment ends for other than stated reasons within five years of their acquisition, the employee is liable for personal income tax on the dividends used to purchase the shares. However, there is no liability for national insurance contributions.

*Inland Revenue Approved Stock Option Plans.* The Savings-Related Share Option Scheme (SRSO) or Sharesave or SAYE Scheme, introduced by the Finance Act 1980, is currently the most popular plan judging by the number of participants. It must apply to all employees, except possibly those with relatively short service. The basic structure of the plan is as follows: the employee enters into a save-as-you-earn (SAYE) contract with a designated bank or building society, agreeing to save a specified monthly amount (GBP 5 to 250) by deduction from after-tax remuneration for three, five or seven years and the employer company grants him share options for the maximum number of shares he will be able to purchase at the exercise price with his SAYE savings. The SAYE contract always includes a tax-free bonus added to savings on completion, the amount depending on the term of the contract and the rates are set by HM Treasury. The share exercise price can be up to 20 per cent under the market value of the underlying shares at the time of the grant. At maturity of the SAYE contract, the employee is entitled to choose whether to exercise the option and retain or sell the shares or take the savings and bonus in cash. These requirements fulfilled, the employee is not liable for personal income tax at grant or exercise. However, he must pay capital gains tax on the sale of shares.

*Company Share Ownership Plan (CSOP).* This was introduced in 1984 as Discretionary Share Option Scheme (DSOP) and re-launched in 1996 under the current name with amended requirements. It is a discretionary plan that is often limited to the executives but can also be broad-based. It is often connected to performance results: that is, a certain goal must be reached before the option can be exercised. The following requirements also apply: the value[169] of outstanding options per employee must not exceed GBP 30,000 at grant; the exercise price may not be less than market value at grant; the exercise period may not be shorter than three nor longer than ten years after grant.[170] These requirements fulfilled, the employee is not liable for personal income tax at grant or exercise.

*Enterprise Management Incentives (EMI).* This was introduced by the Finance Act 2000 to help small, higher-risk companies to recruit and retain highly qualified employees. It applies to companies with gross assets of less than GBP 30 million.[171] The plan can be selective. Approval of the Inland Revenue is not required, but it must be notified of each stock option grant under EMI within 92 days. Options granted must not exceed a total market value of GBP 120,000 per employee or GBP 3 million for the company. These requirements fulfilled, neither employees nor the employer company are subject to personal income tax or national insurance contributions at grant or exercise. However, they must pay capital gains tax at the sale of shares.

*Profit-sharing*

At present there are no approved or conventional unapproved financial participation plans in the form of profit-sharing plans. However, a few unapproved bonus schemes might be both broad-based and profit-connected; if so, they could be considered as cash-based profit-sharing plans. There used to be an approved profit-sharing plan — *Profit-Related Pay (PRP)* or *Approved Profit-Sharing (APS)* — which was exceedingly popular until terminated in 2003.[172] There were 14,275 of these plans in 1998, covering 1.6 million employees. The plan, however, was mainly used as a means of avoiding taxation. Because it did not lead to a wider employee shareholder base, while causing heavy tax loss, the government phased it out in 1999, and completely abolished it in 2002. It was replaced with the SIP. Some employees, however, may have yet to withdraw their shares from the earlier plan.

*Participation in decision making*

There is no direct connection between participation in decision making and employee financial participation; in particular, financial participation plans cannot extend existing rights in decision making. General provisions of labour law, for example equal pay and prohibition of discrimination, also apply to financial participation plans.

## Notes

1. According to EFES from 2001 to 2007, only four share plans and around 40 cash plans were set up.
2. J. Priewe and F. Havighorst (1999) *Auf dem Weg zur Teilhabergesellschaft? Investivlöhne, Gewinn- und Kapitalbeteiligungen der Arbeitnehmer in Westeuropa und den USA — eine vergleichende Bestandsaufnahme*, Friedrich Ebert Foundation Series 'Wirtschaftspolitische Diskurse', No. 123 (Bonn: FES Library).
3. PriceWaterhouseCoopers (2002).
4. Terms and conditions not prescribed by law can be introduced by the employer company upon consultation with the workers' council; in

companies without a workers' council, with the committee for prevention and protection at work; in companies without such a committee, with the union delegation, and in companies without union representation, with all individual employees.

5. A criterion of a later ownership transfer is that no dividends are paid to the employee during the blocking period.

6. The net asset value defined as the amount of company net equity and reserves divided by the total number of shares.

7. For example, if the company grants a 'substantial' number of discounted shares and the purchase of the shares on the stock market may be expected to result in a drop in price (however, this might be difficult to prove if the stock is traded at a large stock exchange on a liquid market) or a two-year blocking period applies.

8. Until 24 December 2002 it was considered as acceptance of the stock option.

9. The percentage of co-operations among industrial enterprises ranged from 8.5 per cent to 10.4 per cent between 1980 and 1988. The corresponding numbers for personnel was 6.8 per cent and 6.7 per cent. Source: NSI.

10. 1,436 or 28 per cent of 5,165 deals. Source: V. Minchev (2004) 'Stakeholders in the Bulgarian Public Companies', *Ikonomika*, issue No. 2, pp. 55–7.

11. See S. Ivanova and S. Keremidchiev (2006) 'Extended Country Report: Financial Participation of Employees in Bulgaria', in J. Lowitzsch et al., *The PEPPER III Report* (Rome and Berlin: Inter-University Centre Split/Berlin), on supplementary CD-ROM, downloadable from the Inter-University Centre website, http://www.intercentar.de, p. 29, according to the calculations of the authors.

12. Joint-stock company offers of any of these incentives to a Council or Board member must be approved by the general meeting for every beneficiary on an annual basis.

13. Articles 12–32 Labour Code were abolished in 1992.

14. Commercial Law: Article 136 paragraph 3 (for the limited liability company), Article 220 paragraph 3 (for the joint-stock company) and Article 253 paragraph 2 (for the partnership limited by shares).

15. D. Tipurić (ed.) (2004) *'ESOP i hravtsko poduzeće'* (Zagreb: Sinenergija – nakladništvo); in many cases analysed in the study, ESOP programmes were stopped or completed, and some programmes had only a few ESOP characteristics in their design.

16. See also J. Lowitzsch (2006), *'The PEPPER III Report'* pp. 118–19, 123 (Table 1).

17. The Statute of Parliament 2000 authorises social partners to participate in the work of Parliamentary committees, thus giving them direct influence over the drafting of laws dealing with such matters as employment and industrial relations.

18. In this context, the term ESOP is applicable to all schemes where employees make an offer to buy shares of the company, the purchase is funded by special credit and a new company is formed to administer the shares.

19. Instead, Vouchers were distributed to 230,000 persons who had suffered under the former socialist regime: refugees, displaced persons, war veterans, war invalids, families of dead or missing soldiers, and political prisoners; these, together with employees, made up the category of small shareholders.

20. A three-quarter majority of votes representing equity capital is required to change the articles of association. Shareholders holding at least 10 per cent of the equity capital have a voice in decisions made by the general meeting on liability of members of the board of directors or of the supervisory board (Article 273 CL); they can also lodge a claim at court to remove a board member for cause. Shareholders owning at least 5 per cent of shares can call the general meeting. A majority shareholder who holds at least 95 per cent of total shares can buy out minority shareholders, at fair compensation, if the general meeting so resolves (Article 300 CL).
21. The draft law is prepared by the legislative committee of Parliament in the course of harmonisation with the EU law and is supported by trade unions and employers' associations; see the website of the Parliament, http://www.sabor.hr, date accessed 12 December 2005 (in Croatian).
22. By October 2001, the market was approaching the 100 level, having fallen from 800 at the peak of a short-lived boom in 1999. During 2002/03 the market continued a long-term decline, reaching a level of 80 in late 2003.
23. Fifty-eight per cent of the enterprises employed one person; 37 per cent two to nine persons; 4 per cent ten to 49 persons, and only 1 per cent had more than 50 employees (this amounts to 99.9 per cent), see Statistical Service of the Republic of Cyprus (CYSTAT) (2001) *Census of Enterprises 2000* (Nicosia: CYSTAT).
24. It has also been observed that salary and wage earners undertake small-scale entrepreneurial activity, and are thus 'multiple-jobholders' – especially with regard to the development of the services sector.
25. English case law is cited in the Cypriot Courts and is of persuasive authority.
26. Private companies limited by shares are those whose articles restrict the right to transfer their shares, limit the number of their members to 50 and prohibit any public subscription to shares or debentures. A public company limited by shares is one whose Articles do not contain these restrictions and thus may obtain a listing on the Cyprus Stock exchange.
27. In most cases, companies of this nature are incorporated as non-profit making organisations. Companies limited by guarantee can be registered with or without share capital and the liability of each member is limited to the amount agreed on in the memorandum of association to be contributed in the event of the company going into liquidation.
28. See Law 277(I) 2004, implementing Directive 2001/86/EC; Law 160(I)/2006, implementing Directive 2003/72/EC and Law 186(I)/2007, implementing Directive 2005/56/EC.
29. See Law 78(I)/2002005, implementing Directive 2002/14/EC and Laws 68(I)/2002 and 43(I)/2003 implementing Directive 94/45/EC.
30. This case is also covered under the provisions of the 28(I)/2001, implementing Directive 98/59/EC.
31. The provisions of the 5th Law on Asset Accumulation and § 19a of the Income Tax Law.
32. S. Würz (ed.) (2003) *European Stock-Taking on Models of Employee Financial Participation* (Wiesbaden: Dr Dr Heissmann GmbH), p. 59.
33. L. Bellmann and I. Möller (2006) *Gewinn und Kapitalbeteiligung der Mitarbeiter. Die Betriebe in Deutschland haben Nachholbedarf,* IAB-Kurzbericht (Nuremberg: Institut für Arbeitsmarkt- und Berufsforschung), p. 13 (data based on questionnaires of 16,000 German companies).

34. A. Hauser-Ditz, M. Hertwig and L. Pries (2006) *Erste Ergebnisse der BISS-Befragung 2005 – Kurzbericht* (Bochum: Ruhr-Universität Bochum, Forschungsprojekt 'Betriebliche Interessenregulierung in Deutschland – Survey und Strukturanalayse' – BISS) (data based on a representative survey of 3,254 German companies).
35. The Christian Democrats proposed to support voluntary schemes at the company level by introducing additional tax incentives for share schemes up to 1,000 Euro per employee annually with the possibility to defer taxation if connected to a retirement savings plan. The Social Democrats favoured a 'Germany Fund' under state guarantee with employees investing in the fund, which in turn would invest in German enterprises, in particular SMEs.
36. See decision of the Federal High Court (Bundesgerichtshof) of 10 March 2008 regarding § 15 para. 4 Law on Limited Liability Companies and § 125 Civil Code; II ZR 312/06.
37. The previous requirement that the benefit was not to exceed 50 per cent of the share value was removed in 2009.
38. D. C. Jones and N. Mygind (1998) *Ownership Patterns and Dynamics in Privatised Firms in Transition Economies: Evidence from the Baltics*, CEES Working Paper Series, Issue 15 (Fredriksberg: Copenhagen Business School, Centre for East European Studies), published also in *Baltic Journal of Economics*, Vol. 2, No. 2, Winter 1999; according to an overview of the distribution of ownership in a sample of 666 Estonian enterprises.
39. D. C. Jones, P. Kalmi and N. Mygind (2005) 'Choice of Ownership Structure and Firm Performance: Evidence from Estonia', *Post-Communist Economies*, Vol. 17, No. 1, pp. 83–107.
40. N. Mygind (2002) *Ownership, Control, Compensation and Restructuring of Estonian Enterprises – Preliminary Results from a Manager Survey*, CEES Working Paper Series, Issue 42 (Fredriksberg: Copenhagen Business School, Centre for East European Studies).
41. Initially, pre-emptive rights, which often also led to the possibility of buying assets or shares under value, were the most popular mechanism. With regard to privatisation in the industrial sector, most influential political forces were opposed to buyouts by employees.
42. Pursuant to §§ 515 paragraph 1, 2 CC, rights attached to shares issued before 1 September 1995 which do not comply with the provisions of the Commercial Code remain valid, whereas rights not attached to shares are void. Minority shareholders of a joint-stock company can be bought out by a majority shareholder holding at least nine-tenths of the shares upon resolution of the general meeting with at least 95 per cent of the votes represented by all shares; in this case a fair compensation to minority shareholders is secured by the provisions regarding takeover bids (§§ 363 paragraph 2 (2) and 363 paragraph 7 (1) CC) and the right to lodge a claim with a court (§ 363 paragraph 8 (2), (3) CC). Minority shareholders have no corresponding sell-out right, that is, they cannot demand that the majority shareholder buy their shares if they wish to sell them.
43. This seems to be justified because management and employees might have insider knowledge, but it could be argued that employees, unlike managers, do not necessarily have full information as to the financial situation of the

company. Notably, employees are not deemed insiders, but rather as third persons who could receive information from insiders, under the same law (§ 191 paragraph 1, 3 SML).
44. Ch. Ioannou (2008) 'Changing Payment Systems in Greece', mimeo.
45. European Commission (2003a), p. 32.
46. See CONFESAL (2006) Report about changes to the Law governing Sociedades Laborales, October 2006, p 6
47. The overall figure for Spanish employees, including management and co-operatives, is 23.7 per cent. Genuine profit-sharing plans and performance-related pay not connected to financial indicators are not clearly differentiated, so that it is not clear whether this data reflects the incidence of profit-sharing correctly.
48. However, it should be made clear that such a distinction refers to taxation only. In labour law terms, shares are payments in kind and, therefore, their value cannot amount to more than 30 per cent of the wage. Payments in kind have an exceptional character and their establishment is only admissible if there is a law, a collective agreement or a pact between the parties authorising it, it can never be unilaterally imposed by the employer. See E. Poutsma (2001), p. 82.
49. By Decree Law 2/2003 from 25 April 2003 regarding economic reform measures; however, this mechanism has not yet been extended to Workers' Companies as postulated by CONFESAL in 2006.
50. European Commission (2003c). Note that these figures include executive plans.
51. This plan evolved from the Plan Partenarial d'Epargne Salarial Volontaire (PPESV) and may be set up as an inter-enterprise (PERCOI) or branch (PERCOB) plan.
52. The incentive systems of 50 companies were surveyed in 2003, the majority of which were large ones in terms of sales and number of employees.
53. Law XXXIX of 1995 on the Realisation of Entrepreneurial Property in State Ownership; Governmental Decree No. 28 of 1991 on Egzisztencia Credit and Deferred Payments Benefits.
54. Law CVI of 2007 on State Property in force since 1 January 2008.
55. Article 58 paragraph 3 of Law XXXIX of 1995 on Realisation of Entrepreneurial Property in State Ownership. This rule applies to ESOP credits as well.
56. Regulated by Law XLIV of 1992 on Employee Share Ownership Programme, which entered into force on 14 July 1992, amended with Law CXIX of 2003 and articles 38–42 of Law CVI of 2007 on State Property
57. Another difference between the American and Hungarian regulation was that under the 1992 ESOP Law there were no 'fairness' rules (this led to disproportionately large manager ownership); however, this was changed with the 2003 Amendments.
58. In absence of such legal regulations, the majority of ESOP organisations ceased to exist after the loans were repaid. Moreover, the established forms of operating the asset (for example setting up a limited company) involve considerable costs See D. Boda, L. Neumann and Z. Vig (2006) 'Extended Country Report: Financial Participation of Employees in Hungary',

in J. Lowitzsch, *The PEPPER III Report* (Rome and Berlin: Inter-University Centre Split/Berlin), on supplementary CD-ROM, downloadable from the Inter-University Centre website, http://www.intercentar.de.

59. Two special rules apply in calculating the ESOP tax base: (1) the tax base should be reduced by the amounts paid by private persons as their own contribution to the ESOP and by the amounts of subsidy paid by other private or legal persons or by the employer company (under general rules these amounts would have been considered income); (2) at the same time, the tax base must be increased by the acquisition value of the shares given to the ESOP participants (under general rules this amount would be accounted among expenditures, thus reducing the profit.

60. See Article 18 paragraph 4 of Law XLIV of 1992 on Employee Share Ownership Programme and Article 66 of Law CXVII of 1995 on Personal Income Tax; Securities acquired from already taxed personal income of the participant of the programme are not taxable.

61. If this deadline expires without success, at the first shareholders' meeting thereafter the company shall withdraw the employees' shares in question with a corresponding reduction in its share capital, or shall decide to sell such shares after transforming them into ordinary, preference or interest-bearing shares.

62. The applicable rules of taxation are determined by the legal relationship between the private person and the provider. In the case of securities provided by employer to employee, such income is considered as income from employment, and the pertinent tax rules have to be applied. See Informant of the Tax and Financial Control Administration (APEH) on the Rules on Securities Allowance in Force from 1 January 2003. Source: Hungarian CD Jogtar, 28 February 2005.

63. Law CXVII of 1995 on Personal Income Tax; Decree of the Ministry of Finance No. 5 of 2003 on the Procedure of Registration of Approved Employee Securities Benefit Programme, and on the Rate of Administration Service Fee for the Initiation of the Procedure.

64. While personal income tax is payable because the shares are regarded as earned income, no social security contribution must be paid. Earlier share benefits were regarded as in-kind benefits, belonging to the highest income tax bracket (44 per cent), and the social security contribution was also payable.

65. In the five-year plan, the monies saved can be left on deposit with the financial institution for a further two years.

66. This provision could prove to be an obstacle to introducing these plans in non-listed companies if the employees – unlike shareholders who are not employees – have to sell the shares to the company after leaving, which in turn might create tax complications arising from the obligatory sale.

67. 'Protocollo sulla politica dei redditi e dell'occupazione, sugli assetti contrattuali, sulle politiche del lavoro e sul sostegno al sistema produttivo' of 13 July 1993.

68. Compare A. Pendleton and E. Poutsma (2004), p. 12.

69. However, pursuant to Law No. 112/08 the value of the discount is deemed income and subject to personal income tax and social security contributions accordingly; the same applies to shares transferred in lieu of remuneration.

70. This condition substantially reduces the possibility of exemption from ordinary taxation for a large number of employees, considering that the number of companies listed on the market is rather low.
71. In 1998, the share of the flexible wage exempted from payment of social security contributions was raised to 2 per cent and in 1999 the tax relief was re-determined to a maximum of 3 per cent.
72. According to another study based upon responses from 915 enterprises spec ifying their ownership structure for 1997, 1998 and 1999, D. C. Jones and N. Mygind (2005) 'Corporate Governance Cycles during Transition: Theory and Evidence from the Baltics', in I. Filatochev and M. Wright (eds) *The Life Cycle of Corporate Governance* (Cheltenham: Edward Elgar), pp. 253–86.
73. Decrees of 1992/93 included a list, proposed by the sector Ministries, of 579 medium and large enterprises to be privatised. Four hundred of these enterprises were to be public offerings, and an additional 147 were to be leased with the option to buy; later this list was expanded to 712 enterprises.
74. Employee stock issued by a private joint-stock company according to Article 255 CL should be differentiated from the stock acquired by employees in the course of privatisation. Limitations attached to employee stock according to Article 255 CL, in particular lack of voting rights, do not apply to privatisation stock.
75. A manager survey conducted in the spring of 2000 provides information on ownership at the time of privatisation or start-up as a new firm for the years 1993, 1996, 1999 and spring 2000 with 405 respondents; for details see J. Lowitzsch (2006), pp. 199, 205 (Table 4). In 1993, approximately 50 per cent of employees were owners in the sample of responding enterprises. However, that proportion fell to about one-third in 1999. Not surprisingly, the proportion of employee owners was highest in employee-owned enterprises, but here also the proportion of owners fell from 76 per cent in 1993 to 66 per cent in 1999.
76. Vouchers and cash quotas were only given to residents and had limited transferability (to relatives, later they could be used in exchange for outstanding housing loans).
77. The most important of these are the Law on Privatisation of State Property and Property of Municipalities of 11 April 1997 as amended (hereinafter referred to as PL), the Law on Securities Market of 16 January 1996 as amended, and the Law on the State Property Fund of 11 April 1997 as amended.
78. Law on Companies from 11 December 2003, No. IX-1889 (Valstybės žinios 2003, No. 123–5574) as amended; according to CL, shareholders have the pre-emptive right to acquire shares or convertible debentures issued by the company, unless the general meeting decides to withdraw the pre-emptive right for all shareholders.
79. From 4 June 2002, No. IX-926 (Valstybės žinios 2002, No. 64–2569) as amended.
80. Where an enterprise, agency or organisation has no functioning trade union and if the staff meeting has not transferred the function of employee representation and protection to the trade union of the appropriate sector of economic activity, the employees shall be represented by the work council elected by secret ballot at the general meeting of the staff (Articles 19 paragraph 1; 21 paragraph 2 LC).

81. European Commission (2003c).
82. By virtue of their nationalisation these two banks had become parastatal entities (independent statutory bodies within the realm of the public sector).
83. This was a trust fund, set up on behalf of employees, in the Bank of Valletta, a formerly state-owned bank, and in Maltacom, a state-owned telecommunication enterprise.
84. Enemalta Corporation Act, 1977 (Chapter 272 of the Laws of Malta).
85. Water Services Corporation, 1991 (Chapter 355 of the Laws of Malta).
86. Consequently, the following conditions apply across the board: (i) authority for the making of discounts must be given by the company's memorandum and articles of association, (ii) the discount must not exceed 10 per cent of the issue price or as prescribed by the memorandum and articles of association, whichever is less, (iii) the amount or rate of discount must be made public, and (iv) in no event may the value of the shares be reduced to below their nominal value as a result of such a discount.
87. Legal Notice 125 of 2001.
88. Rule 36 of the Fringe Benefit Rules (LN. 125 of 2001).
89. The Trusts and Trustees Act, 1988 (Chapter 331 of the Laws of Malta).
90. 'Collective Investment Scheme' defined in Article 2 IS Act is any scheme that aims at 'collective investment of capital acquired by means of an offer of units for subscription, sale or exchange'. It must operate according to the principle of risk spreading and either: (i) the contributions of the participants and the profits or income out of which payments are to be made to them are pooled; or (ii) at the request of the holders, units are or are to be re-purchased or redeemed out of the assets of the scheme or arrangement, continuously or in blocks at short intervals; or (iii) units are, or have been, or will be issued continuously or in blocks at short intervals.
91. Article 22 paragraph 3 and Article 36 paragraph 13 Employment and Industrial Relations Act, 2002.
92. E. Poutsma and H. van den Tillaart (1996); R. h.j. Stikkelbroeck (2001). 'Survey of employee financial participation in the Netherlands' in Nederlands Participatie Instituut, PS Participation Solutions (eds) Nog steeds tijd voor beleid (The Hague: Nederlands Participatie Instituut).
93. F. Beursken (2007) *Werknemersparticipaties in Nederland: Theorie and Parktijk – Een Analyse van AEX ondernemingen*, Masters thesis, University of Rotterdam.
94. As of 2001, the employee could choose between one of two tax alternatives: unconditional options could be taxed at grant and conditional options at vesting, with no tax liability at the moment of exercise if held for more than three years, or tax could be imposed at exercise on the total capital gain.
95. D. Vevera (2005) *Mitarbeiterbeteiligung am Kapital im EU-Mitgliedstaat Österreich – umfassende Erhebung über Verbreitung, Motive und Anforderungen von Arbeitnehmern und Arbeitgebern* (Vienna: Fachhochschule Wiener Neustadt, Arbeiterkammer Wien and Wirtschaftskammer Österreich), p. 54.
96. R. Kronberger, H. Leitsmüller and A. Rauner (2007) Mitarbeiterbeteiligung in Österreich (Vienna: Linde Verlag), pp. 11, 67.
97. Ibid., p. 17.

98. Ibid., pp. 10, 16.
99. Ibid., p. 17.
100. Ibid., p. 57.
101. Ibid., p. 53.
102. In the literature, there is an objection that the economic activities of foundations are restricted by law so that they cannot create reserves and make investments. In addition, this form cannot be used by small companies owing to administrative complexity and prohibitive costs. Therefore they use business forms as associations (Vereine), trusts (Treuhandschaften) and partnerships under civil law (GbR) instead.
103. In some companies, the shares are possessed by employees, whereas the foundation only accumulates and exercises the voting rights. In such cases, the taxation is different.
104. R. Kronberger, H. Leitsmüller and A. Rauner (2007), p. 51.
105. That means, plans relating to turnover as a factor cannot be regulated by an in-house agreement.
106. R. Kronberger, H. Leitsmüller and A. Rauner (2007), p. 67.
107. See J. Lowitzsch (2006), p. 237 (Table 3).
108. Of 30 August 1996, Dziennik Ustaw No. 118, Pos. 561, republished in Dziennik Ustaw 2002 No. 171, Pos. 1397, No. 240, Pos. 2055, with subsequent amendments.
109. Until 2002 Article 52 paragraph 1 PrivL foresaw a maximum of 10 years; the legal regulations for LLBOs are to be found in Article 39 paragraph 1 No. 3 and Articles 50 to 54 PrivL; it is reserved exclusively for Polish nationals and as an exception also legal persons (Article 51, paragraph 1 No. 2 PrivL).
110. Ordinance of the Minister of Finance of 13 May 1993, Monitor Polski 1993 No. 26, Pos. 274, altering that of 7 May 1991, Monitor Polski 1991 No. 18, Pos. 123.
111. Furthermore Article 54 PrivL foresees the possibility to regulate the specific conditions of such leverage by Ordinance of the Council of Ministers including the possibility to reduce the threshold of paying 20 per cent of the net value of the object of the lease stated in Article 51 paragraph 1 No. 3 PrivL to 15 per cent. In this context Article 64 PrivL granted existing Employees Companies the right to renegotiate their contracts within 3 months of the Ordinance coming into power.
112. This regulation had its origin in the harmonisation with the *acquis communautaire*, that is the implementation of the second Council Directive of 1976 (77/91/EEC; Official Journal L 26, 31 January 1977, p. 1).
113. Article 347 paragraph 3 and 348 paragraph 1 CCC provide the possibility to allocate enterprise profits to special funds while not paying them out as dividends to shareholders, thus allow share based profit-sharing.
114. The issuance of shares to be acquired by employees in this case shall not be considered as a public offering but as a 'private subscription' (Article 431 paragraph 2 No. 1 CCC).
115. Dziennik Ustaw 2003 No. 60, Pos. 535. For a detailed analysis of the new law see Zedler (2003).
116. See decision of the Supreme Court of 5 May 1992, I PZP 23/92, Bibl. Prac. No. 25, p. 96.

117. Such as other forms of remuneration, for example, gratifications (gratyfikacja, nagrody, nagrody jubileuszowy), thirteenth salary, commissions (prowizja; used frequently, if not universally, in the case of sales force employees) and various types of bonus schemes. For details see S. W. Ciupa (2001) *Nowoczesna umova o pracę*, 4th edn (Warsaw: Wydawnictwo C. H. Beck); 'Premie i nagrody dla pracowników', *Rzeczpospolita* of 3 October 2005.
118. J. S. Earle and Á. Telegdy (2002) *Privatization Methods and Productivity Effects in Romanian Industrial Enterprises*, Upjohn Institute for Employment Research, Central European University and Budapest University of Economic Sciences, Central European University Labour Project; World Bank (2004) *Romania: Restructuring for EU Integration – The Policy Agenda. Country Economic Memorandum, Vol. 2: Main Report and Annexes*, June (Washington DC: The World Bank); compare also the J. Lowitzsch (2006), pp. 251–2, Tables 1–3.
119. World Bank data from 2004; at the end of 2003 there were about 1,300 state-owned enterprises and another 600 enterprises *de facto* under state control.
120. Although compulsory, interview evidence reported, that in practice it is seldom applied and, if applied, concerns a rather small number of employees.
121. Law on Associations of Employees and Members of the Management in Companies in the Privatisation Process, establishing so-called management and employees' associations (asociaţiǎ salariatilor şi membrilor conducerii). When voucher privatisation came to an end Emergency Ordinance 88/1997 defined a rough legal framework for the employee shareholder associations and referring for the details to the general legal provisions governing associations and foundations; the Ordinance was subsequently changed by Law No. 137/2002 concerning some measures to forward privatisation.
122. Regarding Article 52 of Law 77/1994 the Privatisation Agency is bound by these conditions. Furthermore, the Agency has to accept a certain amount of privatisation vouchers (property vouchers) in exchange for the shares to be transferred.
123. On the Repartition of Profits Obtained by State and Municipal Companies with the State as Single or Majority Owner (Monitorul Oficial al Românie No. 536/2001 as amended) abrogating earlier regulations, for example, Ordinance 23/1996 on the same issue.
124. Supplemented by Governmental Disposition No. 298/25 February 2002 for the approval of the explanatory note regarding the establishing of the amounts making the object of the profit repartition conforming to the Governmental Ordinance No. 64/2001 and their reflection in bookkeeping (Monitorul Oficial al Românie No. 157/2002).
125. A twist appeared in this year, when all the privatised firms were required to issue 34 per cent of their share capital in employee shares: This requirement was abolished within half a year and the privatisation law then only mentioned an option to issue employee shares, not a requirement to do so.
126. For limited liability companies see §§ 114, 122, 123, 125 et seq., for joint-stock companies see §§ 178, 179, 180 et seq. CC.

127. J. Damijan, A. Gregoric and J. Prašnikar (2004) *Ownership concentration and firm performance in Slovenia*, LICOS – Centre for Transition Economics, Leuven, Discussion Paper 142.
128. A. Kanjuo-Mrčela (2002) 'Lastništvo zaposlenih na prelomu tisočletja', *Industrijska demokracija*, No. 10.
129. Združenje svetov delavcev slovenskih podjetij, http://www.delavska-participacija.com.
130. Združenje managerjev Slovenije, http://www.zdruzenje-manager.si.
131. Of 5 December 1992, OG RS 55/1992, as amended. However, a special form of participation of workers was already regulated by Article 168 Company Law as amended in August 1990 (labelled 'the beginning of capitalism'), which authorised the managing body of socially owned companies and public companies to offer the employees the possibility to buy the assets of the company under the conditions defined in the articles of association.
132. The LOT emphasised ownership transformation rather than privatisation, which, nevertheless, was the final goal of the law. Transformation was the interim stage, allowing for the acquisition of ownership by workers and other Slovenian citizens of existing social capital (public funds).
133. The Slovenian Restitution or Compensation Fund has to issue debenture bonds to re-privatisation claimants who did not get their nationalised property returned in kind. The Slovenian Compensation Fund obtained funds from the non-distributed public funds.
134. A. Kanjuo-Mrčela (2002).
135. A draft framework Law on Employee Financial Participation was submitted to Parliament in October 1997 but never discussed. As stated above, a new proposition of the Law on Employee Profit-Sharing was sent to Parliament in April 2005 but was again refused following Parliamentary discussions.
136. Only the articles of association can grant members of the management board the right to participate in profit-sharing in recognition of their work contributions (Article 252 paragraph 1 CL).
137. It is also possible that participation in profits is defined by the meeting of shareholders (Article 276 CL), but, by systematic interpretation of special provisions in conjunction with general provisions, it can also be concluded that in this case the general meeting has to amend the articles of association.
138. Of 6 August 1993, OG RS 42/1993, as amended.
139. Individual specific provisions on employees' co-management are integrated into the special laws for different economic sectors, for example, the Energy Law, Banks and Savings Banks Law, Insurance Company Law.
140. First official discussions about employee Wage-Earner Funds (as they were called at the time) took place in 1981 at Trade Union Organisations general meeting. The idea of Wage-Earner Funds in Finland was attributable to the model of collective Wage-Earner Funds developed in Sweden by Rudolf Meidner. The US ESOP was also a source of inspiration.
141. In 2007/08 the Centre Party held the majority of seats in parliament and was the ruling majority, together with the Coalition Party, whereas the Social Democratic Party is in opposition
142. Based on the data from the doctoral thesis of Mikko Mäkinen (2007) *Essays on Stock Option Schemes and CEO Compensation*, Acta Universitatis

Oeconomicae Helsingiensis, A-291, Helsinki School of economics; and Panu Kalmi (2005) *Inventory Study for the Project 'Change Patterns of Employee Financial Participation in Europe'* at Nijmegen School of Management, mimco.
143. The discussion draws from M. Vartiainen and Ch. Sweins (2002) Employee Ownership Funds in Finland – Functionality and Personnel Outcomes, *Labour Policy Studies*, No. 243 (Helsinki: Ministry of Labour) and Ch. Sweins (2004) Personnel Funds as a Rewarding Tool – a Research of the Finnish Funds, Licentiate thesis, Helsinki University of Technology.
144. It is possible to use other measures of efficiency, for example, quality or physical productivity. At the present time companies do not, however, use this alternative to any extent.
145. Personnel funds are established by a collective decision of employees and two-thirds of all personnel groups must support the establishment of the fund. In the case of corporate groups there can also be a joint fund for all member companies.
146. See J. R. Blasi and D. L. Kruse (1991) for a description on ESOPs and P. Whyman (2004) 'An Analysis of Wage-Earner Funds in Sweden: Distinguishing Myth from Reality', *Economic and Industrial Democracy*, Vol. 25, No. 3, pp. 411–45 for a recent account on Wage-Earner Funds (WEFs).
147. The unionisation rate in Finland is around 70 per cent to 80 per cent; about 90 per cent of all wage and salary earners are covered by collective bargaining agreements. A few collective agreements, however, have included negotiation on performance-based pay.
148. One of the prerequisites for a Personnel Fund is a profit bonus system decided by the employer. An eventual decision on establishing a Personnel Fund shall be preceded by a procedure of information and consultation in accordance with § 19 Co-operation Law 334/2007.
149. At that time, there were only discussions inside the Central Organisation of Trade Unions (LO). A workgroup around Rudolf Meidner proposed that 20 per cent of the profit in companies with more than 100 workers should be invested in Wage-Earner Funds. Approximately 60 per cent of all employees in Sweden worked in such companies. The profits of these companies made up about 80 per cent of the profits in the whole country. The proposal was to create five regional Wage-Earner Funds, which would be co-ordinated with the employment pension funds. Nevertheless, the law was different from the initial proposal. The funds got their assets from 20 per cent tax on the company real profit and from an increase in pension contribution. The public sector also participated in the funds.
150. In 1991, the political right wing won the elections and started to close down Wage-Earner Funds. The draft law brought into the parliament stipulated that the existing funds should be closed down and no new funds should be established. The accumulated capital of SEK 22 billion in shares was intended to be used to enhance private ownership and savings, but this proposition was rejected, because it would lead to volatility of financial markets. The government decided that SEK 10 billion would be invested in research promotion and the remaining amount in subsidies for pension schemes.
151. S. Würz (ed.) (2003), pp. 116–28.

152. This may involve the risk of large social security contributions for the employer in the future.
153. A. Küçükçolak and L. Özer (2007) 'Do Corporate Governance, Independent Boards & Auditors Affect Market and Financial Performance: An Application to Istanbul Stock Exchange', *Review of Business*, Vol. 28, pp. 5, 12 (Table 7); data results from a questionnaire based on the practices of corporate governance principles by the respondents, namely the Istanbul Stock Exchange (ISE) member firms and companies listed on the ISE, and a statistical evaluation of the findings. One hundred and fifteen member firms out of 205, and 243 ISE companies out of 308, were included.
154. Türk Sanayicileri ve İşadamları Derneği – TÜSİAD [Turkish Industrialists' and Businessmens' Association] (1992) *The Privatisation Implementation in Turkey Report, Section 'Social Privatisation Policy and ESOP'*; M. A. Gürol (1994) *Bir sosyal özelleştirme yöntemi – çalışanların pay ortaklığı* [A social privatisation method – employee share ownership] Ankara: HAK- İŞ [Confederation of true trade unions of Turkey], p. 95.
155. Survey on the Implementation of Corporate Governance Principles conducted by CMB of Turkey in 2004; 249 companies out of 303 responded to the survey.
156. In 1984 the first related Law No. 2983 was enacted, followed by Law No. 3291 in 1986. See Republic of Turkey, Prime Ministry, Privatisation Administration, http://www.oib.gov.tr/baskanlik/yasal_cerceve_eng.htm.
157. Law No. 4046 on the Implementation of Privatisation of 27 November 1994 as published in the Official Gazette No. 22124 on 27 November 1994 and most recently amended by Law No. 5398 of 3 July 2005 published in the Official Gazette No. 25882 on 21 July 2005.
158. Law No. 6762 dated 29 June 1956, enacted on 2 July 1956, published in the Official Gazette No. 9353 on 9 July 1956.
159. Article 329 CC widening the exceptions is under consideration. In parallel the Capital Markets Law is subject to an amendment and in this case acquisition of own shares with the object to give them to their employees including by publicly held joint-stock companies is apparently under consideration.
160. In accordance with Articles 468 paragraph 1 and 469 paragraph 3 other than the aforementioned vehicle of a foundation also an association, a co-operative, a corporation or any other organisation for the benefit of employees may be used.
161. On Principles Regarding Distribution of Dividends and Interim Dividends to be followed by Publicly-Held Joint-Stock Corporations Subject to Capital Market Law; Serial: IV, No. 27 published in the Official Gazette No. 24582 dated 13 November 2001, see Article 8.
162. In accordance with Article 3 lit. a) DivComm of the Communiqué on Principles Regarding Exemption Requirements for Issuers and Removal from the Board's Register Serial: IV, No. 9 published in the Official Gazette No. 22154 on 27 December 1994.
163. Communiqué on Principles and Rules on Financial Statements and Reports in Capital Markets Serial: XI, No. 1 published in the Official Gazette No. 20064 on 29 January 1989.
164. Defined by Article 15 paragraph 6 Capital Market Law: in the case of transactions with another enterprise or individual with whom there is a

direct or indirect management, administrative, supervisory or ownership relationship, publicly held joint-stock corporations shall not impair their profits and/or assets by engaging in deceitful transactions such as by applying a price, fee or value clearly inconsistent with similar transactions with unrelated third parties.

165. According to Communiqué on Public Disclosure of Material Events Serial: VIII, No. 20 published in the Official Gazette No. 21629 on 06 July 1993, amended with Serial: VIII, No. 39 published in the Official Gazette No. 25174 on 20 July 2003.

166. A. Küçükçolak and L. Özer (2007), p. 9 (Table 3), p. 12 (Table 7).

167. ifs School of Finance (2007).

168. HM Revenue & Customs – HMRC (2007), www.hmrc.gov.uk/stats/emp_share_schemes/menu.htm, date accessed 10 September 2007. The difference between the data in the comparative tables and in the country profile is attributable to the last update of statistics by the HM Revenue and Customs. The costs of the plan are comprised of tax losses and National Insurance Contribution (NIC) losses.

169. The value is equal to the number of shares multiplied by the exercise price.

170. Before 2003, an additional requirement had to be fulfilled: the exercise period had to be not less than three years after any previous tax-free exercise. This requirement was abolished.

171. Originally, the volume of assets was GBP 15 million (until 2003), but it was considered necessary to substantially increase it.

172. This plan was a broad-based deferred share-based profit-sharing plan introduced in 1978. The employing company had to set up a trust and pay contributions, so that the trustees were enabled to purchase shares of the company to be attributed to employees. The employees were not entitled to withdraw the shares within two years; if the shares were withdrawn after three years, no personal income tax was to be paid on the benefit. The participation of an employee connected with tax relief was limited to 10 per cent of the earnings or GBP 3,000.

# Bibliography


Ackermann, David (2002) 'How to Cash Out Tax-Free, Yet Keep Your Business ... ESOPs – A Practical Guide for Business Owners and Their Advisors', Conference Paper for the National Center for Employee Ownership, San Francisco, California.

Alchian, Armen A. and Demsetz, Harold (1972) 'Production, Information Costs, and Economic Organisation', *American Economic Review*, Vol. 62, No. 5, December, p. 777.

Bachman, Charles and Butcher, Karl (2002) 'ESOP Financing', National Center for Employee Ownership Conference Paper, San Francisco, California.

Badura, Peter (1994) 'Eigentum' in Ernst Benda, Werner Maihofer and Hans-Jochen Vogel (eds) *Handbuch des Verfassungsrechts*, 2nd edn (Berlin et al.: de Gruyter), p. 327.

Barjak, Franz, Heimpold, Gerhard et al. (1996) *Management Buyout in Ostdeutschland* (Halle: Institut für Wirtschaftsforschung).

Bellmann, Lutz, and Möller, Iris (2006) 'Gewinn- und Kapitalbeteiligung der Mitarbeiter: Die Betriebe in Deutschland haben Nachholbedarf', *IAB-Kurzbericht* (Nuremberg: Institut für Arbeitsmarkt- und Berufsforschung).

Ben-Ner, Avner and Jones, Derek C. (1995) 'Employee Participation, Ownership and Productivity: A Theoretical Framework', *Industrial Relations*, Vol. 34, No. 4, pp. 532–54.

Berle Jr., Adolf A. (1959) *Toward the Paraproprietal Society* (New York: The Twentieth Century Fund).

Beursken, F. (2007) 'Werknemersparticipaties in Nederland: Theorie and Parktijk – Een Analyse van AEX ondernemingen', Master Thesis at the University of Rotterdam.

Beutler, Bent, Bieber, Roland and Pipkorn, Jörn (1993) *Die Europäische Union, Rechtsordnung und Politik*, 4th edn (Baden-Baden: Nomos).

Blanchflower, David G. and Oswald, Andrew J. (1988) 'Profit Related Pay: Prose Discovered?', *Economic Journal*, Vol. 98.

Blasi, Joseph R. (1988) *Employee Ownership: Revolution or Ripoff?* (Cambridge, MA: Ballinger Publishing Company).

Blasi, Joseph R., Kruse, Douglas L. and Bernstein, Aaron (2003) *In the Company of Owners* (New York: Basic Books).

Blasi, Joseph R. and Kruse, Douglas L. (1991) *The New Owners: The Mass Emergence of Employee Ownership in Public Companies and What It Means to American Business* (New York: HarperCollins Publishers Inc.).

Boda, Dorottya, Neumann, László and Vig, Zoltan (2006) 'Extended Country Report: Financial Participation of Employees in Hungary' in Lowitzsch, Jens, *The PEPPER III Report* (Rome and Berlin: Inter-University Centre Split/Berlin), on supplementary CD-ROM, downloadable from the Inter-University Centre website, http://www.intercentar.de.

Bradley, Keith, Estrin, Saul and Taylor, S. (1990) 'Employee Ownership and Company Performance', *Industrial Relations*, Vol. 29 (3), pp. 385–402.

Buchko, A. A. (1992) 'Employee Ownership, Attitudes and Turnover: An Empirical Asessment', *Human Relations*, Vol. 101, pp. 711–33.

Bundesministerium der Finanzen [Federal Ministry of Finance] (2007) 'Einheitliche Bemessungsgrundlage der Körperschaftssteuer in der Europäischen Union', *Monatsbericht des BMF*, April, pp. 67–73.

Bye, R. C. (2002) 'The Case for COLI (Corporate-Owned Life Insurance) – Funding the Repurchase Obligation', Conference Paper, National Center for Employee Ownership, San Francisco, California.

Cable, John R. and FitzRoy, Felix R. (1983) 'Work Organisation, Incentives and Firm Performance: An Empirical Analysis of West German Metal Industries', University of Warwick Mimeo Paper, presented at the 9th Meeting of the European Association for Research in Industrial Economics, 24–26 August 1983, Bergen, Norway.

Chang, Saeyoung (1990) 'Employee Stock Ownership Plans and Shareholder Wealth: An Empirical Investigation', *Financial Management*, Spring, pp. 48–58.

Ciupa, S. W. (2001) *Nowoczesna umova o pracę* [The Modern Labour Contract], 4th edn (Warsaw: Wydawnictwo C. H. Beck).

Cohen, S. (1990) 'Autonomous work teams spread in the USA', *Associated Press*, 9 December 1990.

CONFESAL (2006) *Report regarding changes to the Law governing Sociedades Laborales*, October.

Conte, Michael A. and Svejnar, Jan (1988) 'Productivity Effects of Worker Participation in Management, Profit-Sharing, Worker Ownership of Assets and Unionisation in US Firms', *International Journal of Industrial Organisation*, Vol. 6.

Conte, Michael A. and Svejnar, Jan (1990) 'The Performance Effects of Employee Share Ownership Plans' in A. Blinder (ed.) *Paying for Productivity: A Look at the Evidence*, (Washington, DC: Brookings Institution).

Damijan, Janez, Gregoric, Aleksandra and Prašnikar, Janez (2004) 'Ownership Concentration and Firm Performance in Slovenia', LICOS – Centre for Transition Economics, Leuven, Discussion Paper 142.

Defourney, Jacques, Estrin, Saul and Jones, Derek C. (1985) 'The Effects of Workers' Participation on Enterprise Performance: Empirical Evidence from French Co-operatives', *International Journal of Industrial Organisation*, Vol. 3, No. 2 (June).

Deloitte (2007) *International Tax and Business Guides*, http://www.deloittetaxguides.com (database).

Deutsche Bank Research (2007) 'Germany's Mittelstand – an Endangered Species? Focus on Business Succession', *Current Topics*, 387, 29 May 2007, download available at http://www.dbresearch.de.

Earle, John S. and Telegdy, Álmos (2002) *Privatization Methods and Productivity Effects in Romanian Industrial Enterprises*, Upjohn Institute for Employment Research, Central European University and Budapest University of Economic Sciences, Central European University Labor Project.

European Foundation for the Improvement of Living and Working Conditions (2004) *Financial Participation in the EU: Indicators for Benchmarking* (Dublin: Eurofound).

European Foundation for the Improvement of Living and Working Conditions (2004) *Financial Participation for Small and Medium-Sized Enterprises: Barriers and Potential Solutions* (Dublin: Eurofound).

European Commission (2003a) *Report of the High Level Group of Independent Experts on Cross-Border Obstacles to Financial Participation of Employees for Companies having a Transnational Dimension*, December (Brussels : European Commission).

European Commission (2003b) *Transfer of Businesses – Continuity Through a New Beginning, Final Report of the MAP 2002 Project* (Brussels: European Commission, Directorate-General Enterprise and Industry).

European Commission (2003c) *Employee Stock Options, The Legal and Administrative Environment for Employee Stock Options in the EU* (Brussels: European Commission, Directorate-General Enterprise and Industry).

European Union (2007a) *European Commission, Directorate-General Taxes and Customs Union, 'Taxes in Europe' Database*, http://ec.europa.eu/taxation_customs/taxinv.

European Union (2007b) *European Commission, Directorate-General for Employment, Social Affairs and Equal Opportunities, Social Protection Systems in Member States (MISSOC)*, http://ec.europa.eu/employment_social/missoc/2006.

Festing, Marion, Groening, Yvonne, Kabst, Rüdiger and Weber, Wolfgang (1999) 'Financial Participation in Europe – Determants and Outcomes', *Economic and Industrial Democracy*, Vol. 20, pp. 295–329.

FitzRoy, Felix R. and Kraft, Kornelius (1987) 'Formen der Arbeitnehmer-Arbeitgeberkooperation und ihre Auswirkungen auf die Unternehmensleistung und Entlohnung'.

FitzRoy Felix R. and Kornelius Kraft (eds) *Mitarbeiterbeteiligung und Mitbestimmung im Unternehmen* (Berlin and New York: de Gruyter).

Galgoczi, Bela and Hovorka, Janos (1998) *Employee Ownership in Hungary: The Role of Employers' and Workers' Organisations* (Geneva: International Labour Office).

Ganghoff, Steffen (2004) *Wer regiert in der Steuerpolitik?* (Frankfurt/Main and New York: Campus).

Gärtner, Wolfram (1996) *Die Neugestaltung der Wirtschaftsverfassungen in Ostmitteleuropa* (Berlin: Berlin Verlag Arno Spitz GmbH).

Geißler, Rainer (1996) *Die Sozialstruktur Deutschlands*, 2nd edn (Opladen: Westdeutscher Verlag).

Von Gierke, Otto (1889) Die soziale Aufgabe des *Privatrechts* (Berlin).

De Grazia, Sebastian (1962) *Of Time, Work and Leisure* (New York: The Twentieth Century Fund).

Gürol, Mehmet Ali (1994) *Bir sosyal özelleştirme yöntemi – çalışanların pay ortaklığı* [A social privatisation method – employee share ownership] Ankara: HAK-iŞ [Conservative of true trade unions of Turkey].

Guski, Hans-Günter and Schneider, Hans J. (1986) *Betriebliche Vermögensbeteiligung: Eine Bestandsaufnahme* (Cologne: Deutscher Instituts-Verlag).

Guski, Hans-Günter and Schneider, Hans J. (1983) *Betriebliche Vermögensbeteiligung in der Bundesrepublik Deutschland, Teil II: Ergebnisse, Erfahrungen und Auswirkungen in der Praxis* (Cologne: Deutscher Instituts-Verlag).

Guttmann, Edeltraut (1995) 'Geldvermögen und Schulden privater Haushalte Ende 1993', *Wirtschaft und Statistik*, p. 391.

Hamilton, Alexander (1788) *The Federalist Papers*, No. 73 in Alexander Hamilton, James Madison and John Jay The Federalist II (New York: J. and A. McLean).

Harbaugh, Richmond (1993) *Equity-Sharing – Effects on Collective Bargaining Position of Trade Unions*, CERGE EI Working Paper (Prague: Charles University).

Hauser-Ditz, Axel, Hertwig, Markus and Pries, Ludger (2006) Erste Ergebnisse der BISS-Befragung 2005 – Kurzbericht (Bochum: Ruhr-Universität Bochum,

Forschungsprojekt 'Betriebliche Interessenregulierung in Deutschland – Survey und Strukturanalyse' – BISS).

Hecker, Damian (1990) *Eigentum als Sachherrschaft – Zur Genese und Kritik eines besonderen Herrschaftsanspruchs* (Paderborn and Munich: Schöningh).

Heinsohn, Gunnar and Steiger, Otto (1997) 'The Paradigm of Property, Interest and Money and its Application to European Economic Problems: Mass Unemployment, Monetary Union and Transformation', IKSF Discussion Paper No. 10, July.

HM Revenue & Customs – HMRC (2007), *Employee Share Schemes*, www.hmrc.gov. uk/stats/emp_share_schemes/ menu.htm.

Hölscher, Jens (1996) *Bedingungen ökonomischer Entwicklung in Zentralosteuropa*, Vol. 3: Privatisierung und Privateigentum (Marburg: Metropolis).

ifs School of Finance (2007) *ifs ProShare*, http://www.ifsproshare.org.

Ioannou, Christos (2008) *Changing Payment Systems in Greece*, mimeo.

Ivanova, Stela and Keremidchiev, Spartak (2006) 'Extended Country Report: Financial Participation of Employees in Bulgaria' in J. Lowitzsch, *The PEPPER III Report* (Rome and Berlin: Inter-University Centre Split/Berlin), on supplementary CD-ROM, downloadable from the Inter-University Centre website, http://www.intercentar.de.

Jarosz, Maria (ed.) (1995) *Management Employee Buyouts in Poland* (Warsaw: Instytut Studiow Politycznych, Polska Akademia Nauk).

Jarosz, Maria (ed.) (1996) *Polish Employee-Owned Companies in 1995* (Warsaw: Instytut Studiow Politycznych, Polska Akademia Nauk).

Jarosz, Maria (ed.) (2000) *Dziesiec lat Prywatyzacji Bezposredniej* [Ten Years of Direct Privatisation] (Warsaw: Instytut Studiow Politycznych, Polska Akademia Nauk).

Johnson, Shane and Tian, Yisong (2000) 'The Value of Incentive Effects of Non-Traditional Executive Stock Option Plans', *Journal of Financial Economics*, Vol. 57, pp. 3–34.

Jones, Derek C. and Kato, Takao (1995) 'The Productivity Effects of Employee Stock Ownership Plans and Bonuses: Evidence from Japanese Panel Data', *The American Economic Review*, June, pp. 391–414.

Jones, Derek C. and Mygind, Niels (1998) 'Ownership Patterns and Dynamics in Privatised Firms in Transition Economies: Evidence from the Baltics', CEES Working Paper Series, Issue 15 (Fredriksberg: Copenhagen Business School, Centre for East European Studies), published also in Baltic Journal of Economics, Vol. 2, No. 2, Winter 1999.

Jones, Derek C. and Svejnar, Jan (1985) 'Participation, Profit-Sharing, Worker Ownership and Efficiency in Italian Producer Co-operatives', *Economica*, Vol. 52, November.

Jones, Derek C., Kalmi, Panu and Mygind, Niels (2005) 'Choice of Ownership Structure and Firm Performance: Evidence from Estonia', *Post-Communist Economies*, Vol. 17, No. 1, pp. 83–107.

Jones, Derek C. and Mygind, Niels (2005) 'Corporate Governance Cycles during Transition: Theory and Evidence from the Baltics' in Igor Filatochev and Mike Wright (eds) *The Life Cycle of Corporate Governance* (Cheltenham: Edward Elgar), pp. 253–86.

Kalmi, Panu (2005) *Inventory Study for the Project 'Changing Patterns of Employee Financial Participation in Europe'* at Nijmegen School of Management, mimeo.

Kanjuo-Mrčela, Aleksandra (2002) 'Lastništvo zaposlenih na prelomu tisočletja' [Employee Ownership at the End of the Century], *Industrijska demokracija*, No. 10.

Kelso, Louis O. and Adler, Mortimer J. (1958) *The Capitalist Manifesto* (New York: Random House).

Kelso, Louis O. and Hetter, Patricia (1967) *Two-Factor Theory: The Economics of Reality* (New York: Vintage Books, Random House).

Kelso, Louis and Kelso, Patricia Hetter (1991) *Democracy and Economic Power: Extending the ESOP Revolution through Binary Economics* (Lanham, MD: University Press of America).

Kelso, Louis O. (1960) *Lawyers, Economists and Property* (San Francisco, California).

Kester, Gerard (1980) *Transition to Workers' Self-Management: Its Dynamics in the Decolonising Economy of Malta* (The Hague: Spokesman Books for the Institute of Social Studies).

KPMG (2007) *Corporate and Indirect Tax Rate Survey 2007*, http://www.kpmg.com/Global/IssuesAndInsights/ArticlesAndPublications/Pages/Corporate-Tax-Rate-Survey-2007.aspx.

Krelle, Wilhelm (1993) 'Wirtschaftswachstum und Vermögensverteilung' in Kirchenamt der Evangelischen Kirche in Deutschland (ed.) *Beteiligung am Produktiveigentum* (Hameln: Sponholtz), p. 37.

Krelle, Wilhelm, Schunck, Johann and Siehke, Jürgen (1968) *Überbetriebliche Ertragsbeteiligung der Arbeitnehmer: Mit einer Untersuchung über die Vermögensstruktur der Bundesrepublik Deutschland*, two volumes (Tübingen: Mohr).

Kronberger, Ralf, Leitsmüller, Heinz and Rauner, Alexander (2007) *Mitarbeiterbeteiligung in Österreich* (Vienna: Linde Verlag).

Kruse, Douglas L. and Blasi, Joseph R. (1995) *Employee Ownership, Employee Attitudes, and Firm Performance: A Review of the Evidence*, NBER Working Paper, Series 5277 (Cambridge, MA: National Bureau of Economic Research).

Kruse, Douglas L. (1991) 'Profit-Sharing and Employment Variability: Micro-Economic Evidence on the Weitzman Theory', *Industrial and Labour Relations Review*, Vol. 44, April.

Küçükçolak, Ali and Özer, Levent (2007) 'Do Corporate Governance, Independent Boards & Auditors Affect Market and Financial Performance: An Application to Istanbul Stock Exchange', *Review of Business*, Vol. 28.

Leibenstein, Harvey (1987) *Inside the Firm* (Cambridge, MA: Harvard University Press).

Lipton, David and Sachs, Jeffrey (1990) 'Privatisation in Eastern Europe: The Case of Poland', *Brookings Papers on Economic Activity*, 2.

Logue, John, Glass, Richard, Patton, Wendy, Teodosio, Alex and Thomas, Karen (1998) *Participatory Employee Ownership* (Kent, OH: Worker Ownership Institute).

Lowitzsch, Jens, Hashi, Iraj and Woodward, Richard (eds.) (2009), *The PEPPER IV Report – Assessing and Benchmarking Financial Participation of Employees in the EU-27*, with a foreword by the President of the Europgroup, Jean Claude Juncker (Berlin: Inter-University Centre Split/Berlin).

Lowitzsch, Jens, Bormann, Axel, Hanisch, Stefan, Menke, John D., Roggemann, Herwig and Spitsa, Natalia (2008) *Financial Participation for a New Social Europe: A Building Block Approach* (Rom and Berlin: Inter-University Centre Split/Berlin), (available in separate English, German and French editions).

Lowitzsch, Jens (2006) *The PEPPER III Report – Promotion of Employee Participation in Profits and Enterprise Results in the New Member and Candidate Countries of the European Union* (Rome and Berlin: Inter-University Centre Split/Berlin).

Lowitzsch, Jens (2002) *Privatisierung und Beteiligung in Mittelosteuropa – Am Beispiel des polnischen, slowakischen und tschechischen Modells* [Privatisation and Capital Participation in Central Eastern Europe – The Example of the Polish, the Czech and the Slovak Model] (Berlin: Berlin Verlag Arno Spitz GmbH).

Lyon, Larry (1989) *The Repurchase Liability or the Phantom of the ESOP* (San Francisco, California: Menke & Associates, Inc.).

Maillard, Paul (2007) 'Rapport sur la Participation dans les Èntreprise de moins de 50 Salariés, Report to Prime Minister Dominique de Villepin', presented by Senator Alain Gournac, April, Rapporteur: Paul Maillard.

Mäkinen, Mikko (2007) *Essays on Stock Option Schemes and CEO Compensation*, Acta Universitatis Oeconomicae Helsingiensis, A-291, Helsinki School of Economics.

Massie, Jean-Aymon (1999) 'Simplification du Plan Epargne Groupe – ELF', 7th International Employee Ownership Conference, January 1999.

Meihuizen, H. E. (2000) 'Productivity Effects of Employee Stock Ownership and Employee Stock Option Plans in Firms Listed on the Amsterdam Stock Exchanges: An Empirical Analysis', Paper for the 10th Conference of the IAFEP, Trento, 6–8 July 2000.

Mikloš, Ivan (1995) 'Corruption Risks in the Privatisation Process', Klub Windsor Paper, Bratislava.

Minchev, V. (2004) 'Stakeholders in the Bulgarian Public Companies', *Ikonomika*, Issue No. 2, pp. 55–7.

Mygind, Niels (2002) 'Ownership, Control, Compensation and Restructuring of Estonian Enterprises - Preliminary Results from a Manager Survey', CEES Working Paper Series, Issue 42 (Fredriksberg: Copenhagen Business School, Centre for East European Studies).

Nuttall, Graeme (1999) *Employee Ownership: UK Legal and Tax Aspects* (London: Field Fisher Waterhouse LLP).

Nutzinger, Hans G., Schasse, Ulrich and Teichert, Volker (1987) 'Mitbestimmung in zeitlicher Perspektive: Ergebnisse einer Fallstudie in einem Großbetrieb der Automobilindustrie' in Felix R. FitzRoy and Kornelius Kraft (eds) *Mitarbeiterbeteiligung und Mitbestimmung im Unternehmen* (Berlin and New York: de Gruyter).

Offermann, Volker (1994) 'Die Entwicklung der Einkommen und Vermögen in den neuen Bundesländern seit 1990' in Jürgen Zerche (ed.) *Vom sozialistischen Versorgungsstaat zum Sozialstaat Bundesrepublik* (Regensburg: Transfer-Verlag), p. 96.

O'Kelly, Kevin P. and Pendleton, Andrew (2005) 'Common Elements of an Adaptable Model Plan for Financial Participation in the European Union', IAFP Working Paper, December.

Organisation for Economic Co-operation and Development – OECD (1995) 'Profit-Sharing in OECD Countries' in OECD (ed.) *Employment Outlook* (Paris: OECD).

Organisation for Economic Co-operation and Development – OECD (2005a) *Tax Policy Reform Conclusions* (Paris: OECD Centre for Tax Policy and Administration).

Organisation for Economic Co-operation and Development – OECD (2005b) *Tax Policy Reforms in Italy* (Paris: OECD Centre for Tax Policy and Administration).

Papier, Hans Jürgen (2008) 'Art. 14 of the Basic (Constitutional) Law of Germany' in Theodor Maunz, Günter Dürig, Roman Herzog (eds) *Commentary on the Basic (Constitutional) Law of Germany* (Bonn: Beck).

Pendleton, Andrew, Blasi, Joseph, Kruse, Douglas L., Poutsma, Eric and Sesil, James (2002) *Theoretical Study on Stock Options in Small and Medium Enterprises*, Final Report to the Enterprise-Directorate General, Commission of the European Communities (Manchester: Manchester Metropolitan University Business School).

Pendleton, Andrew, Poutsma, Erik, van Ommeren, Jos, and Brewster, Chris (2001) *Employee Share Ownership and Profit-Sharing in the European Union* (Dublin: European Foundation for the Improvement of Living and Working Conditions).

Pendleton, Andrew, McDonald, John, Robinson, Andrew and Wilson, Nicholas (1995) 'The Impact of Employee Share Ownership Plans on Employee Participation and Industrial Democracy, *Human Resource Management Journal*, Vol. 5 (4), pp. 44–60.

Pendleton, Andrew and Poutsma, Erik (2004) *Financial Participation: The Role of Governments and Social Partners* (Dublin: European Foundation for the Improvement of Living and Working Conditions).

Pendleton, Andrew, Robinson, Andrew and Wilson, Nicholas (1995) 'Does Employee Ownership Weaken Trade Unions? Recent Evidence from the UK Bus Industry', *Economic and Industrial Democracy*, Vol. 16, No. 4, pp. 577–605.

Pendleton, Andrew, Wilson, Nicholas and Wright, Michael (1998) 'The Perception and Effects of Share Ownership: Empirical Evidence from Employee Buyouts', *British Journal of Industrial Relations*, Vol. 36 (1), March, pp. 99–123.

PEPPER II Report (1997), KOM (96) 0697 C4-0019/97.

Pérotin, Virginie (2002) *Employee Participation in Profit and Ownership: A Review of the Issues and Evidence*, European Parliament, Social Affairs Series, SOCI 109 EN, 01-2003 (Luxembourg: European Parliament, Directorate-General for Research).

Pérotin, Virginie and Robinson, Andrew (1995) Chapter Four in 'Profit-Sharing in OECD Countries' in OECD (ed.), *Employment Outlook* (Paris: OECD), pp. 139–69.

Peukert, Wolfgang (1992) 'Zur Notwendigkeit der Beachtung des Grundsatzes des Vertrauensschutzes in der Rechtsprechung des Europäischen Gerichtshofes für Menschenrechte zu Eigentumsfragen', *Europäische Grundrechte-Zeitschrift*, Vol. 19.

Phalippou, Ludovic (2007) *Investing in Private Equity Funds: A Survey* (Amsterdam: The Research Foundation of CFA Institute).

Poutsma, Eric (2001) *Recent Trends in Financial Participation in the European Union* (Dublin: European Foundation for the Improvement of Living and Working Conditions).

Poutsma, Eric and van den Tillaart, Harry (1996) *Financiele werknemersparticipatie in Nederland: tijd voor beleid!* (The Hague: Nederlands Participatie Instituut).

PriceWaterhouseCoopers (2002) *Employee Stock Options in the EU and the USA* (London: PriceWaterhouseCoopers).

Priewe, Jan and Havighorst, Frank (1999) *Auf dem Weg zur Teilhabergesellschaft? Investivlöhne, Gewinn- und Kapitalbeteiligungen der Arbeitnehmer in Westeuropa und den USA – eine vergleichende Bestandsaufnahme*, Friedrich Ebert Foundation Series 'Wirtschaftspolitische Diskurse', No. 123 (Bonn: FES Library).

Priewe, Jens (1994) 'Die Folgen der schnellen Privatisierung der Treuhandanstalt', *Aus Politik und Zeitgeschichte, supplement of the weekly journal Das Parlament*, Vol. 43–4, p. 21.

PSE Socialist Group in the European Parliament (2007) *Hedge Funds and Private Equity – A Critical Analysis* (Brussels and Strasbourg: PSE Socialist Group in the European Parliament).

Reich, Charles A. (1964) 'The New Property', *Yale Law Journal*, Vol. 73, p. 733.

Riegel, R. (1986) 'Zur Bedeutung der Niederlassungsfreiheit im Europäischen Gemeinschaftsrecht', *Neue Juristische Wochenschrift*, p. 2999.

Rittstieg, Helmut (1976) *Eigentum als Verfassungsproblem – Zu Geschichte und Gegenwart des bürgerlichen Verfassungsstaates*, 2nd edn (Darmstadt: Wissenschaftliche Buchgesellschaft).

Roggemann, Herwig (1993) 'Eigentumsordnung in Osteuropa', *Recht in Ost und West*, p. 321.

Roggemann, Herwig (ed.) (1996) *Eigentum in Osteuropa* (Berlin: Berlin Verlag Arno Spitz GmbH).

Roggemann, Herwig (1997a) 'Functional Changes of Property Rights in East and West – Comparative Remarks to Post-Socialist Transformation in Eastern and Western Europe', CERGE EI Working Paper (Prague: Charles University).

Roggemann, Herwigh (1997b) 'On the Relation between Ownership and Privatisation in the Post-Socialist Countries' in University of Split, Faculty of Economics (ed.) *Enterprise in Transition* II (Split: Faculty of Economics, University of Split), p. 193.

Roggemann, Herwig (1997c) 'Funktionswandel des Eigentums in Ost und West – Vergleichende Anmerkungen zur postsozialistischen Transformation in Ost- und Westeuropa', *Recht in Ost und West*, Vol. 6, p. 194; Vol. 7, p. 225.

Roggemann, Herwig (1999a) 'Functional Change in Property Rights in the Welfare State: Lessons from the Federal Republic of Germany' in Irwin Collier, Herwig Roggemann, Oliver Scholz and Horst Toman (eds) *Welfare States in Transition – East and West* (New York: St. Martins Press), pp. 25–40.

Roggemann, Herwig (1999b) 'Erster Teil: Einführung' in H. Roggemann (ed.) *Die Verfassungen Mittel- und Osteuropas* (Berlin: Berlin Verlag Arno Spitz GmbH).

Roggemann, Herwig and Lowitzsch, Jens (eds) (2002) *Privatisierungsinstitutionen in Mittel- und Osteuropa* (Berlin: Berlin Verlag Arno Spitz GmbH).

Say, Jean Baptiste (1824) *Treaties on Political Economy; or the Production, Distribution and Consumption of Wealth*, Vol. I, Chapter XIV, On Production, Paris 1803, 2nd American edn, (Boston: Wells and Lilly, Court Street).

Schlomann, Heinrich (1993) in Ernst-Ulrich Huster (ed.) *Reichtum in Deutschland* (Frankfurt and New York: Springer).

Schneider, Hans J. and Zander, Ernst (1990) *Erfolgs- und Kapitalbeteiligung der Mitarbeiter in Klein- und Mittebetrieben*, 3rd ed. (Freiburg im Breisgau: Haufe).

Schwartz, Bernard (1965) *A Commentary on the Constitution of the United States*, Part II (New York and London: Macmillan).

Schweitzer, Michael and Hummer, Waldemar (1993) *Europarecht*, 4th edn Neuwied and Berlin: Metzner.

Sesil, James, Kruse, Douglas L. and Blasi, Joseph (2000) 'Sharing Ownership Via Employee Stock Ownership', World Institute for Development Economics Research (WIDER) Discussion Paper 2001/25 (United Nations University).

Shanahan, Jerry and Hennessy, Liam (1998) *Underpinning Partnership at the Workplace – An MSF Guide to Profit-Sharing, ESOPs and Equity Participation* (Dublin: Amicus-MSF).

Stikkelbroeck, Rik h. j. (2001). 'Survey of employee financial participation in the Netherlands' in Nederlands Participatie Instituut, PS Participation Solutions (eds) Nog steeds tijd voor beleid (The Hague: Nederlands Participatie Instituut).

Skouris, Wassilios (1995) 'Werbung und Grundrechte in Europa', *Europäische Zeitschrift für Wirtschaftsrecht*, pp. 438–9.

Spengel, Christoph (2003) *Internationale Unternehmensbesteuerung in der Europäischen Union* (Düsseldorf: IDW-Verlag)

Stack, Jack and Burlingham, Bo (1992) *The Great Game of Business: The Only Sensible Way to Run a Company* (New York: Doubleday).

Statistical Service of the Republic of Cyprus – CYSTAT (2001) Census of Enterprises 2000 (Nicosia: CYSTAT).

Sweins, Christina (2004) 'Personnel Funds as a Rewarding Tool – A Research of the Finnish Funds', Licentiate thesis, Helsinki University of Technology.

Szóstkiewicz, Halina (1995) 'Trade Unions in Employee-Owned Companies' in Maria Jarosz (ed.) *Management Employee Buyouts in Poland* (Warsaw: Instytut Studiow Politycznych, Polska Akademia Nauk).

Thiel, Jürgen M. (1991) 'Grundrechtlicher Eigentumsschutz im EG-Recht, *Juristische Schulung*, p. 274.

Tipke, Klaus and Lang, Joachim (eds) (2005) *Steuerrecht*, 18th edn (Cologne: Schmidt).

Tipurić, Darko (ed.) (2004) ESOP i hravtsko poduzeće (Zagreb: Sinenergija – nakladništvo).

Tofaute, Hartmut (1998) 'Arbeitnehmerbeteiligung am Produktivkapital – Fortschreibung einer unendlichen Geschichte', *WSI Mitteilungen*, Issue No. 6 (June), p. 376.

Türk Sanayicileri ve İşadamları Derneği – TÜSİAD [Turkish Industrialists' and Businessmens' Association] (1992) *The Privatisation Implementation in Turkey Report, Section 'Social Privatisation Policy and ESOP'* (Istanbul: TÜSİAD).

UK Treasury Public Enquiry Unit (1998) *Consultation on Employee Share Ownership*, December (London: UK Treasury Public Enquiry Unit).

US General Accounting Office (1986) *Employee Stock Ownership Plans: Benefits and Costs of ESOP Tax Incentives for Broadening Stock Ownership*, GAO-PEMD-87-8 (Washington, DC: US General Accounting Office).

US General Accounting Office (1987) *Employee Stock Ownership Plans: Little Evidence of Effects on Corporate Performance*, GAO/PEMD-88-1 (Washington, DC: US General Accounting Office).

US General Accounting Office (1996) *Employee Stock Ownership Plans. Interim Report on a Survey and Related Economic Trends*, GAO/PEMD-86-4BR (Washington, DC: US General Accounting Office).

Uvalić, Milica (1991) *The PEPPER Report: Promotion of Employee Participation in Profits and Enterprise Results in the Member States of the European Union* (in English, French and German), Supplement 3/91 to the brochure 'Social Europe' (Luxembourg. Office for Official Publications of the European Communities).

Vanek, Jaroslav (1965) 'Workers' Profit Participation, Unemployment, and the Keynesian Equilibrium', *Weltwirtschaftliches Archiv*, No. 2.

Vartiainen, Matti and Sweins, Christina (2002) Employee Ownership Funds in Finland – Functionality and Personnel Outcomes, Labour Policy Studies, No. 243 (Helsinki: Ministry of Labour).

Vaughan-Whitehead, Daniel (1992) *Interessement, Participation, Actionariat – Impacts Economiques dans l'Entreprise*, (Paris: Economica).

Vaughan-Whitehead, Daniel (1995) *Workers' Financial Participation* (Geneva: International Labour Organization).

Vaughan-Whitehead, Daniel and Uvalić, Milica (eds) (1997) *Privatisation Surprises in Transition Economies* (Cheltham: Edward Elgar).

Vevera, Daniela (2005) *Mitarbeiterbeteiligung am Kapital im EU-Mitgliedstaat Österreich – umfassende Erhebung über Verbreitung, Motive und Anforderungen von Arbeitnehmern und Arbeitgebern (Vienna: Fachhochschule Wiener Neustadt, Arbeiterkammer Wien and Wirtschaftskammer Österreich)*.

Villinger, Mark E. (1993) *Handbuch der Europäischen Menschenrechtskonvention unter besonderer Berücksichtigung der schweizerischen Rechtslage* (Zürich: Schulthess, Polygraph Verlag).

Vučić, Novica (1972) 'Die sozio-ökonomische Lehre des Jugoslawischen Selbstverwaltungssozialismus', *Osteuropa*, Issue No. 6, p. 430.

Wagner, Klaus-R. (1993) *Management-Buyout: Führungskräftebeteiligung, Arbeitnehmerbeteiligung; Grundlagen – Modellhinweise – Neue Bundesländer – Rechtspolitik* (Neuwied, Kriftel and Berlin: Luchterhand).

Wagner, Klaus-R. (1995) 'Renaissance der Mitarbeiterbeteiligung', *Betriebsberater*, supplement to issue No. 7 of this journal.

Walley, K. and Wilson, N. (ed.) (1992) *ESOPs: Their Role in Corporate Finance and Performance* (Hants: Macmillan).

Watanabe, Susumu (1991) 'The Japanese Quality Control Circle: Why It Works', *International Labour Review*, Vol. 130, No. 1, p. 64.

Weber-Grellet, Heinrich (2005) *Europäisches Steuerrecht* (Munich: Beck).

Weitzman, Martin (1991) 'How Not to Privatise', *Rivista di Politica Economica*, Vol. 81, No. 12.

Whadhwani, S. and Wall, M. (1990) 'The Effects of Profit-Sharing on Employment, Wages, Stock Returns and Productivity: Evidence from UK Micro-Data', *Economic Journal*, 100 (399), pp. 1–17.

White and Case (2001) *The European Company Statute*.

Whyman, Philip (2004) 'An Analysis of Wage-Earner Funds in Sweden: Distinguishing Myth from Reality', *Economic and Industrial Democracy*, Vol. 25, No. 3, pp. 411–45.

Winiecki, J. (2004) 'Kapitalistyczna karawana idzie dalej' [The capitalist caravan is moving on], *Rzeczpospolita*, 16 August 2004, Economy.

World Bank (2004) *Romania: Restructuring for EU Integration – The Policy Agenda. Country Economic Memorandum, Vol. 2: Main Report and Annexes*, June (Washington DC: The World Bank).

Würz, Stefan (ed.) (2003) *European Stock-Taking on Models of Employee Financial Participation, Results of Ten European Case Studies* (Wiesbaden: Dr Dr Heissmann GmbH).

Zimmermann, Gunter E. (1996) 'Neue Armut und neuer Reichtum: Zunehmende Polarisierung der materiellen Lebensbedingungen im vereinten Deutschland', *Gegenwartskunde*, 44, p. 5.

# Index